International
Marketing

International Retail Marketing

A Case Study Approach

Edited by
Margaret Bruce, Christopher M. Moore and Grete Birtwistle

ELSEVIER
BUTTERWORTH
HEINEMANN

AMSTERDAM   BOSTON   HEIDELBERG   LONDON   NEW YORK   OXFORD
PARIS   SAN DIEGO   SAN FRANCISCO   SINGAPORE   SYDNEY   TOKYO

Elsevier Butterworth-Heinemann
Linacre House, Jordan Hill, Oxford OX2 8DP
30 Corporate Drive, Burlington, MA 01803

First published 2004
Reprinted 2005

British Library Cataloguing in Publication Data
A catalogue record for this book is available from the British Library

Library of Congress Cataloguing in Publication Data
A catalogue record for this book is available from the Library of Congress

ISBN 0 7506 5748 0

For information on all Elsevier Butterworth-Heinemann
publications visit our website at www.bh.com

Working together to grow
libraries in developing countries

www.elsevier.com | www.bookaid.org | www.sabre.org

ELSEVIER   BOOK AID International   Sabre Foundation

Typeset by Charon Tec Pvt. Ltd, Chennai, India
www.charontec.com
Printed and bound in Great Britain

Contents

List of figures and tables

Figures

Tables

Preface

International retailing is an essential ingredient for the global economy. International retailing satisfies the increasingly complex and demanding needs of global consumers. Cultural diversity is expressed through the products and services that are provided by global retailers, who are in a position to discover new tastes and preferences, work with global suppliers to bring these products to the consumer speedily and at a fair price. International retailers are able to transfer knowledge and experience across cultural boundaries, and this ensures that they are constantly improving their quality of products and service delivery, and supplying the best of what is available to their consumer base. Retail technology enables responsive demand, real-time pricing, such as bar-coding, point-of-sale systems, e-commerce and customer relationship management schemes, for example loyalty programmes. Global retailers are at the forefront of technology change to manage their operations and consumer interface. Consumers are international in their outlook through travelling for business and/or pleasure, through accessing the Internet, music, television and magazines, and so are looking for new experiences and a global appeal when shopping. Progressive retailers have to meet this demand through keeping abreast of global trends and working with suppliers to optimise the appropriate product mix in store. Sustainability and ethical aspects of retailing are particularly apt when working globally. This is a challenging area for retailers and is an aspect of their quality management. Addressing the dynamics of the market for teenagers and youth market is another demanding area. Young consumers have their own finance and make their own decisions about what products they chose to buy and where from. They tend to be strongly influenced by celebrities, brands and peer-group pressure. Retailers need to understand their shopping habits and cater for the needs of this cohort. In general, consumers are increasingly brand aware and want to have access to luxury products. Own brands, or private labels, have to offer premium quality and a sense of uniqueness to attract and retain consumers' loyalty.

International Retail Marketing addresses all of the major issues affecting international retailing, including logistics and supply chain management, service quality across international boundaries, e-tailing, design, ethical sourcing, luxury brands, young consumers and global trends. This is a book that will be useful to retail managers, suppliers and academics.

Foreword

Yesterday, I returned to the UK from China, with its explosive retail development, and on this day the Safeway Merger Inquiry reported its findings. We indeed live in interesting times!

International retailing is a reality. It started slowly but surely, it will continue for many years, and we will not see *global retailing* for a generation. Retailing touches every person, and even in its early stages of development, *international retailing* is having profound effects on consumers, communities, competing retailers and on their suppliers.

This book on *International Retail Marketing* is very timely. The subject is massive, so the authors, wisely, do not attempt an all-encompassing study. They would shoehorn, pigeon-hole and stereotype too much if they tried. Instead they choose separate important subjects, which reflect what is happening in our industry.

I like the way the book moves easily between such diverse matters as supply chain, young consumers and e-commerce. In this way you get to see both the wood and the trees at the same time! In some ways it is an accurate impression of how a retailer would see it, moving, sometimes jumping, from subject to subject. Each piece is important and has to be dealt with, but it is not a jigsaw, so do not try too hard to force them into a single picture. I also like the way it travels around the world. It is not centred on the US, as so many offerings are.

I am fascinated by our industry, and I am sure the reader of this book will see why.

Sir Terry Leahy, Chief Executive, TESCO

List of contributors

Emma Banister is a Lecturer in Marketing at Lancaster University Management School. Her first degree was in politics and history at Newcastle University and she completed an MSc in Marketing in 1997 and her PhD in 2001, both at the School of Management, UMIST. She took up her appointment at Lancaster University in July 2003 after 3 years spent as Lecturer in the Department of Textiles, UMIST. Her research interests focus on consumer behaviour, specifically symbolic consumption (particularly distastes and the negative meanings associated with products, and young consumers).

Dr. Grete Birtwistle is the Head of the Division of Marketing at the Caledonian Business School, Glasgow Caledonian University. She has extensive fashion retailing experience and her PhD research investigated the area of store image and store positioning for fashion retailers. In particular, she highlighted the importance of retail staff perception of store image factors and that employees should be advocates of the company. She has published a number of articles and made contributions to books, mainly on areas of fashion marketing. Her current research explores ways of increasing the speed in the fashion supply chain and in order to achieve this she is interviewing both suppliers at different stages within the chain as well as buyers and logistics managers from retail companies. She is a Member of the Glasgow Centre for Retailing, and through this forum provides businesses with training courses and consultancy advice. Her main teaching areas are fashion marketing, integrated fashion logistics and integrated fashion communication. She has recently been a Guest Lecturer at Florida State University in Tallahassee.

Margaret Bruce is Professor of Design Management and Marketing at Manchester Business School. She was the Director of Fashion Retailing and Head of Textiles at UMIST. Professor Bruce is an internationally renowned scholar and consultant. Professor Bruce has published over 200 papers and 10 books in these fields, including *Fashion Marketing* (2001, with Tony Hines, Butterworth-Heinemann) and *Design in Business* (2002, with John Bessant, Pearson Education Limited and Financial Times). Her latest research focused on innovation in the extended enterprise and this will be published as *Design Drivers* (Butterworth-Heinemann, 2004). Professor Bruce holds an International Chair of Management and Strategy in Design at ICN Ecole de Management, University of Nancy II, France and an Honorary Professorship at Xi'an University of Science and Technology, China.

Alice W.C. Chu, M.A., M.H.K.I.T.A., is an Assistant Professor at the Institute of Textiles and Clothing, the Hong Kong Polytechnic University where she teaches fashion retailing, retail management and international fashion retailing. Prior to her academic career, she held senior management positions with several fashion retailers including Warner Brothers Studio Store, G2000 Ltd and Goldlion. She has gained commercial experience in export trading, merchandising, product development, marketing and fashion retailing. Alice has developed a strong interest in the effect of store environment on shopping behaviour, store operations, customer service, e-tailing and consumption value. She has also published a number of articles relating to fashion retailing in academic journals and at conferences. She is also an author for a book chapter in *Fashion Marketing: Contemporary Issues*, published by Butterworth-Heinemann in 2001. Her most recent collaboration research activity involves university-funded project on modelling the routing pattern of fashion shoppers in shopping centre. Except research, Alice has also served as a consultant in various retail firms on the development their staff manual and in-house management training programmes. Currently, she is the Leader of the Undergraduate Programme in Fashion Retailing and is the Deputy Chairman of the Retailing Group in ITC.

Stephen Doyle is a Senior Lecturer in the Division of Marketing at Glasgow Caledonian University. Previously based at Napier University, his primary research interests are in the areas of retail design, in-store environment and retailer image, as well as destination image and product design. In addition, he has published chapters on the role of retailing and merchandise in the sport, leisure, festivals and event sectors.

John Fernie is Professor of Retail Marketing and the Head of School of Management and Languages at Heriot-Watt University, Scotland. He was previously Professor of Retailing and Logistics and also the Director of the Institute for Retail Studies at the University of Stirling. He has written and contributed to numerous textbooks and articles on retail management, especially in the field of retail logistics and the internationalisation of retail formats. He is Editor of the *International Journal of Retail and Distribution Management*, published by Emerald, and received the prestigious award of *Editor of the Year in 1997* in addition to *Leading Editor Award*s in 1994 and 1998 and 2000. He is on the Editorial Board of the *Journal of Product and Brand Management*, also published by Emerald. He is an Active Member of the Institute of Logistics and Transport and the Chartered Institute of Marketing in the UK as well as holding office in the American Collegiate Retail Association. In 2001, he became a Member of the Logistics Directors Forum, a group of leading professionals in supply chain management and logistics in the UK.

Dr Tony Hines is currently in the Retail Management Group at Manchester Metropolitan University Business School. His research interests are market-led supply chain strategies, and small firms, and he has a particular expertise in the apparel sector. His recent publications include a highly successful edited book *Fashion Marketing – Contemporary Issues* with Professor Margaret Bruce and a number of academic articles addressing supply chain relationships and their strategic importance in the apparel sector. He has also recently completed *Supply Chain Strategies* a text published by Butterworth-Heinemann. He has been an invited as Plenary Speaker at a number of *World Textile Conferences* most recently in India, Greece, Turkey and the US where he presented papers on supply chain strategies and e-business. In 2003, he was an invited Plenary Speaker at the *Leading Action for Textiles, Clothing and Footwear Conference* in the UK. In November 2000, he was an invited Plenary Speaker at the *International Forum for Fashion Training Institutes* held in London a platform shared with the UK Government Minister for the Creative Industries. He was joint author of a report on the Department of Trade and Industry (DTI) Mission to the US to examine e-commerce developments in the textile and apparel supply chain (July 2000). He has also undertaken market research for the Consumer Association and been an Invited Expert on consumer issues and retailing for the BBC on radio and television.

Tony is one of only three international academics invited to be a Member of the Strategic Planning Committee for the Milano Project in South Korea and is currently working with the Sri Lankan Government to develop executive marketing and supply chain programmes for the Apparel Industry in conjunction with the Chartered Institute of Marketing.

Tony has worked with a number of organisations in the UK and internationally to develop supply chain strategies. He is Editor of the *Textile Institute Journal of Economics, Management and Marketing* a position he has held since 1994. He is a leading marketing educator and holds External Examiner positions at Oxford Brookes University Business School for their South African programmes, Glasgow Caledonian University (MSc Marketing), Bournemouth University (MA Services Marketing), University of Ulster and he is a Senior Examiner for the Chartered Institute of Marketing.

Tim Jackson, Dip.M., M.A, is a Principal Lecturer at the London College of Fashion and Member of the Editorial Panel of *The Journal of Fashion Marketing and Management*. He leads a Post Graduate Certificate in Fashion Buying and Merchandising and chairs the Fashion Management Research Group at the London College of Fashion. Having worked both in retail management and in buying and merchandising for a number of fashion retailers including Dash, Jaeger and Burton Menswear, he has co-written the first UK textbook on fashion buying and merchandising management with David Shaw. Tim is qualified in marketing having gained an MA in Marketing and the CIM Diploma; he has undertaken considerable research into the fashion industry while based at the London College of Fashion and has commented on fashion business issues in the media. In addition to lecturing at the London College of Fashion he has lectured at the University of Westminster and Surrey University and is an External Examiner at both Manchester Metropolitan and Middlesex Universities.

Dr Trevor J. Little is Professor and the Head of the Department of Textile and Apparel Technology and Management at North Carolina State University. His research interests include linking the market and design functions, understanding customer requirement, manufacturing systems and developing new products to fulfil the needs and wants of the consumer.

Ruth Marciniak, BA (Hons), PgD, MBA, is a Senior Lecturer in Retailing at London Metropolitan University where she is responsible for the Retail Management Pathway of the BA (Hons) Combined Studies programme in the Business School. She is currently completing a PhD thesis on e-commerce practices of UK fashion retailers. She has also published in the area of fashion marketing and e-commerce in refereed journals, including the *International Journal of Retail and Distribution Management* and the *Journal of Fashion Marketing and Management*. She has presented academic papers at a number of national and international conferences, including the *British Academy of Management* and the *International Conference on Innovation through Electronic Commerce*.

Professor Christopher M. Moore, MA (Hons), MBA, PhD, is the Director for the Glasgow Centre for Retailing at Glasgow Caledonian University. A graduate of the Universities of Glasgow and Stirling, his doctoral thesis considered the internationalisation of foreign fashion retailers into the UK. His research interests include fashion buying and merchandising, fashion brand development and the internationalisation strategies of luxury brand retailers. His research activities have allowed him to work with many of the key international fashion retailers.

He has recently co-authored with Professor John Fernie and Suzanne Fernie a major new textbook on retailing and marketing, *Principles of Retailing*. He is the Assistant Editor of the *Journal of Customer Behaviour* and sits on the Editorial Panels of a number of leading academic journals.

Professor Moore currently holds the Scotmid Chair in Retailing. Scotmid is Scotland's largest independent co-operative society. As part of his remit as Director for the Glasgow Centre for Retailing, his duties include providing research and consultancy services for major retailers and consumer-facing organisations.

Heva Nejad graduated with a BSc in Textile Science and Technology in 2001 and completed an MSc in International Fashion Retail the following year (both from the Textiles Department, UMIST). The chapter in this book is based upon her MSc dissertation, which explored the effects of celebrity and media on the consumption of fashion by young consumers. Heva is currently working as a trainee buyer for Makro UK Ltd.

Dr Traci May-Plumlee is an Assistant Professor in the Department of Textile and Apparel Technology and Management. She is the Program Director of the Anni Albers Scholars program – a Double Degree Program requiring a BS in Textile Technology and a BA in Art and Design. Traci's current areas of research include product-evaluative criteria, virtual draping in three-dimensional, digital design technologies, and innovative product development to satisfy textile and apparel customer requirements.

Dr Deirdre Shaw is a Senior Lecturer in the Division of Marketing, Glasgow Caledonian University. Her main research interests focus on consumer behaviour with regard to ethical issues, values and consumption patterns, including simplified lifestyles. This research has explored a number of consumption contexts including food, clothing and home interior purchasing. Methodological approaches have included modelling ethical consumer decision-making via structural equation modelling techniques and case studies of simplified consumption lifestyles. Publications include national and international journal articles and conference papers focusing on ethical and responsible consumption choices.

Dr Anne Smith, BSc (Hons), MSc, PhD, PGCE, MCIM, is Senior Lecturer in Marketing, Department of Business and Management, University of Glasgow. Having previously held posts at the Universities of Sheffield, Manchester (UMIST) and the West Indies (Barbados), she has more than 20 years experience of course delivery and design, in both the public and private sectors, in the UK and overseas. Subjects taught range from 'broad-based' management, strategy and marketing courses (including professional qualifications in marketing and accountancy) to specialised modules in service quality and design, service internationalisation and research methodology.

Her research work focuses on the service sector, in particular health and financial services, investigating issues of service quality and design. This work has been published in journals such as the *Journal of Business Research*, *Journal of Marketing Management*, *Services Industries Journal*, *International Journal of Bank Marketing*, and in a co-authored book, *The Management and Marketing of Health Services*. More recently, a major programme of research focusing on cross-cultural methodology and the impact of response styles on international service-quality evaluation and design has been initiated, with colleagues at the University of Swansea, with early findings published in the *International Marketing Review*.

Further major research interests are the process and practice of service innovation and service reorganisation in both the public and private sectors. A current project 'Reorganising for Success', funded by the Chartered Institute of Personnel and Development, in collaboration with colleagues both at Glasgow and at other UK universities has involved a major survey of UK organisations. Initial findings have been published in Management and Practitioner Publications, including the *Mastering Leadership Series* (*Financial Times*).

Ms Dominique A.C. Tomolillo is a graduate of the MSc Fashion Marketing degree from the Division of Marketing, Glasgow Caledonian University.

Dr Kit-lun Yick gained her BA (Hons) in Clothing Management and Technology from Manchester Metropolitan University in UK and the PhD in Fabric Objective Measurement Technology from the Hong Kong Polytechnic University. And then, Dr Yick joined the Institute of Textiles and Clothing, the Hong Kong Polytechnic University as a lecturer in 1996. She specialises in fabric science and technology, fashion technology and clothing production management. Dr Yick teaches a broad range of subjects at different levels, including fashion technology, clothing production management, international textile and clothing industry, apparel, apparel textiles, apparel trade practice, production planning and organisation, etc. She has also involved in supervision of undergraduate and doctorate research students. Her recent research interests include comfort evaluation, modelling of fabric properties, thermo-regulating materials, product development, consumer studies, local retail business, etc. Dr Yick has also served as a consultant to industry in the areas of quality-system implementation, fabric performance evaluation, ethical evaluation process enhancement, production plant development, etc.

Acknowledgements

We would like to thank and dedicate this book to our colleagues for all their support and encouragement, as follows: Dr John Fernie, Heriot-Watt University, Dr Andrew Newman, Manchester Business School, Professor Thomas Froehlicher, Director-General ICN Ecole de Management, University of Nancy II, France, Christine Kratz, Lecturer at ICN Ecole de Management, EPSRC Retailing Network, and British Academy of Marketing Retailing Special Interest Group.

We would also like to thank Nicki Sneath and Holly Bennett, Butterworth-Heinemann for their enthusiasm and commitment to this project. Karinna Nobbs at Glasgow Caledonian University for her effective editorial assistance. Finally, we would like to express our appreciation to our contributors.

Introduction

Retailing is an international business. To satisfy the needs of global consumers, retailers have to meet these through the products they offer, whether these are principally food, fashion or multiple retailers. Consumers experience different cultures when they travel for work or pleasure and they have access to the Internet, television, magazines, etc and they demand products, which reflect these tastes. Retailers are sourcing globally for the fashion or cosmetic or electronic gadget that is new and exciting for their challenging consumer base. Sustainability and fair trade are issues that are coming uppermost for retailers and they have to ensure that they are trading and sourcing ethically. Thus, they have to have in place optimum quality management to do so. One growing market is that of young consumers who have their own finance, are strongly influenced by celebrities and peer-group pressure. This market sector is fast moving, brand-led, difficult to satisfy and fickle. Consumers are increasingly aware of luxury brands, which is particularly challenging for private- or own-label retailers. Own-label or private-label products have to be of a premium quality and at a competitive price to attract and retail consumers. International retailers are under pressure to identify key trends in different regions and deliver the appropriate product mix, at the expected level of service quality to satisfy their global consumers. This entails having effective supplier relationships in place to guarantee product delivery on time and at the agreed price point to meet demand globally. It means monitoring the retailer brand to ensure that it is strengthened, not diluted, by different expectations across the world. It includes keeping ahead of the game in terms of customer care and global trends. It means being aware of competitors that may come into the market through the Internet, through merger and acquisition, and/or through vertical integration. All of these issues are captured in this book.

International Retail Marketing is a primary source for managers in retailing or their suppliers, or those wishing to embark on a career in international retailing. The book is divided into two sections. Section 1 reviews and discusses the main conceptual and theoretical themes facing international retail marketing. Section 2 examines topical issues affecting international retail marketing and is based on contributions from leading experts from around the world. Each chapter concludes with a set of Study Questions.

Moore and Fernie examine the nature of international retailing, how international retailers operate globally, the pressures they face, and approache{[G1]}s to strategic international retail marketing. Retailers are cost driven and to achieve a profitable international retailing business requires consideration of key activities, systems and processes. This is addressed by Moore and Fernie. In Chapter 2, Fernie focuses on logistics and supply chain management for international retailers. Products have to be manufactured, assembled, and transported to the retailer and then distributed to retail outlets throughout the retail operation. This is complex and when systems fail, then this means that anchor products are not in store at the time they need to be. Achieving a fail-safe process that is agile, lean, quick response, and that is able to meet changing consumer needs within tight cost parameters is not easy! Fernie considers the contingent factors impacting on an efficient and effective supply chain. Central to any retailer are the roles of sourcing, buying and merchandising.

Without the right products in stores at the right time and price and presented appropriately to the consumer, then the retailer would be out of business. And yet, these activities are not always given the attention that they deserve and they are clearly a strategic activity. In Chapter 3, Moore gives an intelligent synopsis of retail buying and considers its role as a 'change agent', 'gate-keeper' and 'opinion-leader'. To fulfil these roles, buying needs to be closely linked with the retailers' strategic objectives, predict future trends and create and deliver on the buying plan. Buyers also have to be able to cultivate effective relationships with suppliers to negotiate on price and delivery. Doyle considers store design and visual merchandising in Chapter 4. Atmospherics, layout and visual merchandising are increasingly critical aspects of the retail offering. They serve to attract or detract potential consumers and impact on purchase behaviour and customer retention. Creating zoned areas in stores, for example for teenagers, baby and toddlers, etc. is one approach to meeting different customer needs and assists consumers to navigate around the store.

Section 2 covers a number of major issues affecting international retail marketing and is full of interesting cases and examples. E-commerce hype envisaged a future without 'brick-and-mortar' retailers. This vision has not been proven, as yet. Internet shopping is another channel open to the consumer and can prove to be convenient and cheaper for certain products and services, for example books, compact disks, flights, hotels, etc. This new channel has led to the emergence of new types of retailers and novel trading activities, such as auction sites like e-bay. For many retailers, e-commerce has been adopted to support key operations, such as sourcing and buying, tracking of shipments, billing, ticketing, training, etc. Marciniak and Bruce review e-tailing and the strategic options that this provides. In Chapter 6, Hines focuses on relationship management within the domain of the supply chain management. Investment in partnerships is one approach that is used to guarantee access to new product ideas, to ensure priority of delivery and to maintain a sensitive price. Drawing on examples, Hines argues that supply chains are effectively 'value creation mechanisms for customers' and need to be treated as such, rather than merely taking a cost-driven approach. Where retailers take this perspective, they are able to create a supply chain that meets with their strategic objectives, for example lean and agile as the case of Zara in fashion. Bannister and Nejad address the area of young consumers in Chapter 7. This is a rapidly expanding market in its own right and also young consumers' influence on household purchases, so that they are being referred to as 'brand managers of the home'. Bannister and Nejad segment the market into 'kids', 'tweens' and 'teens', and focus on the influence of celebrity on young consumers. By conducting their own research, they reveal a range of attitudes and influences on purchase behaviour in this sector. Regarding celebrity endorsement, then they appeal to very small-age bands and the celebrity needs to be managed to ensure their values were still appealing to the target segment. Next, Tomolillo and Shaw take the topical issue of ethics in fashion in Chapter 8. Using focus groups, they have asked consumers directly about their perspectives on ethical consumerism and the trade-offs they, as consumers, make between cost, fashion, aesthetics and ethics. Consumers were aware of environmental issues in the production of fabrics and ethical issues in terms of exploitation of women workers in clothing factories. They would like more choice in terms of fashionable and ethical garments. Chapter 9 provides an analysis of global luxury brands. Jackson addresses the thorny question as to whether luxury and fashion are synonymous or not, and then he goes onto question the nature of luxury. Luxury is now being diffused down the social strata and so the meaning of 'luxury' is in itself dynamic. He cites Menkes (2002): 'the word luxury is almost old fashioned. I have a different philosophy on luxury – to me it is the right pair of jeans that fit well and could be any brand. I call it design-led quality.' The connection with design has meant that the luxury brands are acquiring design talent to expand their businesses on the basis of the creative talent and inherent sense of exclusivity that this can bring. Keeping ahead of the 'Jones' and retaining, or expanding the market, is not easy for luxury brands in a climate of copycats and accessibility of fusion lines. Service quality is another concern of international retailers. In Chapter 10, Smith reports on an international survey of consumers' cross-cultural expectations of service in financial services. She notes that without understanding the tacit nature of service expectations, retailers are taking unforeseeable risks in geographical expansion across cultural boundaries. Indeed, the intangible elements of service are often neglected by international retailers who tend to assume a 'mono-culture' throughout their organisation, which can create problems of customer attraction and retention. Birtwistle extends this theme in terms of store image and retail positioning. Consumers have perceptions of stores, which influence their propensity to enter that store and their retention to it. From her research, she has found that a key factor of store image is customer care and service quality and is the 'most significant differentiator, particularly in fashion retailing where staff can have high customer contact.' Thus, store staff have a major role in store image, in addition to that of advertising and merchandising. The final chapters in this section consider trends in Asia and the US. In Chapter 12, Chu and Yick focus on fashion trends in Asia. The markets in cities like Hong Kong are becoming saturated and intensely competitive, as international retailers are using Hong Kong as a base to enter China. With fast-moving fashion markets, no one retailer is able to cater for the diverse range of wants and needs of consumers, so 'portfolio retailing' is becoming more and more common. Portfolio retailers operate a number of different retail formats to meet distinctive market needs and each has its own-tailored merchandising programme to serve the specific needs of a different target group. Hong Kong retailers have expanded in the region into China, Thailand, Korea but these face operational problems and also have to adapt to and reflect the cultural needs of these environments. Brand image and a customer-centred approach to marketing are necessary for success in Asian markets.

Little and May-Plumlee, in Chapter 13, provide an overview of the technological impacts on retailing in US, which have enabled responsive demand, real-time management and optimization, such as point-of-sale systems, bar-coding, e-commerce and customer relationship management activities, like loyalty schemes. They describe a study of US consumers and note the key factors affecting the decision to purchase – fit, colour, style, brand and price. The study also compared intention to buy with point-of-sale figures and from this the authors argue that such data is an accurate predictor of future sales. They suggest that vendor-managed inventory systems using point-of-sale data can provide powerful style and attribute data to support merchandising and product development functions for both local and global consumers.

Perspectives of international retailing

Chapter 1

Retailing within an international context

Christopher M. Moore and John Fernie

The purpose of this chapter is to examine the key themes and issues pertinent to the internationalisation of retailing. Drawing from the relevant academic literature, the aims of the chapter are as follows:

- to define the nature and scope of retailer internationalisation;
- to identify the motivations for international expansion;
- to review the direction of international expansion;
- to consider the methods of market entry that internationalising retailers adopt;
- to review the conceptual frameworks which seek to explain retailer internationalisation.

1.1 Introduction: who are the international retailers?

Retailing is predominantly a domestic market activity. The total business of the vast majority of retailers is done within one particular country and in many cases, within one specific region or district. Consequently, when compared to other sectors, the proportion of foreign assets to total assets within retailing is low. As such, it has been noted that international retailing is still a minority activity for the majority of retailers (McGoldrick, 1995).

That said, even the most perfunctorily review of the structure of the retailing sector indicates that an increasing number of retailers no longer confine their trading activities to the home market. For example, fashion retailers, such as The Gap, Gucci, Escada, Ralph Lauren, H&M, Benetton, Mango and Zara have recognised the international appeal of their brand image, product ranges, and merchandising methods and have sought to exploit these advantages through the development of extensive international store networks. For many of these fashion retailers, their international performance has been impressive in terms of the speed of their expansions, the breadth of their foreign market coverage and the contribution of foreign sales to their total sales income levels. Furthermore, many of these retailers have become household names on a global scale and this is a further testament to the depth of their international success.

However, by virtue of the fragmented nature of the ownership characteristics of fashion retailing, both domestically and internationally, the international sales of each of the leading participants is relatively insignificant in the grand scheme of international fashion expenditure and none of them currently have the capability to disrupt the structure of any significant foreign market in Europe or elsewhere. For example, one of the world's best recognised and most prolific brands, Ralph Lauren, reported sales for the period 2002/2003 of $2.4 billion, of which just over $520 million (21 per cent) was derived from foreign markets.

Table 1.1 Largest grocery retailers in the world by sales in 2000

Group	Country of origin	Net sales in 2000 ($ billion)	Grocery (%)	Foreign (%)	Number of operating countries
Wal-Mart	USA	199,096	40	17	11
Carrefour	France	64,791	71	48	32
Ahold	The Netherlands	52,471	91	82	23
Kroger	USA	50,990	91	0	0
Metro	Germany	48,235	48	44	27
Albertson's	USA	38,999	90	0	0
Kmart	USA	38,531	36	0	0
Tesco	UK	34,400	87	10	11
Safeway	USA	33,275	92	11	3
Rewe	Germany	33,193 (estimate)	73	20	20

Source: Planet Retail (2002)

When compared to the leading international grocery retailers, the international profile of Ralph Lauren is somewhat eclipsed. For example, *Planet Retail* (2002) provides a vivid account of the international significance of what Wrigley (2002) has described as an 'elite group of multinational/trans-national operations' (TNCs). Table 1.1 presents a profile of the world's largest grocery retailers in 2000/2001.

From Table 1.1 it is clear that, while Wal-Mart is easily the world's largest grocery retailer as measured in terms of total sales, it lags behind the other main retail TNCs in terms of the contribution of foreign sales to total sales. However, Fernie *et al.* (2003) note that Wal-Mart's forecasted sales for 2010 are in the region of $700 billion, of which the contribution of foreign markets is estimated to rise to 27 per cent of that total. To envisage the sheer scale of this growth, if international sales were to grow in line with expectations, then the contribution of foreign sales would equate to the equivalent of all of Wal-Mart's sales in 2000/2001.

The emergence and future dominance of what Wrigley (2002) predicts to be a tiny elite of international grocery retailers has, and will be continued to be sustained by, consolidation within the European grocery market in particular. As Fernie *et al.* (2003) observed, to be a truly global retailer, a company needs to achieve credible scale in Europe, which requires a leading position in at least two of the three largest markets: Germany, France and the UK. Figure 1.1 is the overview of Wrigley (2002) on the structure of the European Union (EU) food retail market and the inter-linkages between firms highlights the collaborations that have occurred but also indicates the potential for links/consolidation in the future within the sector.

The purpose of the comparison between the scale of international sales for the grocery elite of Wal-Mart, Carrefour, Ahold and Tesco and that of the leading international fashion retailer Ralph Lauren, is to highlight the fact that when we consider the internationalisation of retailing in the early part of the 21st century, we must recognise two distinct strata or groupings of international retailer. The first is a unique, small and immensely powerful grouping of grocery retailers that has (and will continue) to transform the landscape of global and domestic retailing. Wal-Mart, Carrefour, Ahold and Tesco in particular, are the distinctive groupings. Any review of the international development of retailing must necessarily acknowledge the distinct position that they have achieved.

The second stratum is in effect all of those other retailers, of varying size and influence, who participate within foreign markets. Many of these are immensely important by virtue

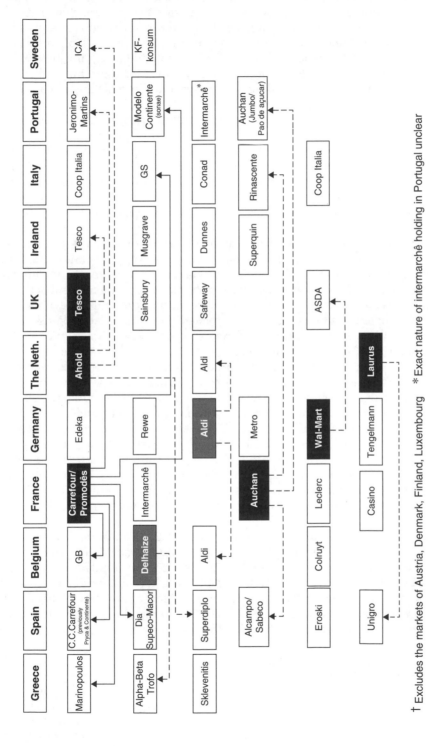

† Excludes the markets of Austria, Denmark, Finland, Luxembourg   * Exact nature of intermarchê holding in Portugal unclear

Figure 1.1 The structure of the EU food retail market and the inter-linkages between firms in that market in mid-2001

of the extent and spread of their foreign market participation. But the dimension which distinguishes these from the grocery elite is that while some are truly global companies, such as Ikea, Benetton and Toys 'R' Us, none of them provide a significant challenge to the retail structure of any of the large national markets of the world. Various attempts have been made to classify this 'other' grouping. Among those identified by Hollander (1970) were the luxury goods retailers (such as Mappin and Webb and Gucci); the general merchandise retailers (such as department store retailers, variety and discount retailers, and mail order firms); speciality retailers; trading companies and direct selling and automatic vending firms.

In many respects, other than for the demise of the trading companies and the emergence of Internet-based retailer, such as Amazon, the classification provided by Hollander remains robust and serves this chapter well in terms of providing an inclusive description of the key groupings of international retailers. The remainder of this chapter, while acknowledging the importance of the elite group of grocery retailers, will seek in particular to redress the omissions of other texts on international retailing (which have tended to ignore the foreign market development of fashion and luxury brand retailers) by focusing upon their international activities.

Before exploring some of the key issues of retailer internationalisation in depth, it is important that three further points are made. The first is that while it is undoubtedly the case that the international expansion activities of retailers have increased significantly over the past two to three decades, it is helpful to note that this is not a recent activity. A number of companies have had long experience of operating stores abroad. For example, as Alexander (1997) noted, Burberry of London opened their first store in Paris in 1909, while Liberty of London opened their first foreign branch some time earlier in 1890. W.H. Smith opened their Parisian store in 1903.

Secondly, it is important to consider the academic justifications for focusing exclusively on retailers international activities. Pellegrini (1994) maintained that studies of retailer internationalisation provide for a deeper understanding of retailers' strategies for strategic management and growth, while Tordjman (1994) suggested that such investigations serve to highlight pan-national differences and convergences in consumer behaviour. Other researchers have proposed that the study of retailer internationalisation provides important insights into our understanding of the nature and characteristics of retailer decision-making (Burt, 1991; Dawson, 1994; Clarke and Rimmer, 1997). From another perspective, Burt (1995) has suggested that the wider availability of information and databases related to retailer internationalisation has served to facilitate the increase in research attention in this area.

Finally a variety of themes relevant to retailer internationalisation has subsequently emerged in the literature as identified by Doherty (2000), and these relate to the scale and extent of retailer expansion (Brown and Burt, 1992); the direction of international expansion (Burt, 1993; Davies and Fergusson, 1995); the motivations for international expansion, as well as the methods of foreign market entry adopted (Alexander, 1990; Williams; 1992; Dawson, 1994; Sparks, 1996). Drawing from these central themes, the focus of this chapter will be to consider the nature and characteristics of these various dimensions.

1.2 The nature and scope of retailer internationalisation

Since the early 1990s, efforts have been made to provide clear definitions of what is meant by retail internationalisation. Brown and Burt (1992) recognised the need to identify what is that retailers actually internationalise: 'Is it management expertise and management systems? Innovative forms of trading? or unique retail brands?'. Without this clarification, they argued, it is impossible to adequately explain whether the international experience of retailers is similar to those of other sectors or whether these are in some way unique.

Hollander (1970) defined multinational retailers as 'those firms that are in some way responsive to the headquarters (HQ) located outside the country, or colony, in which the retail sales are made' (p. 10), while Sparks (1996) noted that researchers in this area have tended to draw from the international marketing literature in order to define the parameters of what constitutes an international retailer. Among the most important contributors to research in the area of international business were Johanson and Wiedersheim-Paul (1975) who (based on their studies of the international expansion activities of Swedish manufacturers), suggested that the term 'international' defined something of the business orientation, management character and the attitude of the firm. Furthermore, they suggested that business internationalisation was essentially an incremental process which begins with the exporting of goods to foreign markets and comes to fruition when the firm established manufacturing sites in the foreign market so as to satisfy the foreign demand.

Likewise, Johanson and Vahlne (1977) stated that the internationalisation of business was essentially concerned with the incremental movement and extension of production, sales and distribution capacity from the home market to a foreign market. The primary interpretation of business internationalisation within the literature has been to see this form of growth as an incremental process where the manufacturers increase their involvement in a foreign market through indirect forms of investment, culminating in the establishment of a subsidiary company for sales and manufacturing in the foreign market (Cavusgil, 1982).

In the 1990s, researchers working in the area of services marketing, and in particular, the internationalisation of service provision, have challenged the appropriateness of transferring manufacturing interpretations to the service sector. Through the identification of the intangible, perishable and heterogeneous nature of service provision, it has been noted that while the internationalisation of manufacturing may advance incrementally, in contrast for service providers, full market involvement is typically required immediately (Dahringer, 1991; Katrishen and Scordis, 1998). Consequently, there have been calls for an understanding of business internationalisation which also recognises the invisible dimensions of foreign market participation, such as the transfer of business know-how and management experience, marketing skills, technological capability and other forms of professional services from one country to another (Clark *et al.*, 1996; Knight, 1999).

Similarly, within the context of the internationalisation of retailing, it has been noted that the definitions of the internationalisation of manufacturing may not readily accommodate the scope, extent and complexity inherent to international retailing. For example, Dawson (1994) has argued that:

> The balance between centralised and decentralised decision-making, the relative importance of organisation and establishment scale economies, the degree of spatial dispersion in the multi-establishment enterprise, the relative size of the establishment to the size of the firm, the relative exit costs if the decisions are reversed, the speed with which an income stream can be generated after an investment decision has been made, different cash flow characteristics, the relative value of stock and hence importance of sourcing; all these items and others, serve to differentiate the manufacturing firm and the retail firm not least in respect of the internationalisation process.
>
> Dawson (1994, p. 270)

While international retailers are typically identified as those firms that operate stores within foreign markets, the internationalisation processes relevant to retailing are much more complex. Drawing from the work of Dawson (1994) and Sparks (1996), it is possible to view retail internationalisation in terms of a continuum of invisible to visible dimensions, as presented in Figure 1.2.

Arguably, the least apparent dimensions and the factors less obvious to external parties are those which relate to the **internationalisation of financial investments**. Examples of pan-national investments include the acquisition of shares in a retail company based in one country by an investing institution (such as a pension fund) that is based in another market. Other inconspicuous examples of retail internationalisation include cross-border shopping, which is often motivated by a consumer's desire to acquire goods from an adjacent country that are perhaps scarce or more expensive within the home market. For example, the movement of day-shoppers from the UK to France in the search of less expensive, good quality wines, illustrates this invisible form of internationalisation in retailing.

A variety of studies have considered the transfer of **retail know-how** from one market to another. Perhaps the most influential was that of Kacker (1988) who suggested that the term 'know-how' is used to signify the 'business concepts, operating policies and techniques employed in a retail business in a given environmental setting' (p. 8).

Furthermore, he identified two dimensions of retailer know-how: the *managerial*, which includes concepts, policies and systems, and the *technical*, which refers to matters related to location planning, visual merchandising, as well as buying and merchandising. The flow of know-how can be unplanned and may occur whenever a firm decides to replicate the practises of another company – perhaps a foreign retailer – without any formal collaboration with that retailer. Conversely, the flow of expertise can be planned, whereby 'there is a purposive transfer of an established technology or innovation from one country to another' (p. 12). This flow of expertise may arise as a result of a franchise arrangement or as a consequence of a joint venture arrangement between the two firms.

The transfer of retailing expertise from one country to another is not a recent phenomenon. It is well documented that British grocery retailers were influenced by the self-service operations of American retailers in the post Second World War era, as evidenced by Sainsburys' development of self-service stores in the UK in the early 1950s (Boswell, 1969). Similarly, Tanner (1992) examined the influence of American trading formats, brands and product ranges on Japanese retailers, who were quick to adopt these dimensions within their stores.

The various forms of transferable retail expertise have been identified by Dawson (1994) and these include store formats; management ideas (such as those associated with promotional methods, measures of productivity and models for the assessment of new store locations); as well as retail technology in the form of management information systems and stock control programmes, design concepts and customer-service initiatives.

Of the various forms of retail internationalisation identified in Figure 1.2, the **internationalisation of sourcing** is the most common and widespread form of retail internationalisation. Often driven by the globalisation of manufacturer brands and/or the desire to

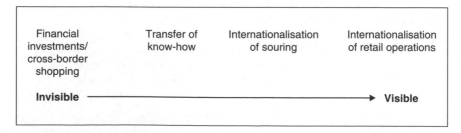

Figure 1.2 The dimensions of retail internationalisation

source cheaper, but better value products from foreign markets, retailers are increasingly sourcing goods and services from markets other than the home market. For example, since the late 1990s, the British retailer Marks and Spencer has radically altered their sourcing strategy. While in the past, Marks and Spencer extensively promoted the fact that the vast majority of their clothing ranges were manufactured in the UK, increased price competition in the clothing sector, as well as escalating manufacturing costs has meant that the majority of Marks and Spencer's clothing ranges are now manufactured outside the UK.

It is not only for cost-saving reasons that retailers may choose to buy their products from abroad. As a means of achieving market differentiation, a buying team may source from a foreign supplier in order to increase the variety and perceived uniqueness of their product ranges. Dawson (1994) noted the 'pulling power' of foreign brands in the move towards international sourcing in that customers often perceive these brands to be associated with quality or fashion. As a result, retailers seek to benefit from these positive associations by stocking these preferred brands. Various studies have identified a relationship between customers' perception of product quality and brand name, and more specifically, the country of origin of the product (Bannister and Saunders, 1978; Bilkey and Nes, 1982; Johansson *et al.*, 1985; Han, 1989; Lin and Sternquist, 1994).

Even if a retailer should elect to source from a domestic supplier, it is likely that the suppliers will themselves have sourced raw materials internationally and/or subcontracted production to foreign companies for product or garment assembly. Often, it is the case that these products are then returned to the original supplier's factories where the goods are finished, pressed and packaged for delivery. By adopting this approach, suppliers, particularly within the European Community countries, have been able to label their garments as having been made within the home market, despite the fact that the substantive manufacturing processes occurred elsewhere.

Clearly, then, there are a number of factors which precipitate the retailer's decision to purchase from foreign suppliers. These factors can be classified in terms of **push and pull** factors. **Push factors** relate to those features of the home market that serve to make domestic buying problematic and less viable, while **pull factors** are those features of the foreign market that make sourcing from that market more attractive. Figure 1.3 provides examples of push and pull factors.

There are a range of methods that can be adopted in order to facilitate international sourcing, and these include indirect sourcing from foreign markets through visits to international trade shows, wholesalers and agents, and through direct means, achieved by setting up international buying offices within the key-souring countries. These international buying offices are established in order to recruit suppliers, oversee production and

Push	Pull
Lack of local expertise	Strength of national brand, e.g. made in Italy within the fashion sector
Lack of production flexibility	Strength of an international supplier's brand, e.g. GUCCI
Prohibitive pricing	High-quality standards
Insufficient number of suppliers to meet demand	Local manufacturing expertise/quality of workforce
Lack of investment in advanced technology	Indigenous expertise, such as Italian tailoring
Lack of new product development/innovation	Advanced technology/manufacturing plant

Figure 1.3 Push and pull factors of international sourcing

manage product supply and availability. In addition, international sourcing can be achieved through the establishment of international buying groups and networks, which function to link manufacturers, wholesalers, agents and retailers across national boundaries.

Dawson (1994) suggested that the shift towards international sourcing by retailers typically develop over four stages:

- The first stage involves domestic sourcing, combined with the use of wholesalers who supply products of foreign origin to the retailer.
- The second stage sees the retailer becomes more proactive in their international souring involvement in that they commission agents to source foreign products on their behalf.
- The third stage typically involves the establishment of a foreign buying office which acts as a link between the buyers based within the home market head office and the local suppliers in the foreign market.
- The final stage of development involves the creation of a worldwide network of buying offices that supply information on supplier opportunities, manage product quality within their precise region and manage the transportation of products from the supplier to the home market.

For those fashion retailers, such as Prada, Gucci and Diesel, who also supply to third-party stockists, the process of securing orders can be done in one of three ways. For example, Comme des Garcons of Japan operates a sales office in central Paris. Retail buyers who wish to stock the Comme des Garcon brand must visit the Paris sales office in order to view the ranges and place orders. Gucci use a different method. Firstly, the prospective stockists must be approved as a Gucci stockist by the company's sales agent in Milan. Once approved, the stockists must visit the agent's showroom in Italy in order to view and place their orders. Alternatively, the Italian jeans brand Diesel has established a wholly-owned subsidiary company in the UK which has the responsibility of managing the retail stores of the company and their wholesale distribution. Buyers visit Diesel's London showroom to place their orders. The decision to establish a wholly-owned subsidiary company is an unusual one in international fashion retailing. Diesel's decision was a reflection of the importance of the British market to the company as a whole. In the financial year 2002/2003, Diesel's annual accounts show that the company had worldwide sales of £422 million of which almost 15 per cent (£60.3 million) were derived from the UK market.

Developments in information and communications technology have served as important facilitating factors in the development of international sourcing programmes. The advent of electronic data interchange has improved the links that exist among retailers, product designers and manufacturers. These have contributed to the emergence of integrated, pan-national supply chains that can efficiently respond to the consumer demand.

The availability of reliable information and communications technology is particularly important for those retailers who choose to source a particular product or product range from a number of different foreign markets. The decision to extend their sourcing across a number of markets may be motivated by the desire to spread risk. For example, if a supplying market is vulnerable to political or economic unrest, then it would be prudent for the buying team to source from other countries too in order to protect the business from supply chain turbulence. Furthermore, especially for the largest retailers, it may be the case that no one national market has the capability to fully meet their demands. In these circumstances, an international sourcing strategy will be required in order to supply the required volume of products.

Driven by what would appear to be an insatiable consumer demand for value for money, product variety and choice, and maximum product availability, it is likely that the internationalisation of retailer sourcing will continue unabated in the years to come.

The **internationalisation of operations** is the most visible dimensions of retail internationalisation. Typically, it is this dimension that identifies the international retailer. The others, such as the internationalisation of financial investments, of know-how and of product and service sourcing, serve as dimensions of the internationalisation process within retailing. Dawson (1994) stated that the internationalisation of operations can be described as 'the operation, by a single firm, of shops or other form of retail distribution, in more than one country' (p. 268). There are a number of important issues which surround the internationalisation of stores, such as the internationalising retailer having to face cultural differences in terms of consumer, employee and general business practices. Burt (1989) in a review of the key trends affecting the European consumer, suggested that demographic, socio-economic and lifestyle changes would provide significant challenges to retailers, not least with respect of required modifications to their store formats, merchandise assortments and the methods of promotion that they used.

The challenges and difficulties experienced by retailers, such as Wal-Mart in Germany, C&A in the UK and Marks and Spencer in Canada and the USA, all serve to illustrate the difficulties inherent to managing store operations within diverse trading markets. The examination of the internationalisation of retail operations has emerged as the central focus of much of the research in this area. These studies have tended to focus upon motivations for choosing to establish operations within a foreign market; the methods of market entry that are used; as well as the strategies that retailers adopt in order to respond to local market differences. Each of these dimensions will be considered later in this chapter.

1.3 The motivations for international expansion

Of the research areas related to retailer internationalisation, which considers the reasons for retail firms involvement within foreign markets has arguably attracted greatest attention. Variously described as driving forces (Treadgold, 1990), international inducements (Hollander, 1970), as well as strategic motivations, (Alexander, 1990), all of these terms relate in some way to those factors that encourage retailers to consider international market involvement as a strategy for growth (Williams, 1991).

While not devised within a retailing context, the Eclectic Paradigm proposed by Dunning (1981) has been recognised as the most widely applied theoretical framework for understanding direct investment, and specifically investment to finance manufacturing activity, within a foreign market (Johanson and Vahlne, 1977). From the literature on retailer internationalisation, a number of authors have acknowledged a debt to Dunning's Eclectic Paradigm, principally as a point of departure for researchers as they seek to investigate and conceptualise retailers' motivations for expansion into international markets (Pellegrini, 1992; Dawson, 1994; Sparks, 1996; Alexander, 1997). And while the applicability and relevance of the model for retailer internationalisation has been questioned, the inherent value of the model lies in its ability to underline the highly specific characteristics of the foreign market participation of the retailers (Dawson, 1994).

Dunning identified three particular advantages which encourage foreign market participation. **Ownership-specific advantages** provide a firm with competitive advantage within a market because of their possession of certain tangible and intangible assets, such as unique products, company size or trademark protection, which are, at least for a period of time, exclusive or specific to the firm possessing them. The desire to maximise the ownership-specific advantages, then encourages the firm to use them itself rather than to sell or lease them. The **internalisation advantages** are ultimately concerned with protecting against or exploiting market failure, and necessitate the extension of the firm's activities through organic growth and vertical integration, rather than through the externalising of these assets through contracts with independent firms. As to whether these advantages result in the extension of the firm's internal activities, such as manufacturing activities, to a foreign market is dependent on whether the firm can utilise and co-ordinate their advantages with factor inputs derived from the foreign market (i.e. **location-specific advantages**). If foreign market participation cannot provide some form of location-specific advantage, such as in relation to lower labour costs, or the opportunity to circumvent import controls and the like, then foreign markets will be served entirely by exports and domestic markets by domestic production.

Dunning makes no direct reference to retailers' foreign investment. However, others, such as Dawson (1994) and Pellegrini (1992) have considered the applicability of the theory to the foreign direct investment of retailers, analysing in particular the three advantage categories within the context of retailing. Dawson (1994) suggested that the ownership advantages of retailers can be readily found in their products, brands and refined sales methods (such as that undertaken by Benetton), but these advantages can be readily obtained through indirect financial agreements in the form of licensing and franchising. Likewise, Pellegrini (1992) maintained that while ownership-specific advantages are often linked to product differentiation, these advantages do not justify, in themselves, the decision to invest abroad when products can be so easily and profitably exported. And while it is acknowledged that location-specific advantages, such as relatively lower fixed and variable costs, may justify why a product ought to be produced within another country; Pellegrini argued that this does not account for why the retailer should be directly involved in the retailing of that product given that there are many examples of retailers enjoying locational advantages through franchising and licensing, thus avoiding direct investment and other associated costs.

Dawson (1994) and Pellegrini (1992) have suggested that the Eclectic Paradigm highlights the inherent differences between direct foreign investment within the manufacturing and retailing sectors. Inextricably linked to these differences in approach to foreign investment are the variations that exist in relation to the organisational and management characteristics of manufacturing and retailing businesses, specifically those related to the nature of decision-making and the balance between centralised and decentralised control, the size of the retail establishment relative to the size of the firm, and the extent of spatial dispersion that may exist within a multi-establishment business. Dawson also identified the key financial differences between the retailing and manufacturing firm and suggested that these clearly impact on their methods of international trading. In particular, he noted the variances in the relative importance of organisational- and establishment-scale economies within retailing, as well as the differences in cash flow characteristics; income streams are generated more speedily after the initial decision to invest is made, lower exit costs, as well as the relatively high value of the stock investment of a retailer.

Hollander (1970) provided a comprehensive account of the motivations underlying a retailer's decision to internationalise, which had a significant bearing on subsequent research in this area (Alexander, 1995). Hollander identified three primary motivation categories:

■ *Inadvertent internationalisation*, which occurs as the result of political events, such as the annexation of a region after military action.
■ *Non-commercial motives*, such as those associated with the advancement of social, ethical, personal or political beliefs.
■ *Commercial motives* derived from the desire to exploit the opportunities available within a stable and economically attractive foreign market.

1.3.1 Push and pull of retailer internationalisation

Alexander (1997) noted that **push and pull** factors have emerged as an important method for interpreting retailers' motives for expanding into foreign markets. Derived principally from the work of Kacker (1985, 1986), the 'push–pull' dichotomy seeks to explain why retailers are pulled towards a foreign market and/or are 'pushed' out of their home market in order to further their growth objectives. Based on a review of the expansion activities of European retailers into the American market, Kacker (1985) claimed that these two sets of factors were the key drivers for the significant growth in European retailer acquisition of American firms from the early 1970s to the mid-1980s. Accordingly, European retailer activity was prompted by 'push' factors, such as domestic government constraints on the size of retail development, and by the 'pull' factors of a stable political and economic climate within the American market.

Alexander (1997) noted that from the late 1980s onwards, empirical research appeared to challenge the premise that retailer internationalisation was principally a reactive response to negative internal market conditions. Williams (1991, 1992) in his analysis of the international activities of British retailers suggested that while the underlying motivations were multi-faceted, for the majority of companies the desire to move into foreign markets was essentially pro-active in nature, driven by the desire to obtain profit growth through the exploitation of a trading formula felt to have pan-national appeal. Issues of home market saturation and limited growth opportunities were far less apparent as motivations for such expansion. Other studies, undertaken by Alexander (1990, 1995, 1996) and McGoldrick and Fryer (1993) likewise suggested that the international participation of British and other European retailers was proactive and growth-orientated.

One explanation for the seeming change in priorities is provided by McGoldrick and Fryer (1993) who suggested that a retailer's motivations for international involvement change over time. As a company becomes more experienced and confident in their international involvement, so then their motives alter and issues of foreign market opportunity and the desire to further exploit their trading competencies become more important. Within this context, Alexander (1995) suggested that for those retailers that had initially become involved in international activities in the past two decades for reasons mainly of home market saturation, the motivation to continue foreign market expansion in the 1990s was now likely to be driven by the desire to maximise the opportunities available to them in other countries. Therefore, the 'pull' factors of retailer internationalisation are likely to become more significant as firms become expert in foreign market trading.

In recognising the different and conflicting positions of the 'reactive and proactive schools', Alexander (1994, 1995) argued that much of the divergence may be attributed to contextual and methodological factors in that the assumptions of the reactive school were founded during a period of economic recession, and the research methodology adopted by academics at this time was to adopt the more distant 'tracking approach'; whereby the understanding of international expansion was based largely on secondary data. In contrast, the perspective of the proactive school was developed at a time of relative economic prosperity and their research approach was empirically based, potentially allowing for a more intimate understanding of the internal processes and thinking of the retailers under scrutiny.

At the beginning of the 21st century, there is perhaps some justification to see such dichotomies as somewhat simplistic and even as being too narrow. With the emergence of the elite group of trans-national grocery retailers (i.e. Wal-Mart, Carrefour, Ahold and Tesco), it is clear that their motivations for international expansion are much more refined and highly developed than those of the retailers who were the focus of academic attention in the 1980s and early 1990s. Tesco, for example, which now achieves 15 per cent of its turnover from outside of the UK and with 65,000 staff overseas, has declared that internationalisation is one of the four defining elements of its corporate strategy. For these retailers, international activity is clearly not a peripheral of accidental activity. Instead, it is a defining element of the corporate philosophy of each.

This shift towards an international corporate perspective is not confined to the elite group alone. For example, the Spanish footwear brand Camper has pursued a rigorous international strategy in recognition of the pan-national appeal of their brand, product range and the relative lack of competition in their market sector. Likewise, for the Italian fashion brand Miss Sixty, international market development is the core priority. The speed of their development within the UK is a clear indication of their commitment to internationalisation. The Miss Sixty group of brands has only be in the UK for 5 years, but the group has opened eight stores, three outlet stores and three concessions within that period and recorded sales of £60 million for the financial year 2002/2003.

1.4 The direction of international expansion

From the literature on the internationalisation of business in general, it is suggested that the direction of international expansion of businesses is determined by the geographical and cultural proximity, as well as the competitive conditions of the foreign market. However, the literature also recognises that the significance of these various factors change over time and that companies are likely to follow an evolutionary pattern of international development (Johanson and Vahlne, 1977; Weidersheim-Paul *et al.*, 1978; Cavusgil, 1982). This evolutionary pattern typically entails an initial entry into markets perceived to be geographically and culturally similar to the domestic market in terms of language, political and trading systems, as well as social mores and traditions. As companies increase in their international trading experience, confidence encourages them to extend into foreign market previously perceived to be impenetrable and remote (Cavusgil, 1980; Welch and Weidersheim-Paul, 1980).

Central to the explanation of this incremental approach to foreign market entry is the concept of psychic distance. Emanating from the export marketing literature, psychic distance is predicated on the belief that a firm's inexperience in foreign market exchange will encourage them to initially export to, and establish operations within, markets perceived to be psychologically proximate to the home market. Utilised essentially as a risk-reducing strategy, increased experience of international exchange encourages participation within markets previously perceived to be psychological distant (Johanson and Vahlne, 1977; Cavusgil, 1982).

The concept of psychic distance is implicit within the models of business internationalisation. The Uppsala Internationalisation Model (Johanson and Weidersheim-Paul, 1975) proposes that the internationalisation of firms occurs in incremental stages and recognises that at the earliest stages of international involvement, the direction of international expansion is typically to geographically close markets. Thereafter, improvements in foreign market intelligence and increased confidence gained from experiential learning encourage firms to enter geographically and culturally distant markets.

There is clear evidence from the literature to support the concept of psychic distance within the context of retailer internationalisation. Hollander (1970) indicated that retailers seek to manage the threat of psychological distance by entering geographically close and culturally similar markets, and this was replicated in the study of Waldman (1978), which found that internationalising retailers adopt a country-by-country expansion strategy, commencing from markets adjacent to the retailer's national border. Later studies by Robinson and Clarke-Hill (1990), Lualajainen (1991), Williams (1991), Knee (1993), Burt (1993, in Europe), Kacker (1985 in the USA) and Davies (1993, in Asian markets) have indicated similar patterns of expansion; although the extent to which the seemingly arbitrary notions of geographical and cultural proximity are meaningful indicators of likely business success have been legitimately questioned (Treadgold, 1988; Burt, 1993, Dawson, 1994). Furthermore, from the services marketing literature, it has been suggested that advances in communications technology, as well as macro-level changes in the form of economic and cultural integration has meant that psychic alienation is now a much less important consideration to international marketers (Ekeledo and Sivakumar, 1998; Majkgard and Sharma, 1998).

Reflecting on the process of market expansion adopted by internationalising retailers, and drawing from the principles established by the various stages theories, Treadgold (1990) proposed that a retailer's international development follows three stages as follows:

- Reluctance
- Caution
- Ambition

The first stage begins with the admission of a lack of opportunity within the home market. As a result, foreign market entry is a reluctant requirement for corporate growth. At the second stage, the cautious retailer enters culturally and geographically close foreign markets. Experiential learning encourages the retailer to become more ambitious in their international aspirations, and their market choice is then based on the nature and extent of opportunities within the foreign market, rather than for reasons of cultural and geographical safety.

While these conceptualisations based on staged development are the useful means of illustrating the various processes that companies follow as they internationalise, they are not without their critics. In relation to Treadgold's application of the stages approach to retailing, it has been suggested that the stages models fail to recognise that retailers, regardless of their size, may make an immediate and significant commitment to a geographically and/or disparate foreign market (through franchising or acquisition), accelerating the process and missing out stages (Davies and Fergusson, 1996), and do so in the knowledge that they can withdraw from the market with relative ease (Dawson, 1994).

Other studies have likewise challenged the importance of psychic distance and have suggested that not all retailers necessarily choose to locate within culturally close markets, but depending on the nature of the retailer's product assortment and market positioning, may choose to locate at an early stage of their international involvement within markets that are geographically and culturally disparate from their home market. For example, the British fashion retailer Paul Smith with more than 200 stores in Japan has become (according to the Paul Smith web site in August 2003) Japan's best selling European fashion brand. At first sight, the choice of Japan as a first market for a small menswear retailer from Nottingham may appear odd, if not bizarre. However, Sir Paul Smith recognised the huge opportunities for his brand in Japan. By virtue of the Japanese interest in excellent tailoring, innovative design, and the allure of an English brand, Paul Smith enjoyed a number of credible advantages. The success the company has achieved within Japan has served as an important income stream and growth platform for the successful development of Paul Smith within the UK and the rest of Europe.

At times, internationalising retailers will enter a culturally proximate market with a view to using that country as a spring board for access into other, less familiar markets. The luxury American accessories retailer Coach announced in Summer 2003 their decision to open a concession within Harvey Nichols Department Store in London, with the prospect of opening a stand-alone store soon after in London. While one of the most successful luxury brands in the USA where it enjoys a 19 per cent market share of the luxury-fashion accessories market, Coach acknowledged prior to the opening of their first London outlet that the brand was relatively unknown within the UK and in Europe generally. However, hopeful of a successful launch, the decision to open their first European store in London was based on the recognition of the prestige of London as a centre for luxury goods retailing and as a key European shopping destination. By introducing the brands to the French, Germans and Italians in London, the company hopes to spread the brands popularity throughout Europe. In addition, Coach believed prior to their UK entry that the first concession would serve as a testing ground for the potential popularity of key products in Europe. As the company president explained in an interview with the *Financial Times* in July (*Financial Times*, 2003a), 'The UK will give us some sense as to what the opportunity size in Europe might be'.

Other fashion companies have likewise indicated the indirect benefit of establishing operations within the British market, not least for the fact that UK participation facilitates a greater exposure within the European fashion press and encourages business partners located within virgin territories to collaborate in franchise agreements. As such, while the direction of a retailer's international expansion may be influenced by considerations of cultural proximity and market adjacency, the development of a platform market such as the UK may be as much driven by the opportunities arising from other markets which emerge as a result of being in a particular market as they are about the opportunities that arise within a particular market.

1.5 Methods of market entry

The choice of market entry that an internationalising retailer adopts is dependent on the market position of the firm, trading format and their international expansion strategy. In recognition of the fact that retailers may elect to adopt a variety of modes of foreign market entry, Treadgold and Davies (1988) argued that the method of foreign market entry adopted by a firm serves to reflect (and is influenced by) the internal competencies of the retailer as well as the trading conditions they perceive to exist within the foreign market. In particular, the selected entry method indicates the level of control that the retailer seeks to exert over their foreign operations, the degree of flexibility required in order to effectively respond to market conditions that their foreign enterprise may face, as well as the mount of resources that the retailer wishes to allocate for overseas expansion.

Five methods of market entry are identified within the international retailing literature. **Non-controlling interest** involves the firm acquiring what is normally a minority stake in a foreign retailer. The advantage of this approach is that it allows the firm to obtain market intelligence at minimal risk. It also allows those who know the market (i.e. the existing management team), to continue to manage the foreign operation. The primary disadvantage to the investing retailer is that it is essentially a passive position. Consequently, investments are typically made without the ability to influence the activities of the new investment.

Internal expansion involves the opening of individual stores in a foreign market using the same format as that used within the home country. This method of expansion is financed using internal resources. There are many advantages associated with this method of expansion. It can be used by any size of firm and experimental openings can be made with minimum risk and at times at a relatively modest cost. This approach affords the internationalising retailer with full control over their operations and allows for adaptation based on experience and different market conditions. Certainly at the early stages of development, this approach also allows for ease of exit since no other external party is directly involved in such a decision.

Internal expansion does have associated disadvantages. By virtue of the reliance on internal resources in order to fund the expansion programme, it may take a long time before a substantial foreign presence can be achieved. Given that the retailer operates in isolation, there is not the benefit of local management knowledge and expertise to draw upon. As such, this approach requires a full locational assessment prior to investment. Furthermore, if the host country is distant from the home market, the distance can cause problems with respect to co-ordination and control.

Merger or takeover is typically characterised by the acquisition of control over an existing retail business within a foreign country. The benefits of this approach are that it allows for substantial market presence to be quickly achieved, management is already in place and cash flow is therefore immediate. This method also provides an opportunity to speedily transfer technology and other forms of know-how from the foreign to the home market and vice versa. Merger or takeover also provides the opportunity to obtain locations quickly for conversion to a chosen format. The disadvantages of this method are that it can be difficult and very costly to exit from the situation if mistakes have been made. In many cases, the process of evaluating the business position of the takeover target can be difficult and in some cases, competitive bidding may not afford the time to allow for a full evalu-ation. There is also the problem that suitable acquisition companies may not be readily available. As such, this may not be an option that is readily available to retailers with international aspirations.

Franchise-type agreements are when the retail formula and the ideas of the franchiser from the originating country are replicated, under contract, by the franchisee in the host coun-try. As has been identified in the literature, this is one of the most favoured approaches to market entry among internationalising retailers. The method affords the advantage of rapid international expansion at a low cost and at low risk to the franchiser. Franchising incorpo-rates the talent and local knowledge of foreign management and provides for the develop-ment of locally competitive marketing policy. Within closed markets, the use of franchise agreements allows for entry barriers to be overcome. As to the associated disadvantages, it may be difficult for the internationalising retailer to recruit suitable franchisees with the required expertise and financial resources. In some cases, the franchisers may find themselves locked in an unsatisfactory relationship and the intricacies of international franchise contracts may make it difficult for the company to extricate themselves from complex legal agreements.

Joint ventures can take a variety of forms, including in-store concessions, involving the letting of retail space by an established retailer in the host country to a foreign retailer; a joint development agreement between two entrant firms in a host country or an agree-ment between an entering and an indigenous retailer. It is not uncommon for one partner in a joint venture agreement to buy out their partner in order to maintain their position in the market. The benefits of a joint venture arrangement are that it often provides for a link with a firm already in the market and this may provide a new market entrant with much needed information with respect to an alien trading environment. This approach also pro-vides a platform on which a firm can decide either to fully enter into the foreign market or to exit at a later point. Like the other methods of market entry, this has certain disadvantages. This approach is only possible if a suitable trading partner can be found. In addition, if the venture is successful, then a joint venture agreement typically requires that the benefits be equally shared. Perhaps the most significant possible disadvantage is that the success of a joint venture is dependent on the business acumen of both the parties. The successful actions of one partner could be diluted by the ineptitude of the other partner in the relationship.

Largely because much of the research relevant to the internationalisation of retailing has focused upon the foreign development of grocery firms, little recognition is given within the literature to the role of wholesaling as a market-entry method. Wholesaling is com-monly used by fashion companies, not only at the early stages of their international involvement, but also in conjunction with their development of a network of retail outlets. Wholesaling is in essence exporting by another name and involves one company supply-ing a range of branded goods to a third-party retail stockist in exchange for payment. Invariably, the international retailer's wholesale division will appoint an agent to act as their representative in a foreign market. The agent is responsible for attracting potential customers; selling ranges to stockists; taking orders and making sure that these are received and processed by the wholesaler. In most cases, the role of the agent is to establish and staff a showroom which is then used to display the stock to prospective stockists. The agent does not normally raise an invoice for the payment of goods; does not take payment from stockists or accept legal title for the merchandise. Agents are usually paid on a fee and commission basis by the international wholesaler but payment is not made until the retail stockist has paid the international wholesaler in full.

Wholesaling provides an important income stream for international fashion retailers. For example, in financial year 2002/2003, wholesaling accounted for $1.18 billion of Ralph Lauren's total turnover. This represents a contribution of 49 per cent to Ralph Lauren's total turnover. In addition, wholesaling provides a low-risk way of testing market reaction to a brand and product range, and assists in the establishment of a customer following prior to the establishment of a store network within a foreign market.

For many fashion retailers, wholesaling remains an important distribution method long after they have established stores on a foreign country. As well as being a low-cost option, wholesaling can provide for significant market coverage at relatively low risk. For example, Quicksilver, the Australian surf brand has over 300 wholesale stockists which augment the 28 Quicksilver stand-alone stores within the UK. It is interesting to note that the company maintains that their retailer stores support their wholesale business, while success from their wholesale accounts encourages increased demand for the full ranges that are available within their retailer outlets.

There are, however, certain problems associated with wholesaling. While some suppliers may set down strict criteria for the evaluation of potential stockists, there is always the risk that the stockist may undermine the reputation of the brand through poor visual presentation, unauthorised pricing discounting or poor customer-service provision. In response to these problems, many international wholesalers require that their agents also monitor the extent to which stockists comply with brand implementation guidelines and standards. This is however a very costly exercise and is the exception rather than the norm within the UK fashion sector.

Considering the various entry methods overall, Sparks (1996) presented these as a continuum; ranging from direct investment of internal resources to fund organic growth, to less direct involvement achieved through non-controlling interests. This continuum represents, according to Sparks, not only differences in the degree of retailer's direct involvement and control over the foreign operation, but also variations in the degree of perceived risk associated with such participation. Thus, for example, growth by means of internal expansion is characterised by a high degree of control and knowledge transfer from the home market to the host, while franchise relationships present lesser degrees of risk, and fewer opportunities for host market control and knowledge transfer for the internationalising retailer.

It is important to note that internationalising retailers often adopt a range of market-entry methods over time and at any one point in time. On examination of the market-entry methods used by the 'elite' group of grocery retailers (i.e. Wal-Mart, Carrefour, Ahold and Tesco), it is clear that these adopt an opportunistic approach to market-entry choice in that they use whichever entry method is best suited to their strategic objectives and the local market conditions. For example, as Burt and Sparks (2003) reported, Tesco has used organic growth in Taiwan; joint ventures with Samsung in South Korea and Sime Darby in Malaysia. Tesco used an acquisition strategy for entry into Hungary, Poland, the Czech Republic, Slovakia, Thailand and Ireland.

With stores in 28 countries, the French retailer Carrefour enjoys the greatest inter-national coverage of all of the European-based international grocery chains. The company has used a variety of market-entry methods, including joint ventures in Belgium, Brazil and Austria. An interesting dimension of Carrefour's international growth was their merger with another French retailer with international interests, Promodes. This merger not only extended the international participation of Carrefour, but also precipitated its transformation from being a hypermarket-only to a multi-format operator – with interests in supermarket and hard discount businesses (Burt and Sparks, 2003). This merger also meant that franchising became an additional operating method for the company in its foreign markets.

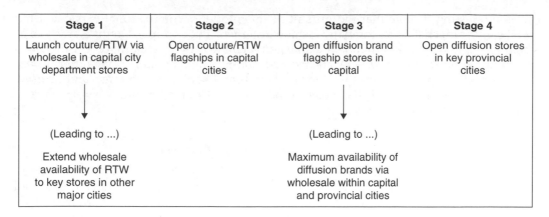

Figure 1.4 The four stages in the international development of fashion designers
Source: Moore *et al.* (2000)

Just as this international 'elite' has used multi-entry methods, other international fashion firms have likewise adopted a range of market-entry methods. What perhaps distinguishes the market-entry strategies of the international fashion retailers from other categories is that these often use a range of entry methods concurrently. For example, the Italian retailer, Benetton operates 50 stores under the Benetton and Sisley fascias within the UK. Of the 50, nine are company owned and the remainder operate under franchise agreements. In addition, Benetton's has a wholesale distribution network which supplies leading department stores, such as House of Fraser and Debenhams. Benetton's mix of operating approaches is motivated by their desire to balance control over brand presentation (achieved through their company-owned stores), with maximum market coverge achieved at minimum risk (via their franchised stores and wholesale accounts).

A review of the market development strategies of the leading international fashion designers highlights the complex web of relationships that develop when they enter new markets. Figure 1.4 illustrates the fours stages of international development that have been adopted by firms, such as Donna Karan, Ralph Lauren, Calvin Klein and Giorgio Armani.

The first stage involves the international designers supplying to prestigious department stores, such as Harrods in London and Saks Fifth Avenue in New York, via wholesale arrangements. As indicated previously, wholesaling serves to establish a brand following at a low cost. Once established, their wholesaling arrangements are extended to key retailers in other major cities. The second stage involves the opening of flagship stores within the key fashion capitals and premium shopping streets – Bond Street in London; Fifth Avenue in New York and Rue Saint Honaire in Paris. Due to the high rental and operating costs associated with these stores, these tend to be viewed as 'loss leaders', which exist in order to promote and support wholesale sales and the movement towards the development of stage three. This third stage in their international expansion involves the development of diffusion brands that are sold in dedicated flagship stores and distributed via the wholesale arrangements. Further discussion surrounding the characteristics of diffusion brands is provided later in this chapter. Generally, it is the diffusion brand, which is the most profitable for the internationalising retailer. This is because their middle market, lower-price positioning facilitates significant sales volumes. Given the crucial role that these diffusion flagship stores play within the market development of these firms, many design houses have sought a stock-market listing in order to finance the international expansion of these diffusion stores. The fourth and final stage involves the expansion of diffusion stores to the key provincial cities of the main operating markets.

It is interesting to note that the pursuit of this model of international expansion has posed significant challenges for many fashion designers. For example, Donna Karan Corp., which lead the way in international expansion facilitated by a stock-market listing, was eventually bought out by the French luxury-fashion conglomerate, LVMH after a poor stock-market performance left the Donna Karan brand somewhat battered and bruised. Similarly, Calvin Klein stock has recently been bought out by Phillips Van-Heusen in February 2003 for similar reasons.

1.5.1 International market de-entry: divestments and withdrawals

While much of the attention of academic researchers has been focused upon the market-entry choices of internationalising retailers, more recent investigations have considered the divestment and strategic withdrawal activities of international retailers. Moore (1997) noted that market entry followed by a relatively swift withdrawal was a common feature of the international expansion of fashion retailers with a mid-market positioning. Reviewing the withdrawal of retailers, such as Jacadi, Naf Naf, Kookai and Next, Moore found that withdrawal was often a result of an irrevocable breakdown in franchise relationships or because of difficulties within the domestic market. In some cases, the decision to divest was due to personality conflicts between senior executives, but was most often attributed to poor market performance and untenable operating costs.

In a more recent review of the international divestment activities of two British retailers, Marks and Spencer and Arcadia, Alexander and Quinn (2002) noted that the latter, the decision to divest, were due to poor trading conditions within the home market, changes in senior management and a lack of integration between the domestic and international markets. Similarly, for Marks and Spencer, the decision to withdraw from their foreign markets was due to inclement domestic market conditions, a change in senior management and a resultant reprioritising of company resources, as well as a disproportionate resource allocation to some international operations.

Alexander and Quinn (2002) make the valid point that the under-performance of foreign operations is often excused or indeed ignored, whenever performance within the home market is buoyant. They also make the point that while retailers may elect to withdraw from international operations at times of home market crisis; the reality is such that such activities rarely appease investors' dissatisfaction with company performance. In the case of Marks and Spencer, the decision to sell off their American operations in 2001 has proved to be a complicated, as well as a costly exercise. In November 2001, the company sold its Brooks Brothers menswear chain for $225 million in cash. This was less than one-third of the amount paid by Marks and Spencer for the New York-based company in 1988. By August 2003, Marks and Spencer had yet to find a buyer for their other American business, Kings Supermarket chain. The chain was bought by Marks and Spencer in 1988 at a cost of $110.3 million. An attempt to sell the business to New York food retailer, D'Agostino for $160 million failed in December 2002. The company explained their failure to secure a buyer for the chain on tough USA debt and equity markets which made it difficult for potential buyers to raise sufficient finds to purchase the chain (*Reuters*, 12 August 2003).

A review of the recent and on-going divestment experiences of Marks and Spencer highlights a variety of dimensions associated with exiting a market. Perhaps one of the most interesting is that their failure to secure a reasonable selling price for of both their American chains serves to highlight that the company had paid over the odds for two businesses in the first place. Furthermore, it is now clear that Marks and Spencer's domestic market successes in the 1980s and 1990s served to eclipse the realities of imprudent acquisition decisions and poor ongoing sales performance in their foreign markets.

1.6 Strategies for managing foreign operations

The final sections of this chapter will consider the various recent conceptualisations that have been developed in order to explain the nature and characteristics of retailer internationalisation. However, prior to this review, it is necessary to first consider the various strategies that retailers adopt in response to the challenges associated with trading in foreign markets. A number of writers have sought to provide typologies of the strategies that retailers adopt in order to manage their international operations and the most significant of these have been integrated into the most recent models of retailer internationalisation. Therefore, this section will initially review the important typologies relevant to the international strategies of the retailers.

As a preliminary point, it is worth noting that the wider literature relating to the internationalisation of business highlights that the strategic approach a firm may adopt within foreign markets is dependent on a complex series of decisions with respect to the firm's attitude towards adjustments to their marketing mix; their policies related to the power of decision-making and the control that they require over foreign market operations (Johnson and Czinkota, 1982; Levitt, 1983; Christensen *et al.*, 1987; Onkvisit and Shaw, 1987).

Furthermore, the general international management literature has used Levitt's ideas on globalisation of markets, published in the *Harvard Business Review* in 1983 as the benchmark for the standardisation versus customisation debate when companies take their products into international markets. Levitt argued that consumers typically have the same needs and aspirations around the world and companies ought to recognise this in relation to their product and service offerings. While there is certainly evidence to prove that a standardised product offer is possible within certain product sectors, such as hotel chains and credit cards, it is also the case that these firms have had to adapt elements of their product offer and change dimensions of their communications strategies in order to reflect the distinctive needs of specific markets.

Academic understanding of the extent to which retailers adapt their strategies in response to foreign market differences has been heavily influenced by the work of Salmon and Tordjman (1989). They identified three strategic approaches to retailer internationalisation:

- International investment
- Global
- Multinational

and suggested that a retailer's choice of strategy is ultimately dependent on the trading characteristics and internal competencies of the company.

The **international investment strategy** involves the transfer of capital from one country to another, with the aim of acquiring part-share or total shares in another operating company. Retailers typically adopt this approach in the early stages of their international involvement in order to diversify their business for reasons of financial and political risk, to gain rapid market share within countries where the organic development of a chain of outlets would involve high risk and high cost, as well as to obtain the trading advantages inherent to that market. A variety of studies have highlighted that this internationalisation strategy has been adopted by British retailers (Wrigley, 1989, 1993, 1996, 1997, 1998, 1999, 2000; Hamill and Crosbie, 1990; Alexander, 1995), especially British grocery retailers seeking to enter the North American market through the acquisition of existing firms.

The internationalising retailer who elects to take an active role in the management of store operations abroad typically must react to two conflicting pressures. The first relates to their need to respond to the specific needs of consumers in particular foreign markets, while the second is to maximise profitability through operational-scale economies (Salmon and Tordjman, 1989). Retailers who adopt a **global strategy** seek to maximise their profitability by maintaining a high degree of control over their foreign store network. Central to this strategy is the faithful replication of a trading concept which is achieved through the standardisation of the retail marketing mix and the faithful replication of the same product range, communications methods, corporate identity, service and price levels within all stores, regardless of their geographical location. Retailers who use this strategy tend to be those who have a distinctive brand identity and/or product range.

Case Example: Tom Ford and Gucci

When Tom Ford assumed the position of Creative Director for Gucci in the 1990s, his main priority was to end the many product-licensing agreements that Gucci had made in the previous two decades. Under the stewardship of the third generation of the Gucci family, the Gucci brand name had been indiscriminately licensed to over 13,000 product lines. Consequently, Gucci products were available within 18,000 outlets worldwide. For a brand that had sought to convey an image of exclusive sophistication, it is perhaps no surprise that the profitability of the company was adversely affected by this explosion in product licensing. Ford recognised that as a result of their promiscuous licensing strategy, Gucci no longer had control over its brand image and identity. By rescinding as many of the licensing agreements as was possible, Ford then embarked on a ruthless brand control campaign that was to become legendary in the fashion sector. Every aspect of Gucci's brand image across the company's international store portfolio came under the personal control of Ford and his staff at the company's HQ in Italy. By retaining full control over the positioning of the brand and radically reducing its availability, Tom Ford had successfully re-engineered the Gucci brand to become one of the world's most profitable and respected fashion brands.

The adoption of a global strategy has one major disadvantage. It does not allow for flexibility in response to local conditions and demands. The adoption of a **multinational strategy** seeks to provide that flexibility through the retention of a basic trading concept or image across a range of geographically dispersed markets, coupled with a commitment to the adaptation of a trading formula in response to local market conditions and the expectations of local customers. Carrefour – identified previously as one of the super-elite international retailers – has adopted this strategic approach throughout their 33-year history of international trading. The company claims that their international merchandising strategy allows for extensive local adaptation and that this is evidenced by the fact that almost 90 per cent of their inventory is local or regional. Furthermore, Carrefour maintains that it actively facilitates the exchange of management know-how and expertise between and among those who manage their many trading markets (Burt and Sparks, 2003).

In a more recent review of the transfer of retail formats into developing markets, such as that of China, Goldman (2001) proposed a refinement of the global versus multinational view. He identified six strategy variants and these are detailed as follows:

1. *The global niche position strategy* – This strategy in effect, is a global strategy in the extreme. Targeted towards a specific global segment, within a highly specific market segment, retailers who pursue this approach religiously replicate their brand formula across all of their trading markets.
2. *The opportunism strategy* – This approach is akin to the multinational strategy in that it allows for the adaptation of formats in response to local market opportunities.
3. *The format pioneering opportunity strategy* – This strategy involves the development of a regional format in response to local opportunities. The format is confined to that specific region only.

4. *The format extension compatible country of origin strategy* – This strategy is in many ways a version of a global strategy in that the home market format is replicated with some changes in response to the specific idiosyncrasies of the local market.
5. *The portfolio-based format extension strategy* – This strategy is similar to the above, but involves the adaptation of a non-domestic format.
6. *The competitive positioning orientated strategy* – This approach is concerned with developing the positive dimensions of the format in response to the competitive conditions of the trading market.

To all intents and purposes, the typology of Goldman (2001) affirms the fact that the global and multinational strategies ought not to be viewed as two discrete and mutually exclusive approaches to trans-national expansion, but are instead two extremes on a continuum of strategic choices. The majority of retailers' international strategies are based largely on a mix of both the approaches.

1.6.1 Towards a conceptual framework of retailer internationalisation

In tandem with the growth in retailers' international involvement in the 1980s and 1990s, there has been the emergence of conceptual frameworks by retail academics. Much of the earlier work drew from the manufacturing sector; most notably, the work of Dunning' Eclectic Paradigm (1981) which was reviewed earlier in this chapter. In essence, his model highlighted that the nature of international expansion is a function of a series of advantages: *ownership specific*, where the product (retail offer) gives competitive advantage; *location specific*, where the host country can offer cost or market opportunities (Eastern Europe and Asia); or *internalisation advantage*, where management innovation or other corporate advantages can lead to success. As was identified previously, there has been criticism of this borrowing of concepts from the general business studies literature on the basis that the internationalisation of retailing differs fundamentally from that of manufacturing. Other examples of the 'theory borrowings' include those models, which explored the stages of international expansion. These have typically been derived from international marketing, specifically in relation to market-entry strategies. Likewise, work in the area of retail international development strategies, such as that of Salmon and Tordjman (1989), which was reviewed in the previous section.

While these various borrowings are in themselves problematic, perhaps the most important problem with many of the previous models resides in the fact that these were derived at a time when retailer internationalisation was small scale in terms of its global impact. At that point, the retailer internationalists were largely niche players and notably fashion retailers who had developed strong franchise agreements.

However, the mid-1990s and the early part of the 20th century have witnessed true internationalisation so many of these earlier works, while valuable in their time, appear to be more applicable to the earlier stages of the internationalisation of retailing. That said, two American works, published in the late 1990s have served to provide a more relevant contribution to our knowledge of this complex area. Sternquist (1997) produced her Strategic International Retail Expansion (SIRE) model primarily for the purpose of explaining the international expansion of USA retailers. The model, presented below as Figure 1.5 is essentially integrative in nature. It joins the eclectic paradigm (on the left side of the diagram), with the stages and the global versus multinational strategy literature.

Sternquist noted that multinational retailers' expansion is typically slower than that of global retailers and that these adapt rather than standardise. Furthermore, this type of retailer tends to concentrate their expansion within a specific geographical area and it is only when they have become sufficiently established in that area that they then move on to another region or area.

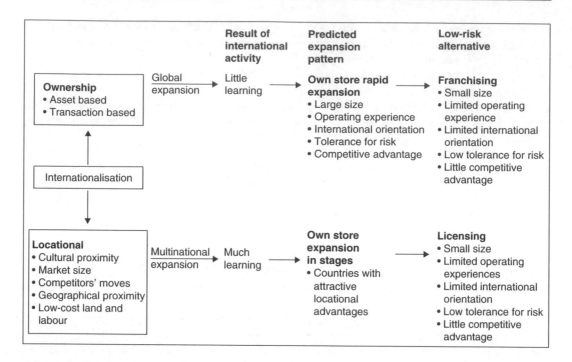

Figure 1.5 Model of SIRE
Source: Strenquist (1997)

Drawing from the behavioural strand of the international marketing literature, the work of Vida and Fairhurst (1998) proposed that the driving force behind a retailers' international expansion are the ownership advantages of the firm and the knowledge, experience and attitudes of management towards specific markets. They propose that as management gain in knowledge and experience from their participation in foreign markets, they become more ambitious in their international aspirations. In particular, their model considered the *antecedents*, which encapsulate the environment within which a decision is taken; the *process* in which expansion or withdrawal decisions are made and the *outcomes* which relate to the strategic options relevant to market selection and the selection of new markets.

More recently, the work of Alexander and Myers (2000) has sought to integrate previous research into a framework which delineates, from a corporate perspective, the internationalisation process. Figure 1.6 details the drivers for change, which precipitate the decision to participate within foreign markets.

Derived from asset-based advantages, such as in the form of the retail format or brand (echoing the work of Dunning), the decision to maximise the opportunity provided by these assets is determined by the internal facilitating competences that exists within the retail organisation (as was suggested by Vida and Fairhurst). Based on the availability of the required internal competencies, decisions relevant to market selection, entry methods and operating approach are made. As the retailer gains in international experience, the internal facilitating competencies are upgraded to accommodate the lessons learnt from its operations in new geographical areas.

Alexander and Myers (2000) have also produced a matrix, which attempts to explain international retail strategies (see Figure 1.7). They use the extension of the retail concept along the *x*-axis and the firm's perspective on internationalisation on the *y*-axis. In terms of measuring the latter, they propose that the company's approach may be either described

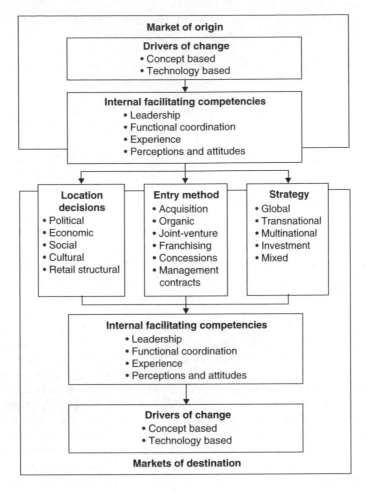

Figure 1.6 Operational organisation of international retailers
Source: Alexander and Myers (2000)

High	Multinational	Global
Market extension		
Low	Proximal	Transnational
	Ethnocentricism	Geocentricism

Figure 1.7 Market and operational organisation
Source: Alexander and Myers (2000)

as ethnocentric or geocentric. An ethnocentric approach is one whereby the retailer adopts a domestic orientation to their international strategy. Those retailers defined as taking a geocentric perspective may, according to Alexander and Myers (2000), 'embrace change rather than replicate an existing formula'.

The matrix identifies four variations of market and operational internationalisation. They classify the proximal retailer as one which provides a similar retail offer to that offered in the domestic market to those customers in psychologically proximate markets. In some cases, this may involve the border-hopping activities, which typified the early internationalisation strategies of retailers in Europe and North America. As such, these foreign markets are viewed as extensions of the domestic market.

The other quadrants in the matrix are much more controversial. The multinational retailer is described as having a high degree of market extension but remains psychologically attached to the competitive mindset of the domestic market. It is Alexander and Myers' contention that firms such as Wal-Mart and The Gap would be categorised as multinational retailers. This group of retailers, while they may achieve a high degree of market extension, retain an ethnocentric perspective when it comes to international involvement.

The global retailer, in contrast, not only engages in high levels of market extension, but they also are prepared to embrace change in response to foreign market conditions rather than to replicate an existing formula. Within this context, they identify Ahold (one of the super-elite international retailer retailers identified previously), as a global retailer. The final category is that of the trans-national retailer. Like the global retailer, this group are prepared to embrace change in foreign markets but operates in a comparatively limited number of markets. It is interesting to note that Alexander and Myers (2000) identified Zara as a trans-national retailer. On face value, this may appear a peculiar categorisation for Zara since they appear committed to a highly standardised operating formula which provides little opportunity for market responsiveness. However, an analysis of Zara's internationalisation model indicates that while their brand image is highly standardised, the processes which support their product development and merchandising strategy are very flexible and allow for the integration of pan-national fashion trends almost as soon as these emerge. Further evidence of Zara's flexibility is evidenced by their approach to trading within the British market. From the outset, the company recognised the allure that their Spanish origins provided for their brand and they clearly understood the distinctive positioning that the company had within the UK as a fashion-forward retailer. As such, the company has tended to focus upon the more fashionable lines within their British stores. In order to exploit their advantages within the British market, the pricing policy within the UK has been more upscale and prices are at least 20 per cent higher than in their home market of Spain.

Burt (2002) in a more recent contribution, noted the inherent difficulties of developing taxonomies of this nature. However, he identifies global retailers as high-fashion firms and grocery retailers, such as Ahold and other specialist companies, as multinational retailers.

1.6.2 *Conceptualising the future: international retail strategies*

While these various conceptualisations have enhanced our understanding of the strategic challenges associated with managing international operations, none of these provided have explored which approach will provide for strategic advantage in the future. With respect to the future developments among the elite trans-national corporations, Wrigley (2002) proposed a bi-polar model, which highlights the contrasting approaches that have been adopted this important group of international retailers (see Figure 1.8).

One approach that he identified is the *Intelligently Federal* model which has been adopted by firms, such as Ahold. With its focus upon local partnerships, best practise knowledge transfer, format adaptation and back-end systems integration, it contrasts markedly with the *Aggressively Industrial* model which provides low format adaptation and maintains maximum central management control. The latter approach is one that is favoured by 'category killers', such as Wal-Mart. While recognising that the debate over which of these

Aggressively Industrial	Intelligently Federal
Low format adaptation	Multiple/flexible formats
Lack of partnerships/ alliances in emerging markets	Partnerships/alliances in emerging markets
Focus on economies of scale in purchasing, marketing and logistics	Focus on back-end integration, assessing economies of skills as much as scale and best practice knowledge transfer
Centralised bureaucracy, export of key management and corporate culture from core	
	Absorb, utilise/transfer, best local management acquired
The global *category killer* model	The *umbrella organisation/ corporate parent* model *versus*

Figure 1.8 Alternative corporate models of globalised retailer operation
Source: Wrigely (2002)

models is likely to succeed in the future has yet to be finally resolved, Wrigley readily acknowledges that questions concerning the sustainability of the low-adaptation approach are inevitable. Acknowledging the key challenge for retailers in the future will be the extent to which they are capable of responding to the demands of 'different cultures', it would appear that Wrigley subscribes to the view that the 'Intelligently Federal' approach is the one most likely to succeed in the long term.

It is much more difficult to conceptualise a model that encapsulates the strategic approach that is most likely to be adopted by those non-elite trans-national/non-grocery retailers, far less one that can be used to predict which strategy is likely to be most effective in the future. By virtue of the range and diversity of the many different types of retailer who operate internationally, any proposed model is likely to be perfunctory and inadequate. However, drawing from the research expertise of the authors in the area of fashion retailer internationalisation, it is possible to identify the factors that are most likely to direct and influence the strategies of international fashion retailers.

No classification of the international fashion retailers appears to exist. Therefore, derived from a database of over 200 fashion companies that operate within foreign markets, it is possible to identify four specific categories of international fashion retailer as detailed in Table 1.2. This categorisation is based on the product and market of the international retailers. Due to the inadequacies of existing databases, it is not possible to base a classification on the nature and extent of the foreign market coverage of the international retailers. The identification of these groupings is especially useful as a means of identifying the convergences and divergences that exist with respect to the operating strategies of fashion retailers within foreign markets.

1.7 International fashion retailers' strategies

Based on over 30 interviews with International Retailing Executives representative of each of the four grouping delineated in Table 1.2, it is possible to identify three key dimensions, which while not exclusive in their importance, nevertheless serve to define the dynamics

Table 1.2 Four categories of international fashion retailer

1. *The product specialist fashion retailers* – These are companies that focus upon a narrow and specific product range, such as Camper Shoes, La Senza, Tie Rack, Nike, Sock Shop and Jacadi. These have a clearly defined target customer group either based on demography (such as childrenswear), gender (such as La Senza and Hom Underwear) or a specific interest (such as sport and Nike and Reebok). While there are some obvious exceptions (i.e. Nike Town concept), these retailers usually operate relatively small-scale stores either within busy customer traffic sites, such as adjacent to airports/railway stations or major mass-market shopping areas, such as Oxford Street in London, and Fifth Avenue, in New York. The competitive differential of this specialist group is inextricably linked to the depth of their merchandise range within specific product categories.

2. *The fashion designer retailers* – Fernie *et al.* (1997) provided a clear definition of the international fashion designer retailers in terms of their having bi-annual fashion show in one of the international fashion capitals (i.e. Paris, Milan, London and New York) and have been established in the fashion design business for at least 2 years. These firms retail merchandise through outlets bearing the designer's name (or an associated name), within two or more countries and market their own label merchandise. In many cases, the merchandise ranges offered by these companies extends beyond clothing to include other lifestyle product areas, such as furniture and household accessories.

   Examples of this group include Gucci, Giorgio Armani, Prada, Valentino and Chanel. These firms typically locate within premium locations within capital and other important cities. Their competitive differential relates to the allure of their brand, their perceived exclusivity and, at times, the innovative nature of their product design.

3. *The general merchandise retailers* – They are retailers that offer a merchandise mix that includes clothing alongside non-fashion goods. Examples include department stores such as Dunnes Stores from Ireland who incorporate fashion ranges with household goods; Marks and Spencer in Hong Kong who sell an edited range of foods alongside their fashion ranges. Their stores are often located within key expatriate locations. The competitive differential of this general group is linked to the breadth, and in some occasions, the depth of their merchandise ranges.

4. *The general fashion retailers* – Unlike the product specialist fashion retailers which tend to concentrate on only a limited range of fashion product categories, the general fashion retailers offer a more extensive range of fashion merchandise and accessories, either to a broad (e.g. The Gap, Next) or highly defined target segment (e.g. Kookai, Miss Sixty, French Connection, Mango). These groups are usually located in 'city-centre' locations so as to allow for maximum customer access. The competitive differential of this group is linked, in part, to the strength of their brand identity, as well as the breadth and depth of their fashion offer.

of contemporary international fashion retailing. These three dimensions present new and significant challenges to the international fashion retailer and their various distribution partners. Arguably these are the issues that will define the success or failure of fashion companies in the future.

The three dimensions to be considered in the remained of this chapter are:

- The customisation of fashion experiences
- Fashion boundary extension
- Fast fashion

1.7.1 Fashion experiences

With more than 166 store worldwide, Prada had typically sought to replicate a broadly similar store environment within each market. It would seem therefore that Prada's approach to store architecture has been symptomatic of the international operating strategy of the typical luxury/high brand – with consistency, coherency and clarity as the essential features. However, the opening of a new Prada store in New York in 2001 and a second in Tokyo a year later, marked a new approach, not only to the international brand positioning of Prada but it could also be argued to the basic assumptions concerning the strategic approach of international designer brands in general.

Prada's store in New York, designed by Rem Koolhaas, is in the site of a former Guggenheim Museum. Emphasising space, light and technology, this development (which Prada describes as an epicentre store), cost in excess of $40 million. The store in Tokyo has few walls. Touch-sensitive screens are suspended from the ceiling and these allow customers to search through the images of the various Prada collections. The changing rooms offer the customer a choice of electronic sounds to match their mood. Designed by the Priztker award-winning Herzog and Meuron, the architects of the Tate Modern in London, the Tokyo store cost $87 million. It is the largest single investment made by an Italian company in Japan since the Second World War (*Financial Times*, 2003b).

The development of the Prada epicentre stores marks a new departure in how luxury and designer fashion brands are presented in stores. In recognition of the consumer back-lash against faceless globalisation and 'predictably corporate' shopping experiences, the most astute retailers in this category have recognised their need to differentiate through the provision of unique, localised and customised fashion experiences. In the past, the store experience was predicated on the belief that every image in every city had to be standardised in order to maintain the integrity of the brand and its positioning. It would seem that this standardisation has been rejected by customers themselves who now expect uniqueness and localisation. This trend provides significant challenges in that how can a brand positioning remain consistent in order to secure the scale economies of standardisation but at the same time be distinctive for specific segments within their specific locations? It would appear that the solution is through the increased customisation of the fashion experience, as one Italian company explained:

> We cannot change the whole product range for one market and then again for another. We would be in a mess. Instead, we all recognise that it is the experience that has to be adaptable. It needs to change to local conditions and tastes. The adaptation must fit in with the values of the company overall and the product range. But is this adaptation of many different store experiences that will mark out the successful companies in the future.

This appears to mark an important shift away from the standardisation of the global strategy in favour of the adaptability of the multinational response. Companies like Prada, with their premium prices, can afford to spend $87 million customising a new store. For retailers in the other three categories identified above, the net margins do not provide for this sort of architectural indulgence. The 'fashion experience' approach of stores, like The Gap, Mango, H&M, Next and La Senza, is to minimise costs and maximise profitability through the replication of a standard store format, which in turn provides for a standardised customer experience. There is little room here for experimentation and innovation. In defence of this approach, one Marketing Director of a leading chain of general fashion retailers made the following point:

> Companies like us are doing something different. Customers come to us for the price and the product. Of course, the experience has got to be good. But it is the main reason why the customer came to us in the first place.

Other mass-market international fashion retailers however have begun to question the long-term sustainability of a standardised store format approach/customer experience.

Camper Shoes of Spain is one of the fastest growing international shoe retailers in the world. The company augments their innovative shoe collections with a store environment strategy that, while centrally controlled, is defined by its commitment to individuality and distinctiveness in each outlet. It would seem that none of their stores is exactly the same. Each has its own quirk and its own design differential.

With the emergence of a more discerning and demanding customer, and the increased proliferation of innovative, individualistic fashion experiences, it is far from certain that the standardised fashion format has a long-term future other than for those international retailers that differentiate by offering a price/product availability trade-off.

1.7.2 Fashion boundary extension

The various economic indicators which track consumer expenditure within the European and American markets have, in the past decade, indicated a consistent decline in the proportion of personal disposable income that is spent on clothing. The decline is due, in part, to price pre-deflation as a result of increased competition and recessional conditions in markets in general. Within the context of the British market, a significant driver for this decline has also been the shift in consumer expenditure in favour of leisure activities, home and communications technology and home products in general.

For international fashion retailers, many of which face stock-market pressure to deliver a satisfactory return on investment, the pressure of this expenditure decline has been considerable. In response to this challenge, some of the most successful international fashion retailers have sought to increase their share of consumer expenditure by extending the boundary of their trading market. The companies have tended to do this in one of three ways, with a number of companies adopting all three approaches.

The first is to engage in **complementary diversification**. This involves extending the coverage of an existing brand into related product areas. For example, Ralph Lauren has increased brand coverage beyond clothing to include perfumes, spectacles, home decorating products, home furnishings, furniture and jewellery.

The second approach is to engage in **market extension** through the development of a diffusion or associate brand, or via the acquisition of an established fashion brand. Of the first option, a diffusion brand has a different name, identity and retail format and is typically a cheaper merchandise range, targeted towards a younger customer. For example, Giorgio Armani operates the Emporio Armani brand as a cheaper, younger diffusion brand. Likewise, the associate brand will differ in name, image and format, and may retail at the same or a higher-price point as the original brand. Often the associate brand is targeted towards an older, often more sophisticated company. Inditex, the company that owns the Zara chain, also operates internationally with an associate brand called Massimo Dutti. This brand is more formal and more expensive than the Zara brand and is targeted towards an older customer segment. By engaging in this form of market extension, Inditex has sought to minimise the risk of single-brand dependency by extending their market participation.

In some cases, a company will seek to extend its market coverage through the acquisition of another corporate brand. This strategy has been adopted most recently by Gucci who, through their development of the Gucci Group of companies have embarked on an acquisition strategy of purchasing:

■ *Declining brands* – such as YSL, which provide an opportunity for rejuvenation.
■ *Young brands* – such as Sergio Rossi, Alexander McQueen, Bedat & Co Stella McCartney, which provide an opportunity for sharp income growth.
■ *Complementary brands* – such as Boucheron which provides for manufacturing and operational synergies.

Diesel: pushing fashion boundaries

From its origins as a jeanswear label (it was the best selling brand in the sector in the UK in 2002; Drapers, 2003) Diesel has expanded the coverage of its core brand to include mens' and womens' casual and outerwear. The brand also includes an accessories line, Spare Parts – the Diesel underwear brand, a footwear line, a perfume range and an accessories range. In order to appeal to the more street-aware customer, the 55 DSL range offers a dynamic fashion/ sports option within stand-alone stores and via wholesale stockists. Younger customers are introduced to the brand through Diesel Baby and Diesel Kids. The StyleLab brand is an associate brand of Diesel. It is positioned as an experimental and fashion-forward range within dedicated stores. The company has sought to extend their offer through the purchase of other brands, such as Martin Margiela, which offers an urban take on fashion trends.

The third method that fashion companies have adopted has been to participate in semi-complementary diversification. The most common approach has been to extend into areas such as hotels (Versace and currently being developed by Camper) and cafes and restaurants (Nicole Fahri, Armani and Lanvin). This form of business growth is essentially high-risk strategy since it involves the retailer straying from their area of core competence. However, through the development of strategic alliances with partners who have expertise in these associated fields, many companies believe that these risks can be avoided and brand synergies maximised.

The pushing of the market boundaries within which fashion companies operate was identified as an inevitable feature by the majority of the industry representatives. It is important to note, however, that these developments may not necessarily be replicated within all foreign markets. The decision as to whether a market can support a diffusion brand or an associate brand is ultimately dependent on the same features which determine entry into a foreign market in the first place. This dimension is reflected in the statement made by a representative from a leading French sportswear brand:

> In ten years time I think that you will see more fashion retailers getting involved in areas that you would not have necessarily expected them to be involved in. In fashion we are about ten years later than food and just look at food. Look at Tesco in the UK. You can buy your food, your mortgage, your life from them. Fashion retailers will become more and more like that.
>
>   But whether it happens within a particular foreign country will depend on the competitive conditions. Customer demand for the product. The associated set-up costs. There is no guarantee that the offer will and should be extended to every single market.

1.7.3 *Fast fashion*

Fast fashion is the term that is used to represent the various strategies that fashion companies use in order to respond commercially to the latest fashion trends. In the past, the fashion cycle was split into two principal phases: Spring/Summer and Autumn/Winter. The development cycle from when a product was designed to when it was available for sale in the store was typically upwards of 6 months in duration. However, in the past decade, and as a result of influence of key players, such as Zara, H&M and Top Shop, the younger fashion market has changed dramatically. The primary manifestation of their influence has been the shrinking of the design-to-retail cycle to as little as 4 weeks. While in the past, the key fashion trends generated by the top fashion designers was not available to the mass market until the following season, firms such as H&M, pride themselves on their ability to replicate and have available in store the key fashion show looks within days of their appearance at the designer's fashion shows.

Three factors have supported the emergence and success of fast fashion. The first is a lean and flexible supply chain, which allows for the rapid turnaround of the latest looks in a manner that is effective and cost efficient. The achievement of quick response flexibility has been made possible through the re-engineering of the methods and timings by which garments are designed, coloured and constructed (Varley, 2001). Interestingly, for those companies seeking to achieve a rapid design to retail turnaround, this has necessitated their sourcing from suppliers closer to their target markets. For example, one British menswear retailer reported that the proportion of good sourced outside of the EU had risen from 10 to over 50 per cent as a result of the firm's commitment to the development of fast fashion in their business.

Secondly, the process of achieving fast fashion is dependent on a rapid and accurate information communications technology system. The transfer and sharing of data among all members of the supply chain is crucial to the concept of fast fashion.

Finally, fast fashion requires an efficient distribution system to service the various participants in the production chain and the international store network. Of the latter point, the use of air-freight has increased dramatically in the past 5 years, especially between countries within the EU.

The issue of fast fashion is all the more complex within international markets. While the variations in the emergence and up-take of new fashion trends across national markets would appear to be dissipating, it is nevertheless clear that trend variations do exist across national markets. Furthermore, while some are 'mega'-fashion trends (i.e. these are not confined to one national market), others are market-bound, and are influenced by particular dimensions of the domestic culture. For those retailers, such as the product specialists and general fashion retailers, the need to be responsive to changes in consumer buying patterns is crucial. Providing a competent response to emergent fashion trends requires an integrated management approach. From the interviews with senior fashion executives, it is clear that the configuration of relationships within international fashion retailing is changing radically. This is illustrated by the following observation made by the Director of Marketing for a fashion retailer that operates in more than 20 countries:

> In the past, the relationship that we had with our subsidiaries in foreign markets and franchise partners was at a distance. I suppose it was transactional. Now, in order to survive, we have developed a new type of partnership where we exchange information about what is happening in the local markets. It is not enough anymore to believe that the brand alone will deliver success.

For many international fashion retailers, the advent of fast fashion has prompted the development of more collaborative relationships within foreign partners. This collaboration is manifested in three specific ways.

The first involves the increased involvement of foreign management and partner companies in the process of new product development. Rather than the internationalising retailer presenting ranges as a 'non-negotiable given' to international partners, many now encourage them to be actively involved in the development of new product ideas and range developments. For example, it has been the case that the management of the Diesel's British subsidiary has been actively involved in the design development of ranges that would be suited to the needs of customers in the UK.

As well as engaging local management in range development, fashion retailers are also developing trend communication networks. These networks are comprised of 'cool spotters', who monitor fashion trends and developments from peripheral, street and underground market segments. By collecting digital images and video clips, they collate information on trends as they emerge and send this data to their client's design team within the home market. Through their development of a network of 'cool spotters', the fashion companies can access the key trends at the earliest point in their gestation. They can then integrate the key trend themes into their latest fast fashion creations.

The third form of collaboration is through the development of 'flash collections'. These are market-reactive fashion collections that are developed in response to highly specific trends within national markets. These collections are available for a limited time period – often no more than 4 weeks – and are available in small batch sizes. As a means of achieving scale economies, these ranges will be available to the three or four markets that appear receptive to the latest trends. The development of 'flash collections' is now regarded as a crucial activity and this is justified by one the Buying Directors of the British subsidiary of a key Italian brand:

> Flash collections are very important for us. They work by being available for a very short period within specific countries. Customers like the fact that we do this thing that is very quick and short-term and it keeps their interest. It might not always make commercial sense to do it. But in order to survive, we need to retain the sense that we are fast and there when it happens.

The development of 'flash collections' has been a further inducement for retailers to source closer to their selling market and to adopt the principles of quick response. It should be noted, however, that while the costs associated with adopting this approach are considerably higher than the 'traditional' sourcing regime, the selling points of these ranges are commensurately higher and often more than compensate for any cost of supply increases.

While it may seem that these various initiatives are confined only to those retailers who operate within the youth market, it is important to note that the trend for fast fashion is also evident among those retailers who target older customers. For example, the German fashion retailer Olsen, who operate retail stores and an extensive wholesale distribution business, is clearly targeted towards women in the 30 plus age bracket. While in the past Olsen operated on a twice-yearly seasonal buying cycle, through their adoption of a new ordering system, 'Time to Market', the company now offers buyers the opportunity to order from their new ranges every 6–8 weeks. As such their latest business-to-business advertising strap-line is 'Time to Market. On Time. On Trend. On Target'. The company maintains that this new approach minimises the business risk by allowing buyers the opportunity to take account of the latest fashion trends in their buying plans.

These three trends clearly challenge the assumption that internationalising fashion retailers will automatically adopt a global approach to the management of their retail operations. It previously appeared that their success was dependent on the faithful replication across all markets of all aspects of the trading and branding strategy. However, the twin drivers of increased market competition, the emergence of a set of customer expectations which demand immediate access to the very latest fashion trends and a consumer expectation of a fashion experience that is distinctive, if not unique, necessitates that the international fashion retailer adopt a much more adaptive and flexible strategic approach.

With these dimensions in mind, Figure 1.9 presents an overview of the possible transformations that may occur in the future with respect to the international strategies of fashion retailers. While it is acknowledged that these various dimensions are not necessarily relevant to every type of fashion retailer, within every foreign market, these nevertheless have at least some relevance for most firms.

A useful summary of the transformations apparent within international fashion retailing is evident in the observations of a Director for International Retail Operations:

> We will look back and see that the fashion landscape was radically altered by the impact of firms like Prada and Zara, Mango and H&M. While they might not be

Global strategy	Drivers ————————→	Market responsive strategy
Standardised retail format and experience	Customer rejection of 'corporate' retail experiences Demand for innovation and distinction	Specific fashion experiences which reflect customer expectations and local sensibilities
Replication of a single concept abroad	Decline in fashion expenditure (leading to the need for market development via diffusion, associate or acquired brands)	Replication of specific brand concepts dependent on market opportunity
Centralisation of product ranging decision-making	Emergence of fast fashion necessitating collaboration in: • Range development • Trend spotting • Range customisation	Collaborative partnerships rather than transactional relationships between members of the supply chain

Figure 1.9 Factors that support the transformation from a global to a market-responsive strategic approach by international fashion retailers

the biggest or most important in world terms, these companies will be seen to have re-shaped how fashion is managed. We can see these are the key movers at the beginning of the 21st century. They are transformational fashion retailers.

1.8 Concluding remarks

This chapter has sought to provide an introduction to retailer internationalisation by bringing together some of the early writings on the subject with the more recent studies that have acknowledged the changing landscape of pan-national distribution. Initial consideration was given to the identification of the key international retailers, and it was acknowledged that the 'elite trans-national grocery retailers', comprising in the main of Wal-Mary, Carrefour, Ahold and Tesco, are clearly in a league of their own. Their distinctiveness is drawn not only from the scale and the extent of the international market involvement, but also from their impact on the market structures of some of the world's most significant national markets.

The chapter also examined the actual dimensions of retailer internationalisation and sought to bring a new dimension to the debate by considering the processes associated with the internationalisation of product sourcing. Furthermore, the motives for international expansion were considered and while the earlier explanations for market development were acknowledged, it was also recognised that many of there explanations now appear inadequate in their ability to explain the strategic decision-making of the elite internationalists in the grocery sector.

Mindful of the fact that most previous studies have tended to focus upon the internationalisation of food retailers, the section that considered the foreign market-entry approaches of retailers recognised the importance of wholesaling as a market development strategy for fashion firms. As was evidenced by the example of Ralph Lauren, wholesaling not only is important at the point of foreign market entry, but also remains significant throughout the period within which a fashion retailer operates within a foreign market. The issues associated with market withdrawal were discussed. Clearly this is an area worthy of future research attention.

The final section considered the various recent conceptual frameworks that have been developed in order to advance the understanding of retailer internationalisation. The culmination of this section involved a review of the topology of Wrigley (2002). Given the importance of the elite grocery retailers to the re-shaping of the contemporary global landscape, it is perhaps fitting that a model (which focuses almost exclusively on the activities of this group) should be presented.

However, given the apparent research neglect with respect to the internationalisation of fashion retailing, it is also appropriate that the chapter should end with a review of the drivers which appear likely to influence and shape the future strategies of the leading international fashion retailers. It will be interesting to note whether and how the trio of influences, namely the customisation of fashion experiences, fashion boundary extension and fast fashion, materialises to have any significant impact on how fashion retailers operate within foreign markets in the future.

References

Alexander, N. (1995) Expansion within the single European market: a motivational structure. *The International Review of Retail, Distribution and Consumer Research*, **5**(4), 472–487.

Alexander, N. (1997) *International Retailing*. London, Blackwell Science.

Alexander, N. and Myers, H. (2000) The retail internationalisation process. *International Marketing Review*, **17**(4/5), 334–353.

Alexander, N. and Quinn, B. (2002) International retail divestment. *International Journal of Retail and Distribution Management*, **30**(2), 112–125.

Bannister, J.P. and Saunders, J.A. (1978) UK customers' attitudes towards import: the measurement of national stereotype image. *European Journal of Marketing*, 12(8), 562–570.

Bilkey, W.J. and Nes, E. (1982) Country of origin effects on product evaluation. *Journal of International Business Studies*, **8**(1), 89–99.

Boswell, J. (1969) *JS 100 – The Story of Sainsbury*. London, J. Sainsbury.

Burt, S. (1989) Trends and management issues in European retailing. *International Journal of Retailing*, **4**(4), 3–97.

Burt, S. (1993) Temporal trends in the internationalisation of British retailing. *International Review of Retail, Distribution and Consumer Research*, **3**(4), 391–410.

Burt, S.L. (2002) International retailing. In McGoldrick, P.J. (ed.), *Retail Marketing*. Maidenhead, McGraw-Hill.

Burt, S. and Sparks, L. (2003) The internationalisation of grocery retailing. In *The Retailing Book: Principles and Applications*. England, Prentice-Hall.

Cavusgil, S.T. (1982) Some observations on the relevance of critical variables for internationalisation stages. In Czinkota, M.R. and Tesar, G. (eds), *Export Management*. New York, Praeger, pp. 276–286.

Clarke, I. and Rimmer, P. (1997) The anatomy of retail internationalisation: Diamaru's decision to invest in Melbourne, Australia. *The Service Industries Journal*, **17**(3), 361–382.

Dahringer, L.D. (1991) Marketing services internationally: barriers and management strategies. *Journal of Services Marketing*, **5**(3), 5–17.

Davies, K. (1993) The international activities of Japanese retailers. *7th International Conference on Research in the Distributive Trades*, Stirling, 8–12 September, pp. 534–543.

Davies, K. and Fergusson, F. (1996) The international activities of Japanese retailers. In Akehurst, G. and Alexander, A. (eds), *The Internationalisation of Retailing*. London, Frank Cass.

Dawson, J. (1994) The Internationalisation of retailing operations. *Journal of Marketing Management*, **10**(4), 267–282.

Doherty, A.M. (2000) Factors influencing international retailers' market entry mode strategy: qualitative evidence from the UK fashion sector. *Journal of Marketing Management*, 16, 223–245.

Dunning, J.H. (1981) *International Production and the Multinational Enterprise*. London, Allen and Unwin.

Ekeledo, I. and Sivakumar, K. (1998) Foreign market entry choice of service firms: a contingency perspective. *Journal of the Academy of Marketing Science*, **26**(4), 274–292.

Fernie, J, Fernie, S. and Moore, C. (2003) *Principles of Retailing*. Oxford, Butterworth-Heinemann.

Financial Times (2003a) Being Miuccia Prada. 21 June 2003.

Financial Times (2003b) Handbag Invasion – Coach the Yankee Luxury Brand. 2 August 2003.

Hollander, S. (1970) *Multinational Retailing*. East Lancing, MI, Michigan State University.

Johanson, J. and Vahlne, J.E. (1977) The internationalisation process of the firm – a model of knowledge development and increasing foreign commitments. *Journal of International Business Studies*, **8**(1), 23–32.

Johanson, J. and Wiedersheim-Paul, F. (1975) The internationalisation of the firm – four Swedish case studies. *Journal of Management Studies*, **12**(3), 305–322.

Kacker, M.P. (1985) *Transatlantic Trends in Retailing: Takeovers and Flow of Know-How*. Westport, Quorum.

Kacker, M.P. (1988) International flow of retailing know-how: bridging the technology gap in distribution. *Journal of Retailing*, **64**(1), 41–63.

Katrishen, F. and Scordis, N. (1998) Economies of scale in services: a study of multinational insurers. *Journal of International Business Studies*, **29**(2), 305–332.

Knee, D. (1993) *Survey of International Moves by Retailers 1991–1993*. Oxford, Oxford Institute for Retail Management.

Laulajainen, R. (1991) Two retailers go global – the geographical dimension. *International Review of Retail, Distribution and Consumer Research*, **1**(5), 607–626.

Levitt, T. (1983) The globalisation of markets. *Harvard Business Review*, **61**(May–June, 92–102.

Lin, L. and Sternquist, B. (1994) Taiwanese customers' perceptions of product information cues: country of origin and store prestige. *European Journal of Marketing*, **28**(1), 5–18.

McGoldrick, P.J. (1995) Introduction to international retailing. In McGoldrick, P.J. and Davies, G. (eds), *International Retailing: Trends and Strategies*. London, Pitman. 11–13.

McGoldrick, P.J. and Fryer, E. (1993) Organisational culture and the internationalisation of retailers. *7th International Conference on Research in the Distributive Trades*, University of Stirling, 6–8 September, pp. 534–543.

Moore, C.M. (1997) La Mode sans frontiers: the internationalisation of fashion retailing. *Journal of Fashion Marketing and Management*, **1**(4), 345–356.

Moore, C.M., Fernie, J. and Burt, S.L. (2000) Brands without boundaries: the internationalisation of the designer retailer's brand. *European Journal of Marketing*, **34**(8), 919–937.

Onkvisit, S. and Shaw, J.J. (1987) Standardised international advertising: a review and critical evaluation of the theoretical and empirical evidence. *Columbia Journal of World Business*, **22**(3), 43–55.

Pellegrini, L. (1992) The internationalisation of retailing and 1992 Europe. *Journal of Marketing Channels*, **1**(2), 3–27.

Pellegrini, L. (1994) Alternatives for growth and internationalisation in retailing. *The International Review of Retail, Distribution and Consumer Research*, **4**(2), 121–148.

Planet Retail (2002) *Grocery Retailing in Europe*. London, M&M Planet Retail.

Reuters (2003) M&S fails to offload remaining US interest. *Reuters News Agency*, 12 August.

Robinson, T. and Clarke-Hill, C.M. (1990) Directional growth by European retailers. *International Journal of Retail and Distribution Management*, **18**(5), 3–14.

Salmon, W.J. and Tordjman, A. (1989) The internationalisation of retailing. *International Journal of Retailing*, **4**(2), 3–16.

Tanner, D. (1992) Kotobukiya Co. Ltd. In Hast A., Pascal, D., Barbour, P. and Griffin, J. (eds), *International Directory of Company Histories*, Vol. V. Detroit, St James Press.

Tordjman, A. (1994) European retailing: convergences, differences, and perspectives. *International Journal of Retail and Distribution Management*, 22(5), 3–19.

Treadgold, A. (1988) Retailing without frontiers. *Retail and Distribution Management*, November/December, 8–12.

Treadgold, A. (1989) Pan-European retail business: emerging structure. *European Business Review*, **1**, 7–12.

Treadgold, A. (1990) The developing internationalisation of retailing. *International Journal of Retail and Distribution Management*, **18**(2), 4–10.

Treadgold, A. and Davies, R.L. (1988) *The Internationalisation of Retailing*. Harlow, Longman.

Turnbull, P.W. (1987) A challenge to the stages theory of the internationalization process. In Rosson, P.J. and Reid, S.D. (eds), *Managing Export Entry and Expansion*, New York, Praeger, pp. 21–40.

Sternquist, B. (1997) International expansion of US retailers. *International Journal of Retail and Distribution Management*, **25**(8), 262–268.

Vida, I. and Fairhurst, A. (1998) International expansion of retail firms: a theoretical approach for further investigation. *Journal of Retailing and Consumer Services*, **5**(3), 143–151.

Waldman, C. (1978) *Strategies of International Mass Retailers*. New York, Praeger.

Weidersheim-Paul, F., Olson, H.C. and Welch, L.S. (1978) Pre-export activity: the first step in internationalisation. *Journal of International Business Studies*, **9**, 47–58.

Welch, L.S. and Weidersheim-Paul, F. (1980) Initial exports – a marketing failure. *Journal of Management Studies*, October, 333–344.

Williams, D.E. (1991) Differential firm advantages and retailer internationalisation. *International Journal of Retail and Distribution Management*, **19**(4), 3–12.

Williams, D.E. (1992) Retailer internationalisation: an empirical enquiry. *European Journal of Marketing*, **26**(8/9), 8–24.

Wrigley, N. (1989) The lure of the USA: further reflections on the internationalisation of British grocery retailing capital. *Environment and Planning A*, **21**, 283–288.

Wrigley, N. (1993) Retail concentration and the internationalisation of British grocery retailing. In Bromley, R. and Thomas, C. (eds), *Retail Change: Contemporary Issues*. London, UCL Press, pp. 41–68.

Wrigley, N. (1996) From high street to main street: the market entry of British food retail capital into the USA. *EIRASS/CIRASS Annual Conference*, Telfs/Buchen, 22–26 June.

Wrigley, N. (1997) British food retail capital in the USA – Part 1, Sainsbury and the Shaw's experience. *International Journal of Retail and Distribution Management*, **25**(2–3), 7–21.

Wrigley, N. (1998) European retail giants and the post-LBO reconfiguration of UK food retailing. *The International Review of Retail, Distribution and Consumer Research*, **8**(2), 127–146.

Wrigley, N. (1999) Corporate finance, leverage restructuring and the economic landscape: the LBO wave in US food retailing. In Martin, R.L. (ed.), *Money and the Space Economy*. Chichester, Wiley, pp. 185–205.

Wrigley, N. (2000) Strategic market behaviour in the internationalisation of food retailing: interpreting the third wave of Sainsbury's US diversification. *European Journal of Marketing*, **34**(8), pp. 891–919.

Wrigley, N. (2002) The landscape of pan-European food retail consolidation. *International Journal of Retail and Distribution Management*, **30**(2), 81–91.

Study questions and guideline answers

1. Retail internationalisation is much more than the opening of stores abroad. Provide a critical review of this statement.

Reponses should consider that retailer internationalisation is not only concerned with the opening of stores abroad. Responses ought to incorporate a review of the transfer of the 'invisible' dimensions, such as know-how, sourcing and finance.

2. Why do retailers internationalise?

Responses ought to consider that the 'push' and 'pull' factors identified in the chapter. In particular, consideration should be given to the fact that motives for international expansion may change over time and that the explanations for international expansion may be influenced by the research methodologies used.

3. Provide a critique of the various methods of market entry that are available to the internationalising retailer.

Responses should consider the five key entry methods and consider the advantages and disadvantages associated with each. Responses should include the dimensions included in Section 1.7.

4. Critically review the strategies for retailer internationalisation proposed in the chapter.

Responses ought to review the defining elements of the strategy framework of Salmon and Tordjam (1989) – principally in terms of **the investment strategy/globalisation strategy/multinational strategy**. Consideration ought to be given to the six-dimensional typology of Goldman (2001).

Chapter 2

Retail logistics

John Fernie

Aims

The aims of this chapter are to discuss:

- the theoretical framework which underpins logistics and supply chain management (SCM) concepts;
- efficient consumer response (ECR) and managing supply chain relationships;
- the application of supply chain concepts in different international markets;
- future trends, most notably the impact of electronic commerce (e-commerce) on logistics networks.

2.1 Introduction

The principles behind logistics and SCM are not new. Managing elements of the supply chain has been encapsulated within organisations for centuries. Decisions such as where to hold stock, in what quantities and how it is distributed have been part of the 'trade-off' analysis that is at the heart of logistics management. It is only in the last 10–15 years, however, that logistics had achieved prominence in companies' boardrooms primarily because of the impact which the application of supply chain techniques can have on a company's competitive position and profitability. Retailers have been in the forefront of applying best practice principles to their businesses with UK grocery retailers being acknowledged as innovators in logistics management.

2.2 Supply chain management: theoretical perspectives

The roots of SCM as a discipline is often attributed to the management guru, Peter Drucker and his seminal article in the *Fortune Magazine* in 1962. At this time he was discussing distribution as one of the key areas of business where major efficiency gains could be achieved and costs saved. Then, and through the next two decades, the supply chain was still viewed as a series of disparate functions. Thus, logistics management was depicted as two separate schools of thoughts: one dealing with materials management (industrial markets) and the other with physical distribution management (consumer goods markets) (see Figure 2.1). In terms of the marketing function, research has focused upon buyer–seller relationships and the shift away from adversarial relationships to those built upon trust (see Ford, 1997). At the same time a body of literature was developing, mainly in the UK, on the transformation of retail logistics from a manufacturer-driven to a retail-controlled system (McKinnon, 1989; Fernie, 1990; Fernie and Sparks, 1998).

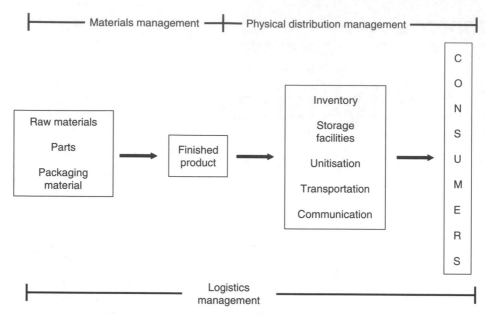

Figure 2.1 Logistics management

In both industrial and consumer markets, several key themes began to emerge:

(a) the shift from a push to a pull (i.e. a demand-driven supply chain);
(b) the customer is gaining more power in the marketing channel;
(c) the role of information systems to gain better control of the supply chain;
(d) the elimination of unnecessary inventory in the supply chain;
(e) the focusing upon core capabilities and increasing the likelihood of outsourcing non-core activities to specialists.

To achieve maximum effectiveness of supply chains, it is imperative that integration takes place by 'the linking together of previously separated activities within a single system' (Slack *et al.*, 1998, p. 303). This means that companies have had to review their internal organisation to eliminate duplication and ensure that total costs can be reduced rather than allow separate functions (including marketing) to control their costs in a sub-optimal manner. Similarly, supply chain integration can be achieved by establishing ongoing relationships with trading partners along the supply chain.

Throughout the 1970s and 1980s attention in industrial marketing focused upon the changes promulgated by the processes involved in improving efficiencies in manufacturing. Total quality management, business process re-engineering and continuous improvement brought Japanese business thinking to Western manufacturing operations. The implementation of these practices was popularised by the book of Womack *et al.* (1990) on *The Machine that Changed the World*. Not surprisingly, much of the literature on buyer–seller relationships focused upon the car manufacturing sector.

During the 1990s, this focus upon lean production was challenged in the US and UK because of an over-reliance on efficiency measures rather than innovative responses. Harrison *et al.* (1999) show in Table 2.1, how lean and agile supply chains differ. Agility as a concept was developed in the US in response to the Japanese success in lean production. Agility plays to US strengths of entrepreneurship and information systems technology.

Table 2.1 Alternative supply chain processes

	Efficient/function (Lean)	Innovative/responsive (Agile)
Primary purpose	Supply predictable demand efficiently at lowest cost	Respond quickly to unpredictable demand in order to minimise stockouts, forced markdowns and obsolete inventory
Manufacturing focus	Maintain high-average utilisation rate	Deploy excess buffer capacity
Inventory strategy	Generate high turns and minimise inventory	Deploy significant buffer stock of parts
Lead-time focus	Shorten lead time as long as it does not increase cost	Invest aggressively in ways to reduce lead time
Approach to supplier selection	Select primarily for cost and quality	Select primarily for speed, flexibility and quality

Source: Harrison *et al.* (1999)

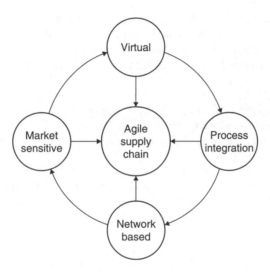

Figure 2.2 The Agile supply chain
Source: Harrison *et al.* (1999)

They have therefore developed an agile supply chain model (Figure 2.2), which is highly responsive to market demand. They argue that the improvements in the use of information technology (IT) to capture 'real-time' data means less reliance on forecasts and creates a virtual supply chain between trading partners. By sharing information, process integration will take place between partners who focus upon their core competencies. The final link in the agile supply chain is the network where a confederation of partners structure, co-ordinate and manage relationships to meet customer needs.

From this background to the evolution of SCM, it is clear that SCM draws upon a range of disciplines with regard to theoretical development. Initially much of the research was geared towards the development of algorithms and spatial allocation models for the determination of the least cost locations for warehouses and optimal delivery routes to distribute to final customers. The disciplines of geography, economics, operational research and mathematics provided solutions to management problems.

As SCM has developed into an integrated concept seeking functional integration within and between organisations, the theories to explain empirical research have been increasingly drawn from the strategic management or economics literature.

The key concepts and theories in SCM are:

- the value-chain concept;
- resource-based theory (RBT) of the firm;
- transaction cost economics;
- network theory.

The thrust of all these theories is how to gain competitive advantage by managing the supply chain more effectively. The concept of the value chain was originally mooted by Porter (1985) and his ideas have been further developed by logisticians, especially by Christopher (1997). In Figure 2.3, a supply chain model is illustrated which shows how value is added to the product through manufacturing, branding, packaging, display at the store and so on. At the same time, at each stage cost is added in terms of production costs, branding costs and overall logistics costs. The trick for companies is to manage this chain to create value for the customer at an acceptable cost. The managing of this so-called 'pipeline' has been a key challenge for logistics professionals, especially with the realisation that the reduction of time not only reduced costs but also gave competitive advantage.

According to Christopher there are three dimensions to time-based competition which must be managed effectively if an organisation is going to be responsive to market changes. These are as follows:

- *Time to market* – the speed at bringing a business opportunity to market.
- *Time to serve* – the speed at meeting a customer's order.
- *Time to react* – the speed at adjusting output to volatile responses in demand.

He uses these principles to develop strategies for strategic lead-time management. By understanding the lead times of the integrated web of suppliers necessary to manufacture a product, he argues that a 'pipeline map' can be drawn to represent each stage in the supply chain process from raw materials to customer. In these maps it is useful to differentiate between 'horizontal' and 'vertical' time.

- Horizontal time is the time spent on processes such as manufacture, assembly, in-transit or order processing.
- Vertical time is the time when nothing is happening, no value is added but only cost and products/materials are standing as inventory.

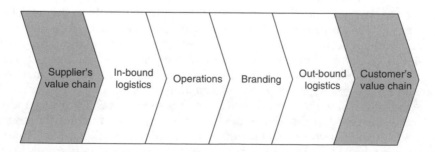

Figure 2.3 The extended value chain
Source: Christopher (1997)

It was in fashion markets that the notion of 'time-based competition' had most significance in view of the short-time window for changing styles. In addition, the prominent trend in the last 20 years has been to source products offshore, usually in low-cost Pacific Rim nations, which lengthened the physical supply chain pipeline. These factors combined to illustrate the trade-offs, which have to be made in SCM, and on how to develop closer working relationships with supply chain partners. Christopher has used the example of The Limited in the US to illustrate his accelerating 'time to market'. The company revolutionised the apparel supply chain philosophy in the US by designing, ordering and receiving products from South-east Asia to stores in a matter of weeks rather than the months of its competitors. New lines were test marketed in trial stores, orders communicated by EDI to suppliers which also benefited from computer-aided design/computer-aided manufacturing (CAD/CAM) technology in modifying designs. The products, already labelled and priced, were consolidated in Hong Kong where chartered 747s air freighted the goods to Columbus, Ohio, for onward despatch to stores. The higher freight costs were easily compensated for by lower markdowns and higher inventory turns per annum.

Along with The Limited, another catalyst for much of the initiatives in lead-time reduction came from work undertaken by Kurt Salmon Associates (KSA) in the US in the mid-1980s. KSA were commissioned by US garment suppliers to investigate on how they could compete with Far East suppliers. The results were revealing in that the supply chains were long (one-and-a-quarter years from loom to store), badly co-ordinated and inefficient (Christopher and Peck, 1998). The concept of quick response (QR) was therefore initiated to reduce lead times and improve co-ordination across the apparel supply chain. In Europe, QR principles have been applied across the clothing retail sector. Supply base rationalisation has been a feature of the last decade as companies have dramatically reduced the number of suppliers and have worked much closer with the remaining suppliers to ensure more responsiveness to the marketplace.

The resource-based perspective builds upon Porter's models by focusing upon the various resources within the firm, which will allow it to compete effectively. Resources, capabilities and core competences are key concepts in this theory. As a supply chain perspective to competitive advantage increases the resource base within which decisions are taken, this theory links to transaction cost analysis and network theory. Thus, firms have to make choices on the degree of vertical integration in their business, to 'make or buy' in production and the extent of outsourcing required in logistical support services. Building upon the seminal work of Williamson (1979), Cox (1996) has developed a contractual theory of the firm by revising his ideas on high-asset specificity and 'sunk costs, to the notion of core competences' within the firm. Therefore, a company with core skills in either logistics or production would have internal contracts within the firm. Complementary skills of medium-asset specificity would be outsourced on a partnership basis and low-asset specificity skills would be outsourced on an 'arms-length' contract basis.

The nature of the multiplicity of relationships has created the so-called network organisation. In order to be responsive to market changes and to have an agile supply chain, flexibility is essential. Extending the RBT, the network perspective assumes that firms depend on resources controlled by other firms and can only gain access to these resources by interacting with these firms, forming value-chain partnerships and subsequently networks. Network theory focuses on creating partnerships based on trust, cross-functional teamwork and inter-organisational co-operation.

In industrial markets, especially the automobile and high-technology sector, a complex web of relationships has been formed. This has led Christopher (1997) to claim 'that there is a strong case for arguing that individual companies no longer compete with other stand-alone companies, but rather, that supply chain now competes against supply chain' (p. 22). Tiers of suppliers have been created to manufacture specific component parts and other

The Benetton Group has around 5500 shops in 120 countries, manufacturing plants in Europe, Asia, the Middle East and India and revenues of more than $1.8 billion. Its interests are in two main areas:

- casual wear, accounting for around three-quarters of its total revenue. Key brands are United Colors of Benetton and Sisley.
- sportswear, accounting for one-fifth of total revenue. Key brands are Nordica, Prince, Killer Loop and Rollerblade.

Much of Benetton's success until the 1990s could be attributed to its innovative operations techniques and its strong network relationships which it has developed with both its suppliers and distributors. Benetton pioneered the 'principle of postponement' whereby garment dyeing was delayed for as long as possible in order that decisions on colour could be made to reflect market trends. At the same time a network of sub-contractors (small- to medium-sized enterprises) supplied Benetton's factories with the labour-intensive phases of production (tailoring, finishing and ironing) while continuing to manufacture the capital-intensive parts of the operation (weaving, cutting, dyeing and quality control) in Treviso in north-eastern Italy. In terms of distribution, Benetton sells its products through agents, each responsible for developing a market area. These agents set up a contract relationship, similar to a franchise, with the owners who sell the products.

Benetton is now beginning to transform its business by retaining its network structure but changing the nature of the network. Unlike most of its competitors, it is increasing vertical integration within the business. As volumes have increased Benetton set up a production pole at Castrette near its headquarter (HQ). This large complex is responsible for producing around 120 million items per year. To take advantage of lower labour costs, Benetton has located foreign production poles, based on the Castrette model, in Spain, Portugal, Hungary, Croatia, Tunisia, Korea, Egypt and India. These foreign production centres focus on one type of product utilising the skills of the region so T-shirts are made in Spain, jackets in Eastern Europe.

In order to reduce time throughout the supply chain, Benetton has increased upstream vertical integration by consolidating its textile and thread supplies so that 85 per cent is controlled by the company. This means that Benetton can speed up the flow of materials from raw material suppliers through its production poles to ultimate distribution from Italy to its global retail network.

The retail network and the products on offer have also experienced changes. Benetton had offered a standard range in most markets but allowed for 20 per cent of its range to be customised for country markets. Now to communicate a single global image, Benetton is only allowing 5–10 per cent of differentiation in each collection. Furthermore, it has streamlined its brand range to focus on the United Colors of Benneton and Sisley brands.

The company is also changing its store network to enable it to compete more effectively with its international competitors. It is enlarging its existing stores, where possible, to accommodate its full range of these key brands. Where this is not possible it will focus on a specific segment or product. Finally, it is opening more than 100 megastores worldwide to sell the full-range focusing on garments with a high styling content. These stores are owned and managed solely by Benetton to ensure that the company can maintain control downstream and be able to respond quickly to market changes.

Figure 2.4 The Benetton group

supplier associations have been formed to co-ordinate supply chain activities. In these businesses the trend has been to buy rather than make and to outsource non-core activities.

Benetton, which has been hailed as the archetypal example of a network organisation, is bucking the trend by increasing vertical integration and ownership of assets in the supply chain (Camuffo *et al.*, 2001). While it is retaining its network structure, it is refining the network from product design through to distribution to its stores (see Figure 2.4).

2.3 Efficient consumer response

The notion of time-based competition through just-in-time (JIT) and QR principles was given further credence in the fast-moving consumer goods (FMCG) sector with the advent of ECR.

ECR arrived on the scene in the early 1990s when KSA produced another supply chain report, ECR, in 1993 in response to another appeal by a US-industry sector to evaluate its efficiency in the face of growing competition to its traditional sector. Similar trends were discerned from their earlier work in the apparel sector; excessive inventories, long non-coordinated supply chains (104 days from picking line to store purchase) and an estimated potential saving of $30 billion, 10.8 per cent of sales turnover.

During the last decade, the ECR initiative has stalled in the US; indeed, inventory levels remain over 100 days in the dry grocery sector. Nevertheless, ECR has taken off in Europe from the creation of an European Executive Board in 1994 with the support of European-wide associations representing different elements of the supply chain: AIM, the European Brands Association; CIES, the Food Business Forum; EAN International, the International Article Numbering Association and Eurocommerce, the European organisation for the retail and wholesale trade.

It was in 1994 that initial European studies were carried out to establish the extent of supply chain inefficiencies and to formulate initiatives to improve supply chain performance (Table 2.2). ECR Europe defines ECR as 'a global movement in the grocery industry

Table 2.2 Comparisons of scope and savings from supply chain studies

Supply chain study	Scope of study	Estimated savings
KSA (1993)	US dry grocery sector	10.8% of sales turnover (2.3% financial, 8.5% cost) Total supply chain $30 billion, warehouse supplier dry sector $10 billion Supply chain cut by 41% from 104 days to 61 days
Coca Cola supply chain collaboration (1994)	127 European companies Focused on cost reduction from end of manufacturers line Small proportion of category management	2.3–3.4% percentage points of sales turnover (60% to retailers, 40% to manufacturer)
ECR Europe (1996 on going)	15 value-chain analysis studies (10 European manufacturers, 5 retailers) 15 product categories Seven distribution channels	5.7% percentage points of sales turnover (4.8% operating costs, 0.9% inventory cost) Total supply chain saving of $21 billion UK savings £2 billion

Source: Fiddis (1997)

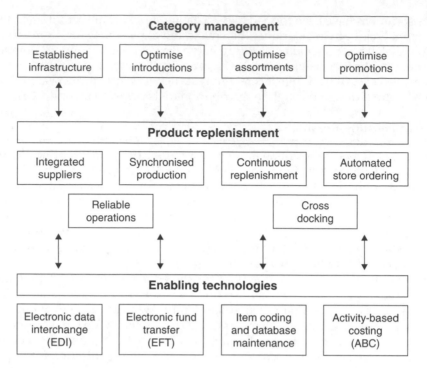

Figure 2.5 ECR improvement concepts
Source: Coopers and Lybrand (1996)

focusing on the total supply chain – suppliers, manufacturers, wholesalers and retailers, working close together to fulfil the changing demand of the grocery consumer better, faster and at less cost'.

One of the early studies carried out by Coopers and Lybrand (1996) identified 14 improvement areas whereby ECR principles could be implemented. These were categorised into three broad areas, namely product replenishment, category management and enabling technologies (Figure 2.5). Most of these improvement areas had received management action in the past, the problem was how to view the concepts as an integrated set rather than individual action areas.

As the ECR Europe movement began to gather momentum, the emphasis on much of the work conducted by the organisation tended to shift from the supply-side technologies (product replenishment) to demand-driven initiatives (category management). This is reflected in the early ECR project reports, which dealt with efficient replenishment and efficient unit loads. While the supply side is still important as reflected in projects on *Transport Optimisation and Unit Loads Identification and Tracking*; the majority of recent projects have focused upon consumer value, efficient promotion tactics, efficient product introductions and collaboration in customer-specific marketing.

Commensurate with this change in emphasis has been the topics under discussion at the *Annual ECR Europe Conference*. At its inception in Geneva in 1996, the concept was being developed and efficient replenishment initiatives were prominent on the agenda. Subsequent conferences have tended to emphasise demand-driven initiatives and emerging issues such as e-commerce.

It can be argued that the early work focused upon improving *efficiencies* within the supply chain and later collaborations have stressed the *effectiveness* of the supply chain. Thus, the focus now is on how to achieve profitable growth as there is little point in delivering products efficiently if they are the wrong assortment, displayed in the wrong part of the store!

The ECR Europe prime objective is to develop best practices and to disseminate these benefits to all members of the food supply chain in Europe. To date it has been highly successful in moving towards this objective. The early conferences were well attended (over 1000 delegates) but events in the 21st century have attracted over 3000 people. ECR initiatives are now formally organised in 14 European countries and the work in these countries is formally recognised through representation on the Executive Board. The Board itself is comprised of 30 senior executives from leading retailers and branded manufacturers in Europe who established the policy agenda to initiate new pilot projects and develop demand and supply strategies.

It is clear, however, that ECR will not be a panacea for all companies. The improvement areas suggested in Figure 2.5 provide a tariff of initiatives from which companies will choose according to their own particular objectives. Each company will have a different starting point and a different agenda depending on the current nature of supplier–retailer relationships. Nevertheless, a common theme applicable to all retailers is the limited number of relationships, which are established with suppliers. The large grocery retailers deal with thousands of suppliers and have only formal partnerships or initiated pilot projects with a small number of suppliers, for example J. Sainsbury has supply chain forums which brings together senior supply chain staff with 19 of their counterparts (suppliers) which account for a large part of Sainsbury's volume business. A criticism of *ECR Europe Conferences* and in those held in the UK, is that these venues are packed with representatives from the largest retailers and their multinational FMCG suppliers. Such concentration, the argument goes, can only lead to restricting consumer choice, high-profit margins and higher prices. So much for the consumer in ECR! With Wal-Mart's entry into the European market, this is hardly true in view of the intense price competition in Germany and the UK, the initial target markets. ECR can in fact enable companies to compete better in such competitive markets. It is true, however, that smaller companies have been slower to hop on the ECR bandwagon because of the time and resource commitments required to carry out ECR initiatives. Nevertheless, smaller companies such as those operating convenience stores have achieved significant increases in sales through working with key suppliers which have acted as 'category captains' in developing assortments within stores.

2.4 The retail supply chain

The implementation of ECR initiatives has been identified as the fourth and final stage of the evolution of grocery logistics in the UK. Fernie *et al.* (2000) classify this as the relationship stage, which relates to a more collaborative approach to SCM after decades of confrontation. The UK is often mooted to have the most-efficient grocery supply chain in the world and a key contributor to the healthy profit margins of its grocery retailers.

The four stages are as follows:

- supplier control (pre-1980),
- centralisation (1981–1989),
- JIT (1990–1995),
- relationship (1995–to date).

The first stage, supplier control, is widespread in many countries today and was the dominant method of distribution to stores in the 1960s and 1970s in the UK. Suppliers manufactured and stored products at the factory or numerous warehouses throughout the country. Direct store deliveries (DSD) were made on an infrequent basis (7–10 days), often by third-party contractors which consolidated products from a range of factories. Store managers negotiated with suppliers and kept this stock in 'the backroom'.

Centralisation, the second stage, is now becoming a feature of retail logistics in many countries and was prominent in the UK in the 1980s. The grocery retailers took the initiative at this time in constructing large, purpose-built regional distribution centres (RDCs) to consolidate products from suppliers for onward delivery to stores. This stage marked the beginning of a shift from supplier to retailer control of the supply chain. There were clear advantages from a retailer perspective:

- reduced inventories,
- lead times reduced from weeks to days at stores,
- 'backroom' areas released for selling space,
- greater product availability,
- 'bulk discounts' from suppliers,
- fewer invoices, lower administration costs,
- better utilisation of staff in stores.

Centralisation, however, required much capital investment in RDCs, vehicles, material-handling equipment and human resources. Centralisation of distribution also meant centralisation of buying with store managers losing autonomy as new headquarter (HQ) functions were created to manage this change. This period also witnessed a boom in the third-party contract market as retailers considered whether to invest in other parts of the retail business rather than logistics. All of the 'big-four' grocery retailers, Sainsbury, Tesco, Asda and Safeway, contracted out many RDCs to logistics service providers (LSPs) in the mid- to late 1980s.

In the third stage, the JIT phase, major efficiency improvements were achieved, as refinements to the initial networks were implemented. The larger grocery chains focused upon product-specific RDCs with most temperature-controlled products being channelled through a large number of small warehouses operated by third-party contractors. By the early 1990s, temperature-controlled products were subsumed within a network of composite distribution centres developed by superstore operators. Composites allowed products of all temperature ranges to be distributed through one system of multi-temperature warehouses and vehicles. This allowed retailers to reduce stock in store as delivery frequency increased. Furthermore, a more streamlined system not only improved efficiency but also reduced waste of short shelf-life products giving a better-quality offer to the customer.

While efforts were being made to improve secondary-distribution networks, initial projects were established to integrate primary with secondary distribution. When Safeway opened its large composite in 1989 at Bellshill in Scotland, it included a resource recovery centre, which washed returnable trays and baled cardboard from its stores. It also established a supplier-collection programme, which was to save the company millions of pounds during the 1990s. Most secondary networks were established to provide stores with high customer-service levels; however, vehicle utilisation on return trips to the RDC were invariably poor and it was efforts to reduce this 'empty running' that led to initiatives such as return trips with suppliers products to the RDC or equipment/recycling waste from stores.

Although improvements to the initial networks were being implemented, RDCs continued to carry 2 weeks or more of stock of non-perishable products. To improve inventory levels and move to a JIT system, retailers began to request more frequent deliveries from their suppliers in smaller-order quantities. Whiteoak, who represents Mars, and therefore suppliers' interests, wrote in 1993 that these initiatives gave clear benefits to retailers at the expense of increased costs to suppliers. In response to these changes, consolidation centres have been created upstream from RDCs to enable suppliers to improve vehicle utilisation from the factory.

The final stage, the relationship stage, is ongoing but is crucial if further costs are going to be taken out of the supply chain. In the earlier third stage, Whiteoak had noted that the transition from a supplier to a retail-controlled network had given cost savings to both suppliers and retailers *until* the JIT phase in the early 1990s. By the mid-1990s, retailers began to appreciate that there was no 'quick wins' such as that of centralisation in the 1980s to improve net margins. If another step change in managing retail logistics was to occur, it had to be realised through supply chain co-operation. The advent of ECR and its promotion by the Institute of Grocery Distribution fostered further co-operation between supply chain members. By the early part of the 2000s, however, increased competition in the retail marketplace fuelled by Wal-Mart's entry into the UK in 1999 has led to a drive for greater operation efficiencies and diversification into non-food areas where margins are greater. The latter has led to a transformation of distribution networks as indicated by recent changes in Asda's network (see Figure 2.6).

Asda was the last of the major grocery retailers to centralise its distribution. As the super-store pioneer in the UK, the company stocked more lines, including non-food lines, than its competitors. It also focused on branded products and suppliers delivered them direct to their nationwide network. By the mid-1980s, however, Asda reviewed its marketing and distribution strategy. Backdoor congestion at stores where 50–60 vehicles per day jostled to unload coupled with the huge administration costs of each store manager dealing with thousands of suppliers led to the decision to centralise its buying and distribution functions. The increase in own label penetration of its product mix reinforced the centralisation decision. By centralising, late Asda gained experience from a maturing distribution industry which had implemented networks for other retailers. Owing to the size and distribution of the Asda store network, a small number of large distribution centres were built: six RDCs and two national distribution centres stocking slow-moving grocery lines and non-food merchandise. Most of these distribution centres (six) were contracted out to LSPs.

Throughout the 1990s Asda developed more distribution centres and re-structured its network as store numbers increased from 130 to 230 in a decade. The success of the George brand led to the opening of a new state-of-the-art automated clothing centre in 1999. Although this depot was contracted out, the new grocery additions to the network were run 'in-house' by Asda. Nevertheless, with its creation of seven consolidation centres to co-ordinate the fresh produce chain, it contracted out the management of these freight movements to an LSP. It was in this year that Wal-Mart purchased Asda and embarked on the further development of general merchandise products. By 2005, 20 supercentres are planned with 50 per cent of sales space being devoted to non-food lines. Furthermore, by implementing Wal-Mart's Retail Link systems into Asda, it was anticipated that existing stores would release more space for selling these higher margin lines. For example, in September 2001 Asda re-launched its Home and Leisure business, introducing up to 5000 new lines, around 2000 of which were sourced through Wal-Mart's global network. The existing network is as follows:

- National Distribution Centres – Brackmills, Corby, Ince, Lutterworth, Whitwood.
- Composite RDCs – Dartford, Grangemouth, Lutterworth, Washington, Wigan.
- Other RDCs – Chepstow, Didcot, Wakefield, Washington.

This network services 256 Asda stores on a daily basis with the national centres holding slow-moving grocery (Lutterworth) or non-food lines (Brackmills and Ince, clothing and Whitwood and Corby, Home and Leisure). A further rationalisation of this network will occur in 2003 when much of the home, clothing and leisure products will be routed through a new depot in Yorkshire.

Figure 2.6 Asda's changing distribution network

The most radical initiative to impact on the grocery supply in the 2000s is the implementation of factory gate pricing (FGP) by the major multiple retailers. Initiated by Tesco and Sainsbury, FGP is the price retailers are willing to pay excluding transport costs from the point at which the product is ready for shipment to the RDC of retailers. In essence, this is the next step on from '*ad hoc*' backhauling and the consolidating of loads. In theory, FGP optimises the entire transport network throughout the supply chain. Instead of a series of bi-lateral transport contracts between LSPs and retailers/manufacturers, transport resources would be pooled to maximise vehicle utilisation. The larger retailers and LSPs can see the major benefits of FGP. With increased international sourcing LSPs have been keen to offer services in managing product flows across countries, and continents. Technologies are now available to track such movements and cost visibility should enhance openness in negotiations. Suppliers, however, have shown most concern with FGP. While the desegregation of product price from transport price leads to dislocation of current practices, many suppliers fear that retailers will then scrutinise product cost demanding further price reductions.

2.4.1 Differences in logistics 'culture' in international markets

ECR initiatives launched throughout the 1990s have done much to promote the spirit of collaboration. Organisations are having to change to accommodate and embrace ECR and to dispel inherent rivalries which have built up over decades of confrontation. The UK has been in the vanguard of implementing ECR with Tesco and Sainsbury claiming to have saved hundreds of millions of pounds in the late 1990s/early 2000s. The rate of adoption of ECR initiatives has varied between companies within international markets. Table 2.2 shows that the Kurt Salmon report hoped for an improvement of supply chain time from picking line to consumer from 104 to 61 days in the US. A comparative study of European markets by GEA Consultia in 1994 shows that all of the major countries hold much less stock within the supply chain. Indeed, the UK figure is now around 25 days. Mitchell (1997) argues that few of the largest European retailers (mainly German and French companies) have proven to be ECR enthusiasts. Many of those French and German retailers are privately owned or franchise operations and they tend to be volume and price driven in their strategic positioning. By contrast, UK and Dutch firms are essentially publicly quoted, margin-driven retailers who have had a more constructive approach to supplier relations. While accepting that there are key differences in European markets, in general there are differences between the US and Europe with regard to trading conditions. Mitchell (1997, p. 14) states that:

■ The US grocery retail trade is fragmented not concentrated as in parts of Europe.
■ US private label development is primitive compared with many European countries.
■ The balance of power in the manufacturer–retailer relationship is very different in the US compared with Europe.
■ The trade structure is different in that wholesalers play a more important role in the US.
■ Trade practices such as forward buying were more deeply rooted in the US than Europe.
■ Trade-promotional deals and the use of coupons in consumer promotions are unique to the US.
■ Legislation, especially anti-trust legislation, can inhibit supply chain collaboration.

While legislation has imposed controls on US retailers in terms of pricing and competition policy, there are significant fewer controls on location, planning and store choice issues. This has resulted in US retailers being able to operate profitably on much less sales per square metre ratios than the higher priced, fixed costs associated with the more 'controlled' markets of Europe.

To understand how different country logistics structures have evolved, it is necessary to understand the nature of consumer choice and the range of retail formats prior to seeking explanations for the nature of logistical support to stores through supplier relations, cost structures and other operational factors.

2.5 Consumer choice and retail formats

US tourists coming to Europe are probably puzzled at store opening hours and the restrictions on store choice compared with their own country. Although liberalisation of opening hours is beginning to happen across Europe, the tight planning restrictions on store sizes and location have tended to shape format development. Furthermore, cross-national surveys of attributes influencing a consumer's choice of store has shown the strong influence of price in France and Germany compared with the UK where price tends to be ranked behind convenience, assortment range, quality and customer service. (It can be argued however that as Wal-Mart becomes more established in the UK, the price spread between it and the UK competition may lead consumers to revalue these store attributes.) In the US price and promotion are also strong drivers of store choice; however, US consumers spend their food dollar in a variety of ways, including eating out which has always been more common than in Europe. Indeed, the KSA survey on ECR was initiated because of the competition from warehouse clubs and Wal-Mart into the traditional supermarket sector.

A partial explanation for the high-inventory levels cited by KSA in their survey is that US consumers do buy in bulk. With such an emphasis on price and promotion, consumers shop around and stockpile dry goods in garages and basements. Compared with their European counterparts, who neither have the space nor the format choices, US consumers have their own household 'backroom' warehouse areas.

In Europe the pattern of format development follows a broad north–south division. The southern Mediterranean and eastern European markets continue to have a predominance of small, independent stores and the supply chain is manufacturer controlled. This is changing, however, as northern European retailers enter these markets. In northern Europe, retailers have developed large-store formats but in different ways. For example, it is not surprising that Wal-Mart chose Germany as its entry market for Europe because of its strong discounter culture. This is reflected in its large number of hypermarkets and hard discounters, but the German consumer also shops at local markets. In France, the home of the hypermarket, large-scale formats co-exist with 'superettes' and local markets whereas in the UK and the Netherlands fewer formats are evident with superstores and supermarkets, respectively, dominating their markets.

In these northern European countries different logistics networks have evolved in response to format development. As discussed earlier in the chapter, many of the largest supermarket chains in the UK, which have a portfolio of superstores, have developed composite distribution to improve efficiency throughout the supply chain. Here all product categories – produce, chilled and ambient – are consolidated at a RDC for onward distribution to stores in composite trailers which also can carry a mix of products. In Holland, Albert Heijn has utilised cool and ambient warehouse complexes to deliver to their smaller-sized supermarkets whereas the German and French retailers have numerous product category warehouses supplying their wide range of formats (with hypermarkets, depending on spread of stores, products may be delivered direct by suppliers).

2.6 Manufacturer–retailer relationships

A major feature of retail change in Europe has been the consolidation of retail activity into fewer, large corporations in national markets. Many grocery retailers in Europe were small privately owned family companies 30 years ago and they were dwarfed by their multinational-branded suppliers. This is no longer the case. Some may remain privately owned but along with their PLC counterparts they are now international companies which have grown in economic power to challenge their international branded suppliers. Although the largest companies are predominantly German and French in origin, a high degree of concentration also exists in the Netherlands and the UK. Indeed, the investigation by the Competition Commission on the operation of multiple retail grocery companies in the UK illustrates this shift in power from manufacturer to retailer.

An indication of the growth of these European retailers has been the way in which they have been able to dictate where and when suppliers will deliver products to specific sites. Increasingly, the product has been of the distributor-label category. This is of particular significance in the UK where grocery chains have followed the Marks and Spencer strategy of premium value-added brands that compete directly with the manufacturers' brands.

The implications of these changes in power relationships between retailers and their suppliers have been that manufacturers have been either abdicating or losing their responsibility for controlling the supply chain. In the UK, the transition from a supplier-driven system to one of retail control is complete compared with some other parts of Europe. As mentioned earlier, most grocery retailers in the UK not only have centralised over 90 per cent of their products through RDCs but also have created primary consolidation centres further back up the supply chain to minimise inventory held between factory and store. The implementation of FGP further reinforces the trend to retail supply chain control. Although this degree of control is less evident in other European markets and in the US, the spate of merger activity in the late 1990s and the expansion of retail giants (Wal-Mart, Carrefour, Tesco, Ahold) with their 'big-box' formats into new geographical markets is leading to internationalisation of logistics practice.

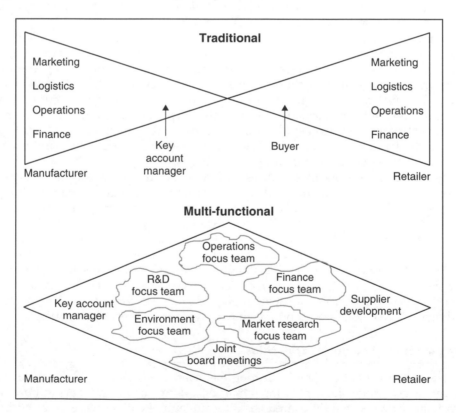

Figure 2.7 Transformation of the interface between manufacturer and retailer

Despite these shifts in the power balance, it is generally accepted that to apply ECR principles, the greatest challenge for European retailers is the breaking down of cultural barriers within organisations to move from a confrontational culture to one of collaboration. Organisations will change from a traditional functional 'internal' structure to that of a multi-functional 'external' structure. The changing organisational forms are shown in Figure 2.7 which depicts the traditional 'bow tie' and the new cross-functional team approach.

To achieve the significant supply chain savings mooted in ECR reports, companies are having to change their attitudes although the politics and inherent rivalries built up over the decades will take years for this *Cultural Revolution* to take place. It was significant that J. Sainsbury was *the* retailer represented at the ECR session in Paris in 1999 in *'ECR – the human side of change'*. Sainsbury was initially cynical about the benefits of ECR but have made significant progress in recent years and are aware of the time and resources required to modify working practices. One of the Roland Berger consultants represented at this session commented that the Anglo Saxon countries were more pro-active in implementing cultural change to move to a trusting partnership approach than the French or German companies.

Despite these possible drawbacks, the speed of change is remarkable. Surveys conducted throughout the 1990s on manufacturer–retailer relationships in the UK initially showed that partnerships would not work. By 1997 a sea change in attitude was happening. Who would have thought even then that the main grocery retailers would be sharing electronic point of sale (EPOS) data?

2.7 Logistics cost structures

A critical aspect of these organisational changes which have been evolving in response to ECR initiatives is how to share both the benefits and *costs* of the initiatives. Until the mid-1990s much of the emphasis on logistics costs focused upon the company or industry channel costs rather than overall supply chain costs.

The advent of activity-based costing (ABC), one of the enabling technologies identified in Figure 2.5, has allowed for a 'process' approach to be taken to supply chain activities. For example, much of the initiatives undertaken on product replenishment had clear benefits for retailers but required extra work (i.e. extra costs) to further up the supply chain. Thus, the *Cultural Revolution* referred to in the previous section is necessary for retailers to establish 'ground rules' on attributing costs as well as benefits when seeking supply chain efficiencies. ECR Europe launched the *Profit Impact of ECR* project in September 1997 and has developed a software-modelling tool, 'the wizard' which helps trading partners to identify the activities which are impacted on when applying ECR initiatives.

Although the tools are being developed to improve existing practice, logistics costs do vary considerably in different countries. This was aptly shown in the UK in 1999 and 2000 when road-haulage companies and other supporting businesses organised blockades in major cities and oil refineries in protest at hikes in fuel duty after successive budgets have made fuel costs the highest in Europe. Fuel costs are only part of the cost equation; labour costs in warehousing and transport, property prices and interest rates lead to differences in European markets. With the implementation of the EMU and standardisation of interest rates, distortions created by national governments' fiscal policies should be less significant than the past. For example, high relative interest rates in Britain were often the reason cited for destocking by British retailers and innovations pertaining to JIT distribution. Also, the cheaper land costs in France and Spain have been responsible for more speculative forward buying of stock and for holding more inventory in hypermarkets. This is similar to the US where the cost trade-offs in the logistics mix differ because of relatively cheaper fuel and land costs but greater geographical distances to cover.

2.8 Role of the logistics service provider

One area of collaboration that is often overlooked is that between retailer and professional logistics contractors. Historically, the provision of third-party services to retailers varied markedly from country to country. In the UK where centralisation of distribution occurred early a major market was created for third-party providers to manage RDCs. In the rest of Europe, less enthusiasm for 'contracting out' was initially shown with a tendency for companies to retaining warehousing 'in-house' and possibly contract out the transport. Financial conventions differ by country and in Germany, for example, strong balance sheets are viewed positively compared with the UK; also the opportunity cost of capital (investing in logistics infrastructure compared with retailing assets) may result in retaining rather than outsourcing these functions.

In recent years, however, the role of LSPs has been enhanced. This can be attributed to the internationalisation of retail and transport businesses and the need for greater co-ordination of supply chain activities. The supply chain is now more complex than before. Retailers are optimising traffic loads to minimise empty running and are backhauling from suppliers and recovering packaging waste from recycling centres. As efficient replenishment initiatives are implemented, consolidation of loads is required within the primary distribution network. LSPs are better placed to manage some of these initiatives than manufacturers or retailers. Furthermore, the internationalisation of retail business has stretched existing supply chains and third-party providers can bring expertise to these new market areas. Some British companies have utilised British logistics companies as they opened stores in new markets. Similarly, the world's largest retailer has utilised the expertise of a British logistics company (Tibbet & Britten) to provide logistical support to stores acquired in Canada and Germany. Indeed, the internationalisation of Tibbet & Britten from its UK base has been significant in the 1990s in that it could report in the early 2000s that over a third of its sales was now in North America, where major structural changes are occurring in the grocery market.

2.9 The internationalisation of logistics practice

The gist of our discussion on differences in logistics cultures was to show that implementation of best practice principles has been applied differentially in various geographical markets. Nevertheless, the impetus for internationalisation of logistics practice has been achieved through the formal and informal transfer of 'know-how' between companies and countries. ECR Europe conferences, their sponsoring organisations and national trade associations have all promoted best practice principles for application by member companies. Many of the conferences initiated by these organisations have included field visits to state-of-the-art distribution centres to illustrate the operational aspects of elements of ECR. At a more formal-level companies transfer 'know-how' within subsidiaries of their own group or through formal-retail alliances.

To illustrate how logistics expertise is being transferred across international boundaries, we will look at two European case studies, Tesco and Ahold. Both are global players although their history of internationalisation is very different. Tesco internationalised late and concentrated primarily in Europe; Ahold has around 60 per cent of its sales in the US and is only beginning to refocus its attention on the European market.

2.9.1 Tesco in Ireland and Poland

Tesco's most recent acquisitions in Europe (in Ireland and Poland) offer an insight into how changes in logistics practice can be implemented in different markets. In the wake of its acquisition of Wm Low in Scotland, Tesco plc turned its attention to Ireland in 1997 with the acquisition of 110 supermarkets from Associated British Foods. In the South, Power Supermarkets were part of this acquisition and at the time Power had plans to consolidate distribution. With the takeover, Tesco inherited a 'push' logistics system:

- only 12 per cent of volume was centralised;
- high stockholding levels at store (2 weeks);
- high stockholding levels at depot (4+ weeks);
- up to 600 deliveries per week per store;
- unknown supply chain costs.

Tesco initiated a 3-year plan to transfer Tesco UK 'know-how' to Tesco Ireland. This involved

- consolidation of all product categories, initially through third-party contractors (except one inherited warehouse);
- move to a composite 'chilled' distribution facility by 2000;
- the use of best practice ECR principles developed in the UK to Ireland;
- the upgrading of systems technology to achieve this.

In essence, Tesco Ireland is focusing upon replenishment areas of ECR in the first instance before tackling the demand side of ECR with regard to product assortments, promotion and new product launches.

What is interesting about Tesco's entry into Ireland is that it has speeded up the process of consolidation throughout Ireland. Superquinn also had a supplier-driven logistics system and in a matter of 2 years began to put in place the centralised distribution. The Musgrave Group, which operates franchised convenience stores and supermarkets in both northern and southern Ireland, had centralised ambient products prior to Tesco's entry. Since 1997, Musgraves has taken the lead in Ireland in implementing a supply chain strategy. Two new chilled distribution centres have been opened and the company has been active in ECR projects, which has resulted in organisational changes within the company.

Tesco's entry into Poland has posed a very different set of challenges to logistics managers, the acquisition of the Savia supermarket chain in 1995 followed on from a series of acquisitions in Hungary, the Czech Republic and Slovakia a few years earlier. In all of these cases, Tesco has adopted a similar strategy – gradually introducing the Tesco brand and opening larger supermarkets and hypermarkets. Whereas the supply chain is supplier-led, this has a different meaning to the push system pre-1997 in Ireland. In Ireland, much of the discussion on Tesco's entry to the market was about the possible fate of Irish suppliers. In Poland, this is not the case in that most goods will be locally sourced; however, there is a need to improve operational relationships with respect to quality, packaging and delivery. ECR is not an agenda item for management!

2.9.2 Ahold in Europe

Ahold has benefited from the transference of logistics practice because of its relationships in retail alliances in addition to synergies developed with its expanding web of subsidiaries. During the 1990s Ahold partnered with Casino of France and Safeway of the UK in the European retail alliance. In 1994, a 'composite' distribution centre was very much a UK phenomenon; now it has been developed by Safeway's European partners. Not only have these logistics practices been applied in France and the Netherlands but also in the parent companies' subsidiaries in the US, Portugal and the Czech Republic.

In the Netherlands, Albert Heijn (Ahold's Dutch subsidiary) has developed a state-of-the-art distribution system based on a modified UK 'composite' model. Since Heijn's stores

are much smaller than those of the superstore operators in the UK, these composite distribution centres comprise three independent units unlike in the UK where all products are
stored in one facility. The three centres have a fresh centre dealing with the cool chain: an
RDC for ambient and non-food products and a *returns centre* for reallocation and recycling
of returned products and handling materials.

ECR initiatives, especially those pertaining to efficient replenishment, have been a feature
of Albert Heijn's supply chain strategy with cross-docking and continuous replenishment
being a feature of their relationships with key suppliers such as Coca Cola and Heineken. On
a global basis Ahold attempts to synchronise best logistics practices across its operating subsidiaries. Clearly, this is quite a challenge as the company operates in Latin America, Asia
Pacific and the US. Like J. Sainsbury, Ahold has retained the local store names in the US post
acquisition, but has initiated best practice principles to achieve supply chain efficiencies.

2.10 Future challenges

Clearly, there has been a transformation of logistics within retailing during the past
25 years. Centralisation, new technologies, both in materials handling and information
handling, ECR and the implementation of best practice principles have resulted in logistics
becoming a key management function within retailing. But what of the future? Are we about
to experience evolution or revolution of retail logistics? Much depends on the pace of retail
change in the two areas identified in earlier chapters as drivers of change in the future,
namely, the extent of the internationalisation of retail businesses and the eventual size of
the e-commerce market. These two key strategic factors are interlinked, however, as the
Internet brings together consumers seeking products and services in international markets
and retailers join with their suppliers in global exchanges such as World Wide Retail
Exchange (WWRE) to reap the benefits of reduced costs by streamlining procurement.
Much of what was discussed in the previous section will continue. The large global retailers
will force further consolidation of retail markets in North America, Europe and South-east
Asia. Their presence in these markets will necessitate a review of their supply chains on
how to provide logistics support to new markets as they develop.

The biggest challenge facing retailers is how to respond to the market opportunities
offered by e-commerce. Shopping from home is hardly a new experience for consumers.
Mail order shopping arose in many markets because of the lack of fixed stores in rural
communities and catalogue and other non-store offerings have developed throughout the
20th century. Compared with the US, however, where 'specialogues' for upscale consumers became the norm 20 years ago, the bulk of the mail order business in the UK is still
rooted in traditional catalogues targeted at lower socio-economic group consumers (it was
the lure of cheap credit which provided a catalyst for growth in this market in the first
place). The traditional players such as GUS and Littlewoods have the logistical infrastructure in place but until digital television takes off as the medium for e-commerce ordering,
Internet consumers are the 'wrong' segment for traditional catalogue shopping.

Success in the e-commerce market will be largely dependent on getting fulfilment and
therefore logistics right. If time constrained, consumers are to be lured to e-commerce
shopping, they have to be persuaded that the retail offer is better in terms of quality, value
and *customer service*; that is, getting the product delivered when specified (Christopher's
'time to serve'). Take, for example, the situation in the US between Thanksgiving and
Christmas, the period when Internet ordering is at its peak. In 1999, 40 per cent of online
shoppers reported problems from finding products to late delivery and high-shipping
costs (*Retail Week*, 21 July 2000). The creation of a healthy third-party market in the UK
using the logistics infrastructure of traditional mail order companies (N. Brown, GUS) and
more recent specialists (Zoom) offers a solution to the fulfilment problem.

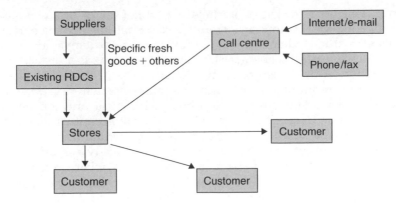

Figure 2.8 Logistics model for store-based picking of e-commerce orders

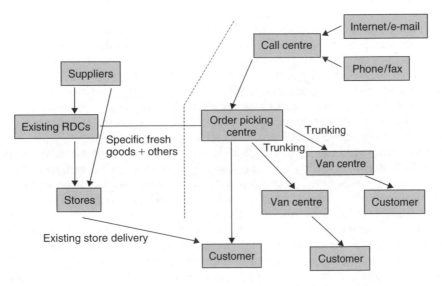

Figure 2.9 Logistics model for dedicated order-picking model of e-commerce orders
Source: Retail Logistics Task Force (2000)

Much of the recent attention on e-commerce has focused upon the grocery sector, which is coming through the experimental phase with a greater commitment to online retailing. The initial reticence is understandable in that major supermarket operators invest heavily in property assets and they did not wish to cannibalise their existing store customers with a competing e-commerce offer. Over time it has been shown that online retailing can complement the store offer and can indeed lead to switching of customers from one chain to another. The development of the online grocery market with a profile of Tesco.com can be found in the chapter on Electronic Commerce and Retailing. Here, we will focus upon fulfilment models. Currently, there are two main logistics models for grocery e-commerce: the store-based order-picking model and the dedicated order-picking model as illustrated in Figures 2.8 and 2.9, respectively. The store-based system used by Tesco makes use of existing distribution assets in that products pass through RDCs to stores and their store staff pick and distribute orders to customers. The advantages of this system are the speed of implementation and the relatively lower initial investment costs. This system offers customers the full range of goods available in the local store; however, 'out of stocks' occur because the online shopper is competing with in-store customers. It also permits the pooling of retail inventory between conventional and online markets, improving the ratio of inventory to sales.

Tesco's approach is interesting because it is reminiscent of Asda's late acceptance of centralised distribution. Asda's decision of not to centralise in the 1970s like some of its regional competitors meant that it could achieve national penetration quickly (compared to the national leader of the time, J. Sainsbury which has only opened an RDC in Scotland in 2000!). Now Tesco is delivering 'direct' from stores rather than centralising its e-commerce operation because it gives greater market penetration.

Conflicts between conventional and online retailing are likely to intensify at the back of the store as well as at the 'front end'. Back store-room areas, where much of the assembly and packing of home orders is undertaken, will become increasingly congested. Over the past 20 years the trend has been for retailers to reduce the amount of back storage space in shops as in-store inventory levels have dropped and QR replenishment become the norm. This now limits the capacity of these retail outlets to assume the additional role of online fulfilment centre.

Furthermore, it has been estimated that 50 per cent of distribution costs is tied up in store. Our discussion on delivery options has been the so-called 'last mile' problem. In the case of Tesco, 5 per cent of sales is tied up in the last 50 yards (*The Grocer*, 14 September 2002). Out of stocks on the shop floor are getting worse despite JIT replenishment techniques because of the haphazard nature of backstores. Shelf stackers are having difficulty finding products now – what will the situation be like as online fulfilment competes for the same space. Where sufficient land is available, shops can be enlarged to accommodate a higher volume of home-shopping business. New shops can also be purpose built to integrate conventional retailing and online fulfilment. The Dutch retailer Ahold has coined the term 'wareroom' to describe a dedicated pick facility co-located with a conventional supermarket.

Most of the purpose-built fulfilment centres so far constructed are on separate sites. They overcome most of the problems of fulfilling orders from existing shops. They can be designed specifically for the multiple picking of online orders, incorporate mechanised picking systems and provide much more efficient reception facilities for inbound and outbound vehicles. As their inventory is assigned solely to the online market, home shoppers can have greater confidence in the availability of products at the time of ordering. All of these come at a high price, however, both in terms of capital investment and operating costs. It is estimated, for instance, that Webvan's fulfilment centres cost an average of $36 million. Dedicated pick centres must generate a high throughput to earn the electronic tailers (e-tailers) an adequate rate of return. They also require a high throughput to support a diverse product range. It is very costly to offer a broad range in the early stages of an e-tailing operation when sale volumes are low. Offering a limited range, however, can significantly reduce the appeal of online shopping and retard market growth. The collapse of Webvan which tried, from an early stage, to offer a range of 55,000 items through purpose-built centres provides a salutary warning to other new entrants to the electronic grocery (e-grocery) market.

In summary, the shop-based fulfilment model has low start-up cost but is likely to prove more expensive in the longer term as retail outlets become more congested and service quality for both conventional and online shoppers deteriorates. The fulfilment centre model, on the other hand, has high initial capital and operating costs, but is likely to prove more cost effective in the longer term.

The relative efficiency of the two fulfilment models is likely to vary geographically. Companies might find it more cost effective to serve home shoppers in some areas from shops and in other areas from pick centres, depending on sales densities and local competition.

Other complicating factors are the size and service area of the fulfilment centre. There has been much debate about the optimum size of pick centres and, by implication, the number of centres required to serve the national market. One large UK supermarket estimated that it would require 18 such centres to provide national coverage, while another e-grocery business has indicated that five to six strategically located centres might suffice. Similar principles of warehousing planning apply to pick centres as to distribution centres at a higher level in the supply chain. The more centralised the system, the lower will be the capital investment and inventory levels. Fewer pick centres, however, means longer average distances to customer's homes and higher delivery costs. The cost of transporting orders over longer distances can be reduced by inserting an extra tier of satellite depots between the pick centre and the home (Figure 2.9). Orders bound for the same district can be trunked in a consolidated load to a local 'satellite' depot (or 'van centre') where they are broken down for onward delivery in small vans (Retail Logistics Task Force, 2001). Webvan operated a hub-satellite system of this type, with each pick centre supplying orders through a network of 10–12 satellites. The satellites do not need to be separate buildings. The use of demountable vehicles, as proposed by the UK e-grocery Ocado for the south-east of England, allows the local break-bulk operation to be 'depot-less' and thus more cost effective.

2.11 Solutions to the last mile problem

In the UK, it has been estimated that the average cost of order processing, picking and delivery for groceries is around £13 per order. As the charge to the customer is normally £5 per order, it is clear that unless the order value is high, retailers will make a loss on every delivery they make.

The cost of the delivery operation is strongly influenced by time constraints, in particular the width of the 'time windows' when orders are dropped at customers' homes. In deciding how wide a time window to offer online shoppers, e-tailers must strike a competitive balance between customer convenience and delivery efficiency. From the customer's standpoint, the ideal would be a guaranteed delivery within a very narrow time interval, minimising the encroachment on his/her lifestyle. It is very costly, however, to provide such 'time-definite' deliveries. Nockold (2002) modelled the effect of varying the width of time windows on home-delivery costs in the London area. The window was initially set at 3 hours. He then reduced it by 25 per cent, then 50 per cent and finally eliminated this time constraint. These options had the effect of cutting transport costs by, respectively, 6–12, 17–24 and 27–37 per cent. His conclusion was that by having completely open delivery times, cost savings of up to a third were attainable.

Normally to achieve this degree of flexibility, it must be possible to deliver orders when no one is at home to receive them. Unattended delivery can take various forms. According to market research, the preferred option for around two-thirds of British households is to leave the goods with a neighbour (Verdict Research, 2000). This applies mainly to non-food items, however. Owing to their bulk and the need for refrigeration, few online grocery orders are left with neighbours. Instead home-based reception (or 'drop') boxes are being promoted as a technical solution to the problem of unattended delivery. These boxes can be divided into three broad categories:

- *Integral boxes* – generally built into the home at the time of construction.
- *External fixed boxes* – attached to an outside wall.
- *External mobile (or 'delivery') boxes* – moved to and from the home and secured there temporarily by (e.g. a steel cable linked to an electronic terminal).

These boxes come in various sizes and offer different types of electronic access. Most are well-enough insulated to maintain the temperature of frozen and chilled produce for 6–12 hours. In a comparison of fixed and mobile boxes, Punakivi *et al.* (2001) conclude that their operating costs are similar, assuming that the latter are only collected at the time of the next delivery. Mobile boxes, however, have a capital cost advantage because they are shared between many customers and can achieve much higher utilisation rates.

In the US, unattended reception was pioneered, unsuccessfully, by Streamline. Their Stream boxes were generally located in customers' garages which were equipped with keypad entry systems. Home-access systems do not require the use of a reception box. One system, which is currently being trialled in 50 homes in the English Midlands uses a telephone-linked electronic keypad to provide delivery staff with controlled access to garages and out-buildings. The keypads communicate with a central server allowing the 'home access' agency to alter the pin codes after each delivery. It is claimed that this system cuts average drop times from 10 to 4 minutes and, if coupled with a 5-hour time window, would allow delivery productivity (measured in drops per vehicle per week) by 84 per cent. Home-access systems offer greater flexibility than drop boxes and are much cheaper to install than an integral reception unit. Their main disadvantage is that they pose a significant security risk both to the goods being delivered and the home itself.

A more radical means of cutting transport costs is by delivering to local collection points rather than to the home. These collection points can be existing outlets, such as corner shops, post offices or petrol stations, purpose-built centres or communal reception boxes. Few existing outlets have the capacity or refrigeration facilities to accommodate online grocery orders. This has led one property developer to propose the development of a network of specially designed collection centres (or 'e-stops') to handle a range of both food and non-food products. A much cheaper option is to install banks of reception boxes at central locations within neighbourhoods where orders can be deposited for collection. One company has adapted left luggage lockers into pick-up points for home-ordered products. Their size, shape and lack of refrigeration limits their suitability for the collection of online grocery orders. As e-grocery sales expand, however, there will be an increasing demand for communal reception facilities at apartment blocks.

The use of collection points economises on transport by sharply reducing the number of delivery locations and increasing the degree of load consolidation. It achieves this, however, at the expense of customer convenience, by requiring the online shopper to travel to the collection point to pick up the order. If the collection can be made in the course of an existing trip, say from work or to a petrol station, the loss of convenience may be acceptable. For most online grocery shoppers, however, this is unlikely to prove an attractive option.

Punakivi and Tanskanen (2002) have made a comparative study of the delivery costs for several 'last mile' options, using point of sales (POS) data from one of the largest supermarket chains in Finland. The dataset contained 1639 shopping baskets of 1450 anonymous household customers. In their analysis, five home-delivery concepts were modelled (see Table 2.3). These ranged from the standard Tesco model of attended reception within 2-hour delivery slots to unattended delivery to shared reception boxes in 'central locations'. Not surprisingly, the more the customer controlled the delivery time windows, the higher were the delivery costs. The results of the modelling exercise show that transport costs for unattended delivery to shared reception boxes were 55–66 per cent lower than attended delivery within 2-hour windows.

2.12 Outsourcing of home-delivery operations

Most deliveries of online grocery orders are currently made on a dedicated basis either by the e-tailers themselves or third-party distributors working on their behalf. Most of the larger e-grocers have been keen to retain direct control of the 'last mile' to ensure a high level of service and maintain customer contact. This carries a transport cost penalty, however. By outsourcing home deliveries on a shared-user basis, e-grocers could collectively

Table 2.3 Comparison of home-delivery concepts

Case	Home delivery concept and description	Example
1	Attended reception with 2-hour delivery time windows Delivery hours 8:00–22:00 Customer locations based on POS data Number of orders per day varies from 20 to 720	Peapod.com, USA Tesco. com, UK
2	Home-based reception box concept Delivery time window 8:00–16:00 Customer locations based on POS data Number of orders per day varies from 20 to 720	SOK, Finland Streamline, USA
3A	Delivery box concept, with pick up of the box on the next delivery Delivery time window 8:00–16:00, pick up on next delivery Customer locations based on POS data Number of orders per day varies from 20 to 720	Homeport, UK
3B	Delivery box concept with pick up of the box on next day Delivery time window 8:00–16:00, pick up next day Customer locations based on POS data Number of orders per day varies from 20 to 720	Homeport, UK Sainsbury, UK Food Ferry, UK
4	Shared reception box concept Time window 8:00–16.00, 'by end of working hours' 5, 10, 20 and 30 selected central locations of the shared reception box units Capacity of the shared reception box units varies: 8, 16, 24 and 32 customer-specific lockers per unit Utilisation rate of shared reception box units in the analysis: 50% and 75% Number of orders (20–720) per day varies according to the combination of above elements	Hollming, Finland Boxcar Systems, USA ByBox holdings, UK

Source: Punakivi and Tanskanen (2001)

reduce their transport costs by increasing drop densities and consolidating loads. A 'common distribution system' for grocery home deliveries would have to interface with different company IT systems and probably require the insertion of an additional consolidation point in the home-delivery channel (Retail Logistics Task Force, 2001). Adding another node and link would offset some of the consolidation benefits. It is worth noting, though, that the Swiss online grocer LeShop manages to provide a low-cost, next-day delivery across Switzerland by channelling home orders through the national postal service.

2.13 Summary

This chapter has outlined the theoretical constructs underpinning SCM and their applications to the retail sector. It was shown that the notion of time as a driver in competitive advantage is reflected in concepts such as JIT in manufacturing and QR and ECR in the FMCG. If the aims of ECR are to be realised by meeting consumer demand better, faster and at less cost, supply chain integration will be necessary between and within companies.

Considerable progress has been made to realise these objectives in the past 10–15 years. Fashion retailers such as The Limited, Zara and Benetton have gained competitive advantage through efficient management of their supply chains. The traditional adversarial approach between grocery retailer and supplier has also weakened as ECR initiatives were implemented throughout the 1990s. In the evolution of grocery logistics in the UK, this was identified as the relationship stage since 1995. Whether FGP initiated by leading retailers will lead to conflict and mistrust again remains to be seen.

What was clear from the discussion on international markets is that collaboration and the implementation of ECR is more advanced in the UK than in other countries. Differences in logistics networks across markets can be explained by factors other than the nature of manufacturer–retailer relationships, for example, the range of retail formats and their spatial distribution, variations in logistics costs in relation to land, labour and freight costs, and the relative sophistication of the LSP market.

Nevertheless, the consolidation of retail markets throughout the world and further internationalisation by the retail giants will result in more global sourcing and the adoption of logistics best practice principles across international markets as illustrated by the cases of Tesco and Ahold.

Finally, the main challenge facing retailers in the future is how they unlock the potential of e-commerce. The chapter on Electronic Commerce and Retailing showed how this market was developing but most dot.com failures resulted from fulfilment problems. The two models discussed here outlined the pros and cons of the store-based model compared to the picking-centre model for meeting consumers' orders. Although the store model is currently the most successful, increased backdoor congestion in store warehouses will ultimately lead to the development of picking centres in the future. Regardless of which model is adopted, the 'last mile' problem remains unsolved. The standard 2-hour delivery window offered by most retailers does not maximise the utilisation of their vehicle fleets. Thus, a variety of technical solutions, involving unattended reception boxes, have been mooted to reduce these costs. The relative success of unattended delivery options will depend on their acceptability by customers who will have to be persuaded to switch from attended delivery within narrow time windows.

References

Camuffo, A., Romano, P. and Vinelli, A. (2001) Back to the future: Benetton transforms its global network. _MIT Sloan Management Review_, Fall, 46–52.

Christopher, M. (1997) _Marketing Logistics_. Oxford, Butterworth-Heineman.

Christopher, M. and Peck, H. (1998) Fashion logistics. In Fernie, J. and Sparks, L. (eds), _Logistics and Retail Management_, London, Kogan Page, Chapter 6.

Coopers and Lybrand (1996) _European Value Chain Analysis Study – Final Report_, ECR Europe, Utrecht.

Cox, A. (1996) Relationship competence and strategic procurement management. Towards an entrepreneurial and contractual theory of the firm. _European Journal of Purchasing and Supply Management_, **2**(1), 57–70.

Drucker, P. (1962) The economy's dark continent. _Fortune_, April, 265–270.

Fernie, J. (1990) _Retail Distribution Management_. London, Kogan Page.

Fernie, J. and Sparks, L. (1998) _Logistics and Retail Management_. London, Kogan Page.

Fernie, J., Pfab, F. and Marchant, C. (2000) Retail grocery logistics in the UK. _International Journal of Logistics Management_, **11**(2), 83–90.

Fiddis, C. (1997) _Manufacturer–Retailer Relationships in the Food and Drink Industry. Strategies and Tactics in the Battle for Power_. London, FT Retail and Consumer Publishing, Pearson Professional.

Ford, D. (ed.) (1997) *Understanding Business Markets*. London, Academic Press.

GEA Consultia (1994) *Supplier–Retailer Collaboration in Supply Chain Management*. London, Coca Cola Retailing Research Group Europe.

Harrison, A., Christopher, M. and van Hoek, R. (1999) *Creating the Agile Supply Chain*, Corby, Institute of Logistics and Transport.

McKinnon, A.C. (1989) The advantages and disadvantages of centralised distribution. In Fernie, J. (ed.), *Retail Distribution Management*. London, Kogan Page, pp. 74–89.

Mitchell, A. (1997) *Efficient Consumer Response: A New Paradigm for the European FMCG Sector*. London, FT Retail and Consumer Publishing, Pearson Professional.

Nockold, C. (2001) Identifying the real costs of home delivery. *Logistics and Transport Focus*, **3**(10), 70–71.

Porter, M. (1985), *Competitive Advantage: Creating and Sustaining Superior Performance*, Free Press, New York.

Punakivi, M. and Tanskanen, K. (2002) Increasing the cost efficiency of e-fulfilment using shared reception boxes. *International Journal of Retail and Distribution Management*, **30**(10), 498–507.

Punakivi, M., Yrjola, H. and Holmstrom, J. (2001) Solving the last mile issue: reception box or delivery box. *International Journal of Physical Distribution and Logistics Management*, **31**(6), 427–439.

Retail Logistics Task Force – DTI Foresight (2000) *@Your Service: Future Models of Retail Logistics*. London, DTI.

Retail Logistics Task Force – DTI Foresight (2001) *@Your Home: New Markets for Customer Service and Delivery*. London, DTI.

Slack, N., Chambers, S., Harland, S.C., Harrison, A. and Johnson, R. (1998) *Operations Management*, 2nd edition. London, Pitman Publishing.

Verdict Research (2000) *Electronic Shopping, UK*. London, Verdict.

Williamson, O.E. (1979) Transaction cost economics: the governance of contractual relations. *Journal of Law and Economics*, **22**(October), 223–261.

Womack, J.P., Jones, D. and Roos, D. (1990) *The Machine that Changed the World: The Story of Lean Production*. New York, Harper-Collins.

Study questions

1. Discuss the key concepts and theories of SCM and their application to fashion retailing?
2. Outline the history of ECR and discuss its implementation in the markets of different countries?
3. Comment on the four stages of the evolution of grocery logistics in the UK, to what extent will FGP negate the collaborative efforts by suppliers and retailers in the relationship (4th) stage?
4. With the aid of examples show how logistics best practice/principles are being applied internationally?
5. Review the advantages and disadvantages of the two main fulfilment models for grocery e-commerce and discuss some of the solutions proposed for overcoming the 'last mile' problem?

Chapter 3

The anatomy of retail buying

Christopher M. Moore

The purpose of this chapter is to consider the issues associated with the management of buying and merchandising within retail organisations. The aims of the chapter are as follows:

- to review the importance of effective and efficient buying and merchandising within retail organisations;
- to identify the principle buying activities;
- to examine the nature and characteristics of retail buying structures;
- to review the mechanisms by which buyer's performance is reviewed and evaluated;
- to review the key stages in new supplier evaluation and selection.

3.1 The importance of buying and merchandising

The main purpose of the retail buyer's role is to translate the company's business positioning statement into reality through the appropriate selection of a merchandise assortment. The buyer does not operate within a vacuum – but must instead create a merchandise range that meets the marketing objectives of the organisation and is within the bounds of agreed budgetary parameters. As such, the success of the retail organisation is inextricably linked to the performance of the buyer since it is they who have the responsibility for providing optimal customer service through the procurement of the right products that are available at the appropriate time, in appropriate quantities (McGoldrick, 2002). It is through their efficient and effective procurement of goods that sufficient profits are made which ensure the continuance of the business in the long term.

Given the importance of the buyer's role, various attempts have been made to identify the requisite skills and competences of a successful retail buyer. Varley (2001) suggested that the successful buyer must be a numerate and be an effective communicator. Furthermore, she suggests that the buyer ought to be skilled in market analysis and should have the confidence to be an effective negotiator. Given their ever-increasing involvement in range development and product selection, it is also clear that retail buyers are also expected to possess flair and be creative.

Hirschman and Stampfl (1980) provided what has become the seminal categorisation of the retail buyer's role. Their categorisation recognised three primary functions.

The first is as **change agent**, where the buyer influences consumers' purchase behaviour by offering new and often innovative products and services to the market. For example, those buyers with the responsibility for developing new assortments for an own-brand range or those who introduce new products, perhaps sourced exclusively from foreign suppliers, who typically fall into this category.

The second is as **gate keeper**, where the buyer assumes responsibility for the flow of product from suppliers to end consumers. As such, these buyers assume a relatively passive role and their companies act principally as a pipeline for product and service distribution. Those buyers who purchase manufacturer brands and products and who take no role in the process of developing and branding a product; assume this gate keeper role.

The third is as **opinion-leader**, where the buyer influences consumer opinion but does not necessarily prompt a purchase from their company. Consumers may only use the retailer as a source for ideas and information. As an example, Liberty, the up-market London department store retailer has long been identified as a source of inspiration for other retailers, who may provide cheaper copies of Liberty's ranges. Similarly, consumers, who perhaps for economic reasons, are unable to purchase directly from Liberty, may instead customise ranges purchased from other retailers in the 'Liberty style'.

In summary, the buyer plays a hugely important role within a retail organisation. It is their responsibility to ensure that appropriate ranges are available to customers at the correct time, in the right quantities and at the right quality. Fundamentally, it is the buyer's responsibility to ensure the profitability of the business through the appropriate selection of goods.

3.2 The principle buying activities

It is impossible to provide an infallible review of the activities of a retail buyer by virtue of the fact that the buyer's remit will differ according to the retailer that they buy for and the market sector within which the company operates. As such, the experience of the owner–manager–buyer of an independent fashion boutique will be radically different from that of a buyer employed by a specialist wine retailer. The former may be responsible for buying across a very wide range of product areas from a large number of suppliers, whereas the latter may concentrate on buying a very few types of product from a limited number of suppliers.

Despite these inherent differences, it is possible to identify a number of generic buying and merchandising activities which, irrespective of corporate structure, must be completed as part of the procurement process.

3.2.1 Analysis of trading market opportunity

Fundamental to the buyer's role is the delivery of goods and services that will satisfy their customers current and future needs. In order to achieve this requirement, it is necessary for the buyer to have an in-depth understanding of their customers' buying behaviour trends. Based on a clear knowledge of the trends in purchasing behaviour, buyers must effectively anticipate their customers' new product and service requirements. Furthermore, buyers must also competently identify new market opportunities as these emerge. Based on this information, the buyer must then develop a buying plan.

3.2.2 The development of a buying plan

As part of the development of a buying plan, the buyer must detail the nature and characteristics of the merchandise range that is to be offered to customers. The buying plan will determine the breadth (the range of different product categories) and the depth (the choice of products within a specific category) of the assortment. An important dimension of the buying plan is the setting of financial targets for the assortment. These targets will include forecasts for future sales and profit margins within each product category. These targets are then used to set the retail price levels for each specific product. Furthermore, the buying plan will typically include a more detailed breakdown of the buying budget in terms of sales and profit contribution by week, month, quarter, as well as full year.

3.2.3 Management of the supplier strategy

The success of a buying strategy is ultimately dependent on the support of an efficient and appropriate supplier strategy. It is the responsibility of the buying and merchandising department to select an appropriate and reliable supply base. In recent years, the nature of buyer–supplier relationships within retail marketing channels has changed significantly. As markets have become more dynamic and competitive, and as the expectations of consumers have become more complex, it has been in the interest of buyers and their suppliers to develop what Dawson and Shaw (1989) described as collaborative, rather than confrontational, relationships. One of the most important drivers for this change in the nature of channel relationships has been the recognition of the costs associated with selecting a new supplier. This is because considerable time is taken up as part of the process of searching, evaluating, selecting, negotiating and establishing a rapport with a new supplier. Therefore, in order to minimise these costs, buyers have sought to develop effective supplier selection strategies that provide for the successful identification and selection of suitable suppliers to the business.

Having identified an appropriate supply base, it is necessary for the buyer to agree the terms of trade with their suppliers. These terms are typically concerned with

- drawing up product specifications;
- forecasting, reviewing and agreeing order quantities;
- negotiating prices and discount arrangements;
- agreeing delivery schedules and re-order protocols.

As well as agreeing terms of trade with suppliers, the buyer will also monitor supplier's performance, in areas such as product quality, stockholding management and other forms of costs management.

As more retailers take a more active involvement in the supply chain through the development of own-branded ranges, many buyers also consider the extent to which suppliers positively contribute to product innovation. As retailers seek to achieve competitive advantage through their provision of innovative and unique product ranges, the extent to which a supplier can provide support through the provision of exclusive deals becomes an important consideration.

3.2.4 Product development for own-brand ranges

As has been identified, an ever-increasing number of retailers are developing own-brand ranges. These initiatives are motivated by the desire to secure competitive advantage through the exclusive distribution of products that are specifically tailored to meet the requirements of the retailers' target customers. Furthermore, own-brand ranges provide profit margins that are higher than those provided by manufacturers' brands. This development has in many cases resulted in the retail buyer assuming significant control over the supply chain, not least in terms of determining product specifications. This shift in power – in favour of the retailer – has meant that supplier must adhere to strict performance criteria, particularly in relation to product quality standards, and availability levels.

While the procedures inherent to the development of own-brand ranges are product and company specific, it is possible to identify key stages of that process. As a preliminary, it is necessary for the buyer to thoroughly review consumer, competitor and product trends and developments with the market. With this information to hand, the buyer must then review the company's existing ranges in terms of their previous and future sales performance and the competitive advantage that these provide. In some instances, buyers will be able to use internal financial data in order to measure the direct profit contribution of a product category or a specific product. By comparing market trend data with an analysis of the strengths and weaknesses of the current product ranges, the buyer will then be in a position to identify the areas development with respect to the products that will be marketed under the company's own brand name (Davidson *et al.*, 1988).

Having identified broad areas of opportunity, it is then necessary for the buyer to further develop and refine their product requirements so as to clearly and adequately brief their suppliers. This process of refinement will usually require that the buyer attend trade shows, exhibitions and fairs, so as to gain further inspiration for their new products. Furthermore, ideas may come from their appraisal of competitors' ranges and inspiration may also come from the ideas provided directly from customers. With respect to the latter source of inspiration, it is common for buyers to convene customer focus groups that serve, through the use of brainstorming techniques, to identify new product opportunities.

Derived from these various sources, the buyer will then construct a brief for their suppliers that will provide a detailed sketch of their requirements with respect to the proposed new product. In particular, the brief will provide details of the broad specifications for the product, as well as details of the required price points.

Whenever it is believed that a new product development is innovative and unique to the market, buyers may insist that their suppliers sign a confidentiality agreement which prohibits them from providing information to any competitors about the new product or the processes are used to manufacture it. The period of required confidentiality may extend to a number of years and buyers will readily sue any breach of these agreements on the basis this may undermine the competitive advantage of the retailer.

Based on these specified briefs, suppliers will be expected to provide product samples on the basis of agreed specifications. In addition, initial costings for products will be agreed. Whenever the investment requirements are high, it may be the case that the buying team test the commercial viability of a product by undertaking further consumer research. This may involve the adoption of user studies, which includes gaining feedback from consumers about products as they use, eat, drink or wear them. Based on their feedback, modifications may then be made to the product specification.

Particularly, whenever a number of new products are developed simultaneously, such as by a fashion retailer as they develop a seasonal collection, it is common for all of these to be considered as part of a buying range review. As part of the range review, senior management will ratify which products are to be accepted and which product projects are to be terminated. Decisions relevant to whether a product is accepted or rejected in the range review will be based on cost price estimates, sales projections, competitor and market analysis, as well as the findings of quality and performance testing reports.

Larger retailers, with sufficient resource capability, may instigate a trial of any new products prior to a full launch. These trials are typically contained to a small number of stores that are identified on the basis of their match between their typical customer profile and the target audience for the newly developed product. Based on the results of these trials, production commitments to manufacturers will be finalised.

After a new own-brand product has been launched, it is the responsibility of the buying team to monitor its performance by considering such dimensions as sales levels, profit contributions, supplier's performance levels and customer satisfaction levels as evidenced by the number of complaints received. Depending on the outcome of these performance reviews, the buyer may decide to continue with the supply of these products or they may cease production and develop a strategy for the swift liquidation of the unwanted stock.

If the product is to be retained, it is the buyer's responsibility to ensure that all products are available in order to meet current and future demand. As part of this process, it is also necessary to consider the impact of a newly launched product on existing lines. Where sales of an existing product are adversely affected by a new launch, it may then be necessary for a buyer to either reduce the stockholding of the existing product or to eliminate the product all together.

3.2.5 Marketing of products and presentation at point of sale

While the primary responsibility for the marketing and presentation of products may reside with marketing professionals, it is also likely that buyers will be active in the decisions relevant to the promotion of product ranges. Given that buyers are actively involved in the procurement and often the development of new product ranges, it is appropriate that they be involved in decisions relevant to their marketing and promotion. Their involvement typically relates to packaging, presentation, marketing communications and promotional decisions.

Given the increasingly competitive and congested nature of product markets, it could be argued that decisions relevant to the marketing and presentation of products are fundamental to their success. As such, the involvement of buyers in such decision-making is not only important but also essential.

3.3 The nature and characteristics of retail buying structures

The structure of a retailer's buying department is inevitably dependent on the size of the company, its ownership status and its culture. However, these distinctions aside, it is possible to identify three organisational structures for a retail buying department as follows: centralised, decentralised and a combinative. Each of these will be defined and examined in turn.

A **centralised** buying structure involves all of the buying structures being managed and controlled by buyers collectively in one place – typically at the retailer's head office. This structural form is almost universally adopted by medium- and large-size retailers for a variety of reasons. Perhaps most importantly, a centralised buying structure allows for economies of scale in buying since orders are consolidated for all outlets in the chain, rather than individually, on an outlet-by-outlet basis.

The consolidation of the buy as part of a centralised buying structure radically reduces any duplication of effort across a number of different outlets, which in turn allows for a more effective use of manpower. Centralisation allows expert buyers to concentrate on buying and procurement decisions, while management at store level can focus upon customer-service matters. Furthermore, centralisation provides for a single point of communication for the supply base which also allows for a tighter control over the supply chain in matters of quality, production and service delivery. In particular, centralisation allows buyers to negotiate terms of supply with the advantage of scale economies, which typically allows them to negotiate strongly on pricing and other support issues. With buyers located in a central location with a more efficient and effective information resource base, it could also be suggested that centralisation enables the procurement team to strategically identify and manage market-trend information as it emerges.

It is important to note, however, that the adoption of a centralised buying structure is not without its problems. For example, while centralisation provides for a consistent merchandise range across the company, it reduces the retailer's flexibility to respond to local trends, needs and opportunity. The rigidity of centralisation typically means that the intimate knowledge that store management has of their local market is under-utilised and is not integrated into the buying decision-making process. This in turn may result in local management becoming demotivated as a result of their non-involvement.

With respect to the latter point, it could be argued that with the implementation of electronic point-of-sale (EPOS) programmes, this allows for local market information to be easily integrated into buying decisions. Indeed, it could be suggested that the information provided by EPOS systems is likely to be more reliable than that provided by intuition of local managers. However, it must also be acknowledged that EPOS systems can account only for those items that have been sold; they are not capable of identifying and accommodating those items that local markets may want but which are not stocked by the retailer.

A **decentralised** buying structure is in the main adopted only by small retail companies, such as family-owned, single-outlet businesses. Under such a structure, buying is done at store level, often by the store manager. The advantages of decentralised buying are in effect the disadvantages of centralised buying. Of these, perhaps the most significant advantage of decentralised buying is the opportunity it provides for retailers who adopt such a structure to respond to the needs of their local market.

Similarly, the disadvantages of decentralisation are the advantages of a centralised approach. An obvious disadvantage of decentralisation is the fact that it does not provide for the scale economies of centralised buying. In order to overcome this issue, many small independent retailers who operate decentralised buying join with other independent retailers in a buying group. A number of different buying groups exist, such as Spar, Intersport and UniChem, and their purpose is to provide independent retailers with the opportunity to benefit from economies of scale through their consolidated buying. Through their participation is in a recognised buying group, retailers are given the opportunity to access leading brands and products that otherwise may not be available to them by virtue of their small buying scale.

A **combinative** structure is the third approach that a retailer may adopt. As part of a combinative approach, the authority to purchase operates at both a central and a local level. This may involve the central buyers adopting 70 per cent of the lines that are to be stocked, while the remaining stock is bought by local managers. This approach has been utilised by multinational food retailers whose central managers buy mega-brands that are sold in all of their operating markets, while their local management are responsible for sourcing products from local suppliers in order to satisfy local customer tastes.

A procurement split, as such as the 70/30 per cent split that is detailed above, is not the only way in which procurement is managed in a combinative structure. The most commonly adopted alternative involves a centralised buying team assembling a range of products from which local managers can select according to the needs of their customers. While a catalogue approach does not provide the local manager with the freedom to select the products or brands of their choice, it does allow them a limited opportunity to influence the products that they will sell.

As customers become more demanding in terms of their desire to access specialist and exotic products, they also expect retailers to provide product ranges that are tailored to their local requirements. A combinative buying structure provides something of a compromise which on the one hand, allows for economies of scale while on the other provides an opportunity for buyers to respond to local market trends and opportunities.

3.4 Evaluating buyer's performance

Given the importance of buying to the success, or otherwise, of a retail organisation, it is crucial that the company establishes credible mechanisms which allow for the assessment of buyer's performance. The critical success factors that are used in order to evaluate buyer's performance will be dependent on the nature and characteristics of the buyer's company. For many retail organisations, the measurement of a buyer's performance is directly linked to the rewards and remunerations that they receive.

McGoldrick (2002) identified the importance of financial measures in the assessment of buyer's performance and in particular, noted that gross and net margin performance was an important indicator. Furthermore, he notes that the extent to which the buyer's activities serve to provide a competitive differential for the company was an important consideration in the evaluation of performance. In recognition that the strategic contribution of the buyer often extends beyond the provision of sound contract terms, it is possible to identify three categories of evaluation in terms of *financial and resource performance measures; customer satisfaction indicators* and *innovation and market-development measures*. Each of these categories is detailed below:

3.4.1 Financial and resource performance measures

The financial and resource utilisation dimensions used to measure buying function performance include:

- *gross and net margin performance* as measured by levels achieved against budget and the previous year's margin levels;
- *optimisation of sales level* as measured by levels achieved against budget and previous year's sales levels;
- *level of market share achieved* as measured by levels achieved against target level and previous year's market-share level;
- *minimal level of markdowns* as measured by levels achieved against targets and last year's markdown levels.

3.4.2 Customer satisfaction indicators

The customer satisfaction indicators include

- *minimal level of out-of-stock ranges* as measured by levels achieved against target;
- *minimal level of customer complaints and returns* as measured by levels achieved against target;
- *consistent quality of goods* as measured by levels of customer returns and complaints, as well as rejections and the results of company quality control checks.

3.4.3 Innovation and market-development measures

The innovation and market-development measures include:

- *development of distinct competitive advantages* in terms of product ranges, price levels and quality as measured against the competition;
- *level of success achieved in relation to new product development introductions* as measured by previous year's performance, the terms of the development strategy and the competition;
- *speed of reaction to changes in demand at the macro- and micro-level* as measured by minimal levels of sell-outs and the profitable optimisation of sales;
- *level of development with respect to the creation of new market segments* as measured against previous year's performance levels and planned development levels.

The extent to which retailers will use all or at least some of these measures will be dependent on their size, management structure and the characteristics of the sector within which they operate.

3.5 New supplier selection and evaluation

Bailey (1990) identified that the selection of an appropriate and reliable supply base was arguably the most significant and important buying activity. Furthermore, Varley (2001) noted that the successful implementation of the buying strategy was inextricably linked to the strength, or otherwise, of the relationships between buyers and their suppliers.

Dawson and Shaw (1989) provided what could be categorised as the definitive categorisation of buyer–supplier relationships and their categorisation noted four distinct relationship types:

1. **Conventional** – whereby the relationship between the buyer and the supplier is purely transactional.
2. **Contractual** – whereby buyers and their suppliers are bound together as a result of some formal agreement or contract, such as in the form of a franchise.
3. **Administered** – whereby one member of the supply chain co-ordinates the activities of all others in the chain; it could be suggested that forms such as Marks and Spencer often adopt this sort of role in their supply chains.
4. **Corporate** – whereby the supply chain is vertically integrated in that the retailer owns their own manufacturing capability.

As well as providing a classification of the types of buyer–supplier relationships within retailing, Dawson and Shaw (1989) also noted that with the advent of retailer's own brands, there has been a change in the style of buyer–supplier relationships. Rather than establish adversarial relationships that are characterised by conflict and 'one-upmanship', short termism and non-cooperation, buyers are instead seeking to create collaborative relationships with their suppliers. Their determination to generate more productive and co-operative relationships with suppliers is based on their recognition of the high costs associated with new supplier selection and the lost opportunities that may result as a consequence of adversarial relationships.

This desire to develop 'win–win' buyer–supplier relationships has encouraged the emergence of collaborative relationships which seem to achieve high degrees of responsiveness to customer demand, flexibility in production and replenishment decisions close to the point of sale (POS), effective communication in the supply chain through the sharing of information and a commitment to achieving a 'joint approach' to problem solving.

In terms of identifying the number of suppliers to engage, retail buyers may be tempted to concentrate their procurement to a few suppliers because this concentration provides for scale economies and higher level of profitability.

Furthermore, concentration allows the retail buyer to increase their influence and control over their suppliers and this may allow them to achieve exclusivity in supply. High levels of procurement concentration do pose certain risks, not least those associated with reduced flexibility should production problems emerge or radical changes in consumer demand arise. There is also the possibility that complacency in product and service quality levels may emerge as a result of the buyer becoming overly dependent on the supplier.

As a means of resolving these issues, buyers are increasingly adopting a tiered suppliers' strategy which results in their committing perhaps 65 per cent of their buy is from one large supplier, while the remainder of the buy is spread over a number of smaller buyers. This approach allows the buyer to benefit from scale economies while also allowing for some flexibility in response to changing market conditions.

In terms of the process of selecting a new supplier, it is common for the buyer to consider a number of key dimensions that measure the extent to which a supplier's capability

Product
- Range of products available in the suppliers' portfolio – a buyer may be more interested in a supplier that can provide a variety of different products at the same time.
- Quality of goods and services.
- Value for money of the range, principally in terms of the cost prices and the service benefits made available.
- Product development potential of the supplier.
- Exclusivity potential, which is especially important for those retailers that market their goods under their own brand.

Terms of trade
- Cost price levels.
- Payment cycle requirements: 30, 60 or 180 days.
- Range and conditions of discounts.
- Level of investment required by the retailer in terms of their providing either financial or technical support to the supplier.

Reputation of the supplier
- Customer portfolio, as evidenced by the number and reputation of customers and the number of which that may be competitors.
- Suppliers' statements on corporate social responsibility.
- Reputation for ethical and safety standards, in relation to factory/workers' conditions.
- Reputation of the senior management and personnel within the supplier's company.
- Financial standing of the supplier, especially in terms of the risk of insolvency.
- Technical capability and reputation for quality management.

Systems support
- Communication systems for buyer–supplier relationship management.
- Stock management systems.
- Customer-service systems, such as in relation to the handling of faulty goods and the crediting procedures that are to be used when these goods are returned.
- Administrative support for stock and financial processing.

Marketing support
- Reputation of the supplier's brand, if appropriate.
- In-store merchandising support available from the supplier.
- Promotional activities proposed by supplier in order to support product in the market.
- Advertising support proposed by supplier in order to communicate the product in the market.

Figure 3.1 Key buyer considerations

matches the buyer's supply needs. Among the considerations that are crucial for the buyer to consider are given in Figure 3.1.

The complexity inherent to the process of selecting a new supplier is dependent on a number of factors. If the new supplier is to provide a product range that is potentially lucrative or a high commercial risk, then it is likely that greater time and effort will be expended as part of the new supplier selection process. If, however, the retailer has extensive experience in a particular procurement area, then it is possible that the procedure for selecting a new supplier will be kept to a minimum.

In broad terms, the process of selecting a new supplier follows seven discrete stages as follows:

Stage 1   New supplier research and identification
Through their use of supplier directories, the Trade Press, specialist supplier-recruitment agents, trade contacts, as well as their own personal contacts, buyers will explore the nature and characteristics of the supplier base within the market. It is important to note that supplier identification is often based on the recommendation of buyers employed by other retailers. This is because the buyer community is usually very small and buyers invariably develop strong information networks.

Stage 2   Make an initial enquiry/contact with potential supplier
This stage will often involve the buyer, or an agent operating on their behalf, contacting a supplier in order to enquire about the capability and their interest in supplying to the company. For the larger corporate chains, it is often the case that prospective suppliers come to the buyers at the headquarters (HQ) with a view to presenting their products and new ideas. As such, these larger firms benefits from their market position, since they are often able to access the best suppliers with the latest ideas in advance of their smaller competitors.

Stage 3   Visit to supplier factory
At this stage, a member of the buying team, or their agent, may visit the supplier's factory with a view to assessing their production capabilities and the quality of their human and plant resources. At this stage, the buyer may seek confirmation and assurances that the supplier operates in a manner that is ethical and conforms with relevant legislation, such as in relation to employee's health and safety. For those suppliers that operate abroad, an agent may undertake this task on behalf of the retailer. Given the importance of this task, it is common for fashion retailers in the UK to operate buying offices within their principal supplier markets in order that they can fully control the supplier approval process.

Stage 4   Product sampling
If the buyer is satisfied with the supplier's capabilities and reputation, the next stage in the evaluation process would involve the supplier providing samples of their products. For retailers with own-branded merchandise, the samples that are provided may be based on their explicit specifications. As part of the evaluation process, the buyer may require that product tests be undertaken. For fashion buyers, their testing may involve soliciting the opinion of garment technologists who may test the colour-fastness of products, as well as construction quality and ease of garment care. Furthermore, buyers may also seek the feedback of consumers who have been commissioned to wear and use the products within a domestic setting. As retailers seek to improve their quality standards and levels of customer satisfaction, many more are using customer feedback as an important element of the new supplier selection process.

Stage 5   Negotiation of terms of trade
It is only when the buyer is satisfied that the supplier has the capability to reliably supply the company that consideration will be given to the details of the terms of trade. As part of this evaluation process, consideration is given to cost price levels, payment cycle requirements, the conditions associated with securing discounts, as well as any investment that is required from the supplier with respect to marketing support.

Stage 6 Range period

Provided that the buyer is satisfied that the terms of trade support the firm's strategic objectives, it is common for the buyer to arrange a trial period for new supplier. The purpose of this stage is to measure customer reaction to the suppliers' products, especially in terms of quality. In addition, the trial stage will also enable the buyer to evaluate and communicate the suppliers' competence in managing their end of the supply chain.

Stage 7 Formalisation buyer–supplier relationship

Depending on the outcome of the previous six stages, if the buyer is satisfied that the supplier is reliable, efficient and is capable of providing the required product range at an acceptable price, then the decision is made to formalise the buyer–supplier relationship. At this point, a contract is usually created which binds the supplier and the buyer in a legal relationship. Both sides are bound by such a contract and it is only if the terms of the contract are broken that either side has then the opportunity to rescind the terms of the contract.

3.6 Summary

The purpose of this chapter was to consider the issues associated with the management of buying within retail organisations. In order to support this aim, the chapter considered the importance of effective and efficient buying and merchandising within retailer organisations. In particular, the roles of the buyer as change agent/gate keeper/opinion leader were considered on the basis that each dimension indicates the various ways in which a buyer can influence the nature of the supply chain.

The chapter also considered the principle buying activities and identified these as being relevant to the analysis of trading market opportunity, development of the buying plan, management of the supplier strategy, product development of own-brand ranges and marketing of products, and presentation of products as POS.

A review of the nature and characteristics of retail buying structures was provided and consideration was given to the relative advantages and disadvantages of centralised, decentralised and combinative buying structures. Furthermore, consideration was given to the criteria that may be used in order to evaluate buyer's performance and in particular, the importance of financial and resource performance measures, customer satisfaction indicators, and innovation and market-development measures was considered.

The chapter concluded by examining the reasons for the emergence of more collaborative forms of buyer–supplier relationships within the retail supply chain. Finally, the chapter delineated seven key stages that are integral to the evaluation and selection of new suppliers.

References

Bailey, P.J.H. (1987) *Purchasing and Supply Management*. London, Chapman and Hall.

Davidson, W.R., Sweeney, D.J. and Stampfl, R.W. (1988) *Retailing Management*. New York, John Wiley and Sons.

Dawson, J.A. and Shaw, S.A. (1989) The move to administered vertical marketing systems by British retailers. *European Journal of Marketing*, **23**(7), 42–52.

McGoldrick, P. (2002) *Retail Marketing*, 2nd edition. London, McGraw-Hill.

Murphy, R. (2001) B2C online strategies for fashion retailers. In Hines, T. and Bruce, M. (eds), *Fashion Marketing: Contemporary Issues*. Oxford, Butterworth-Heinemann.

Varley, R. (2001) *Retail Product Management – Buying and Merchandising*, 1st edition. London, Routledge.

Webb, B. (2001) Retail brand marketing in the new millennium. In Hines, T. and Bruce, M. (eds), *Fashion Marketing: Contemporary Issues*. Oxford, Butterworth-Heinemann.

Study questions and guideline answers

1. **Outline the measures that can be used in order to review the performance of the retail buyer.**

Consideration ought to be given to the key performance measures such as those described below.

Financial and resource performance measures

The financial and resource utilisation dimensions used to measure buying function performance include:

- *gross and net margin performance* as measured by levels achieved against budget and the previous year's margin levels;
- *optimisation of sales level* as measured by levels achieved against budget and previous year's sales levels;
- *level of market-share achieved* as measured by levels achieved against target level and previous year's market-share level;
- *minimal level of markdowns* as measured by levels achieved against targets and last year's markdown levels.

Customer satisfaction indicators

The customer satisfaction indicators include:

- *minimal level of out-of-stock ranges* as measured by levels achieved against target;
- *minimal level of customer complaints and returns* as measured by levels achieved against target;
- *consistent quality of goods* as measured by levels of customer returns and complaints, as well as rejections and the results of company quality control checks.

Innovation and market-development measures

Innovation and market-development measures include:

- *development of distinct competitive advantages* in terms of product ranges, price levels and quality as measured against the competition;
- *level of success achieved in relation to new product development introductions* as measured by previous year's performance, the terms of the development strategy and the competition;
- *speed of reaction to changes in demand at the macro- and micro-level* as measured by minimal levels of sell-outs and the profitable optimisation of sales;
- *level of development with respect to the creation of new market segments* as measured against previous year's performance levels and planned development levels.

2. **Identify and describe the criteria that a buyer could use in order to evaluate a new supplier.**

New supplier evaluation ought to include those given in Figure 3.2.

3. **Provide a critique of the various structures that exist in order to support the retail buying function.**

Buying structures ought to consider the following.

A **centralised** buying structure involves all of the buying structures being managed and controlled by buyers collectively in one place – typically at the retailer's head office. This structural form is almost universally adopted by medium- and large-size retailers for a variety of reasons. Perhaps most importantly, a centralised buying structure allows for economies of scale in buying since orders are consolidated for all outlets in the chain, rather than individually, on an outlet-by-outlet basis.

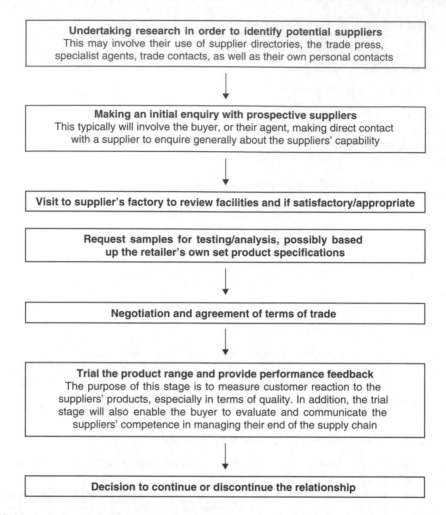

Figure 3.2 New supplier evaluation

A centralised buying structure radically reduces any duplication of effort across a number of different outlets, which in turn allows for a more effective use of manpower. It allows expert buyers to concentrate on buying and procurement decisions, while management at store level can focus upon customer-service matters. Furthermore, centralisation provides for a single point of communication for the supply base which also allows for a tighter control over the supply chain in matters of quality, production and service delivery. In particular, centralisation allows buyers to negotiate terms of supply with the advantage of scale economies, which typically allows them to negotiate strongly on pricing and other support issues. With buyers located in a central location with a more efficient and effective information resource base, it could also be suggested that centralisation enables the procurement team to strategically identify and manage market-trend information as it emerges.

It is important to note, however, that the adoption of a centralised buying structure is not without its problems. For example, while centralisation provides for a consistent merchandise range across the company, it reduces the retailer's flexibility to respond to local trends, needs and opportunity. The rigidity of centralisation typically means that the intimate knowledge that store management has of their local market is under-utilised and is not integrated into the buying decision-making process. This in turn may result in local management becoming demotivated as a result of their non-involvement.

With respect to the latter point, it could be argued that with the implementation of EPOS programmes, allows for local market information to be easily integrated into buying decisions. Indeed, it could be suggested that the information provided by EPOS systems is likely to be more reliable than that provided by intuition of local managers. However, it must also be acknowledged that EPOS systems can account only for those items that have been sold; they are not capable of identifying and accommodate those items that local markets may want but which are not stocked by the retailer.

A **decentralised** buying structure is in the main adopted only by small retail companies, such as family-owned, single-outlet businesses. Under such a structure, buying is done at store level, often by the store manager. The advantages of decentralised buying are in effect the disadvantages of centralised buying. Of these, perhaps the most significant advantage of decentralised buying is the opportunity it provides for retailers who adopt such a structure to respond to the needs of their local market.

Similarly, the disadvantages of decentralisation are the advantages of a centralised approach. An obvious disadvantage of decentralisation is the fact that it does not provide for the scale economies of centralised buying. In order to overcome this issue, many small independent retailers who operate decentralised buying join with other independent retailers in a buying group. A number of different buying groups exist, such as Spar, Intersport and UniChem, and their purpose is to provide independent retailers with the opportunity to benefit from economies of scale through their consolidated buying. Through their participation in a recognised buying group, retailers are given the opportunity to access leading brands and products that otherwise may not be available to them by virtue of their small buying scale.

A **combinative** structure is the third approach that a retailer may adopt. As part of a combinative approach, the authority to purchase operates at both a central and a local level. This may involve the central buyers adopting 70 per cent of the lines that are to be stocked, while the remaining stock is bought by local managers. This approach has been utilised by multinational food retailers whose central managers buy mega-brands that are sold in all of their operating markets, while their local management are responsible for sourcing products from local suppliers in order to satisfy local customer tastes.

Chapter 4

Retail store design

Stephen Doyle

4.1 Introduction

The purpose of this chapter is to first and foremost highlight the significance of store design as a key consideration for all retailers (Doyle and Broadbridge; 1999). In so doing, it will integrate the principles of design with their application in the retail context through relevant exemplars. This chapter will identify that store design is not solely concerned with the establishment of interiors that may be perceived as attractive and/or functional, but has implications for the public face of the retailer. It also suggests that retail design is a management issue and that design is a creative response to a set of given conditions.

The objectives of this chapter can thus be expressed as follows:

- to highlight the significance of store design in the context of efficiency, experience and differentiation;
- to demonstrate that effective retail design is a co-ordinated balance between the physical and aesthetic dimensions of the retailer;
- to provide insight into retail design at the micro- and macro-level;
- to propose a framework appropriate for retail design management.

4.2 Definitions of design

The term design is somewhat mercurial, possessing a variety of meanings both stated and implied. Design can be described as an activity or series of activities co-ordinated for the purposes of a tangible outcome (Bruce and Cooper; 1997), and store design would certainly fit in with such a definition. In addition, it can be considered as the output of the process of designing, the object or system resultant from the input of designers and other involved parties (e.g. craftsmen/women, manufacturers). Once again, such a meaning has relevance to retail store design in as much, as after the planning process there exists a physical manifestation of the design. A more philosophical definition was proposed by Forty (1989) and Oakley (1990) when they described design as being concerned with improvement and resolution. What is common to all definitions is the emphasis that design is concerned with planning, with recognising the purpose of the 'design' and the needs of the users, and these should be reflected both in the form that the solution takes and the effectiveness with which it functions.

4.2.1 Background

The importance of design within the context of retailing has been long recognised, and arguably, the application of the principles of design pre-date any academic consideration of the subject. In essence, before the seminal paper of Martineau (1958), an understanding and incorporation of design was manifest in retailing, not least through the need to make clear the nature of the product offer. Store design, then as now, dealt with issues such as customer enticement, customer flow, cost management, operational efficiency, competitive distinction and image. Reflections on the early department stores reveal how effective such retailers were in incorporating design within their overall retail strategy.

In considering the department store, there has to be found a multiplicity of issues that reflect the retailer's keen awareness of the importance of store design, and in what may be considered large scale. Here we see a new form of retailing emerge in the mid-19th century, capitalising upon the product of the industrial revolution, not just in merchandise terms (although mass production helped facilitate a form of mass retailing) but in terms of architecture, urban landscape, communication and customer distribution throughout the stores. Steel frames enabled the construction of large, multi-floored buildings that comprised expanses of open space, uninterrupted by supporting walls, thereby creating a free-flow environment. In this alone is demonstrated the integration of technology to redefine the physical parameters of stores, and in this respect, we see store design as a progressive, problem-solving activity. In incorporating what were new building techniques and materials, the 'problem' of small-scale stores was resolved. Similarly, such large-scale shops required an effective method of encouraging customers to 'shop' the whole area and so escalators and lifts where integrated into the architecture to transport customers vertically throughout the departments. In this component of department store design we see the importance of integrated thinking. We may postulate that customers would have been less likely to navigate a store the size of, for example La Samaritaine (Paris), Marshall Fields (Chicago) or Selfridges (London) if some form of mechanical aid was not available, and so, store design is essentially about appropriate holism.

Such holism is apparent in the exterior elements of the department stores as well. In order to entice the customer in, the department store made good use of plate glass, a material only recently available to architects, thus the visual links between the street and the store were large, dramatic and radical. Such windows facilitated merchandise 'tableaux' that communicated in a new way, the stores' contents and indeed the newness of the store concept. If the windows were conceived to cause interest, multiple entrances were devised to ease access to the store itself, and in so doing, the retailer needed to consider how to manage the movement of customers throughout a large area from a variety of points of ingress. The stores were therefore zoned and subsequently directories could be placed throughout, as were stairs, escalators and lifts. Such dilemmas may not seem particularly unusual in the current retail environment, but in the 19th century these were new problems that needed new design solutions. Thus, while Underhill (1999) stresses the need for contemporary retailers to provide good directional signage, precedents for this had not been established in a store the scale of the department stores. In this respect, the manifestation department store provides is a useful case study of store design, incorporating all aspects of design, from conceptualisation through management to actualisation.

One element that has not yet been touched upon was the need for competing department stores to create an identity that distinguished each from the other. Hence, while there evolved a common architectural language that identified these edifices as department stores, such stores also needed to determine a way in which they could differentiate themselves from their competitors. Each store interpreted the language in differing ways, through its use of typeface, architecture, motif, store-fittings, features, technology and the merchandise that it offered. Such competition had an impact on the physical landscape that the stores and the public inhabited, enriching them in developmental and aesthetic terms.

In this brief historical foray into store design, we can witness the influence of factors external to the retailer on the retailer's vision. Societal, economic and technical changes all conspired to make the department store a possibility. The form that it took was the result of informed design. This reflects what Bruce and Cooper (1997) suggest is the way that designers think and work, whereby they suggest that 'designers use a combination of intuition, understanding and current knowledge to develop a design solution' (p. 13). Furthermore, it endorses their proposal that 'When designers approach problems, they question every aspect continuously, they push ideas laterally and they have the continual desire to take risks with solutions' (p. 13). In the example of the department stores, what is highlighted is the output of the creative interaction between clients and designers in possession of intuition, knowledge and current understanding. Such interaction resulted in an establishment of a new retail form.

The department stores present a valid point of introduction into the subject of store design, not simply because they provide an exemplar of the overarching importance of store design. Nor is it because many remain in a relatively undiluted form that allows us to witness the essence of the design, although that is a useful characteristic. Instead, it is principally because, as the result of coherent design, they embody the issues that remain significant to retail design today. Similarly, as Kent (2002) emphasises the increased need to design retail spaces that enhance experience, similar philosophies are recognised in the departments stores, where in essence, social experience formed a substantial part of their remit (e.g. Zola; 1883) and such was readily incorporated into their designs through the inclusion of restaurants, cafes and rooftop gardens. Kent (2002) stresses role of department stores in the contemporary 'development of experiential branding' (p. 294), whereby branding has evolved from a '2D approach to the creation of an identity to the visualisation of external architecture and the creation of internal spaces' (p. 294). This is an important point to develop the remainder chapter since it serves as a reminder, that above all else, store design should be relevant to its purpose and to its users.

4.3 The design principles

Derived from Mayall (1979), Doyle and Broadbridge (1999) proposed the application of nine design principles as a guide to retail store design. These principles stressed the benefits of an integrated approach to design to the retailer and to the wider community. What these principles also recognise is the strategic and commercial value of retail store design as a means by which the retailer can construct an environment that is both aesthetically and functionally attractive to the customer and also effective and efficient for the business of retailing. The remainder of this chapter will explore the philosophy and application of the design principles.

4.3.1 *The principle of totality*

This principle is concerned with the overarching nature of design, stressing that no single element should be considered separately from the other elements that comprise the design. In essence, totality suggests that there should be synergy among the design features and that consideration should be taken of all stakeholders' perspectives. In respect of retail store design, users relates not only to customers, although from a marketing viewpoint they should be central to the design solution. It will also include directors, managers, staff and shareholders all of whom will be impacted on in some way by the store design. This may be in terms of the comfort or efficiency of the working environment; the extent to which the store design helps position the company; the cost of the design or the lost revenue in respect of the better alternatives offered by competitors. As Oakley (1990) stressed 'design is an inescapable concern of every business, of every manager' (p. 5).

Totality also stresses the relationship between form and function, emphasising that both should co-exist in any design solution. This is the overarching guiding principle that draws together all of the principles that are derivatives of it. Totality indicates that the design should take cognisance therefore, not only of the users but also of non-users, of the resources available, of the positioning of the retailer, of the nature of the products and the influence of suppliers, of technology and its associated costs (installation and main-tenance), of competitors and of the design of other stores within the chain (if appropriate). Doyle and Broadbridge (1999) in fact suggest that the incorporation of design principles into the strategic and operational thinking of the retailer provides a framework that encourages functional collaboration.

4.3.2 The principle of time

The principle of time recognises the finite nature of designs and the dynamic nature of the environment in which retailers exist and compete. The durability of a store design may be dependent on the nature of the retailer, whereby, for example a retailer such as Liberty of London places great emphasis upon its heritage and therefore retains a substantial part of its original store design as testament to its longevity and as a source of its difference. However, even such retailers need to recognise that old technology may not be acceptable to modern customers and operations, while 'old' surroundings may be. Furthermore, while retaining the core features, Liberty of London has undertaken substantial renovation work (completed in 2002) to its Regent Street store so that the retailer is able to emphasise its relevance in terms of the present as well as the past.

Durability may also be influenced by geographical location. In countries – such as France, Italy and Spain – retailers, including restaurants, cafes appear less prone to the whims of fashion and so store interiors and exteriors tend to be more long term than their UK equivalents. Time is thus not simply concerned with the physical durability of the store but also of its psychological durability in respect of the acceptability of the design. However, where the lifespan of the design is likely to be brief, then the materials used to construct the store environment should reflect this in cost terms.

It is also pertinent to consider time not only in respect of the whole design, but also in respect of certain components of the design. The architecture and layout may remain func-tional and aesthetically effective, but the fixtures and fittings, the paint and the carpets for example, components which reveal wear and tear, may undermine the overall effect and thus, even in circumstances whereby the retailer sees no reason to renew or renovate the store design, renewal of elements that comprise the design may need renewing.

4.3.3 The principle of value

The principle of value may be viewed as appropriateness or fitness for purpose rather than simply being a cost-based construct. Value underscores the fact that store design is contextual, whereby users of a store will evaluate the design based on their experiences and expectations, which in themselves may be influenced by other retailers, be they com-petitors or not. Reflection upon the store design of competitors or retailers seeking a simi-lar position will help identify the factors that users view as significant benchmarks. This is not to suggest that the principle of value is best achieved through mimicry. Instead, it sug-gests that, regardless of the manifestation of the store design, it must seek to satisfy, in par-ticular, its chosen market and therefore to accentuate or adopt the key features that are pertinent to that market.

4.3.4 The principle of resource

All retail store designs face resource constraints. This may be in the form of finance, but may also include knowledge, technology, land, space, materials, planning consent and existing features. It is the responsibility of the design process to maximise the benefits gained from using these resources. As in any aspect of resource management there may be conflict, such that the desire to increase selling space may have to be at the expense of storage facilities. This may be achievable if the retailer's operations or supplier's relations allow the stock held to be minimised, such has been the case with Marks and Spencer's recent in-store expansions. However, where this is achieved at the expense of the retailer's ability to actually maintain stock reserves that allow effective trading then, in essence, such a design proposal is flawed. This returns us to the first principle, that of totality.

The resources used in retail store designs relate not only to the experiences of customers, although, as previously suggested, these should be a priority. They must reflect the position of the retailer such that they augment that position. When used effectively, the lavish or creative use of resources may in themselves become noteworthy and newsworthy. The Prada Gugeheim (2001) in New York received substantial news coverage, partly because of the building that it occupied; itself a resource and partly because of the physical and technical features that have been incorporated to suggest a forward thinking, intelligent, luxury brand. Furthermore, Prada views the store not simply as a retail space, but also as a means of making a contribution to the community, whereby, when not functioning as a shop, it functions as a public venue.

Resources represent the key parameters of store design. Every design proposal should be based on a realistic analysis of the resources available, perhaps most significantly finance. Consideration should be given to identifying the areas where resource investment is most needed and is likely to provide the greatest benefit. If a store is being refitted, it may be possible to recycle materials to enable expenditure elsewhere. In this respect, design is fundamentally the issues of management. It is rare that store design is not influenced by some constraints. Such constraints should not necessarily be viewed as limiting creativity, but as establishing the framework within which the creative process takes place. It is therefore incumbent upon the retailer to clearly define available resources prior to undertaking any store design activity.

4.3.5 The principle of synthesis

Synthesis relates to a process of bringing together separate components such that they form a coherent whole. These components may be described as the building blocks of design and include concepts, knowledge, materials and people all of which need to be articulated such that the final solution is cognisant of the many factors that influence store design. Doyle and Broadbridge (1999) argue that synthesis may also 'apply to the synthesising of bonds between the groups' (p. 79) underlining the need for planning and control of the design process and its outcomes.

In the context of store design, synthesis may operate a number of varying levels. At the micro-level, retail store design may be concerned with the management of factors that relate to a single store. At the macro-level, synthesis may apply to the management of retail design within the streetscape, and be managed under the umbrella of planning regulations. In this respect there may exist some conflict, the individual store seeking to emphasise its distinctiveness through visual or physical aspects of design, while planners may be seeking to achieve visual or physical harmony at the town or city level (Frey, 1999). Shopping centres/galleries/malls might exist between these two extremes, whereby there is an overarching cohesiveness resulting from the primary architecture if the building, but within, each individual store is vying to demonstrate its personality within the confines of the collective.

4.3.6 The principle of iteration

The key characteristic of the principle of iteration is that it emphasises the need for continued review of the retail store design. This review may take into account (among other things) the condition of the interior and exterior, the changing needs and expectations of customers, the activities of competitors, technological developments, legislation and merchandise factors. The principle of time proposes that all design becomes progressively less appropriate over time, reaching a point of obsolescence. The principle of iteration exists to remind the retailer that, with judicious monitoring of the design solution it may be possible to minimise the impact and costs of such progressive obsolescence. Major refurbishment costs not only in terms of materials and labour, but also in terms of lost trade resulting from customer inconvenience. Such activities in themselves present a design problem, for example, with the shop in partial disarray, how does the retailer navigate the customers safely and conveniently through the store. Temporary signage may be required as will merchandise reviews, since it may not be possible to present the complete range. What might the impact be on the customer's perception of merchandise presented in temporary areas? This will depend on how influential the store environment is in modifying the customers' behaviours.

In the 1990s, Selfridges, London underwent substantial interior refurbishment resulting in the temporary closure of the central escalators. In these conditions, customers needed to have alternative means of shopping the shop vertically. In this case, part of the rationale was to re-instate Selfridges as a major retail force and so the principle of iteration comprised part of its competitive strategy. This example demonstrates the need for retailers to continually revise the store design or components thereof to ensure that store maintains its relevance in a market that is influenced not only by established retailers, but also by new entrants to the marketplace. Continued review of the store design enables the retailer to make major or minor adjustments at appropriate key times, but also to plan for the implications of major work in respect of customer experience and operations, whereby these implications become in themselves issues of retail design.

Under this principle the issues discussed have thus far tended to focus upon major change. However, the most obvious examples of the need for iteration relate to merchandising and seasonality. Window displays, as previously discussed, provide a valuable design tool for communicating to the customer. Unchanging windows may suggest unchanging merchandise, and while consistency may be commendable, tedium is not. Over time the message will be diluted as its newness is diminished to a larger segment of the passing population. Windows can provide entertainment as well as information. They can enhance the public spaces beyond the shop, or they can detract from it; regular reflection is therefore worthwhile. The second example could be partially related to this. Seasonal changes allow the retailer to adjust not only the merchandise, but introduce temporary changes to the store interior and exterior, thereby creating an environment, that while structurally stable, is continuously evolving. These may be communicated to the outside world through the widows, but in addition, we may reflect upon the adornment, at Christmas, of the Liberty building in London with a large bow, representing the emporium as a large gift, or the hanging of Christmas lights, by retailers, in the streets. These are temporary design components that, once the season has progressed, are obsolete and therefore to be removed, but are nevertheless a useful example of how design and design elements may not necessarily be permanent and should therefore be frequently considered.

4.3.7 The principle of change

As the core of design is changed, whereby what currently exists can be improved upon. Conversely, it may be argued that if the changes are not improvements then they should not be made. The process of design is thus reflective; change should have a purpose. Change may be prompted by internal factors, external factors or by both. In this respect retail store design is contextual. Hence, the design of a store may be altered as a response to competitor's activity. It may also be altered to reflect the changing nature of customers or customers' expectations. Retailers may use design as a means of repositioning a store or re-affirming the store's position by publicly demonstrating its willingness to invest in the fabric, technology or decor of the building. In this context, the retail design may be interpreted as a metaphor for commitment and longevity. Design as metaphor may be witnessed in the form, materials, concepts and associated expenditure of flagship stores in as much as these stores exist to communicate an image and identity to the customer, the investor and to the competition. Similarly, banking has historically used architecture as a means of communicating solidity, wealth and respectability. These exemplars highlight that the dichotomy between form and function may in fact be a false one, revealing that the form a retail store design takes may serve a communication purpose.

A further example demonstrates the relationship between form and function that exists in the retail context. David Linley & Co. Ltd. undertook to change the retail space of the company's flagship store in London. At the heart of this change was the need for expansion, reflecting the success of the company and the increasing product range that it offered. The increased interior space and store frontage addressed a number of issues simultaneously. At a functional level, the revised store design provided more trading space, a more pleasant environment for customers and likewise for staff. In addition, the new design made clears the links between the design function of the company and the products/services that it offered by means of a glass wall that acted as a visual conduit between the two spaces. This stressed the importance of design to the retailer. The increased frontage enabled the company to display a greater array of products and to be more visible. All of these elements have an element of form and of function.

However, perhaps the most succinct example of this relationship exists in the shop entrance. Prior to the expansion, the shop entrance was a single door that was located around the corner from the shop front. After the renovation, the store proudly welcomed its customers through large, double doors positioned centrally to the front of the shop. This new door proclaims a number of things about the company. It is more open, more accessible (reflecting the evolving product range). In addition, it is easier to access and so has improved the functional aspect of the door. This is a distillation of the relationship between form and function, with form and function existing as correlates and where the relationship has been strengthened through design change.

4.3.8 *The principle of relationship*

The previous section logically leads us to the principle of relationship and this is apposite since this principle stresses that design should be purposeful, contextual and thus relate to the specific of the given situation. Without context, without relationship then it could be argued that store design is only partially informed and only partially complete. Stores that are intended to be shopped by parents with children should take into consideration the needs of both parties in their design. This may be reflected in safety, in facilities (the decision to have a creche becomes a design issue when considering where to locate it, how much space to afford it, of what should it comprise and so on), space, access and décor. The extent to which a retailer emphasises these components may communicate to the customer the extent to which the retailer values their custom. At the heart of this is, first and foremost, customer knowledge and understanding. However, such knowledge and understanding should pertain to all relevant parties, including staff and potential customers. Benetton, Milan demonstrated a high level of insight and commitment to parents and children by dedicating a large proportion of its sales floor to a mechanised, fantasy woodland for children. In practical terms, it provides a distraction for children, possibly even a reward or a destination for children; all of which are conducive to an enhanced retail experience for all parties.

4.3.9 The principle of competence

Design, like any other aspect of retailing, requires management. Doyle and Broadbridge (1999) suggest that the greater the resource limitations, particularly fiscal, the greater the need for management to be subsumed internally over the long term. However, where there is limited expertise within the organisation, then there may be an argument for employing a design professional early on in the design process to ensure a satisfactory solution and the avoidance of expensive mistakes. The ability to make this decision alone may be indicative of the degree of competence of the retailer's management. In addition, competence relates to the retailer's ability to identify the nature and timing of design change and provide the contextual information necessary in accord with the principle of design.

Competence may thus be a shared attribute between internal and external professionals, each assuming responsibility for their own specific remit. At a base level, the retailer is responsible for decisions relating to expenditure on the design (be that process or product of) and the designer for the effective utilisation of the budget. Developing the relationship further, the designer may need information from the retailer about the customer, operations, site, lease tenure, attitude to risk, additional resources, features to be retained, scope of the change, etc., with the designer's competence being affected by the retailer's ability to provide these insights. Similarly, the retailer's competence either to retail effectively or to recognise what may be critical information, is partially dependent on the designer's competence. Ultimately, this highlights that the appropriateness and effectiveness of a store design is the result of managing creativity within a given framework, regardless of whether that creativity is managed internally, externally or both.

4.3.10 The principle of service

The principle of service stresses the impact of retail store design on the wider world and not just persons immediately involved with the retailer on a transactional or investment basis. Mayall (1979) somewhat idealistically suggested that 'a design must satisfy everybody, and not just those for whom it is directly intended' (p. 167). Whether design can satisfy everybody is debatable given the diverse nature of humankind. However, as Doyle and Broadbridge (1999) suggest, it is possible for retail design to have both empathy and sympathy for its environment and the general users of that environment. In addition, it is possible for retail store design to actively pursue significance to a wider audience than the retail customer.

Such a phenomenon is exemplified by Prada 'Guggenheim', New York, which received a *GE Edison Award of Merit* for lighting. The store design places an emphasis not upon the merchandise but upon the architecture of the building and the multi-functionality of the building. Poyner (2001) expressed this as returning the retailer to the population, suggesting that retailers have a social responsibility to integrate with and maintain the physical and social fabric of the environment. Thus the Prada store is designed such that, by day it functions as a retail outlet and by evening it can serve a wider population as a social venue. In addition, Prada has assumed responsibility for maintaining and opening access to a building of local significance to New York. On its opening, the store received substantial news coverage, partly because of the building that it occupied; partly because of the physical and technical features that have been incorporated to suggest a forward thinking, intelligent, luxury brand and partly because it attempted to integrate a social dimension to its design.

The integration of service or social responsibility in respect of store design is not specific to luxury goods retailers. Neighbouring the ASDA Hamilton (Scotland) is a large public area, used on an *ad hoc* basis by local residents as recreational space and more formally for activities such as farmers' and local traders' markets. Visually, the area is linked not only by its proximity to the retailer, but also by the consistent use of materials that comprise the public space and the retail space. Seating, sculpture, shelter and stained glass all combine to establish a facility that enhances not only the retailer but also the local environment, providing a facility that is for the benefit of customers' and non-customers' alike. In this respect, the store design is attempting to satisfy beyond its customer base.

Associated with a design policy, such as this, does have resource implications and it may be argued that in the cases of both Prada and ASDA, the retailers should have concentrated upon managing and designing retail spaces that are solely for retail purposes. However, it may also be suggested that retail design that attempts to deliver benefits to the wider population derives associated benefits in terms of publicity and goodwill. It may also be argued that, should retailers ignore the principles of service, then, if retailers are judged by the company they keep, as may be suggested by gravity models of location theory (McGoldrick, 2002), then the extent to which that company accepts it has a responsibility to the landscape will affect the overall attractiveness of a location.

4.4 Conclusions

This chapter demonstrates that retail design is more than interior decoration. It emphasises that store design is significant to all retailers, regardless of the sector, regardless of the product and regardless of the position. Every retail outlet reveals some degree of design input, be it at the elevated and highly considered level of a flagship fashion store or the less apparent design consideration that may be manifested in a local cornershop. What is common and consistent is that decisions have to be made in relation to the location of goods, the flow of customer traffic, security, storage, lighting, etc. and each of these decisions are design decisions that are influenced by the type of retailer, the type of retail manager, the resources available and customer expectations. It is therefore inappropriate to view retail design as being significant to high-involvement retailers (Doyle, 2002); retail design affects all retailers.

What is also demonstrated by this chapter is that retail design product and process, whereby the product is the result of the process. The effectiveness of the product (the store design) is influenced by the effectiveness with which the process is managed and the nature of the process inputs, such as customer knowledge and operational awareness, thus while retail design may be most obviously manifested in the visual and physical characteristics of the store, it has pertinence for the overall efficiency of the store and thus the experience of customers and staff alike. In fact, the principles are proposed by Mayall (1979) suggest that design should consider a wider remit than just users, but should consider the experience of non-users, which in respect of retail design may be reflected in the store's impact on the landscape or its use of non-renewable resources.

The principles themselves serve to demonstrate the myriad factors that require consideration and management in respect of store design, emphasising the short-term and long-term implications; the need for appropriateness and relativity; the benefits of change and the significance of design decision upon the wider world, to the extent that that wider world may be altered for better or worse. In addition, the principles stress that design in its broadest terms is holistic and that retail design is primarily about providing a coherent and capable retail solution, one that addresses customer's needs and serves to distinguish the retailer from its competitors. The principles therefore exist as a guide to achieving this within the constraints of the business and the context of the sector.

References

Bruce, M. and Cooper, R. (1997) *Marketing and Design Management*. London, Thomson Business Press.

Doyle, S.A. and Broadbridge, A. (1999) Differentiation by design: the importance of design in retailer repositioning and differentiation. *International Journal of Retail and Distribution Management*, **27**(2&3), 72–81.

Doyle, S.A. (2002) Forty, A. (1989) *Objects of desire: Design and Society*, London, Thames and Hudson.

Frey, H. (1999) *Designing the City*. London, E&FN Spon.

Kent, T. (2002) 2D23D: management and design perspectives on retail branding. *Proceedings of 7th International Conference on Retailing and Commercial Distribution*, University of Gloucester, 10–12 July, pp. 286–297.

Martineau, P. (1958) The personality of the retail store. *Harvard Business Review*, **36**(January–February), 47–55.

Mayall, W.H. (1979) *Principles in Design*. London, The Design Council.

McGoldrick, P. (2002) *Retail Marketing*. London, McGraw-Hill.

Oakley, M. (1990) Design and design management. In Oakley, M. (ed.), *Design Management: A handbook of Issues and Methods*. London, Basil Blackwell.

Poyner, R. (2001) Meet me at the checkout. *The Business, Financial Times Weekend Magazine*, 1 December, 16–22.

Underhill, P. (1999) *Why We Buy. The Science of Shopping*. New York, Simon & Schuster.

Zola, E. (1883) *Au Bonheur des Dammes*.

Study questions

1. Retail design is influenced by context. Considering a variety of sectors, how might such contextuality be manifest?
2. How does the position of retailers influence the design solution? What positioning benefits might store design provide?
3. In what ways might new store design differ from the redesign of an established store?

Issues and cases

Chapter 5

The scope of e-commerce in retail strategy

Ruth Marciniak and Margaret Bruce

Aims

The aims of this chapter are:

- to define retail strategy;
- to define electronic commerce (e-commerce) and its scope within retail strategy;
- to explain how e-commerce may evolve within retail organisations;
- to explore positioning models within e-commerce;
- to determine market opportunities via e-commerce;
- to examine retailer choices surrounding the integration or separation of e-commerce activities within the organisation.

5.1 Introduction

The shakeout of dot.com retailers, such as the spectacular failure of the fashion electronic retailer Boo.com, makes e-commerce an easy target and gives credence to the view that retailers operating on the high street can relax as far as the Internet is concerned. This is further entrenched by reports that consumers are still wary about buying online, despite a plethora of safe shopping initiatives designed to build up trust in the market. However, while the Internet has not killed the high street, as media reports in the late 1990s would have had us believe, the high street should not be complacent about the impact of e-commerce. Rather the challenge is to combine the best of the 'bricks' and 'clicks' worlds to provide environments that best meet consumers' needs. While developing retail strategies appropriate for e-commerce is no different from developing any other kind of strategy, wherein the retailer identifies a range of strategic options and assesses the most appropriate to achieve its objectives, understanding of how the market operates in this environment is vital.

5.2 What is retail strategy?

Strategy is concerned with planning and the long-term survival and success of a business. It defines the direction for a firm; it specifies where the business is going and determines how it will get there. It also guides the company towards its financial objectives (Davies and Brooks, 1989). The essence of strategic planning lies with the consideration of current alternative strategic decisions, given possible threats and opportunities. In all, a major objective of any organisation is the acquisition of a competitive advantage, which results from its appropriately selected strategic choices (Siomkos and Vrechopoulos, 2000). The impact of e-commerce within an industry will be affected by the strategic choices of those operating within it.

Central to strategy thinking is the view that it should identify the method of achieving differential advantage (Day and Wensley, 1988). Such an advantage may be based on cost leadership or differentiation through branding, and/or focus on a niche market (Porter, 1980). Within retail strategy, a rationale for differentiation is as Dawson (2000) suggests, consumers are not homogeneous, and therefore an essential factor of retailer competition is the attempt by a retailer to be different from other retailers in order to better satisfy the particular consumer. Here he points out differentiation on non-price factors, such as customer service, is more subtle and is wider ranging than differentiation on price.

Adopting the rational perspective, McGoldrick (2002) offers logical steps in formulating retail marketing strategy starting with a strategic audit, in order to identify significant factors at play in the internal and external environments. Next is identification of the retailer's strategic direction and routes to competitive advantage, followed by customer targeting and positioning strategies. Thereby offering an identification, development and selection model, wherein the process of strategy is typified as being a linear progression through a number of distinct steps, identified as being, analysis, formulation and implementation. Here it is assumed that the decision-maker is a boundly rational individual who wishes to avoid uncertainty, searching for new solutions only when confronted with new problems. Likewise in their textbooks, Newman and Cullen (2002) offer a similar framework for the strategic planning process, as does Gilbert (2003). Such a view is encompassed in the definition of strategy of Ansoff (1965) where he sees it as a valid managerial instrument, which encompasses decision rules and guidelines, which guide the process of development of an organisation.

In examining the concept of the traditional rational perspective of strategy, it is taken for granted that decision-making takes place, for example decisions with regard to what customer segment, what market position, what trading format, what merchandise. In view of this, concerns of the rational perspective are about rational choice between alternatives involving how decisions come about and how they are subsequently implemented. Here traditionally the strategic process is seen as a procedure based on rigorous logic and extensive knowledge of all pertinent factors wherein intentional and actual decisions are seen as being well correlated (Hendry, 2000). Decision-makers enter the decision-making process with known objectives (Eisenhardt and Zbaracki, 1992), for example an objective to build strong merchandise and brands or alternatively, enhance relationships with customers via offering various channels to market.

5.3 Definition and scope of e-commerce

The attractiveness of the Internet as a commercial medium is due to its ability to facilitate the global sharing of information and resources and therefore its potential to create market opportunities (Hoffman *et al.*, 1996). e-commerce is identified as being one of the most promising applications of information technology (IT) in recent years (Gunasekaran *et al.*, 2002), encompassing the buying and selling of information, products and services via computer networks (Kalakota and Whinston, 1996). Bloch *et al.* (1996) extend this to include 'support for any kind of business transactions over a digital infrastructure.' Thus broadening the definition to absorb activities such as the provision of information to customers, marketing and support activities, in effect all the activities which are common to the combined efforts of each of the three channels conventionally used in the retail buying and selling process, these being, communications, transaction and distribution channels.

Consequently, in an online environment a web site is able to advertise products, allow consumers to pay for them and in the case of digital software distribute the product via a download (Li *et al.*, 1999). With regards to non-digital products, communications and transaction functions are achieved on a web site but not distribution. Therefore, depending on the product, from a business to consumer (B2C) perspective, e-commerce has the potential to be used in all phases of a commercial transaction.

The remit of e-commerce is wide as it is not just about facilitating individual business transactions, it also involves the management of relationships that leads to and arise from transactions. Gunasekaran *et al.* (2002) identified five ways in which e-commerce can contribute to the firm's economic efficiency:

- shrinking distances and timescales;
- lowering distribution and transaction costs;
- speeding product development;
- providing more information to buyers and sellers;
- enlarging customer choice and supplier reach.

In all, e-commerce is a generic title that describes a range of technologies and practices that are available to potentially improve the efficiencies of trading relationships. However, despite these identified efficiencies and in view of increasing levels of e-commerce activity by retailers, it still remains uncertain how the technology can contribute towards a strategic advantage (Dawson, 2000; Hart *et al.*, 2000). As the above illustrates the medium is able to fulfil the utilities of the channels involved in retailing; however, for it to be a truly successful medium for consumer spending the technologies will need to match or exceed the utility provided by the traditional high-street retail formats (Alba *et al.*, 1997). Such utilities include immediate delivery, credit facilities and choice of method of payment, display, personal assistance in selecting goods, return services and warrantees. In terms of online retailers delivering such utilities, much debate has taken place with regards its potential success.

For instance, Hart *et al.* (2000) report that to date, most of the commentary on the significance of the Internet to retail marketing has been anecdotal; offering exaggerated speculative forecasts of its future potential. Yet the Internet presents a sufficiently distinct retail environment that has attracted both the practitioners and the retailers alike yet there lacks a sound theoretical framework to guide e-commerce decisions (Cowles *et al.*, 2002). Evidence suggests that there is a desire to devise such a framework as Reynolds (2000) infers:

> Rarely has the retail and consumer services sector been faced with a strategic challenge of such significant complexity and uncertainty, which has grown in terms of that significance so rapidly.
>
> Reynolds (2000, p. 417)

While the adequacy or otherwise of e-commerce is debated, retailers have busied themselves developing their e-commerce business models. To date, as reported in the media, some of the most successful web sites are those belonging to 'pure-play' or Internet-only retailers. Such examples include Amazon.com and Ebay; neither of which had ever even previously operated a physical retail storefront. Along with the 'pure-plays', Internet retailers are also comprised of firms who have existing high-street stores and/or mail order facilities. They may be either a large retailer serving most of the UK market or a small retailer serving a specialised niche market. Typically, the large retailers have adopted a 'wait and see' approach towards the Internet (Rowley, 2002). For instance, they may have established an Internet presence early on, but it may be only recently that they have launched transactional facilities. Such an example of this within the UK is John Lewis. Further to this, a number of pure-play retailers have taken the decision to move into the high street. Examples of this include Confetti who bought over Jerrys Home Stores. Undoubtedly, there is much movement evident between the various selling channels within retailing.

What is evident is that some companies have engaged in e-commerce activity without any consideration towards a return on investment (Damanpour and Madison, 2001). One of the reasons for this may be that many businesses fear that without an Internet presence, the firm will get left behind. A further reason is that firms have been seduced by suggestions that e-commerce provides opportunities to access bigger markets at lower costs. For instance, Bloch *et al.* (1996) propose that e-commerce offers cost advantages to firms via less-expensive product promotions, while Benjamin and Wigand (1995) suggest that it offers a more cost-effective distribution channel and overall reduction in physical distribution costs. Bloch *et al.* (1996) also advocate that e-commerce can enable a company to implement customer focus strategies through better customer relationships. Together with various reports regarding the growing numbers of consumers who now have access to the Internet and use it for purchasing, it is understandable that e-commerce is seen as an attractive way forward for many firms (Mintel, 2001) as the characteristics of virtual markets presented to firms via e-commerce are seen as new opportunities for wealth creation (Amit and Zott, 2000).

To date, of those who have launched web sites, some have met with financial success. However, other firms have either relatively little success, their sites have yet to pay significant dividends, or have gone out of business. Evidence suggests these companies have set themselves up without consideration of the strategic implications of developing, implementing and running a web site. For example, Neal and Veitch (2000) indicate that more than a third of 102 UK-based web sites surveyed by the Trading Standards Institute, including those of high-street shops and well-known online specialists were problematic. For instance, 38 per cent of orders did not arrive on time, and 17 per cent of orders were unfulfilled because of system crashes, out-of-stock items, forgotten orders or companies collapsing.

A major challenge facing retailers who are entering the electronic business (e-business) environment is the nature of retail operations involved as they are conceptually the opposite to physical store retailing. As shown in Table 5.1, such retail facets as physical space, tangible inventory and customer traffic are very different between the two environments (Cowles *et al.*, 2002). As such traditional practices of high-street retailers are challenged in a virtual retail environment.

Table 5.1 Challenges to retail operations: physical store versus virtual store

	Physical store	**Virtual store**
Space	Shelf space	Navigability
	Square footage	Design of web pages
Inventory	Tangible	Intangible
	1. See-and-touch products	1. Handling not possible
	2. Leave the shop with the product	2. Wait for delivery
	3. Shipping not appropriate	3. Shipping costs incurred
	4. Physical communication with sales staff	4. Virtual communication with sales staff
Customer traffic	Size of store	Bandwidth

5.4 Appropriate goods and services for selling online

Considering any retail strategy appropriate for selling goods or services online, one must consider what types of products or services would sell most effectively via this medium. Here there exists much speculation. It is viewed that currently the Internet can only realistically reproduce two of the five human senses, these being sight and sound (Phau *et al.*, 2000). Therefore suggesting that products pertaining predominantly to these senses will do well selling online. Furthermore, Phau *et al.* (2000) consider that the Internet is more suitable for selling intangible or service-related products, especially those that are highly differentiated. For this reason, they suggest that Internet retailers should therefore 'focus on computer-related products, or products which allow trial sampling or those that are high on information content.' Examples of such include computer software, compact discs (CDs), online newspapers, online video/music, and online financial and stock information. In support of Phau *et al.* (2000), the classification system of Peterson *et al.* (1997) in identifying the nature of products and services they consider will sell well online and, also includes intangible and differentiated products. However, they also consider that high-cost low-frequency purchases such as hi-fi systems, rather than low-cost high-frequency products (e.g. groceries) will sell well. One may conclude from this that both of these studies suggest that the Internet potentially offers an extremely limited range of products and services for sale to the consumer. One must ask the question then, why have so many businesses whose core products do not fit into the classification of either Phau *et al.* (2000) or Peterson *et al.* chosen to sell their goods online? In particular, fashion goods, which according to a Pricewaterhouse Coopers (2000) survey, the share of Internet users who reported buying clothes online, has increased. Certainly as Tapscott *et al.* (2000) point out, conventional wisdom suggests that easy to describe products such as books, video games and CDs will do well selling online. As well as being able to be sampled by customers as Phau (2000) suggests, they are also standardised products, easy to deliver and high-margin goods. However, Tapscott *et al.* (2000) also point out that perhaps the most attractive consumer market for physical goods is groceries. Despite the fact that typically they offer low margins, can rot in transit and their packaging and handling requirements vary, the size of the market is huge and no other kinds of goods are purchased with such regularity. In terms of clothing, in comparison to an avid CD buyer, the enthusiastic fashion clothes buyer will be spending far higher amounts due to the higher unit cost of the product. Further to this, the product incurs much higher margins than CDs and therefore makes the sector a more attractive proposition.

5.5 What is e-commerce strategy?

Rowley (2002) points out that strategy formulation in e-commerce is similar to strategy formulation for other business contexts. However, in the eagerness of businesses racing to capitalise on the dot.com boom of the late 1990s, they neglected to consider that the rules of business in an e-commerce environment are no different to other retail environments, namely focus on the customer, acquire the right competences and understand the competition. In her paper, Rowley (2002) identifies key questions that all business strategy is concerned with. Further to this, she also identifies factors that are unique to e-commerce strategy formulation. Each of which is outlined in Table 5.2.

In all, as Burt and Sparks (2002) point out, when examining e-commerce, what is being considered is process innovation, whereby technology provides the capability for a reconfiguration of existing businesses together with the scope for introductions of new operations. Process innovation in terms of B2C e-commerce arises from the ability of the Internet to provide electronic links between dispersed sources of information and the enhanced

Table 5.2 Business strategy and factors pertinent to e-commerce strategy

Business strategy factors	E-commerce strategy factors
Market(s) to be in	One-to-one customer connectivity
Distinctiveness of product/service compared to competitors	Direct access to customer profiles
Appropriate competences necessary to achieve objectives	Need to accommodate rapid change
Anticipated changes in marketplace position	Evolving virtual alliances
Anticipated competitor activities	
Future customer expectations	

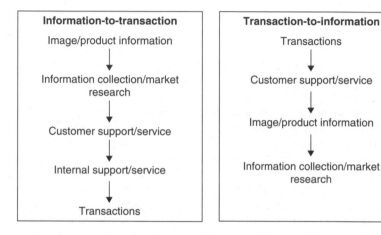

Figure 5.1 Evolutionary stages of web site development

collection of real-time data. Such is this ability that it gives rise to the unique aspects of e-commerce identified above by Rowley (2002), which potentially serve to create competitive advantage.

5.6 Stages approach to e-commerce evolution

Various explanatory models exist that offer a stepwise approach to explain how an e-commerce strategy evolves, based on classification of style and content of web sites and level of exploitation of the technology, such models have been produced by Quelch and Klein (1996), Coleman (1998), Stroud (1998) and Martin and Kambil (1999). Typically different steps are taken depending on whether the firm is an Internet start-up or a large established retailer indicating that existing well-established large retailers tend to adopt the information-to-transaction approach: where a company supplies images and product information and then evolves to offer transactions such as selling to customers. UK firms Marks and Spencer and the Arcardia group both adopted this approach when they first launched their web site. Whereas start-ups adopt a different approach as they tend to move from transaction to information: here a company's initial purpose for a web site is primarily to sell its products and subsequently provide information such as customer support (Figure 5.1). These models suggest a rationale linear approach to the development of Internet technology adoption, such as the models offered below based on Quelch and Klein's work.

However such linear models of Internet technology adoption as offered above, may be problematic. For instance, it is suggested that attempts to use linear models tend to oversimplify complex issues and circumstances (Kai-Uwe Brock, 2000) and their effectiveness and generalization has also been questioned (Wolfe, 1994; Matlay, 1999; Fallon and Moran, 2000). Such models adopt a situational control perspective, which assumes the characteristics of technology determine the actions with regard to the use and consequence of the technology (Markus and Robey, 1988). In all, the rationalist approaches adopted in the above models may not be helpful in reflecting how process really occurs. For instance, Supri *et al.* (2000) suggest that effective adoption and implementation of Internet technologies may rely more on individual factors such as organisational size, structure and mix of available resources. Such a view supports the emergent perspective of technology wherein actions cannot be predicted; rather they emerge from complex social interactions.

5.7 Positioning in e-commerce

In terms of where the firm positions itself in the environment, Porter (1996) argues that strategic positions emerge from three sources, these being:

■ Firstly, *Variety-based positioning* wherein decisions are made with regard to the product or service varieties the firm selects. Such a position embodies specialist retailing, where merchandise width, depth and availability of a product range is offered; for example, the UK-based wine warehouse company, Majestic Wine Warehouse Ltd's Majestic online web site.
■ Secondly, *needs-based positioning* based on the needs of a selected group of customers; for example, Selfridges & Co Department Store which attracts a young affluent cliental who are looking for high-fashion quality goods.
■ Thirdly, *access-based positioning* based on segmenting customers who are accessible in different ways. This may be applied to companies such as Tesco's various store formats; Extra, Metro, Express and of course Tesco online, based on the customers' shopping intentions.

Here Porter (1996) advocates that it is important that a firm selects a strategic position that is different from its rivals, hence the need for understanding what is happening within the external environment and the need for keeping abreast of competitors activities.

Alternatively, further types of positioning models have been adopted in creating electronic business (e-business) ventures. For instance, initiatives such as price comparison sites where consumers have the opportunity to locate and compare product offerings (Alba *et al.*, 1997). Such a model is attractive as the Internet provides opportunities for capitalising on what Kuttner (1998) suggests, the near-perfect market, which unlike in the high street that relies on consumer ignorance, prices are easily accessed available for all to see in order to make price comparisons. However in reality the Internet has proved to be a more complex environment. Perhaps a more robust model is where retailers have sought to aggregate markets via a focused differentiated strategy, referred to as metamediaries (Sawhney, 1999). Through exploiting consumer's time-pressed lifestyle, such retailers seek to aggregate information, products and services and offer them all in one web site. Typically such products or services offered on these sites are with high involvement such as weddings or holidays.

A further example of a differentiated strategic positioning implemented by an e-business is by offering itself as both a product and service provider. The most classic example of this is Amazon.com who, along with its product offerings, also offers services such as book reviews and book suggestions. Such services have the potential to lead to new kinds of relationships with customers, which are dependent on Internet technologies such as e-mail for mediations, for example notifications and recommendations (Maes, 1998).

5.8 Market opportunities via e-commerce

The strategic potential of the e-commerce can be understood by applying the product–market matrix of Ansoff (1965) (see Figure 5.2) which has laid the firm foundation for thinking through alternative strategic directions: market penetration, product development, market development and diversification as it functions to illustrate the main growth vectors available to a company.

Documented below are current examples of growth strategies pursued by various retailers used to illustrate each of the four segments of the matrix.

5.8.1 Market penetration

The Internet can be used to sell more existing products into existing markets. This can be achieved by using the Internet for increasing the awareness of the firm as illustrated by UK supermarkets such as Tesco and Sainsburys' plus the bookseller WH Smith and numerous clothing retailers including the Arcadia Group and Next. All of these retailers pursue a multi-channel strategy selling both via the web, the high street and/or mail order to their existing customers. Finlay (2000) suggests that market penetration fits strategically for a firm when its present customers can be induced to buy more and typically, when a company wants to attack the market share of their competitors, they will undertake market penetration as a way of increasing their own share in the market.

Given that generally the market for consumer goods within the UK is mature, then penetrating these markets by targeting consumers who are looking for convenient ways to shop via a web site would seem to be a viable growth strategy. Typically for these multi-channel retailers, it is not important to them where the customer shops, that is, using the firm's web site or in the high-store or mail-order catalogue, the key is that they shop with them. Evidence suggests that those who do shop using all the channels the retailer has, buys four times more often online than the average online customer (kiosk.com, 2001). These results offer a very strong validation of the importance of a multi-channel strategy and while good, present challenges to retailers in terms of how to tap into these shoppers. Firstly, it is important to identify the channel with the highest-value customer. They also need to co-ordinate their customer data across all channels and invest in the systems to understand that data and install real-time inventory tracking across all channels.

5.8.2 Market development

The success of a firm selling to new markets, with the same or similar product and/or services as are currently offered, would be classified as market development; for example,

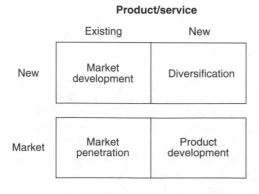

Figure 5.2 The product market matrix

selling to new customer groups and or new geographical areas. The Internet facilitates this, given that it is a worldwide medium. Hence a firm's web site plus its offerings are accessible for all to see. However the success of this growth option requires that the firm's product or service satisfies the requirements of any new customer group (Doyle, 1992), which may be different from those of the original customer market (de Chernatony and McDonald, 1995). For example, offering a web site in only one language will not swiftly facilitate the creation of worldwide customers, as languages, cultures and local market conditions vary throughout the world. Therefore, providing a web site for other geographical areas is a major challenge.

In all, firms need to balance the decreased costs of distribution associated with marketing communications and transaction facilities using the Internet with the increased costs of support in terms of the resources required to target different audiences. For instance, according to Duncan (2001) after English, the languages that are likely to get the greatest return on translation investment are French, German and Spanish, and looking into the future, he predicts Chinese. He suggests that consumers are far more likely to complete a transaction online, if the web site is in their own language rather than English. In order to reach 70 per cent of the consumer audience in Europe, the content of the web site would need to be translated into five languages. Further, in terms of market development and meeting the needs of different local markets, Duncan identifies additional considerations, which need to be tackled, such as tax, value-added tax (VAT) and different local legal requirements. While offline businesses also require to do this, those operating in online environments also require to have an understanding of data protection and approaches to registration of domain names for each of the local markets. Overall Finlay (2000) suggests that market development fits strategically when a firm is strong in marketing, unsaturated markets exist, economies of scale are significant and the competitive arena is becoming global. Examples of such companies who have pursued market development as a growth strategy via e-commerce include Amazon.com, when embarking upon their initial e-commerce strategy of selling books to the UK market.

5.8.3 *Product development*

The Internet has facilitated the development of new products and services that are delivered via a download to an existing target market. Here product or service development as a growth strategy emphasises developing the product or service itself, with the offer placed in the firm's current markets. Examples of such Internet-based products include online newspapers, magazines, market reports, films and music. As yet there exists no standard for downloading and securing payment for music over the Internet. The recording industry is currently in the process of working towards this, however it is also in the process of addressing the activities of web sites such as Napster, who offered a song-swapping service and were liable for copyright infringement damages (Milmo, 2001).

Undoubtedly, one of the best growth opportunities in e-commerce in the UK would be the widespread adoption of online-banking services. Indeed the industry has made great strides to provide this, for example Barclays Bank, Abbey National and the Royal Bank of Scotland all have a number of initiatives to deliver new services to existing customers. Online banking provides an opportunity for growth as it can facilitate the offering of further new services for customers. For instance, an online-bank customer is likely to access their account from home on a regular basis, more so than, for example, a customer who buys their car insurance online. This subsequently provides the bank with an opportunity to offer the existing customer new services available from their portfolio. Alternatively, the bank may act as a broker for an insurance company, promoting their services on the bank's web site.

A further rationale for service development on the Internet is cost, as launching a new mortgage, insurance or loans product is very expensive for a bank in terms of investments required to undertake market research, advertising and mail shots, while the cost of undertaking these activities via an online environment are believed to be significantly lower. Cost savings can also be made in administrative tasks, for instance funds can be transferred between accounts and responses made to queries without any bank staff needing to intervene.

From the consumer's perspective, a number of benefits may be accrued such as access to banking services 24 hours a day, the facility to check current account balances and pay bills from home, all contributing to raising customer-service standards by giving consumers new and more convenient ways of handling their money. However to date, a number of banking services are unable to be fully developed, for example, current UK Internet-based accounts are restricted to banking within the UK, also the facility for customers to trade in the currency of their choice and dabble with overseas stock exchanges is not available.

However evidence suggests that consumers would prefer personal attention rather than use the new services offered via the Internet. Indeed a vast majority of bank customers think that an online banking service is not important for their relationship with their bank. According to a survey by Deloitte Consulting, less than one-third of customers rate electronic banking (e-banking) as an important service, and of those only 22 per cent actually use it. Further to this a poll found that more than 30 per cent of customers do not even know whether their bank provides online services at all (Bachelor, 2001). In terms of strategic fit, Finlay (2000) suggests growth through product or service development is appropriate if the firm's brand reputation is high, hence its reputation can feasibly be attached to new offers. Further to this, it is appropriate if the competitive arena is characterised by rapid technological developments; the business has especially strong research capabilities and economies of scope are significant. All of these apply to the UK banking industry. However at present, there is a major divide between what consumers want and the kind of new service development, which the high-street banks are keen to push.

5.8.4 Diversification

With regards to this quadrant of Ansoff's matrix, new products and/or services are developed which are sold to new markets. A firm diversifies when it changes the scope of its capabilities. Amazon.com is a good example of a firm who has followed this growth strategy. For while the company began by selling books in one market, the US, moving gradually onto audio and video products, it quickly moved into new geographical markets, for example the UK. Its most recent new market is France. According to McDonald (2000) the firm is keen to concentrate on the European market because of its high population density, which means lower transportation and shipping costs. As well as developing into new markets, in July 1999 it began an expansive product diversification strategy consisting of having 18 million items of merchandise across 14 different categories with the purpose being to cross-sell products to its huge customer base (Stephens, 2000). Such a diversification programme includes adding electronic equipment such as digital video devices (DVDs), lawn and patio furniture, garden products, hardware supplies and latterly cars to the list of products its web site sells on its US site. Visiting the US site is akin to a giant virtual shopping mall, a one-stop shopping for e-commerce, while the firm's UK site includes, along with books and CDs, cameras, computer software and electrical goods plus an auction facility. Advantages of such a strategy include embedding the firm's brand as a leader in online retailing plus the ability to capture customer data about purchase behaviour from each product shipment and subsequently use in direct marketing activities.

Such diversification has led critics to consider that it could prevent Amazon.com from achieving any sustainable long-term profitability due to the fact that its too diversified range of products may increasingly stress its complex distribution infrastructure. As a result inefficient order processing and shipping may ensue if they have over-taxed their resources (Stephens, 2000). A final point, made by McIntoch (2000) is that consumers associate Amazon with initially books and now CDs, rather than other consumable goods and for this reason considers that the problem Amazon.com may have is the fact that is it first and foremost known for being a successful bookseller. Finlay (2000) points out that while the growth in size of the organisation as a result of diversification may be an advantage to the firm, the costs may be significant. As he points out, it is unlikely that unrelated diversified firms will add value unless there are managerial or financial synergies. This will be dependent on how successful Amazon.com have been in fusing its operations together.

5.9 Clicks and bricks retailing: integration or separation?

In order that a firm may maximise its returns, strategic choices need to be made in terms of identifying, developing, protecting and deploying resources. However, the retailer has the choice whether to integrate existing resources into their e-commerce activities or treat their e-commerce as a separate arm of the business, thereby deploying separate resources. Gulati and Garino (2000) point out that within this decision wide ranging permutations exist in terms of which aspects of a business to integrate and which to keep distinct. Here they identify four business dimensions, namely brand, management, operations and equity, which they consider as key in determining the degree of integration. Each of these is evaluated in turn.

5.9.1 Brand

The choice to extend a retailer's existing brand online or to keep it separate is a choice between trust and flexibility (Gulati and Garino, 2000). Extending the retailer's current brand to its e-commerce activities gives the retailer's web site instant authority as oppose to a pure-play retailer who has to invest heavily in order to establish and build up the company's brand name as was the case of Boo.com. Further to this, as indicated in the study of consumer searches on the Internet by Ward and Lee (2000), here they typically rely on brand names when searching for products and services. Established brand names contribute to the legitimacy of the web site and therefore act as promoters of online transactions as, with recognisable names, customers will be less fearful of credit card fraud. Brand integration of the online store and physical store further contributes to building the brand as it offers consumers choice in terms of how and where they shop for retailers goods. For instance they may view product offerings at home via the retailers' web site before making a visit to the store to make their purchase, or vice versa. However, the failure to provide sufficient breadth and depth and brand selection via the retailer's accompanying web site is a common problem as highlighted by Cowles *et al.* (2002). In terms of flexibility, Gulati and Garino (2000) point out that the online retailer is forced to offer the same goods online as offline, otherwise differences in availability of products may lead to customer dissatisfaction. If a different product mix is used online to offline, then the retailer should consider selecting an alternative brand name.

Further to this, if using the same brand name on as offline, flexibility is further thwarted if the retailer has thoughts about targeting a different target segment using its web site. If this is the desire of the retailer then again consideration of an alternative brand name or sub-brand name should be given. The car- and bike-accessory UK retailer, Halfords has adopted this approach by developing separate sites each aimed at its key customer segments, Bikehut.com, which targets cyclists and Ripspeed.com, for motoring enthusiasts (Sweney, 2002). Likewise, if different pricing strategies are to be employed, an alternative brand name or sub-brand should be given. In all, Gulati and Garino (2000) indicate, the use of a sub-brand successfully side steps the trade-off between trust and flexibility. Here they draw upon the example of the US toy retailer KB Toys who adopted the online sub-brand KB Kids in order to leverage the existing brand to sell products beyond toys. This was achieved via a joint venture with a 'pure-play' company, BrainPlay.com, who are established online retailers of children's products.

5.9.2 *Management teams and operations*

Gulati and Garino (2000) suggest that integrated management teams can 'better align strategic objectives, find and exploit synergies, and share knowledge' (p. 113). Alternatively, a separate management team for each online and offline areas of the business, with separate business models for each are able to innovate more freely.

Questions surrounding whether the retailer should integrate or separate its management teams revolve around whether current management has the skills and competences to develop an e-commerce channel. Alternatively, if it is anticipated that major channel conflict may arise between different channels, then Gulati and Garino (2000) suggest that management teams should be separate. Likewise if the company considers that e-commerce threatens the current business model, again the activities should be separate.

Burt and Sparks (2002) consider the retail process as comprising of the sourcing of products, stockholding, inventory, store merchandising, marketing effort, customer selection, picking and payment and distribution of goods to the consumer. Decisions with regards to integrating these must be based on the strength of the retailers existing retail operations. For example, Next Plc took the decision to integrate its existing distribution and information systems, integrating them to their e-commerce activities, as they had existing competences in this area, through their years of experience in home shopping, when they initially launched their web site. Gulati and Garino (2000) point out that such integration can provide significant cost savings. Here they draw upon the US retailer Office Depot as an example of such. The company offer added value in the form of convenience to its customers through providing information regarding store locations and each store's inventory online. Therefore customers, wishing to purchase via a store, are able to check the site to ensure that the product they want is in stock at the store they wish to visit, and if so, go to the store to make their purchase. As a consequence the retailer has reported that their web site has actually increased traffic to its physical outlets.

Further to this, Gulati and Garino (2000) point out that Office Depot has benefited through purchasing leverage as a result of integration of its operations. Asda offers a further example of integration. Following Tesco, rather than using dedicated warehouses for its home delivery, it has now taken the decision to use in-store pickers at their retail stores. The rationale for their decision is that they claim fulfilling in-store helps to get their full range of products on their web site. For instance, in-store they can handle 11,000 products, whereas the warehouse could only handle approximately 2000 (Goddard, 2002).

In order to make such a decision the retailer needs to consider whether their existing distribution systems translate well to the Internet. Further to this, they need to assess if their information systems provide a good foundation on which to build their e-commerce platform.

5.9.3 *Equity*

A major decision for bricks and clicks retailers is, which elements of their business to own and what to outsource. Integration of all the operations, allows the retailer to capture the entire value of its e-commerce business. However as Gulati and Garino (2002) point out, separation of functions through outsourcing, can help attract and retain talented individuals and can provide access to outside capital. Outsourcing can also save the business from starting the Internet channel from scratch. Rather drawing upon the competences of already established companies in the field serves to gain a competitive advantage. Outsourcing of call centres is a common decision for e-commerce retailers. As is using third-party companies to support the retailers logistics and distribution functions. An example of this being Ocado, who fulfils the grocery retailer Waitrose's home-shopping deliveries (albeit, Waitrose own 40 per cent of this company). Decisions surrounding whether or not to integrate operations into the company or to outsource revolve around whether the retailer is having trouble attracting or keeping talented key people within specific operations.

In all, Gulati and Garino (2000) point out that whichever bricks and clicks approach to adopt in terms of the integration separation, the decision is about the retailer's ability to manage the trade-offs between the two. It is not simply a question of either/or. Rather a way forward is to consider each element of the business; here a balance may be struck between the flexibility that separation offers and the economies that come with integration within each of the functions identified.

5.10 Conclusion

E-commerce presents an alternative opportunity for retailers to market and sell their goods online. However, the full potential of such has not been fully realised. As a subject area, e-commerce is surrounded both by ambiguity and uncertainty. The extent to which new business models will prove either defensible or profitable is open to debate (Reynolds, 2000).

While there is evidence of an eagerness of existing retailers to have an Internet presence, in such eagerness it is likely that firms may neglect to question whether their web initiative targets their existing customer group, whether it attracts a new customer group and most significantly, what value is the site offering to any customer group. Such neglect could result in failure. A further reason for failure is the inability to develop a business model that reaches profitability, which could result from lack of foresight in calculating total operating costs or by overestimating the size of the market for online shopping (Ring and Tigert, 2001). Another reason is a failure to understand the infrastructure required in the operation of a transactional web site. For instance, loading 10,000 consumer items in a van and distributing them to a retail store is much cheaper than sending 10,000 vans to deliver the same goods individually to 10,000 doorsteps and makes for a much more complex operation. As Reynolds (2000) points out, 'due to the fragmentation of merchandise and service mix and consequently wide variation in fulfilment requirements this generates across categories' (p. 431).

The literature surrounding e-commerce adoption sees the process as mechanistic and goal driven. For instance it is assumed that retailers, regardless of size or type, online intentions are to be global, they desire to be completely networked with the marketplace and fully transactional. Such linear models that offer explanations for the development of an e-commerce strategy are too simplistic. They also fail to consider the capabilities of the firm planning the e-commerce strategy or the content of such strategies in terms of resource implications and decisions regarding how the adopter will use the technology to position themselves within the marketplace. Rather first and foremost, the main consideration is as Burt and Sparks (2002) point out, is to establish how tasks and activities are performed within an electronic retail channel.

The expenditures involved in implementing and maintaining e-commerce are high and not to be underestimated. This situation is typical to any new technology adopter.

Gradually retailers are becoming to understand e-commerce more, so there is less pressure to surge ahead at all costs. Clearly benefits of e-commerce are not solely derived from revenues from online purchases. The medium also helps retailers to learn a great deal about their customers. The benefits of tracking consumer behaviour online, including immediate reaction to sales by demographics, geography and income, are significant. Such a strategy embracing this will result in retailers running their businesses more effectively and ultimately contribute to the success of the firm.

References

Alba, J., Lynch, J., Weitz, B., Janiszewski, C., Lutz, R., Sawyer, A. and Wood, S. (1997) Interactive home shopping: consumer, retailer and manufacturer incentives to participate in electronic marketplaces. *Journal of Marketing*, **61**(July), 38–53.

Amit, R. and Zott, C. (2000) *Value Creation in E-Business* [http://elab.insead.edu/pdf/ebusiness-valuecreation.pdf].

Ansoff, I. (1965) *Corporate Strategy*. New York, McGraw-Hill.

Bachelor, L. (2001) Why consumers avoid e-banking. *The Guardian*, 6 July.

Benjamin, R. and Wingand, R. (1995) Electronic markets and virtual value chains on the information superhighway. *Sloan Management Review*, **Winter** 62–72.

Block, M., Pigneur, Y. and Segev, A. (1996) *On the Road of Electronic Commerce – A Business Value Framework, Gaining Competitive Advantage and Some Research Issues* [http://www.stern.nyu.edu/~mbloch/docs/roadtoec/ec.htm].

Burt, S. and Sparks, L. (2002) E-commerce and the retail process: a review. *Journal of Retailing and Consumer Services* (in press, corrected proof, available online 17 December).

Coleman, K. (1998) Make your web site a business success. *E-Business Advisor*, 12–17.

Damanpour, F. and Madison, J. (2001) E-business e-commerce evolution: perspective and strategy. *Managerial Finance*, **27**(7), 16–33.

Davies, G.J. and Brooks, J.M. (1989) *Positioning Strategy in Retailing*. Paul Chapman.

Dawson, J. (2000) Retailing at century end: some challenges for management and research. *International Review of Retail Distribution and Consumer Research*, **10**(2), 119–148.

Day, G S. and Wensley, R. (1988) Assessing advantage: a framework for diagnosing competitive superiority. *Journal of Marketing*, **52**(April), 1–20.

de Chernatony, L. and McDonald, M. (1995) *Creating Powerful Brands*. London, Butterworth-Heinemann.

Doyle, P. (1992) Managing the marketing mix. In Baker, M. (ed.), *The Marketing Book*. London, Butterworth-Heinemann.

Duncan, S. (2001) It's a small world after all business. *Revolution*, 31 October, 26–29.

Eisnehardt, K.M. and Zbaracki, M.J. (1992) Strategic decision making. *Strategic Management Journal*, **13**, 17–37.

Finlay, P. (2000) Strategic management. *Financial Times*, Pearson Education Limited

Gilbert, D. (2003) *Retail Marketing Management*, 2nd edition. Essex, Pearson Education Limited.

Goddard, C. (2002) We shop so you don't have to. *Revolution*, 6 February, 22–25.

Gulati, R. and Garino, J. (2000) Get the right mix of bricks and clicks. *Harvard Business Review*, May–June, 107– 114.

Gunasekaran, A., McNeil, R.D. and Shaul, D. (2002) E-learning: research and applications. *Industrial and Commercial Training*, **34**(2), 44–53.

Hart, C., Doherty, N. and Ellis Chadwick, F. (2000) Retailer adoption of the Internet – implications for retail marketing. *European Journal of Marketing*, **34**(8).

Hendry, J. (2000) Strategic decision making, discourse and strategy as social practice. *Journal of Management Studies*, **37**(7), 955–977.

Hoffman, D.L., Novak, T.P and Chatterjee, C. (1996) Commercial scenarios for the web: opportunities and challenges. *Journal of Computer-Mediated Communication*, **1**(3) [http://www.usc.edu/annenberg/journal.html].

Kai-Uwe Brock, J. (2000) Internet technology and the small firm. In Carter, S. and Jones-Evans, D. (eds), *Enterprise and the Small Business*. Financial Times; Prentice-Hall.

Kalakota, R. and Whinston, A. (1996) *Frontiers of Electronic Commerce*. Addison-Wesley.

kiosk.com (2001) *Latest Study Underlines Importance of Multi-channel Customers*. 17 October [http://www.kioskcom.com/article_detail.php?ident = 954].

Kuttner, R (1998) The net: a market too perfect for profits. *Business Week*, 11 May, 20.

Li, H., Kuo, C. and Russell, M.G. (1999) The impact of perceived channel utilities, shopping orientations, and on the consumer's on-line buying behaviour. *Journal of Computer-Mediated Communication*, **5**(2) [http:www.ascusc.org/jcmc/vol5/issue2/hairong.html].

Markus, M.L. and Robey, D. (1988) Information technology and organisational change: causal structure in theory and research. *Management Science*, **34**(5), 583–598.

Maes, P. (1998) *Software Agents and the Future of Electronic Commerce* [http://pattie.www.media.mit.edu/people/pattie/ECOM].

Martin, L. and Kambil, A. (1999) Looking back and thinking ahead: effects of prior success on manager's interpretations of new information technologies. *Academy of Management Journal*, **42**, 52–61.

Matley, H. (1999) Vocational education and training in Britain: a small business perspective. *Education and Training*, **41**(1).

McDonald, T. (2000) Don't cry for Amazon. *E-Commerce Times*, 10 October.

McGoldrick P. (2002) *Retail Marketing* 2nd edition Berkshire: McGraw-Hill.

McIntoch (2000) Amazon car sales face bumpy road. Can the leading e-tailer sell absolutely anything it wants? *Guardian*, 24 August.

Michel, S. (2000) *The Post Boo Fall Out New Media Age*, 25 May, p. 20.

Milmo, D. (2001) Poptones postpones web plans. *Media*, 29 March.

Mintel (2001) *Home Shopping*. Mintel Publications.

Neal, D. and Veitch, M. (2000) E-tailers must change or fail. *IT Week*, 14 October.

Newman, A.J. and Cullen, P. (2002) *Retail Environment and Operations*. London, Thomson Learning.

Ody, P. (1997) Home shopping. In Fernie, J. (ed.), *The Future for UK Retailing*. London, Financial Times Business Ltd.

Peterson, R.A. Balasubramanian, S. and Bronnenbery, B.J. (1997) Exploring the implications of the Internet for consumer marketing. *Journal of the Academy of Marketing Science*, **25**(4), 329–346.

Phau, I. and Poon, S.M. (2000) Factors influencing the types of products and services purchased over the Internet. *Internet Research: Electronic Networking Applications and Policy*, **10**(2).

Porter, M.E. (1980) From competitive advantage to corporate strategy. *Harvard Business Review*, 43–59.

Porter M.E. (1996) What is strategy. *Harvard Business Review*, November/December.

Pricewaterhouse Coopers (2000) Clothes online: shoppers versus buyers. *E-Retail Intelligence System* survey at wysiwyg//17/http://www.emarketer.com/estats/20000712_pwc.html.

Quelch, J.A and Klein, L.R. (1996) Internet and international marketing. *Sloan Management Review*, **Spring**, 60–75.

Reynolds, J. (2000) E-commerce: a critical review. *International Journal of Retail and Distribution Management*, **28**(10), 417–444.

Ring, L.J. and Tigert, D.J. (2001) Viewpoint: the decline and fall of Internet grocery retailers. *International Journal of Retail and Distribution Management*, **29**(6).

Rowley, J. (2002) Synergy and strategy in e-business. *Marketing Intelligence and Planning* **20**(4), 215–222.

Sawhney, M. (1999) *Meet the Metamediary* [http://swahney.kellog.nwu.edu/metamed/metamediation.htm].

Simomkos, G.J. and Vrechopoulos, A.P. (2000) *Strategic Market Planning for Competitive Advantage in Electronic Commerce* [http://www.eltrun.aueb.gr/press/tech.htm].

Stephens, R. (2000) Amazon's diversification strategy questioned. *E-Commerce Time*, 4 October.

Stroud, D. (1998) *Internet Strategies*. MacMillan Business.

Supri, S., Baldock, R. and Smallbone, D. The impact of new technology on SME management: the case of the printing industry. Paper presented at *The 2000 Small Business and Enterprise Development Conference*, Manchester Metropolitan University.

Sweney, M. (2001) Amazon predicts break even in UK. *Revolution*, 31 October, p. 11.

Sweney, M (2002) Halfords web site to get £250k overhaul. *Revolution*, 18 September, p. 5.

Tapscott, D., Ticoll, D. and Lowy, A. (2000) *Digital Capital*, Nicholas Brealey Publishing.

Wolfe, R. (1994) Organisation innovation: review, critiques and directions for research. *Journal of Management Studies*, **31**(3), 405–443.

Study questions and guideline answers

1. To what extent do the dot.com failures of recent years assist or obstruct further developments in e-commerce?

Certainly dot.com failures have contributed to a certain amount of negativity surrounding online retailing to the extent that one may perceive that it mere hype, which has no future. However, such an obstructive view would be naïve.

The experience of dot.coms has offered something for other retailers to learn from and in fact, drawing on the work of Rowley, evidence suggests that some retailers have deliberately adopted a 'wait and see' approach before embarking on developing their web sites. Examples of such companies are John Lewis. In the meantime, they have established a web presence in order to stake out their ground while at the same time learning from the mistakes of others. Such mistakes include the decision of Boo.com, who on the day of their launch in November 1999, launched in 18 countries simultaneously, with seven different language versions of the site. The complexity of such cannot be underestimated.

Gradually traditional 'bricks and mortar'. The failure rate of dot.com businesses has now slowed down and online transactions make up a small but increasing proportion of overall consumer spending in retailing.

Retailers have set up their own transactional web sites, and it could be argued, assisted by learning from the past experiences of the first dot.com companies.

Further reading

Cellan-Jones (2001) *Dot.bomb: The Rise and Fall of Dot.com*. Britain Aurum Press.

Malmsten, *et al.* (2002) *Boo Hoo: A Dot Com Story*. Random House Business Books.

2. Assess the advantages or otherwise, that high-street retailers may have over their 'pure-play' counterparts in facilitating e-commerce activities.

Established high-street retailers typically are already well recognised in the marketplace via the high-street and or catalogue retailing. They have an established brand name, loyal customer following and time-honoured experience in the retail business. Such factors facilitate alternative channel developments such as e-commerce. Competences in logistics and direct marketing are seen to be particularly important, for example Next brought their experience and established logistics infrastructure, which supported the catalogue side of the business, to their e-commerce activities. As a result, their web site to date has proved to be very successful for the company.

However the Italian fashion retailer Diesel, whose transactional part of the web site, serving the UK market only, had to be withdrawn because it was alienating its customers in the rest of Europe who were not able to buy from the site. The reason for this being, Diesel did not have an established infrastructure to serve all the European markets. Therefore indicating it not just about brand loyalty and an established high-street retail operation, further competences also need to be in place.

A competence a high-street retailer may not have is the technological know-how of the pure-play retailers. However here as indicated in the chapter, retailers may outsource these skills and have done so to success. Further to this, they may possibly like the creativity, foresight and enthusiasm, which the pure-play retailer will have.

Further reading

Kaufman-Scarborough, C. and Lindquist, J.D. (2002) E-shopping in a multiple channel environment. *Journal of Consumer Marketing*, **19**(4), 333–350.

Koontz, M.L. and Gibson, I.E. (2002) Mixed reality merchandising: bricks, clicks – and mix. *Journal of Fashion Marketing Management*, **6**(4), 381–395.

Reynolds, J. (2002) Charting the multi-channel future: retail choices and constraints. *International Journal of Retail and Distribution Management*, **30**(11), 530–535.

3. What would be the principal objectives in developing sub-brands specifically for each of a retailer's channels (e.g. high-street store, catalogue and web site)? Evaluate such a decision.

Sub-brands serve to further define a retailer's offering. While a retailer's own brand has value, this is also passed on its sub-brand or brands. A sub-brand also has a value of its own, overall benefiting from the halo effect of the master brand.

Adopting a strategy of sub-branding for the retailer's various alternative channels, as is the case with Halfords as outlined in the chapter, allows the retailer to position products and services associated with the sub-brand at either the cheaper or upper end of the market, without affecting the overall brand of the retailer (as Mark and Spencer has done offline with its Autograph range). Likewise it can use the sub-brand to attract an alternative target market. Using different channels to achieve this makes such a strategy even more explicit.

However a weakness is that promotion budgets are required to support each of the sub-brands. Further to this, whereas branding activity serves to reduce confusion in the marketplace as brands communicate messages with regards to, for example prestige, reputation and reliability, hence facilitating consumer choice, sub-branding can be a source of confusion. As the consumer can become confused about the source of the sub-brand and may be unaware of the connection between the brand and the sub-brand. Alternatively, if it is well known that the sub-brand is part of the master brand, anything that may tarnish the master brand will also tarnish the sub-brand.

Further reading

DeGraba, P. and Sullivan, M.W. (1995) Spillover effects, cost savings, R&D and the use of brand extensions. *International Journal of Industrial Organisation*, **13**(2), 229–248.

Grime, I., Diamantopoulo, A. and Smith, G. (2002) Consumer evaluations of extensions and their effects on the core brand: key issues and research propositions. *European Journal of Marketing*, **36**(11).

4. For an online retailer who currently sells solely to its domestic market, what is the inevitability that they may internationalise?

There is no inevitability that an online retailer may progress to sell to international markets despite business models that suggest this as the final stage of evolvement for these retailers. The decision to internationalise must be part of the overall retail strategy for the company, rather than the case being that having access to global markets automatically makes one an international or global retailer. As the chapter indicates market development into new countries requires an understanding of the needs of different local consumer markets in terms of culture, values, attitudes and aspirations.Together with knowledge regarding legislative requirements and local business practices.

Further reading

Colla, E. (2003) International expansion and strategies of discount grocery retailers: the winning models. *International Journal of Retail and Distribution Management*, **31**(1), 55–66.

Jamal, A. (2003) Retailing in a multicultural world: the interplay of retailing, ethnic identity and consumption. *Journal of Retailing and Consumer Services*, **10**(1), 1–11.

Chapter 6

The emergence of supply chain management as a critical success factor for retail organisations*

Tony Hines

Aims

The aims of this chapter are:

- to identify and discuss the chronological developments that have led to the emergence of supply chain management (SCM) as a separate practice and discipline;
- to know and apply the underlying supply chain concepts to recognise existing supply chain complexities and develop appropriate retail strategies;
- to discuss contemporary supply chain issues and their influence in developing appropriate retail strategies;
- to evaluate a range of supply chain strategies, relationships and structures in contemporary retailing organisations;
- to locate and develop your own research agenda in this field.

The purpose of this chapter is to discuss the emergence of SCM, the underlying concepts and its development as an important influence upon successful retailing strategies and operations. The chapter begins with a discussion of historical developments generally and in organisational management that have created the necessary conditions for the emergence of supply chains as an important focus for retail managers. It then moves onto address contemporary issues that occupy the mind space of practising managers in retailing. Empirical examples demonstrate the importance of the supply chain phenomena in creating successful strategies, structures and relationships that enhance organisational value. Finally, future directions are considered before outlining a new research agenda for this developing and important aspect of business management.

*This chapter is based on work published in Hines, T. (2003) *Supply Chain Strategies – Customer Focused and Customer Driven*, Oxford, Butterworth-Heinemann.

6.1 Introduction

The term supply chain management, the SCM, was a phrase first coined in the early 1980s to describe the range of activities co-ordinated by an organisation to procure and manage supplies (Oliver and Weber, 1982). Initially the term referred to an internal focus bounded by a single organisation and how they sourced and procured supplies, managed their internal inventory and moved goods onto their customers, (Macbeth and Ferguson, 1990; Harland, 1995). The original focus was later extended to examine not simply the internal management of the chain. It was recognised that this was inadequate and that the reality in managing supplies meant that supply chains extended beyond the purchasing organ-isation and into their suppliers and their supplier's supplier (Christopher, 1992). It is recognised that there may be tiers of suppliers. Additionally it is recognised that the organisation may have a customer who has other customers where their supplies are incorporated into other products or bundled in a particular way to provide a different product.

You may ask yourself the question why is managing a supply chain seen as important:

- Firstly, customers have so much choice nowadays from an enormous field of competitors that delays in supply mean delays for the customers' who probably are not willing to wait when they can obtain the same or similar substitute product elsewhere.
- Secondly, perhaps when you realise that the average retailer's balance sheet has inventories worth over 50 per cent of the total value of assets it brings the issue into focus.
- Thirdly, the average manufacturing company spends over 50 per cent of every sale on raw material, components and maintenance repair operations (MRO) purchases then it becomes crystal clear why managing the supply chain is so significant.

In this context managing the supply chain is a critical success factor (CSF) in retailing (Leidecker and Bruno, 1984; de Wit and Meyer, 1998; Barney, 1999).

6.2 Historical developments

Organisations historically structured themselves into functions, namely purchasing, pro-duction, distribution, marketing and accounting. These functions managed discrete parts of the organisation. In a business environment where organisations were in competition with one and other it was important to control the internal organisation in order to com-pete. As business networks have developed and become more complex the boundaries of organisations have become less discrete and somewhat blurred (Barney, 1999). Some com-mentators have gone so far as to suggest that this blurring of boundaries may mean that it is not organisations that are in competition any more but rather supply chains (Christopher, 1996). Functional structures have become historical straightjackets rather than practical. As a consequence 'functional silos' restrict intra-organisational and inter-organisational devel-opment necessary to compete in the modern business environment (Slack *et al.*, 2001).

6.2.1 Metaphorical descriptors: pipelines, chains and networks

It is interesting to examine both developments in the management literature and in prac-tice. Much of the concern with supply chains developed from the purchasing and oper-ations' management literature throughout the 1980s and 1990s, which have their roots in earlier organisational and management literatures relating to marketing, purchasing sup-ply and economics disciplines. Metaphors have always been adopted to describe these organisational structures. In practice journals in the apparel sector throughout the 1970s and 1980s the term 'pipeline' was used to discuss the flows of raw materials through manufacturing processes and onto the final customer (Hunter *et al.*, 1990). The term 'supply chain' first appeared in a US *Outlook* article (Oliver and Weber, 1982). In the 1990s 'supply networks' became fashionable (Christopher, 1996). However, it does not help students or researchers in this area that commentators develop new terms frequently even though they are essentially referring to the concept of managing supply chains. For example, 'commodity chains' have been used to describe global production networks (Gereffi, 1994). The next two subsections provide a discussion of the focus of analysis and the major themes that have emerged from the literature.

6.2.2 Levels of analysis

Early work referencing supply chain structures focused upon internal operations from the point of entry into the firm until it exited to the customer (Macbeth and Ferguson, 1990). Indeed Oliver and Webber (1982) were referring to the integration of internal business functions and the flow of materials and information coming into and going out of the business when they originally coined the phrase. This particular definition equates closely to the traditional materials management perspective (Houlihan, 1984; Jones and Riley, 1985; Stevens, 1989). As Harland (1995) recognised the term SCM has had different meanings for different writers. Many early studies and some later studies (Hakansson *et al.*, 1976; Burt, 1984; Campbell, 1985; Heide and Miner, 1992; Lamming, 1993) have focused upon the dyadic aspect between a supplier (manufacturer or distributor) and buyer (retailer or distributor). In supply chain terms these are only two links of the chain.

6.3 Themes in the literature

A number of themes may be observed from a study of the eclectic literature referring to supply chains. This section discusses some of those important themes.

6.3.1 Transaction costs

Themes emerge from the literature often reflecting the contextual concerns of the time. For example, *transaction costs* were of prime concern from 1937 with active research conducted in the 1940s and 1950s, and the main discipline through which the studies were conducted was economics (Coase, 1937; Heckert and Miner, 1940). There have been a few later studies on this theme such as Williamson (1979), Ellram (1994) and Hobbs (1996). A main focus of transaction cost analysis has been concerned with 'power'. Power is important in the transaction process since it determines the negotiation which is often based on price alone. Within this theme power is seen as important within the exchange process between two or more parties. In retail buyer–supplier transactions power has moved from suppliers in the 1940s, 1950s to the retailers in the 1960s, 1970s, 1980s, 1990s, 2000s with increasing concentration of retail buying in the hands of a few large retail organisations in most sectors including food and fashion.

6.3.2 Manufacturing supply chains and efforts to lower inventory costs

Since the First World War and more particularly after the Second World War *manufacturing management* and *industrial management* provided the context and the focus for research examining aspects of what we now recognise as SCM. For example, Forrester (1961) examined the 'bullwhip' effect of managing inventories and recognised that the further-up the supply chain from the end customer one examines inventories; it will be subject to amplified swings of over- and under-supply as a consequence of errors in the demand forecast.

Research into the dynamics of supply chains and modelling the effect of changes to teach managers about the consequences has been a major theme since Forrester first examined the 'bullwhip' effect in the 1960s when systems thinking became popularised in management. The temporal dimension is important since simultaneously throughout the 1960s and 1970s interest was growing as computer power developed in mathematical programming applying optimisation-modelling techniques to supply chain inventories. Since then many studies have concentrated on simulation and pipeline modelling (Fisher *et al.*, 1994; Goodwin and Franklin, 1994; Fransoo and Wouters, 2000; Shapiro, 2001). Ellram (1991) on the other hand, examined vertical integration suggesting that organisations that owned their supply chains were much more likely to be able to manage them effectively.

This tradition has been maintained through the works of different researchers:

- Lamming (1993) examining innovation strategies and lean supply in the automobile sector;
- Ford (1990) and much of the work of the Industrial Marketing and Purchasing Group examining a variety of supply chain interactions across different industrial settings;
- Hines (1994) examining the world-class suppliers;
- Hines and Rich (1994) examining continuous improvement;
- Slack *et al.* (2001) examining operation managements.

The work examining value streams and value stream mapping conducted by Hines *et al.* (2000) builds on previous studies conducted into lean production (LP) and agile manufacturing. Investigations into a number of specific techniques such as LP, Just-In-Time (JIT), World-Class Manufacturing (WCM) and Total Quality Management (TQM) continue in this tradition. Harrison and Storey (1996, p. 63) classify these several operational supply chain concepts as New-Wave Manufacturing (NWM). One could add to this list quick response (QR) originally developed through pipeline management projects in the US textile industry conducted by Kurt Salmon Associates (KSA) and others (Hunter *et al.*, 1990; Hunter, 1992; Hunter and Valentino, 1995). QR is viewed as a derivative method of JIT by some commentators. Harrison and van Hoek (2002, p. 160) view QR as an application of JIT and lean thinking whereby the customer demand is satisfied by producers and suppliers reacting quickly when demand is known rather than making for stock. Others view QR as a 'management paradigm and a methodology' (Lowson *et al.*, 1999).

6.3.3 *Time compression and responsiveness*

Most of the emphasis in QR was focused upon 'pipeline' modelling to reduce time throughout the supply chain (KSA, 1987). However, in practice much of the controllable element was dyadic between the organisation initiating demand and their immediate supplier (Iyer and Bergen, 1997). In some respects it could be argued that the success of QR might be dependent on a number of dyadic relationships that are co-ordinated effectively. Questions arise over who can effectively co-ordinate and who is allowed to? Take the example of a large clothing retailer who contracts the manufacture of own label fashion. The retailers often co-ordinate all suppliers including the textile mills supplying fabrics to the manufacturer, the trim suppliers, production schedules and quality of the converter (contract clothing manufacturer), and logistics services to move goods between each one and deliver to the final destination. Each supplier in the chain has a dyadic relationship with the retail co-ordinator.

Efficient consumer response (ECR) is an extension of QR it was developed as part of a grocery industry analysis conducted by KSA in the US (KSA, 1993). This work was conducted a few years after they had done their work in the textile industry on QR. The purpose of ECR being to integrate SCM with demand management to create smooth flows of product through the supply chain to satisfy consumer demand efficiently (at lowest cost). The four pillars of ECR are: product assortment, promotion, replenishment and new product introductions. The focus of ECR is between the retail organisation and its suppliers whereas the focus for QR is on manufacturing capability and efficiency to deliver promptly.

6.3.4 Recent concerns with ethical trading and environmental issues

More recently sourcing and purchasing research has shown some interest in the ethics of buying products from low-cost offshore destinations where there is an impact on the indigenous environment and community that may be considered detrimental (Green *et al.*, 1998). For example, the well-publicised allegations against companies like Nike and GAP for the use of under-age labour in their supplier factories in Indonesia and Bangladesh. Concerns with damage to the environment with pesticides used to protect cotton crops. Excessive pollution caused by dyeing plants not complying with industry-wide standards on treatment of waste product. There have been countries where the local population is deprived of the nutritional value by exporting food products such as bananas. The issue of food miles has been raised whereby produce that could be supplied by a local farming community has been sourced from countries that may be many miles from the markets in which they are sold. There is a double concern regarding the impact of such decisions on the farming community that could supply the goods in the markets where they are sold and the concern that the transport pollution causes which is not fully costed nor paid for by those importing the goods.

6.3.5 Strategic perspectives

More recently the focus has shifted from what one may describe as operations management towards a strategic management perspective (Macbeth and Ferguson, 1990). Alliances and partnerships have provided the central focus for large-scale studies into supply chain strategies that have been adopted by some of the leading world organisations in major industrial sectors: automobiles, aerospace, electronics, textiles, retailing and supporting service industries (Lamming, 1993; KSA, 1993, Berry *et al.*, 1994; Kanter, 1994; 1997; Hines *et al.*, 2000; Burt *et al.*, 2003). Strategic capabilities are examined by Croom and Batchelor (1997), still following the traditions of manufacturing management. Themes in the mainstream strategy literature such as core competences (Prahalad and Hamel, 1990), capabilities (Stalk *et al.*, 1992) and competing through time advantages (Stalk Jr, 1988) have developed in parallel with research themes into supply chain strategies.

6.3.6 Supply chain structures and relationships

The term supply chain conjures up an image of a linear structure with a chain and links between suppliers and buyers at each link (i.e. dyads). Indeed it is often represented in this way pictorially. However, the reality is much more complex. It has been recognised that the structure is more akin to a network structure between a number of suppliers and a number of buyers (Christopher, 1992). It has also been recognised that the supply chain may be hierarchical with first-, second-, third-tier suppliers and so on. In other words, the structures between one organisation and a supplier may be further complicated by an array of arrangements at each tier point.

   In the 1980s and early 1990s there was a great deal of interest in why Japanese firms were so successful. Much of the success was attributed to the total quality approaches and continuous improvement (Kaizen) philosophy based on the works of Demming and Juran. Demming's fourth point of his fourteen points on quality advocates that organisations' work more closely with fewer suppliers (Demming, 1986). This is a practice that has been adopted by many retailing organisations throughout the 1990s following practices adopted by automobile manufacturers a decade earlier.

The literature on relationships in the supply chain discusses the traditional 'arms length' approach of purchasing in which adversarial relationships are a common feature on one pole and the 'partnership' approach which often adopts the analogy of marriage at the other pole. Often the focus of these studies examines the relationships existing between firms rather than the key business relationships within a supply chain context. Examples of the first category focusing on firm relationships would be Kanter's (1994) examination of strategic collaboration, Porter's (1980) value chain approach, Axelrod's (1984) evolution of relationships, Ford and Farmer's (1986) work on make or buy decisions and Cheao and Scheuing's (1992) study of purchasing relationships. The work of Carlisle and Parker (1989) represented a turning point in recognising that supply chain relationships and purchasing negotiations went beyond the adversarial discussions focused on price alone. Ellram (1991) recognised that these relationships could be much more complex and introduced the concept of networks to explain the types of relationships existing between suppliers and buyers to deliver products and services to the end customer. Around the same time a number of researchers were examining Japanese supply chain practices in the automobile industry discussed earlier. Womack *et al.* (1990) introduced the notion of tiers of suppliers as did Lamming (1993), together with the 'lean supply' concept; Sako (1990) suggested that companies adopting a partnership approach performed better than those that did not.

An interesting alternative perspective that runs counter to much of the relationship literature is offered by Cousins (2002) who identifies three key propositions:

- Firstly, partnership relationships do not exist. Rather there is a range of collaborating relationships and they are all competitive.
- Secondly, organisations do not trust each other but rather they manage risk based on business objectives.
- Thirdly and importantly, the relationship itself is a process not an entity and as such focuses on definable outcomes. For example, cost reduction through value engineering or joint product development and problem solving.

The relationship observed will have been defined by the definable outcomes. This point of view is supported by Cox (1997), who argued that the collaborative approach was not necessarily more effective than a competitive strategy in the supply chain.

6.3.7 Empirical evidence

What differentiates much of the early work in the purchasing and supply literature from the later work examining contemporary supply chain issues are the shifts in focus that have occurred. Table 6.1 illustrates the timeline dimension. These issues are highlighted further through the empirical discussion that follows.

A capability to manage supply chains can prove to be a core competence for an organisation. There are numerous examples of business success and failure being dependent on supply chain capabilities. Amazon.com is a relatively new electronic retailing (e-retailing) organisation whose very survival and growth has been built around technical and organisational developments related to managing the virtual store and fulfilling customer orders. One important aspect of their development has been their ability to build relationships with organisations external to Amazon who already possessed capability to fulfil their promotional promises.

Table 6.1 Purchasing and supply literature timeline

	From (pre-1990)	To (post-1990 to present)
Analytic focus	Predominantly internal focus	Predominantly external (dyadic, chain, network)
	Operations	Strategies
	Exchange/transactional focus	Relationship/structure focus
	Functional processes	Integration
	Cost efficiency (inputs/outputs)	Value added (outputs–inputs)
	Physical processes	Financial, informational and virtual processes
	Product quality (only major concern)	Service quality and total quality approaches
	Simple (e.g. dyadic structures and relationships)	Complex structures (e.g. networks)
	Traditional linear supply chains	Digital supply chains
	Inventory management	Information and customer service

Source: Purchasing and supply chain literature 1930s to present day after Hines (2003)

6.4 Why quick response?

QR is an approach to SCM based on the concepts of reducing inventory holding cost, postponing the commitment of resources in manufacture until a clearer picture of demand is known and having flexible manufacturing systems that are able to respond. QR techniques were pioneered in the textile industry during the 1980s. In 1986, the KSA a major US consultancy were employed by the 'Crafted with Pride Council' a joint textile industry body to examine US apparel and textile supply chains. They went about the task by process-mapping activities in the pipeline and discovered it took 66 weeks total time for all manufacturing operations to be completed and for the processes to move raw materials through production and into the retail stores. However, the total time taken in actual production processes (spinning, weaving, wet processing, cutting, sewing, assembly, packaging and distribution to retailers) took only 11 weeks. This meant that 55 weeks were wasted in inventory delays, mostly in the warehouse waiting for the next operation to call them out. This wasted time costs the US Textile and Apparel pipeline $25 billion according to KSA (1987). This was around 20 per cent of the total industry turnover and it was a cost that had been simply passed on to the consumer until faced with competitive pressure from overseas imports.

Another major success in applying QR principles during the 1980s to manage their supply chain was the Italian-fashion knitwear retailer, Benetton. It is not simply QR but the network of suppliers that is important to provide flexibility for Benetton as orchestrator of processes. More recently the company has transformed its organisation to develop larger retail formats and exercise more control over its supply chain through vertical integration (Camuffo *et al.*, 2001, pp. 46–52). The company has recently established 10 'production poles' outside Italy and they are either wholly owned as in the case of Spain, Portugal, Tunisia, Hungary and Croatia or a 50 per cent joint venture in the likes of South Korea, Egypt and India.

It is interesting that Benetton is similar in size of turnover $1.8 billion to Zara the Spanish-fashion retailer, which is often credited with bringing products to market quickly. Zara too is heavily vertically integrated with in-house production in 23 production centres supported by a network of outsourced production suppliers in smaller firms in Spain and Portugal close to its home base in North-west Spain. This is in stark contrast to the majority of their competitors (Top Shop – Arcadia, GAP, H&M, Next, M&S and BhS) who mainly outsource production.

Since 1993 Giordino, a US-fashion retailer developed successful QR techniques that today are practised by other retailers such as GAP and The Limited. In the UK retailers like

Marks and Spencer and Arcadia have also adopted QR principles for some of their more fashionable lines.

QR is a 'pull system' and relies on consumer demand information being used by all parties in the supply chain. As a consequence much of the early concerns were focused on the use of electronic data interchange (EDI) and compatibility between retailers' and various suppliers' systems (KSA, 1987; Hunter, 1990). It is a system that demands close co-operation between parties in a supply chain. A major concern for fashion retailers is that they do not really know whether consumers will like this season's fashion until they see it and try it in store. It is not like many fast-moving consumer goods (FMCG) categories such as detergent. Soap powder demand is much more predictable and does not have the complexities of a fashion item. Soap powder is bulk material, packaged in various sizes and promoted for example, through coupons offering two for the price of one (buy one get one free). Fashion apparel may have five style variations, ten colours, ten size variations and fashion is perishable. Thus one simple garment may have 500 variables ($5 \times 10 \times 10$) to account for in the decision processes that the retailer makes. It is further complicated by the lack of standard sizing which often means that consumers purchase different size garments from different retailers. For example, a consumer buying size 12 at M&S may need to purchase size 14 at Next.

Returns (consumers returning to store a garment previously purchased) are also more of a problem with fashion. Goods are returned because they do not fit properly. This may be due to sizing problems or it may be due to a whim. For example, the consumer just did not like it when they tried it on again at home or their partner did not like it. No one looks at soap powder and says 'I don't like the packaging on that let's take it back to the store'. So what is all this got to do with QR? Well if bulk manufacturing and all the associated costs can be postponed until consumer demand is known rather than simply forecast there is less likelihood of wasting resources. Historically, retail buyers would have relied on forecasting fashion demand well in advance of the season and be committed to orders perhaps 18 months in advance of the selling season (i.e. six seasons ahead). Forecasting is, however, notoriously inaccurate in fashion. Forecast inaccuracy is also expensive. Supposing your gross margin is 50 per cent and you over-forecast on just a single line by 50 per cent effectively you have no margin and should you need to reduce prices further to shift the stock then you will be incurring cost. This is why QR is so attractive for fashion retailing. QR means a retailer is able to lower risk by trying a product in a small quantity. If the garment sells, they need to be able to replenish the items quickly to maintain availability of product and hence provide customer service.

Some of the problems being able to apply the principles of QR reside in the textile areas of the supply chain. Textile production has two main sources: agriculture and chemicals. Each source has its own time cycle. Natural fibres such as wool or cotton take the best part of a year to develop. Man-made fibres can be made more quickly but production needs to be booked into the textile mills well in advance of the apparel manufacturing cycle. These cycles inevitably have consequences for retail purchasing and replenishment cycles. Many of the most successful QR practitioners are able to shorten these cycles by using 'greige' fabric that can be died late in the process. This allows them to achieve the flexibility they require to respond quickly to consumer demand information.

6.5 Mass customisation

In recent years a number of retailers and suppliers have experimented with 'mass customisation'. These experiments have usually involved the production of relatively simple garments with customisations being limited but attractive enough to individual consumers for them to be willing to pay a premium over and above volume factory production prices.

Two areas of focus have pre-occupied those advocating the approach. Firstly, the development of camera technology that has been employed to take more body measurements than simply waist, leg, chest and collar sizes. These camera measurements have the advantage of being digitally accurate and digitally storable on smart-card technology. Measurements can be instantly transferred to simple computer-aided design and computer-aided manufacturing (CAD/CAM) equipment for customised production. Designs can also be customised (number of pockets, buttons, zips, styles, colours) from previously stored images or may be taken from designs presented by the customer. The second area of focus has been quick dyeing techniques that allow fabrics to be coloured to a chosen design pattern at the point of sale. I have seen examples of prototype production equipment in development in the US, UK and South Korea. The equipment is mainly used presently for simple garments (T-shirts, simple dresses and shorts). It is both retail organisations and suppliers of clothing and textile products who see the potential benefits that these improving technologies have to offer. One major US supplier said they could foresee the day that every large store had a customisation unit contained within it for certain clothing lines.* Levis has also had a widely publicised experiment with customising jeans. Consumer benefits are clear if they can have a smart card that holds their personal data that retailers can use when they supply them with a garment they can be sure it will fit them. From a retailer's point of view the advantage is the consumer is more likely to be satisfied and as a consequence returns will be minimised and inventories will be lower if they are able to customise products in store. Mass customisation may not simply offer the quickest response of all but it may offer an accurate response lowering the risks for both consumers and retailers.

Key success factors in the fashion industry are often cited as responsiveness and flexibility. This has a specific meaning in a supply chain context. Flexibility means being able to adjust production quantities, styles, sizes and colours in line with the market demand. Responsiveness is being able to adjust the whole supply chain to the needs of the market.

6.6 Electronic-business strategies, fulfilment and digital supply chains

Contemporary supply chains are described differently by various commentators using terminologies that shape contemporary views on the topic. The adjectives applied include: flexible, responsive, agile, lean, value-adding networks and value streams. Supply chains are more than the term suggests. They are value creation mechanisms for customers. They are not simply 'supply' focused nor are they necessarily 'chains'. Supply chains are dynamic, efficient, effective response networks delivering customer requirements flexibly and on time. These high-performance networks consist of customers, suppliers and information travelling through organisational 'arterial systems'. These arterial systems cut across functional, organisational and geographical boundaries. Supply chain strategies, structures and relationships are highly complex. Configurations will differ within retail organisations and between retail organisations.

Supply chain efficiency is critical to customer satisfaction. Retailers and their electronic-tailing (e-tailing) operations are dependent on fulfilling the marketing promise. This is achieved through successful supply chain strategies and operations that are integrated and capable of delivering. Systems integration and effective use of information and communication technologies (ICT) is a key requirement. This might take the form of

---

*Interview conducted with board members at the VF Corporation in North Carolina, USA, May 2000.

electronic-procurement (e-procurement), electronic-design (e-design) collaboration, order tracking and delivery systems using satellite technology for logistical operations and so on.

What distinguishes the traditional supply chain approach from a contemporary view is the capability for customers to self-design products/services at a price they find acceptable. Collaboration is not simply between a supplier and buyer but it may be possible through digital supply chains to collaborate with the ultimate consumer. This electronic enabler (e-enabler) may offer scope for those retail organisations and suppliers such as Levi to transform experiments on customising products into a mainstream commercial strategy. The storage of expensive items that no one wants to buy is not necessary in a 'digital supply chain'. Information, time compression, responsiveness and the flexibility to switch production and delivery routing may all be achieved through the application of 'digital SCM'.

6.7 Future directions and research agenda

A number of important themes have been examined within this chapter. The themes selected are my interpretation of important developments that have brought us to where we are today. From roots firmly located in purchasing, supply and operations the concept of 'SCM' as we now understand owes much to developments in other disciplines: strategy, economics, marketing, organisational behaviour and information technology (IT). It is the integration of these disciplines in terms of thinking and applications in terms of practice throughout the management process that is important in helping to understand the current issues and the future directions that research can take.

Integration is the key to managing these complex processes both internally and externally between firms that co-exist in the numerous supply chains that each organisation has. The delivery of a single garment to a retail store may have a network of suppliers stretching around the globe and that is only one supply chain configuration that the retailer has to manage within a range, within a store and within all its stores. The variety of contact points and the number of different relationships that exist in this business to fulfil customer needs are highly complex. An important point to remember is that they are business arrangements and business relationships driven by the motive for profit through exchange. Therefore, examining the exchange processes and how they are managed has much to offer to gain a better knowledge and understanding of how these processes work and change through time. Also to assess the impact of global sourcing and purchasing strategies on both the supplying country and their population and the purchasing country population add an important new dimension considering ethics and green issues. Longitudinal studies, quantitative research, ethnography, phenomenology and social interactionism are all methods that could be employed effectively in this context.

Comparisons drawn between different types of supply chain are always interesting. In this respect comparative case study research has much to offer. Why have Benetton chosen to take greater control of their supply chain by vertically integrating operations and expanding the number of production centres overseas. This is not simply a cost-reduction exercise although that may be an important outcome. They have taken this decision to gain control over the supply chain to minimise risks as much as anything and to establish centres close to where they think their markets may expand. Fashion and fads in retail strategy could be explored to examine if the decisions taken are influenced by patterns of development elsewhere in the sector. For example, were Benetton influenced by Zara's success in establishing new markets in Europe outside of Spain quickly and effectively because they were a vertically integrated company applying 'fast-fashion' concepts (never repeating) and adopting QR tools. Have other retailers copied or are they copying aspects of the ways in which these companies manage their supply chains or do they do things differently and if so what?

We already know from the literature that many of the ideas and supply chain concepts have developed in manufacturing and in particular in automobile manufacture. Is managing the supply chain in the retail sector different to managing an automotive plant or an electronics plant? Is customisation more or less important in fashion retail supply chains than in the computer industry where companies like Dell have led the way? What is different and what is similar about these organisations, their supply chains, their business operations, their marketing and their businesses? These are all interesting questions that when answered we would all learn something from that would help explain different aspects of SCM. Comparative research and research conducted that is interdisciplinary would offer some useful insights in this context.

Whatever aspects of SCM, researchers examine it is evident from the discussions within this chapter that SCM is critical to the successful business management of retail organisations. Researchers from different disciplines have much to offer in contributing to these debates.

References

Axelrod, R. (1984) *The Evolution of Co-operation*. London, Penguin.

Barney, J.B. (1999) How a firm's capabilities affect boundary decisions. *Sloan Management Review*, **Spring**, Boston, MIT.

Berry, D., Towill, D.R. and Wadsley, N. (1994) Supply chain management in the electronics industry. *International Journal of Physical Distribution and Logistics Management*, **24**(10), 20–32.

Burt, D.N., Dobler, D.W. and Starling, S.L. (2003) *World Class Supply Management – The Key to Supply Chain Management*, 7th edition. Boston, MA, McGraw-Hill Irwin.

Campbell, N.C.G. (1985) An interaction approach to organisational buying behaviour. *Journal of Business Research*, **13**, 35–48; reprinted in: Ford, D. (1990) *Understanding Business Markets – Interaction, Relationships, Networks*. London, Academic Press.

Camuffo, A., Romano, P. and Vinelli, A. (2001) Back to the future: Benetton transforms its global network. *Sloan Management Review*. Boston, MIT, pp. 46–52.

Carlisle, J.A. and Parker, R.C. (1989) *Beyond Negotiation: Customer–Supplier Relationships*. Chichester, Wiley.

Chao, C.N. and Scheuing, E. (1992) An examination of the relationships between levels of purchasing responsibilities and roles of those in purchasing decision making, *First PSERG Conference*, Glasgow.

Christopher, M.G. (1992) *Logistics and Supply Chain Management-Strategies for Reducing Costs and Improving Services*. London, Financial Times/Pitman Publishing.

Christopher, M.G. (1996) *Marketing Logistics*. Oxford, Butterworth-Heinemann.

Coase, R.H. (1937) The nature of the firm. *Economica*, **V**.

Cox, A. (1997) *Business Success: A Way of Thinking about Strategy, Critical Supply Chain Assets and Operational Best Practice*. Lincolnshire, Earlsgate Press.

Cousins, P.D. (2002) A conceptual model for managing long term inter-organisational relationships. *European Journal of Purchasing and Supply Management*, 71–82.

Croom, S. and Batchelor, J. (1997) The development of strategic capabilities – an interaction view. *Integrated Manufacturing Systems (UK)* **8**(5), 299–313.

Demming, W.E. (1986) *Out of the Crisis: Quality, Productivity and Competitive Position*. Cambridge, Cambridge University Press.

De Wit, B. and Meyer, R. (1998) *Strategy – Process, Content, Context*. London, Thompson Learning.

Ellram, L.M. (1991) Supply chain management: the industrial organisation perspective. *International Journal of Physical Distribution and Logistics Management*, **21**(1), 13–22.

Ellram, L.M. (1994) A taxonomy of total cost ownership models. *Journal of Business Logistics*, **15**(1), 171–191.

Fisher, M., Obermeyer, W., Hammond, J. and Raman, A. (1994) Making supply meet demand in an uncertain world. *Harvard Business Review*, **72**(3), 83–93.

Ford, D. (1990) *Understanding Business Markets – Interaction, Relationships, Networks*. London, Academic Press.

Ford, I.D. and Farmer, D. (1986) Make or buy – a key strategic issue. *Long Range Planning*, **19**(5), 54–62.

Forrester, J.W. (1961) *Industrial Dynamics*. Boston, MIT Press.

Fransoo, J.C. and Wouters, M.J.F. (2000) Measuring the bullwhip effect in the supply chain. *Supply Chain Management*, **5**(2), 78–89.

Gereffi, G. (1994) The organisation of buyer-driven global commodity chains: how US retailers shape overseas production networks. In Gereffi, G. and Korzeniewicz, M. (eds), *Commodity Chains and Global Capitalism*. Westport Conneticut, Greenwood Press, pp. 95–122.

Goodwin, J.S. and Franklin, S.G. (1994) The beer distribution game: using simulation to teach systems thinking. *Journal of Management Development*, **13**(8), 7–15.

Green, K., Morton, B. and New, S. (1998) Green purchasing and supply policies: do they improve companies' environmental performance? *Supply Chain Management*, **3**(2), 89–95.

Hakansson, H., Johanson, J. and Wootz, B. (1976) Influence tactics in buyer–seller processes. *Industrial Marketing Management*, **4**(6), 319–332.

Harland, C.M. (1995) Supply chain management: relationships, chains and networks. *British Academy of Management Proceedings*, Sheffield, pp. 62–79.

Harrison, A. and Storey, J. (1996) New wave manufacturing strategies – operational, organisational and human dimensions. *International Journal of Operations and Production Management*, **16**(2), 63–76.

Heide, J.B. and Miner, A.S. (1992). The shadow of the future: effects of anticipated interaction and frequency of contact on buyer–supplier co-operation. *Academy of Management Journal*, **35**(2), 265–277.

Hines, P. (1994) *Creating World Class Suppliers: Unlocking Mutual and Competitive Advantage*. London, Pitman.

Hines, T. (2003) *Supply Chain Strategies – Customer Focused and Customer Driven*. Oxford, Butterworth-Heinemann.

Hines, P. and Rich, N. (1994) Focusing the achievement of continuous improvement within the supply chain: an automotive case study. *3rd International Conference of the International Purchasing and Supply Education and Research Association*, University of Glamorgan, March, pp. 219–233.

Hines, P., Lamming, R., Jones, D., Cousins, P. and Rich, N. (2000) *Value Stream Management – Strategy and Excellence in the Supply Chain*. London, Financial Times, Prentice-Hall.

Hobbs, J. (1996) A transaction cost analysis of quality, traceability and animal welfare issues in UK beef retailing. *British Food Journal*, **98**(6), 16–26.

Hogarth-Scott, S. (1999) Retailer–supplier partnerships: hostages to fortune or the way forward for the millenium? *British Food Journal*, **101**(9), 668–682.

Houlihan, J. (1984) Supply chain management. *Proceedings of the 19th International Technical Conference*, BPICS, CA.

Hunter, N.A. (1990) *Quick Response in Apparel Manufacturing*. Manchester, The Textile Institute.

Hunter, N.A. and Valentino, P. (1995) Quick response – ten years later. *Journal of Clothing Science and Technology*, **7**(4).

Hunter, N.A., King, R.E., Nuttle, H.L.W. and Wilson, J.R. (1993) The apparel pipeline modelling project at North Carolina State University. *Journal of Clothing Science and Technology*, **5**(3/4).

Iyer, A.V. and Bergen, M.E. (1997) Quick response in manufacturer–retailer channels. *Management Science*, **43**(4), 559–570.

Jones, T.C. and Riley, D.W. (1985) Using inventory for competitive advantage through supply chain management. *International Journal of Physical Distribution and Materials Management*, **15**(5), 16–26.

Kanter, R.M. (1994) Collaborative advantage: the art of alliances. *Harvard Business Review*, **72**(4), July–August.

KSA (1987) New technology for quick response: how US apparel manufacturers can capitalize on their proximity to the US market. *Getting Started in Quick Response*, Arlington, Technical Advisory Committee, AAMA.

KSA (1993) *Efficient Consumer Response – Enhancing Consumer Value in the Grocery Industry*, Kurt Salmon Associates, Inc. (KSA), Washington, USA, The Research Department, Food Marketing Institute.

KSA (1997) The ABCs of strategic alliances. *Womens Wear Daily Reprint in WDinfotracs*, NY, USA, WDinfotracs.

Lamming, R. (1993) *Beyond Partnership Strategies for Innovation and Lean Supply*. Hemel Hempstead, Prentice-Hall.

Leidecker, J.K. and Bruno, A.V. (1984) Identifying and using critical success factors. *Long Range Planning*, **17**(1), Oxford, Pergamon Press.

Lowson, B., King, R. and Hunter, A. (1999) *Quick Response – Managing the Supply Chain to Meet Consumer Demand*, Chichester, Wiley.

Macbeth, D.K. and Ferguson, N. (1990) Strategic aspects of supply chain management. Paper presented at *OMA-UK Conference on Manufacturing Strategy-Theory and Practice*, Warwick, June.

Oliver, R.K. and Webber, M.D. (1982) Supply chain management: logistics catches up with strategy. *Outlook*, Booz, Allen and Hamilton Inc., USA.

Porter, M.E. (1980) *Competitive Strategy – Techniques for Analyzing Industries and Competitors*. New York, Free Press.

Prahalad, C.K. and Hamel, G. (1990) The core competencies of the corporation. *Harvard Business Review*.

Sako, M. (1990) *Prices, Quality and Trust: Interfirm Relations in Britain and Japan*. Cambridge, Cambridge University Press.

Shapiro, J.F. (2001) *Modeling the Supply Chain*. Pacific Grove, CA, Duxbury Thomson Learning.

Slack, N., Chambers, S. and Johnston, R. (2001) *Operations Management*, 3rd edition. London, FT/Prentice-Hall.

Stalk Jr, G. (1988) Time – the next source of competitive advantage. *Harvard Business Review*, **4**, 41–51.

Stalk, G., Evans, P. and Shulman, L.E. (1992) Competing on capabilities: the new rules of corporate strategy. *Harvard Business Review*, **70**(2), 57–69.

Stevens, G.C. (1989) Integrating the supply chain. *International Journal of Physical Distribution and Materials Management*, **19**(8), 3–8.

Womack, J.P., Jones, D.T. and Roos, D. (1990) *The Machine that Changed the World*. London, MacMillan.

Study questions and guideline answers

1. Several management disciplines converge to create the catalyst for the development of theoretical frameworks used in SCM. Discuss.

The important thing to recognise is the eclectic nature of the disciplines underpinning SCM. Purchasing, operations, financial and economic concepts have been drawn into the subject to provide the theoretical frameworks that underpin SCM. In addition general management, marketing and strategic concepts have more recently become influential in shaping SCM developments.

For example, economics provided 'transaction costs' and 'Pareto analysis (ABC)'; finance provide some of the tools used in benchmarking, balanced scorecards, inventory management and in activity-based management systems; purchasing provides many of the theoretical frameworks to do with supplier selection, choices and negotiations; operations management provides many of the efficiency methods and tools, such as control charts, statistical process-control, process-mapping, value stream analysis, lean manufacturing, quality control and WCM. General management provides the managerial contextualisation and indeed some of the innovation concepts and quality management developments that are important: Kaizen, TQM, Business Process-Re-engineering (BPR) to name but a few. More recently strategic planning frameworks such as those developed by Porter (1980, 1985), for example *Value Chain Analysis* examining internal strengths and *Five Forces Analysis* examining organisational influences in the industry and vice versa. A good discussion would be able to identify these and other developments chronologically using some of the wider literature sources cited in this text to provide the evidence and develop appropriate arguments.

2. Explain why SCM is now seen as a CSF for contemporary retailing organisations.

There are many reasons why SCM has developed and been adopted as a central strategy within retailing organisations. When we say it is a CSF we mean that SCM is one of a small number of things that retail organisations must do well in order to be successful. Being successful in this context is delivering customer satisfaction that leads to higher profit, a strong balance sheet and year-on-year growth. For large retailers this will be reflected in their share price on the stock market.

The discussion could identify the following influences:

(a) The changes that have taken place in retailing during the past 40 years have greatly influenced the need for retailers to control more of what they do. Size, power, retail structures and organisation are all part of the changes that have influenced what retailers do and control. Retail organisations have generally become larger (more outlets, bigger retail spaces, larger geographical coverage, widening product ranges, offering more consumer choice and generally lowering prices). In order to achieve these changes the retail organisations have had to take greater control of their supply networks and structure them to be efficient and effective. SCM has therefore become critical to success in terms of achieving the objectives of lower prices, wider choice and growth.

(b) Extending consumer choice and to meet the more sophisticated consumer demand for everything, everyday from anywhere in the world has meant developing new skills to manage customer demand effectively and to increase profit while offering increasingly better value for money. Sourcing suppliers from anywhere in the globe is the norm with larger retailing organisations. Ensuring deliveries arrive on time, at the right price, in the right place and provide the consumer with the right performance/quality level demands supply chain competence.

(c) Recent retail developments particularly in food, such as Tesco Metro, M&S Simply Food, Sainsbury and local co-operative small format stores, are all part of a trend to provide smaller local stores with limited but quality ranges designed to supplement the 'big shop' as well as different consumer groups, for example, the less mobile who depend on local stores. These developments already add to the 'convenience store' sector with the likes of Spar, Londis and other local, regional and national chains. These types of store present a number of challenges for supply chain managers in terms of numbers of deliveries, siting and size of distribution depots and the selection of suppliers.

For the larger chains where they have to manage a number of different formats (in-town high street, out of town, shopping malls, retail parks and convenience stores) supply chain strategies and operations are central to their efficiency (hence their cost base) and their effectiveness (hence profit).

This guideline is not exhaustive but rather an indication of some of the issues that could be discussed in addressing the question.

3. Cost and customer service are two critical issues that have historically been viewed as conflicting objectives requiring 'trade-offs'. Explain why in contemporary retailing organisations the two may be viewed as compatible.

Cost and customer service would have historically been viewed as polemic constructs. However, modern management concepts might suggest that the two far from being 'traded-off' against each other may be achieved in tandem. This is because the assumption that increasing customer service always means an increase in cost is somewhat flawed. This lesson was learned from Japanese manufacturers who were able to lower cost while simultaneously improving the service offered to customers. Strangely the Japanese learned this from the US quality gurus 'Demming and Juran'. It was internalised and the

Japanese refer to the approach as 'Kaizen' which is what we understand as TQM. TQM is a continuous improvement model that requires organisations to strive for small-scale improvements continuously. The aim is to improve service and focus is on the customer. This service improvement does not necessarily require cost to increase but it uses the resources you have in a more efficient manner to lower unit cost.

Deming is best known for his 14-point plan, which is general enough to apply to most organisations and still have relevance for the modern supply chain manager. Perhaps the most important of his 14 points for the modern supply chain manager is the fourth one which states:

> end the practice of awarding business on the basis of the price tag. Instead minimise total cost. Move towards a single supplier for any one item, on a long-term relationship of loyalty and trust.

Deming (1982)

Juran (1988) refers to the 'quality trilogy' as quality planning, quality control and quality improvement. Objectives must be clearly set annually to increase performance and reduce costs.

4. **Select one major theme from the 'empirical evidence' and for a retail organisation of your choice and explain why it is important and how it influences their supply chain relationships and/or strategies.**

The final discussion question is open to choice. It is an extending activity requiring you to do some wider reading and research before addressing the question. Obviously, there is no specific answer guideline beyond this since each answer will make different choices.

Your focus may come from a number of themes developed within this chapter, for example time compression, cost, efficiency, quality, flexibility and responsiveness.

Chapter 7

Young consumers: the influence of celebrity on clothing choices

Emma Bannister and Heva Nejad

Aims

The aims of this chapter are:

- to explore the culture of celebrity within the female children's market;
- to investigate the means by which celebrities can effectively be used to target consumers;
- to outline the particular challenges and pitfalls which marketers may encounter when using celebrity endorsement as a marketing tool within this market;
- to inform the reader about the tools open to practitioners functioning within the children's market.

7.1 Introduction

This chapter focuses on a segment of consumers who in the recent years have come to the forefront of marketers' attention, young consumers between the ages of 8–13 years. Marketers identify these consumers as 'tweens', a term that reflects the similarities of their behaviour to another important yet slightly older segment, the teenagers. In recent years commentators, the media, marketers and parents have suggested that children are becoming skilful consumers at a younger age, which if harnessed effectively provides an enormous potential opportunity for marketing. In the wake of Marks and Spencer's recent decision to sign up David Beckham as the inspiration behind their boys' wear collection, this chapter seeks to provide an insight into the world of the young consumer and celebrity. More specifically we seek to explore one aspect of this market potential, the fascination of girls of this age with the culture of celebrity and the possible influences of celebrities on their clothing and fashion choices. Findings from a small study which looked at this subject, will be provided against a backdrop of relevant literature in this area.

7.2 Young consumers

During the past decade, the role of children as consumers has grown. Recent figures suggest that the UK pre-school market alone is worth 4.3 billion and the total UK children's market is worth 30 billion (including annual pocket money which is currently 2.3 billion a year) (Hollis, 2002). In addition to this market specifically attributed to children, they are increasingly involved in decisions about purchases made by the family unit (Mill, 1989; Gregan-Paxton and Roedder, 1995) and have been referred to as 'third parents' and 'brand managers' of the home (Mill, 1989). Decision-making skills emerge throughout childhood, and the complexities of strategies develop in tandem with age (Gregan-Paxton and Roedder, 1995), with the literature suggesting that children are exhibiting more fully developed decision-making skills at increasingly earlier ages.

Marketers divide the 'under-18 market' into distinct subgroups. With categories such as 'kids', 'tweens' and 'teens', they attempt to demonstrate how children's levels of consumerism develops rapidly, from the abilities to pester and influence (while 'kids') into independent, sophisticated consumers during their teenage years (Fry, 2000). The research that is reported in this chapter focuses on an age group, which is frequently categorised as 'tweens'. Datamonitor (*cf*. Fry, 2000) classifies tweens as between 10 and 13 years, but the term often includes younger children of 8–12 years of age (suggested the idea of pre-teenage). Children of this age group are said to be more sophisticated consumers than younger children and they are likely to be influenced by peer pressure (reflecting greater amounts of time spent with friends rather than family). They are also likely to understand and recognise brands and the value they represent, gaining a degree of financial autonomy which allows them relative independence.

However, parental involvement in consumption is one of the reasons that this segment of children is so valuable for companies. Children's ability to bring their parents shopping with them means that two markets can effectively be targeted simultaneously, providing the opportunity for 'cradle to grave' marketing (Lynn, 2002, p. 39). The attempt by marketers to secure brand loyalty at a young age is also an important motivator. Some consultants have estimated that the successful 'recruitment' of a 5-year old by a brand could be worth 100,000 in profits throughout their life (Lynn, 2002).

In order to ascertain what encourages children to purchase some products and not others, marketers need to form an in-depth understanding of the children's market. Market researchers specialising on the children's market believe that television helps to make children aware and attuned to what products are in the market (Hall, 1987). Ironically prime-time evening programmes attract the greatest numbers of child viewers, rather than Saturday morning children's programmes – as many mistakenly believe (Shipp, 1993). For the age group we explored, a more major influence was suggested: 'Among tweens, marketing is driven not so much by television or cartoons as by pop singers' (Lynn, 2002, p. 42).

7.3 Marketing to children

Marketing to children has increasingly begun to mimic the adult market, with brands extended in many different directions (Lynn, 2002) necessitating 'grown-up' marketing strategies (Marquis, 1994). Children are more aware of the value of money than previous generations and are better prepared for adulthood. They have economic sophistication, but like adults they are choosy about what they spend their money on (Marquis, 1994). Marketers need to strike a balance as a too 'child-like' approach towards advertising turns off children, while an adult pitch may offend the parents (who remain an important consideration).

The identification of, and reliance on, brands can begin as early as 2 years old (Hite and Hite, 1994). Brand reliance can be expressed as a preference formation, which Hite and Hite (1994) show is influenced by parents and reinforced by advertising. Although very young children may not understand the concept of a brand, they recognise the brand name and packaging (Hite and Hite, 1994), and recent studies suggest this awareness can begin as early as 2 years old (Hollis, 2002). Young children tend to rely on visual brand attributes when forming preferences and making choices among brands of consumer goods. They experiment with brands, retailers and products, and the results of this experience will have a lasting effect on their future brand choices. Children within the age group providing the focus for this study (8–13 years old) have begun to develop ideas of independence, they are anxious to be accepted (Phillips, 1999), they are too sophisticated for babyish things, yet they are still too naïve to be trusted with teenage freedom (Hall, 1987).

As children spend much time in the company of others, whether at home, at school or while playing, it is also important to understand the social context of consumption. Auty and Elliot (2001) describe the need to be liked by one's peers to be a more important driver of choice than the need to express one's identity. In their findings, younger adolescents were found to be more susceptible to normative social influence and the easiest way to gain approval was to be like the people one chooses to be liked by, thus choice moves from psychological considerations to those of culture.

Marketing to children is often portrayed to be irresponsible, aiming to 'brainwash' children into buying products. However, others would argue that it is an indirect effect of the way in which children have changed. Children are media literate from a very early age, and their tastes and opinions are fashioned by a multiplicity of influences. These include their parents, peers and others they become exposed to through media. The challenge for marketers is to make their products attractive to children, harnessing those influences that they can have some influence over, which are often those that operate through the media.

7.4 The celebrity endorser

The celebrity endorser is a ubiquitous feature of modern marketing (McCracken, 1989) and millions of pounds are spent annually on celebrity endorsement contracts (Tripp *et al.*, 1994). Friedman and Friedman (1979) classify three types of endorsers: the celebrity, the professional (or recognised expert) and the typical consumer. They describe *celebrity endorsers* as individuals who are known to the public (e.g. actors, sports figures, entertainers, etc.) for achievements in areas other than that of the product-category endorsed. McCracken (1989) defines a celebrity endorser as any individual who enjoys public recognition and who uses this recognition on behalf of a consumer good by appearing with it in an advertisement. This definition is broad enough to encompass not only film and television actors and stars, but also individuals from the world of sport, politics, music and so forth (McCracken, 1989). As well as promoting established brands, celebrities are used to promulgate new brand images, reposition brands or introduce new ones (Erdogan *et al.*, 2001).

The use of celebrities has become a common practice for companies competing in today's cluttered media environment – with one in five marketing campaigns in the UK now featuring celebrities (Erdogan *et al.*, 2001). The use of celebrities as endorsers, attempts to create positive effects in the minds of consumers, operating alongside consumers' own culturally formed meanings. Companies invest large sums of money to align their brands and themselves with endorsers (Erdogan, 1999). Erdogan (1999) suggests the rising popularity of this phenomenon is due to increasing consumer consciousness and new product proliferation, encouraging marketers to use attention-creating media stars to assist product marketing. Initially, this strategy seems to be a no-risk/all-gain situation, but, as with any dynamic marketing communication strategy, there are potential hazards. Individuals can change and endorsement relations can sour. Companies have limited control over celebrities in comparison to non-celebrities, whose characters they develop to create a spokesperson. In a sense, celebrity endorsement strategies can be a double-edged sword, which makes selecting a celebrity endorser from other alternatives potentially very challenging (Erdogan, 1999).

Celebrity endorsements are expensive. Depending on the status of the celebrity, remuneration could run into millions of pounds for several years. Overall, the use of celebrities

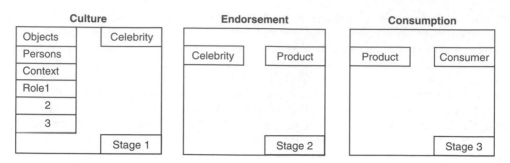

Figure 7.1 Meaning movement and the endorsement process
Source: McCracken (1989, p. 315)

as spokespersons in advertisements constitutes a significant investment in intangible assets by the sponsoring firm – an investment that management hopes to offset with greater future sales revenues and profits (Agrawal and Kamakura, 1995). On balance, investors seem to positively value the use of celebrities in advertisements and celebrity endorsements are not only on the rise, but the average compensation paid to celebrities is also increasing (Agrawal and Kamakura, 1995). However, for this strategy to work, companies need to identify the appropriate celebrities who will potentially enhance the value of investing in advertising (Agrawal and Kamakura, 1995).

7.4.1 The endorsement process

Advertisers believe that messages delivered by well-known personalities achieve a high degree of attention and recall for some consumers (Ohanian, 1991). This can be strengthened by an appropriate connection between the celebrity and the product endorsed, or by the celebrity's personification of some aspect of the product (Ohanian, 1991). McCracken (1989) uses a 'meaning transfer perspective' to illustrate the process by which the symbolic properties identified with the celebrity endorser move between the celebrity, the consumer good and the consumer (see Figure 7.1).

Celebrities become typecast and this becomes useful for the purpose of endorsements. Without typecasting, they are unable to bring clear and unambiguous meanings to the products they endorse (McCracken, 1989). McCracken (1989) demonstrates how the meaning that resides in the celebrity 'adds value' to products through offering distinctions of gender, age and status, with greater precision than can be offered by anonymous actors or models. Celebrities also offer a range of personality and lifestyle meanings that an anonymous model cannot provide. Models and actors 'borrow' or 'act out' the meanings they bring to the advertisement. Celebrities on the other hand 'own' their meanings because they have created them in films, political campaigns or athletic achievement, thereby having particular meanings that cannot be found elsewhere (McCracken, 1989). In the final stage of the process, the consumer claims the meanings that have become associated with the product (via the celebrity) and use these meanings to support their self-concept.

7.4.2 Celebrity effectiveness

The literature suggests the effectiveness of celebrity endorsement is moderated by several factors: celebrity attractiveness and credibility, product–celebrity match, message and product type, level of involvement, number of endorsements by celebrities, target receiver characteristics and overall meanings (e.g. personality, value, standards) (see Erdogan,

1999). In addition, economic visibility of endorsers, regulative issues, compatibility with the overall marketing strategy and potential risks must be considered.

Although the sponsoring company is the underlying source of any advertising message, in most cases the individual models depicted in the advertisement serve as visible communicators. Creating a good campaign featuring a celebrity is an inexact science (Cooper, 1984). The main guidelines are to use a fresh face and have a logical connection between the person and the product (Cooper, 1984). The three underlying factors of sources credibility are expertise, trustworthiness and attractiveness (Ohanian, 1991). Expertise is defined as the knowledge that the communicator seems to possess to support the claims made in advertisements (Ohanian, 1991). Trustworthiness refers to the consumers' confidence in the source for providing information in an objective and honest manner (Ohanian, 1991). Through the increasing use of celebrities as endorsers, attractiveness has become an important dimension of source credibility. Ohanian (1991) indicates that consumers tend to form positive stereotypes about attractive people and that physically attractive communicators are more successful than unattractive communicators.

Research by Kamins (1990) emphasised the importance of considering the appropriate match (in terms of attractiveness) between the celebrity spokesperson and product type. His findings indicated that for appearance-related products, the use of a physically attractive celebrity would significantly enhance spokesperson credibility and consumers' attitude towards the advertisement, relative to the use of a physically unattractive celebrity. However, Kamins (1990) suggests that if awareness is the goal of the advertising campaign, then the extent to which the celebrity is recognised – as opposed to attractiveness – may be the most important strategic variable to consider.

While celebrity endorsement can create initial interest and attention, advertising practitioners should recognise that it will not necessarily result in attitude changes towards a product. Ohanian (1991) states that for celebrity endorsements to be truly effective, attempts should be made to employ celebrity spokespersons who have direct connections with their endorsed products and who are perceived to be experts by the target respondents. Tripp *et al.* (1994) investigated the effects of the number of products endorsed by a celebrity and the number of exposures by the consumer to the celebrity, on consumers' attitudes and purchase intentions. As the number of products endorsed increased, consumers' perceptions of celebrity credibility, celebrity likeability and attitudes towards the advertisement became less favourable. These results were independent of the extent of consumers' exposure to the celebrity.

7.4.3 *Possible negative consequences of celebrity endorsement*

The use of celebrities as part of the marketing communications strategy is a fairly standard practice for companies seeking to support corporate or brand imagery (Erdogan, 1999) and differentiating themselves from competitors in a saturated market. However, at times, celebrities' qualities may be inappropriate, irrelevant and undesirable. Therefore, according to Erdogan (1999), a major question is how can companies select and retain the 'right' celebrity among many competing alternatives, and simultaneously manage this resource while avoiding major pitfalls.

Combining a popular face with a product does not necessarily lead to effective advertising. Marketing campaigns that use celebrities face a potential risk, because they have little control over the celebrity's future behaviour (Till and Shrimp, 1998). Any negative news about a celebrity may reduce the celebrity's allure, and therefore the appeal of the brand that the celebrity has endorsed. While a well-known personality may help create an immediate identity or persona for a product, the benefits may turn negative if the spokesperson suddenly plummets in popularity, gets into an embarrassing scrape, or loses credibility by

Table 7.1 Pros and cons of celebrity endorsement strategies

Potential advantages	Potential hazards	Preventive tactics
Increased attention	Overshadow the brand	Pre-testing and careful planning
Image polishing	Public controversy	Buying insurance and putting provision clauses in contracts
Brand introduction	Image change and overexposure	Explaining what is their role and putting clauses to restrict endorsement for other brands
Brand repositioning	Image change and loss of public recognition	Examining what life-cycle stage the celebrity is in and how long this stage is likely to continue
Underpin global campaigns	Expensive	Selecting celebrities who are appropriate for global target audiences, not because they are hot in all market audiences

Source: Erdogan (1999, p. 295)

endorsing too many other brands (Cooper, 1984). An example of the latter is provided by Steve Redgrave, the Olympic rower, who was the face for 'cholesterol – busting' Flora Pro-Active and a few months later was advertising for Walker's crisps (Norman, 2001). In addition, during the World Cup in 2002, some sponsors watched their chosen stars become injured, crash out of the tournament early or, in the case of 7Up and Ireland's Roy Keane, not even make it to the opening match (Day, 2002). Widely publicised incidents suggest that celebrity endorsers may at times become liabilities to the brands they endorse (Till and Shimp, 1998). Worldwide examples of this include O.J. Simpson's indictment and later acquittal on murder charges while endorsing Hertz rental cars, and Pepsi Cola's series of debacles with three tarnished celebrities – Mike Tyson, Madonna and Michael Jackson. Mike Tyson was the face of Pepsi until 1991 when he was charged and then convicted of rape. Also in 1989 Pepsi was forced to drop a campaign starring Madonna after fundamentalist Christians called for a boycott of the product following the controversial like a Prayer video in which crucifixes were burnt. Michael Jackson was charged with child abuse in 1994, but reached a settlement out of court. There was also embarrassment for the British supermarket chain Sainsbury, when Jules Oliver, the wife of celebrity chef Jamie Oliver (the face of the Sainsbury advertisements) was recently photographed leaving another supermarket (Waitrose) with her arms full of shopping bags.

Advertising managers therefore need to investigate fully the cost of hiring a celebrity and balance this with celebrity trustworthiness and controversy risk. Prior endorsements and celebrity, familiarity and likeability are also likely to be important factors along with the risk of celebrities overshadowing brands, and the stages of the celebrity's life cycle (Erdogan *et al.*, 2001). Table 7.1 provides a useful summary of the pros and cons of celebrity endorsement strategies, along with the strategic measures to manage these effects.

7.5 Children's media

As well as understanding the process by which a celebrity effectively becomes associated with a product, it is important for marketers to understand the main channels by which children gain their knowledge about celebrities. We will briefly discuss the two main media channels that effectively reach out to children, and particularly girls, of this age – television and magazines.

As children's roles as consumers have increased, so has concern over children's abilities to evaluate advertising and promotions, and their abilities to make informed judgements as consumers. Television provides a lucrative medium for marketers attempting to tackle the children's market (Lynn, 2002). In fact, particularly for younger children, it is sometimes difficult to separate television shows from their commercial element – in terms of the supporting merchandise that accompanies the shows. For example, a new programme to hit the screens this year on the BBC, *Rubba-Dubbas*, was actually commissioned because of the merchandising opportunities that it offered. HIT Entertainment's Director of Corporate Development, Nigel Birrell, acknowledges: *When we invest in a new project we want to know that there will be substantial merchandising on the back of it* (*cf.* Lynn, 2002, p. 40).

When children watch television they attempt to fulfil a need for entertainment as well as escapism (Ableman and Atkin, 2000). Children tend to view certain shows regularly and develop attachments to frequently viewed characters, which increase the likelihood that they will be influenced by these images (Hoffner, 1996). The nature of portrayals on television undoubtedly interacts with viewers' traits and prior experiences, to determine their perception of and attraction to television characters (Hoffner, 1996). Noble (1975) contends that identification with characters involves sharing their experiences and desiring to be like them, whereas para-social interaction involves coming to know and imaginatively interacting with characters. Para-social interaction involves the sense of a close personal relationship with a character. There is anecdotal evidence that both male and female viewers are drawn to and imagine themselves as interacting with opposite-sex characters (Hoffner, 1996).

In addition, there are a wealth of UK magazines that target the children's market. In a study by Emap (1999, *cf.* Fry 2000), called *Youth Facts 5*, magazines beat all other media when judged by criteria such as relevance, difference and accessibility. Emap claims that overall young people could give more reasons for involvement with magazines than for any other medium (Fry, 2000). Pop magazines are suggested to provide the most popular medium for reaching 10–13-year olds (Fry, 2000). As a general rule, the girls who make up the majority of the readership of children's magazines start out reading younger titles such as *Live and Kicking*. They then move onto glossy magazines such as *Bliss*, *17* and *Sugar*. While pop stars like Britney Spears and pop groups like S Club 7 remain an important part of the editorial mix in these older titles, the emphasis shifts to fashion, beauty, boys and real-life problems (Fry, 2000).

7.6 A study of young female consumers and celebrities

This study focused on young female consumers, as preliminary work suggested that celebrities were more important as advertising tools for girls than boys at this age, particularly for the product category under study (clothing). The study focused on young girls' understanding of fashion and style, and the influence of celebrity on their perceptions. It was also intended to consider the means by which the participants gained their knowledge about celebrities.

The study therefore focused on the third stage of the diagram of McCracken (1989) shown in Figure 7.1, the transferral of product meanings to the consumer (via the endorsement process), exploring the considerations that marketers should take into account when using celebrities as part of their marketing communications to children.

One of the major challenges to researchers and marketers is to form an understanding of how children see and interpret the world and market research is necessarily becoming more sophisticated in this area. Children have a different perspective to adults, so understanding their consumer behaviour requires a different approach. Until recently, research tended to focus on children's parents, with the assumption that they would ultimately pay for products (McGee and Heubusch, 1997). However, new types of qualitative research endeavour to more effectively explore the reasons why children feel and act the way they do. These insights can go a long way towards developing the messages that children will hear and the products that they will buy (McGee and Heubusch, 1997).

It is important to consider a child's cognitive abilities when designing experimental procedures that are appropriate for them. Peracchio (1991) identifies the importance of considering the following: familiarity with factual information, context, verbally presented information and the goal of the experimental task. When conducting research with adults it is important to devise a research environment and a task and/or questions that they are able to complete. This is even more important and also perhaps more challenging when the participants of the study are children.

Qualitative research methods were used in an attempt to gather well-grounded and rich descriptions, and explanations of processes occurring in local contexts (Miles and Huberman, 1984). A particular strength of qualitative research, for both researchers and practitioners, is its ability to focus on actual practice *in situ*, looking at how social interactions are routinely enacted (Silverman, 2000). Qualitative research concentrates on words and observations, attempting to describe people in their natural situations (Krueger, 1994). Taking into consideration the source of data for this research (young consumers), the nature of this demographic group and the research objectives, it was decided that qualitative research methods would be the most suitable. Specifically, focus groups were chosen, in order to create opportunities for the participants to interact with each other, important considering the nature of the topic under study.

7.6.1 Focus groups

The focus group discussions were intended to be comfortable and enjoyable for the participants and provided an opportunity for them to share their ideas and perceptions. A pilot group was conducted initially, followed by four further focus groups. Each group had between four and six participants. In each case the researcher recruited one participant and then this participant recruited their friends as additional group members. The participants were then invited to attend by a letter from the researcher, which was given to each participant's parents. In effect, the groups functioned as 'friendship groups', which while adversely affecting the representativeness of the sample meant that the participants felt comfortable with each other and a more 'natural' setting could be achieved.

The focus groups were held in the home of the child that was first recruited, as these were surroundings that were familiar and comfortable for each group member. A question guide was employed, but the groups were only very loosely structured, with the discussion following the natural flow of the conversation. The discussions focused on television programmes, magazines, television personalities, fashion and style, and the effectiveness of the use of celebrities in marketing to children.

At the beginning of each focus group session, the participants were divided into pairs and were asked to complete a projective technique. Each pair was given two or three pieces of cardboard with a photograph of a current pop star's head fixed at the top (Kym Marsh[1], Myleene Klass[2], Holly Valance[3], Britney Spears[4], Victoria Beckham[5] and Geri Halliwell[6]). Pairs in each group were given the same set of clothing and were asked to 'dress' the celebrities. The purpose of the exercise was to create an awareness of the topic

---

[1] Member of pop group Hear'Say created from television series pop stars.
[2] Member of pop group Hear'Say.
[3] Teenage pop star who started her career on the Australian soap opera Neighbours.
[4] The US teenage pop star who started her career at a young age on the Disney Show in the US.
[5] Solo artist famous for being part of the Spice Girls group and married to footballer David Beckham.
[6] Solo artist, previously a member of the Spice Girls.

under discussion and to start off a natural conversation between the participants. It was also to provide stimuli for the children to refer back to during the session.

Each focus group (including the discussion accompanying the projective technique) was recorded on audiocassette and transcribed in its entirety prior to analysis. Once the initial categorisation was accomplished, the data within each category was coded further to find emergent patterns or themes within each category. Once the analysis within the categories was established, analysis across the categories took place.

7.6.2 Findings

The children enjoyed and became highly involved in the projective task, creating complete outfits for the celebrities, which often included accessories such as sunglasses, hats, bags, jewellery and even make-up. These collages then became prompts to aid the discussion of style and fashion, and the influence of celebrities over product choices. All four groups chose similar if not identical outfits for the celebrities. The participants' responses suggested a high awareness of these celebrities in the media, often selecting clothing because they said something similar had been worn by them recently or simply because they thought it would suit the celebrity. These responses suggest the children had fairly set ideas about the clothing and fashion associated with certain pop stars, which suggests high media awareness, which would need to be matched by marketers should they wish to tackle this market and harness their fascination with celebrities effectively.

7.6.3 Awareness of celebrities

The children in the study were very aware of the concept of celebrity, but their responses were predominantly restricted to those people involved in music and television. The older children (those of 12- and 13-year olds) were able to expand upon this, stating that celebrities were usually famous for having accomplished something. The girls were interested in learning more about the celebrities' private and public lives and would explore different channels to discover these details, and liked to discuss these lives with their friends.

7.6.4 Celebrity personality

The participants discussed celebrities' personalities at great length, and in general seemed to pick up information relevant to this from watching television. The children considered personality and appearance to be indelibly linked, and the two were almost always discussed in conjunction with each other.

There was some discussion about what the 'true' or 'real' personality of some celebrities was, with the indication that celebrities would sometimes act rather than reveal their true personality. Humour was a highly valued attribute, and for those celebrities featured on television programmes, this gave them an edge over less favoured presenters on rival television stations. Participants also commented on those celebrities that did not appeal to them. Ironically this dislike was often attributed to personality traits that are associated with a great deal of confidence (e.g. arrogance).

For example:

> *Edith (8):* I don't really like her [Victoria Beckham] as she thinks she's a big shot.
>
> *Claire (11):* I think Geri [Halliwell] is really proud of herself and it just makes you think why? It kind of stops you liking her.
>
> *Samantha (10):* It's not just being proud it's also the way she [Geri Halliwell] talks, she's rude and it's just irritating.

7.6.5 Celebrities and clothing

Television and magazines seemed to be the main media channels by which the children discovered information about celebrities. They seemed to follow the lives of particular celebrities very closely, and were able to visualise and verbalise the clothing they associated with them. The projective technique revealed a high level of agreement between the choices assigned to particular celebrities by participants. The participants seemed to actively seek out information regarding celebrities' clothing and also stories which informed, supported or challenged their ideas about celebrities' personalities.

When the participants discussed the clothing worn by celebrities, they often drew upon other characteristics, which they associated with the celebrity. The meanings they associated with the clothing seeming to support theories of symbolic consumption (e.g. Holman, 1980):

> Rosie (10): She's [Victoria Beckham] not a show off, like she won't wear loads of jewellery to show she's got money. She'll wear clothes that normal people would wear.

> Edith (11): I think Geri's clothes show that she I don't know how to put it, that she likes herself. She likes her figure and her boobs a bit of a show off. She knows that she's famous, and she wants to show it off.

> Catherine (13): Her [Kym Marsh] clothes show that she's stylish and sophisticated and she's in show-biz.

It was apparent that celebrities were generally expected to wear different clothing to everyday people; this meant they could wear outrageous clothing without being ridiculed or subject to peer pressure:

> Samantha (12): The accessories separate the normal person from the show-biz person.

> Hannah (13): You know, no one normal could wear the stuff that say Sophie Ellis-Bextor wears or like what Bjork wore at the Oscars [*A dress with swan feathers and swan head looped around the neck-line*], but they can and they get away with it. No one's going to laugh at them. They're famous and a lot of sad people would probably try to copy them but they'd just be laughed at.

Occasionally, the participants suggested that a celebrity's outfit might be suitable for everyday wear and worn by 'ordinary' consumers. Certain celebrities were described as being more similar to them and down to earth. One of the names that kept being mentioned was that of Myleen Klass, formerly of the band *Hear'Say*. The children may have been influenced by Ms Klass' position (along with the other Hear'Say members) as a face of the high-street fashion store, *River Island*. It was difficult to know the causal relationship — whether she had been chosen to model for the store because of her dress style, or whether her endorsement of the brand had led to the perception of her clothing style as being more 'down to earth':

> Erica (12): I think her [Myleene Klass] clothes show that she's more down to earth, and I think she's more like quiet.

> Sarah (12): She's [Myleene Klass] more normal so she wears plainer clothes like that.

> Susan (12): I would probably wear the stuff she [Myleene Klass] does. You know they're more simple and similar to what I wear already. She doesn't go over the top with her dressing like most of them do, so it's not really show-biz.

The findings also suggested the importance of clothing to these young people in terms of forming judgements (positive and negative) about others – particularly celebrities.

7.6.6 Recognition of celebrities' fashion and style

The participants discussed the ever-changing nature of fashion and considered fashion to be a concept to be followed. While it was possible for one individual to start a fashion, it only became considered fashionable when it was widely accepted and worn in public:

> *Claire (11):* I think Geri Halliwell is fashionable rather than stylish because she'll sometimes wear what she wants, but then she'll see someone and they'll be getting all the attention and confidence so then she'll take what they're wearing and she'll just change it a little bit, but she's basically just copied what they wear and just made it suit her.

> *Erica (12):* Britney Spears sets a lot of trends off, like Skechers trainers and everything. A lot of people will buy them now 'cause Britney's been advertising them.

As well as noticing when a celebrity looked good, the participants liked discussing when particular celebrities had made what they considered to be 'fashion mistakes':

> *Roberta (11):* I like Britney Spears, I like her fashion. I like what she wears and her hair, but sometimes she comes out on *CD: UK* and I think oh she looks absolutely awful. Most of the time she looks really pretty, but I think as she can get it wrong she's probably putting it on to get attention and that's probably why I would say it's more fashion than style.

> *Laura (12):* Like sometimes she'll [Britney] wear stuff like big glasses and stuff that I don't think even suit her and sometimes the clothes and shoes that she wears, you can tell she's wearing them without thinking whether they're nice or not just because she thinks it's fashionable or trendy.

In addition, some celebrities were suggested to represent avoidance groups and had a negative influence on consumption decisions:

> *Edith (12):* I don't like people like Marylin Manson and people who dress like that.

> *Samantha (12):* Yeah they [Marylin Manson look-alikes] think they're being different but all look the same. How can that be different? They're still following a trend – even if it's a horrible one.

Some celebrities were not regarded as relevant role models for the participants. For example, supermodels were identified as being more suited to an older age group:

> *Catherine (13):* I don't like supermodels. They just wear shocking stuff that no one would wear and then off the catwalk they just dress too old. Kate Moss is probably the only one I like.

Celebrities seemed to provide a point of reference with regards to fashion and style yet it was primarily pop stars that the participants mentioned, perhaps reflecting these participants' status as the primary target market for single sales in the UK music industry. The celebrities helped the participants to form their notions about fashion and style, and validate their opinions about these concepts.

7.6.7 Celebrity endorsement

The various age groups seemed to demonstrate differing levels of awareness of celebrity endorsement. The 8- and 9-year olds were not aware of any celebrity endorsements. The participants were shown two high-profile campaigns featuring international celebrities. One was a *Skechers'* advert featuring Britney Spears and the other featured a photograph of Mary-Kate and Ashley Olsen[7], yet the participants did not recognise either promotion. When asked if they would choose any of the products from these ranges, there was a difference in response to each range. They unanimously said they would be interested in both product ranges, but they mentioned the need for parental permission:

> Davina (9): I would like to buy them [the clothes] if my mum would let me, but I don't think she would.

> Michelle (9): I'd buy the trainers, but I'd have to ask my mum first before I buy the Mary-Kate and Ashley clothes.

The 10- and 11-year olds were aware of the two promotions that were shown to them but could not name any other celebrity endorsements. They were sceptical about buying either the *Skechers'* trainers or the clothing endorsed by the Olsen twins as they were not familiar with them, but were prepared to look at the styles available to see if they would like them:

> Maggie (10): Well I don't know if I would buy them, because I haven't seen what they [Mary-Kate and Ashley Olsen] have designed.

The children discussed the clothing that Mary-Kate and Ashley wore in their television programme, *Two of a Kind*. This programme functioned as a kind of advertisement for their endorsed clothing range suggesting a blurring of programming and commercials, which was mentioned in the literature review:

> Roberta (11): Some of the trousers that they've [Mary-Kate and Ashley Olsen] worn on TV I quite like and some of the tops, some of the dresses. I suppose I'd like some of the clothes and not others.

> Samantha (10): I didn't like a lot of the clothes they wore on their programme so I don't think I'll like their clothes in the shops that much.

The children tended to like the trainers in the Britney Spears *Skechers* promotion, but they questioned the use of Britney, suggestive of the risks of using celebrity endorsement in this fickle market:

> Claire (11): You can hardly see the trainers, she's trying to promote the trainers by looking good in the clothes she's wearing.

> Rosie (11): What are they trying to promote? Britney looking good or the trainers?

The oldest children in the study (12- and 13-year olds) were aware of both the promotions shown and could also name other celebrity endorsements. This seemed to indicate a more developed awareness of this marketing technique:

> Louise (12): David Beckham and Nike.

> Hannah (13): I think J-Lo either is promoting or has her own brand of clothes and perfume.

---

[7] Teenage twins from the children's television series *Two of a Kind* who have launched their range of clothing in the US and recently for George at Asda.

Carla (12): I think Gareth was doing Pepsi a while ago.

Samantha (12): I think Britney does Pepsi, but she just looks daft in it.

This older age group were not keen on buying the clothes by Mary-Kate and Ashley Olsen. They thought due to the nature of their characters in their television programme their clothes would be too young and meant for a younger age group. These views demonstrate how closely targeted celebrity endorsements need to be within this age group:

Catherine (13): To be honest I think they're nice for little kids but not for my age.

Erica (12): I don't really like watching them anymore. I liked them when I was younger but not anymore. I don't really think I would wear the stuff they've got out. It's probably meant for people in a younger age group.

In addition none of the 12- and 13-year olds thought they would buy the *Skechers* trainers. Their objection was that people would buy them due to Britney Spears promoting them without necessarily liking them. Also they stated that the trainers were expensive, but the image was not worth the price:

Laura (12): People just buy them 'cause it's her [Britney Spears].

Carla (12): You know everyone wears them and everyone knows you're wearing them 'cause of Britney and that's just sad. You can't do that.

Susan (12): I bet people don't even look at the trainers and just buy them 'cause they think oh if Britney's wearing them they must be cool.

Hannah (13): No I think they're really expensive and they don't look that expensive.

Overall the 12- and 13-year olds were aware that the product and endorser were separate entities. They accepted that the endorser would bring consumers' attention to the product. They claimed that the actual product would determine their decision to buy the product, not the endorser. Of course it is difficult to identify whether the behaviour of the participants would accurately reflect their claims as they also acknowledged that others would buy products because of the endorser, suggesting that celebrity endorsement was a strategy that would prove effective within this market:

Samantha (12): At first when I look at telly or something or a magazine, I'd see them [the endorser], but then I'll think I'm not buying you [the endorser], I'm buying the product, so I'd look at the product and think do I want it or not?

Louise (12): At the end of the day I'd have to like the product before I buy it.

A clear difference across the three age groups can be seen. While the youngest children were not aware of endorsers, they were keen to purchase the products they endorsed, although they felt the need for parental involvement in clothing purchasing decisions. The 10- and 11-year olds did not cite the need for parental permission, and their insistence that they would need to see the product before purchase seemed to indicate their greater sophistication. They associated the products with their previous experience with the endorser(s) on television programmes and the image that was communicated. The eldest age group of participants (12–13-year olds) were aware of greater numbers of endorsers and were able to recall celebrity names and brands. The age and image of the endorser were important to this group. There was also the need to be different from others, so a product considered too popular was not appreciated.

7.6.8 Appropriate endorsers

All three age groups were asked who they would like to see endorse a range of clothing for their age group, and which celebrities would effectively encourage them to take an interest in and purchase the products. There were differences between the celebrities chosen by the age groups. The children seemed to be very age aware, particularly the older children, not wanting to select a celebrity more applicable to a younger age group.

The 8- and 9-year olds chose either Britney Spears or Kylie Minogue and all of them chose Victoria Beckham. The 10- and 11-year olds unanimously chose Britney Spears and one girl chose equestrian Pippa Funnel, while another chose Rachel from S Club 7. The choices suggested that they valued celebrities who wore clothing they could both relate to and wear, in everyday situations. The 12- and 13-year olds chose Holly Valance and Cat Deely. In contrast to the previous age groups, they were adamant that they would not like Britney Spears as an endorser, citing that she appeals more to a younger age group. One of the participants stated that she 'acts too young' (despite being at least 7 years older than all of this group!) which again shows the importance of age appropriate behaviour to these rapidly maturing young consumers.

One of the participants demonstrated a fairly good understanding of the economics of celebrity endorsement when she commented on the existence of a fame/expense ratio:

> Hannah (13): If J-Lo did anything it would probably be too expensive for us.
> When they're that famous they can charge what they want, you know Mary-Kate
> and Ashley they're average priced, but someone that big would be too expensive.

Again this demonstrates the importance of successfully matching the celebrity to the product, in the sense that the celebrity needs to seem realistic and give out the 'right' signals about the value of the product and its 'affordability'.

A number of important lessons can be learnt from these young consumers for marketers aiming to reach this segment of the market through endorsement. An endorser will not necessarily appeal to all age groups, and there is the need for different endorsers and marketing campaigns for each target group. Marketers need to appreciate that unlike adult consumers, clear differences in consumption preferences will exist for the different age groups (even within the fairly narrow segment of consumers within this study).

7.6.9 Media preferences in the endorsement process

All three age groups had clear views about their favourite television programmes and magazines. An insight into the viewing habits of the children reveals how the viewing varies across age groups, and also gives a sense of the kinds of celebrities that the children were being exposed to.

The 8- and 9-year olds named their favourite television programmes as those specifically for children such as *Sabrina the Teenage Witch, Blue Peter, S Club 7* but they also enjoyed mainstream soaps like *Coronation Street* and *Emmerdale*. The 10- and 11-year olds chose programmes, which tended to occupy peak-time-viewing slots such as *E.R., Top of the Pops, Pet Rescue, The Simpson's* and *Casualty* (many of which tended to target adult viewers). The 12- and 13-year old girls again mentioned adult targeted programmes such as *Eastenders, Bad Girls, Big Brother, The Simpson's* and *Graham Norton*. They also mentioned *SMTV* and *CD: UK* which are children's shows featuring comedy/music and music, respectively, and ironically capture a high number of young adult viewers.

The magazines preferences of the children also varied enormously between age groups. The 8- and 9-year olds read magazines aimed at young children: *Kids, Girl Talk, Go Girl* and *Archie* comics. They also acknowledged reading magazines that their mothers bought for themselves. The 10- and 11-year olds read a larger variety of magazines, which were sometimes targeted at interests and hobbies (e.g. *Pony*). This age group were particularly keen on music magazines such as *CD: UK, Top of the Pops* and *Smash Hits*. However, on the whole they were not loyal to one particular magazine and stated that they would change the magazine they read either according to the magazine cover (including which celebrity was featured) and anything else that came across as interesting at the point of sale. The 12- and 13-year olds showed similar reading habits to the 10- and 11-year olds (particularly the music magazines), yet many of the magazines they read seemed to have more emphasis on fashion and boys (such as *Mizz* and *Bliss*). However, the girls were also anxious to avoid buying anything that they perceived to be too old for them as the following dialogue demonstrates:

> *Louise (12):* Sometimes I'll get Sugar, but it's a bit too old for us.
>
> *Laura (12):* Sugar's a bit too grown-up for us.
>
> *Edith (12):* Bliss is more for our age [than Sugar] and more interesting.

The children's choice of media (both magazines and television) reflected the different goals that these children had in their consumption behaviour generally. The younger children liked things that fit our traditional view of what it is to be a child (e.g. *Winnie the Pooh*) and programmes with magical undertones (e.g. *Sabrina*), and they favoured magazines that dealt with things associated with childhood such as animals and activities. However, compare these media choices with the oldest age group (television targeted at adults and magazines which deal with teenage issues) and it becomes clear that although there are only 5 years between the children in this sample, the type of media (and therefore the type of celebrities) that they are exposed to is a world apart. This has huge implications for celebrity endorsements, as children will be familiar and comfortable with very different types of celebrities, and seemed to have set ideas about which celebrities were suitable for their particular age group.

7.7 Conclusions

This review of the literature and preliminary findings should provide an insight into the effectiveness with which celebrities can be used to target children, but also reveals some of the challenges and pitfalls that accompany such a strategy. A small sample of girls was able to reveal just how important celebrities were to these young consumers, but it also suggested that celebrities would have to prove some fairly high credentials in order to be effectively used to increase the value of a brand or product. More worryingly for marketers, the study also indicates the very small age bands that marketers may have to work within, if they are hoping to fully harness the power of the celebrity. One of the most striking observations was how clearly the children identified themselves and their allegiances in age terms. Of course more research would need to be carried out before committing marketing spend to this theory, but it does suggest that advertisers need to think very carefully when using endorsers for this market as what might provide an attractive proposition for a 9-year old could be considered babyish by a 13-year old and so forth.

The participants looked to media channels to inform them about details of celebrities' 'private' lives, and celebrities' clothing was also taken to provide an important signifier of character and personality traits. This suggests the care with which a celebrity endorser's image needs to be managed – and the difficulties associated with managing this, as marketers have very little control of a celebrity's image when they are not under the direct control of the company.

Television and magazines played a significant role in the lives of the participants. While they enjoyed television programmes targeted specifically at children, they also cited mainstream soaps, music programmes and programmes targeted at adults as being among their favourites. Younger age groups tended to be interested in magazines that covered their main hobbies and interests. The older age groups tended to be more discerning in their choice of magazines, which could change weekly according to the magazine content and cover.

The findings of this study indicate that while the age group under study have some similar characteristics, their needs and views should not be treated as uniform. This is highly important for retailers and marketing practitioners, as perhaps it is too simplistic to talk about children in such broad categories. Girls of 12 and 13 years may share more similarities with older teenagers than the 8- and 9-year olds and this should be reflected in promotions and also in terms of clothing designs and the way in which fashions are presented and categorised on the shop floor. In order to investigate this phenomenon effectively it may be that this age group would need to be further segmented, which makes it even more difficult for the celebrity endorsement process to function effectively, as rarely is product use and segmentation by age quite this precise (and it may be uneconomical to have varying celebrities for different age groups). It also needs to be considered that the preferences of children are likely to vary considerably from one group of friends, school and location to another.

References

Abelman, R. and Atkin, D. (2000) What children watch when they watch TV: putting theory into practice. *Journal of Broadcasting and Electronic Media*, **44**(Winter), i7, 143.

Agrawal, J. and Kamakura, W.A. (1995) The economic worth of celebrity endorsers: an event study analysis. *Journal of Marketing*, **59**(July), 56–62.

Armistead, C. (2001) Eat my shorts! *Guardian*, 20 November.

Auty, S. and Elliot, R. (2001) Being like or being liked: identity vs. approval in a social context. *Advances in Consumer Research*, **28**, 235–241.

Cooper, M. (1984) Can celebrities really sell products? *Marketing and Media Decisions*, **19**(September), 64–67.

Day, J. (2002) Stars fail to shine for world cup sponsors. *Guardian*, 21 June.

Erdogan, Z.B. (1999) Celebrity endorsement: a literature review. *Journal of Marketing Management*, **15**, 291–314.

Erdogan. Z.B., Baker, M.J. and Togg, S. (2001) Selecting celebrity endorsers: the practitioner's perspective. *Journal of Advertising*, **41**(13), 39.

Friedman, H.H. and Friedman, L. (1979) Endorser effectiveness by product type. *Journal of Advertising Research*, **19**(October), 63–71.

Fry, A. (2000) Brands cash in by targeting tweens. *Marketing*, 12 October, 39.

Gregan-Paxton, J. and Roedder, J.D. (1995) Are young children adaptive decision makers? A study of age differences in information search behaviour. *Journal of consumer Research*, **21**(4), 567–580.

Hall, C. (1987) Tween power; youths' middle tier comes of age. *Marketing and Media Decisions*, **22**(October), 56–62.

Hite, C. and Hite, R. (1994) Reliance on brand by young children. *Journal of the Market Research Society*, **17**(2), 185–193.

Hoffner, C. (1996) Children's wishful identification and parasocial interaction with favourite television characters. *Journal of Broadcasting and Electronic Media*, **40**(Winter), 389–402.

Hollis, L. (2002) We know what she wants. *Guardian*, **G2**, 6 November, p. 14.

Holman, R.H. (1980) Clothing as communication: an empirical investigation. *Advances in Consumer Research*, **7**, 372–377.

Kamins, M.A. (1990) An investigation into the 'match-up' hypothesis in celebrity advertising: when beauty may only be skin deep. *Journal of Advertising*, **19**(1), 4–14.

Krueger, R.A. (1994) *Focus Groups – A Practical Guide for Applied Research*, 2nd edition. Sage Publications Ltd.

Lynn, M. (2002) I'm Britney, buy me. *Business Life* (British Airways), April, p. 38.

Marquis, S. (1994) The young ones. *Marketing*, 10 March, pp. 22–24.

McCracken, G. (1989) Who is the celebrity endorser? Cultural foundations of the endorsement process. *Journal of Consumer Research*, **16**(3), 315.

McGee, T. and Heubusch, K. (1997) Getting inside kids' heads. *American Demographics*, **19**(1) 52–56.

Miles, M.B. and Huberman, M.A. (1984) *Qualitative Data Analysis: A Sourcebook of New Methods*. Sage Publications Ltd.

Mill, K. (1989) Pre-teen buying power. *Marketing and Media Decisions*, **24**(4), 96–99.

Noble, G. (1975) *Children in Front of the Small Screen*. Beverly Hills, CA, Sage Publications Ltd; cited in Hoffner (1996) *Journal of Broadcasting and Electronic Media*, **40**(Winter), 389–402.

Norman, M. (2001) Diary. *Guardian*, 8 August.

Ohanian, R. (1991) The impact of celebrity spokespersons' perceived image on consumers' intention to purchase. *Journal of Advertising Research*, **31**(February/March), 46–54.

Peracchio, L.A (1991) Designing research to assess children's comprehension of marketing messages. *Advances in Consumer Research*, **18**, 23.

Phillips, D. (1999) Tween beat. *Entrepreneur*, **27**(September), i9, 126.

Shipp, H. (1993) New ways to reach children: marketing strategies aimed at children. *American Demographics*, **15**(August), 50–54.

Shrum, L.J. (1998) Development of a cognitive process model to explain the effects of heavy television viewing on social judgement. *Advances in Consumer Research*, **2**, 144–148.

Shrum, L.J., O'Guinn, T.C., Semenik, R.J. and Faber, R.J. (1991) Processes and effects in the construction of normative consumer beliefs: the role of television. *Advances in Consumer Research*, **25**, 289–294.

Silverman, D. (2000) *Doing Qualitative Research – A Practical Handbook*. Sage Publications Ltd.

Tripp, C., Jensen, T.D. and Carlson, L. (1994) The effects of multiple product endorsements by celebrities on consumers' attitudes and intentions. *Journal of Consumer Research*, **20**(4), 535,13.

Study questions and guidelines answers

1. **Provide some examples of what you consider to be well-matched celebrity-brand endorsements and some that you would question. Why is this the case?**

Students should outline some current marketing campaigns and outline the reasons why they feel they are effective. They should draw on the target consumer segment for the product or brand and the characteristics of the celebrity, which in their mind make them appropriate (e.g. personality, celebrity status, what they are famous for and previous advertising campaigns). They should be able to identify that different kinds of celebrities will work well for different products, for example informational campaigns may need someone with a degree of credibility for the item being advertised.

2. **Try to remember when you were the age of the children in this study. Can you think of any famous people you admired? Compare them to the celebrities outlined in this study and reflect on how marketing to children has changed.**

This will depend on how old students are. However, it is likely that they will note that attitudes towards celebrity have changed since they were children, with more celebrity endorsements and more publicity surrounding the lifestyles of the rich and famous. They also should be able to identify that more products and marketing specifically target children and children are encouraged to be more commercially aware. Some students may suggest reasons why this is the case, such as demographic changes in society, rising incomes, working families, etc.

3. **What differences do you think there would be (if any) for marketers seeking to use celebrity endorsement as a tool for products targeting boys? Suggest some celebrities and outline the reasons why they might appeal to boys of this age**

Answers should point out that boys and girls tend to be interested in different things and that this will affect the type of celebrities who will most effectively encourage them to consume. Sport is likely to be more popular with boys, particularly football, and this is reflected in the star-status that many footballers receive. This might actually make it easier for marketers to identify celebrities that will appeal to all age segments of the boys' market, as tastes might tend to be more consistent. Answers might also comment on the differences in boys' and girls' television-viewing habits, magazine consumption and the types of music they enjoy listening to and the magazines they are exposed to as well. Answers should also emphasise the importance for marketers to study these habits in order to gain an insight into their world.

4. **Do you think celebrity endorsement is an effective marketing strategy? How might its effectiveness vary between different segments of consumers?**

With this question it is hoped that students will question the effectiveness of celebrity endorsement for all market segments. However, it is also hoped that they will be able to identify different kinds of celebrities for different markets.

5. **You are given the responsibility of marketing a range of clothing to consumers of a similar age and with a similar lifestyle to you. Who would you decide upon, why and how?**

Through this question students should identify which celebrities appeal to them and why, linking their interests and lifestyles with a particular celebrity and providing reasons for their answer. The answer should also suggest the marketing channels that could be utilised, to ensure that the right market is reached.

Chapter 8

Undressing the ethical issues in fashion: a consumer perspective

Deirdre Shaw and Dominique A.C. Tomolillo

Aims

The main aims of this chapter are:

- to explore the nature of ethical issues in fashion purchasing;
- to examine the role of ethics in today's fashion marketplace;
- to gain an insight into the ethical issues that concern ethical consumers in the context of fashion purchasing;
- to give an insight into other issues that impact ethical consumer decision-making in the context of fashion purchasing;
- to gain an understanding of the ways in which all of the identified issues influence ethical consumer's decision-making with regards to fashion purchasing.

It is just really difficult trying to be an ethical consumer. I mean I guess the food sector has kind of got it cracked but the fashion industry seems a bit more off-the-beaten track. There is just so much to consider when you buy clothes, where it is produced, how it is produced, what it is made of. It is difficult, it is just difficult!

8.1 Introduction

The last three decades have seen a significant growth in ethical concern among consumers, which has resulted in an increase in demand for 'ethical' choices in the marketplace (Doane, 2001). Ethical consumers are characterised by their deep-seated concern for environmental, social and animal issues (Mintel, 1994). Thus, in addition to being influenced by traditional choice criteria, including price and product quality, ethical consumers are also demanding that organisations adopt more moral and socially aware principles (e.g. Shaw and Clarke, 1999; Mason, 2000). The progressive increase in consumer ethical consciousness is understood to have been propelled by a combination of factors, including increased media coverage of ethical issues and the rise of pressure group activities (Kalafatis et al., 1999). Ethical consumers believe that by making ethical choices they have the power to encourage and support businesses which avoid exploiting or harming humans, animals or the environment (Kalafatis et al., 1999; Anon, 2002). In this sense it is understood that these consumers use their buying decisions to demonstrate their beliefs and opinions, therefore, likening their purchase to a 'vote' (Smith, 1990). Thus, in today's competitive marketplace, businesses are continually faced with the challenge of developing brands which are deemed desirable and, more pertinently, ethically acceptable by the increasingly discerning consumers of the society (e.g. Gabriel and Lang, 1999). This demand for change is highlighted in the quote detailed above, from a participant of the present study.

While research has been carried out to explore ethical consumer choice in the context of food purchasing (e.g. Shaw and Clarke, 1999; Shaw *et al.*, 2000), as the participant quote above highlights, only limited research has been undertaken to determine the issues which ethical consumers associate with fashion and clothing purchases (e.g. Dickson, 1999, 2001; Shaw and Duff, 2001). This chapter will, therefore, explore the impact of ethical issues on decision-making in a fashion context. The authors will draw on research that used focus groups, in-depth interviews and a belief elicitation questionnaire to develop an improved understanding in this area.

8.2 Defining fashion and clothing in an ethical context

It is important to clearly define the concepts 'fashion' and 'clothing' in the context of this research. Although these terms are often used interchangeably it is argued here that while closely related, the terms 'fashion' and 'clothing' actually represent different concepts. In establishing an understanding of the fundamental differences between clothing in the generic sense, and 'fashionable' clothing, it is useful to refer to one of the classic human motivational theories developed by psychologist Abraham Maslow (1970). Maslow's model is based on the assumption that individuals have a hierarchy of needs and it is only when lower-level needs are satisfied that the consumer can progress to achieve their higher-level needs (Foxall and Goldsmith, 1994). Maslow's need hierarchy states that individuals move through physiological, safety, belongingness, self-esteem and self-actualisation needs. In relating the identified physiological needs, or basic needs, to the concept of clothing, and more pertinently fashion, Bohdanowicz and Clamp (1994) argue that such needs can be compared to an individual's need for a warm winter coat. More specifically, in attempting to satisfy his or her physiological needs, the consumer is likely to be concerned with the functional aspects of the coat as opposed to the symbolic or fashionable qualities of the garment (Bohdanowicz and Clamp, 1994). After accomplishing their physiological needs, Maslow maintains that consumers then actively seek to fulfil their need for safety (Foxall and Goldsmith, 1994). Bohdanowicz and Clamp (1994) relate this to consumers who avoid purchasing children's nightwear that has been produced using flammable materials. In viewing the latter stages of Maslow's hierarchy of needs, represented by the need for belongingness, self-esteem and self-actualisation, one is able to clearly differentiate between the values associated with clothing in general and fashion. More specifically, it is suggested that the need for belongingness and self-esteem, motivate individuals to seek fashionable clothing as a means of gaining acceptance from their peers and also as a demonstration of their social standing (Gabriel and Lang, 1999; Easey, 2002). In describing self-actualisation, which is often interpreted as an individual's desire to grow psychologically (Daft, 1995; Mullins, 1996), Bohdanowicz and Clamp (1994, p. 16) draw attention to the values and beliefs of ethical consumers and their motivation to frequent retail outlets which share and convey their own personal values and beliefs:

> The fashion marketer can observe this motivational force [self-actualisation] at work in both the creative dresser, whose whole appearance is a well-thought-out design in itself, and in the 'consumer with a conscience' who would shop at Lynx and Oxfam as an externalisation of their beliefs.

Although the hierarchy of needs of Maslow (1970) provides a framework within which to explore the role that fashion plays in driving and motivating consumers, and ethical consumers, towards their own personal goals (Easey, 2002), it is unable to address ethical consumers' perceptions of fashion. Moreover, although can be understood that many ethical consumers frequent ethical retail outlets as a means of satisfying their need for self-actualisation, it remains unclear whether these consumers are positively influenced by the retail outlets and the values that they represent, or by the garments sold in these stores. In addressing this issue, an investigation of ethical clothing retailers identified that 57 per cent of a sample of 1000 ethical consumers either disagreed or strongly disagreed with the statement: 'I would buy from a socially responsible clothing business, only if I really liked the product'(Dickson, 1999, p. 51). In relating these findings to Maslow's hierarchy of needs, it appears that ethical consumers' need for self-actualisation is more closely related to the issue of ethics than to the aesthetic qualities of the garment. However, as Dickson (1999) fails to establish the respondents' views towards fashion, it is impossible to determine whether the samples' apparent disregard for the style of 'ethical' garments is indicative of their views towards fashion or a pronounced ethical obligation towards the issue as a key driver in behaviour (Shaw *et al.*, 2000). Further, the studies of Dickson (1999, 2001) are specific to the US clothing market and as such fail to represent the views of ethical consumers elsewhere. Additionally, it is understood that many of the studies of Dickson (1999, 2001) review an individual ethical issue in isolation rather than in relation to other issues that may be of concern to consumers. As noted by Shaw and Clarke (1999), studies that concentrate on single issues of concern fail to recognise the complex network of issues which ethical consumers consider. Although Shaw and Duff (2001) examine a range of ethical issues in relation to the UK fashion market, they too neglect to determine ethical consumers' perceptions of fashion. In highlighting the possible role and relationship of clothing and fashion to the ethical consumer it is now necessary to explore the nature of these ethical concerns in the marketplace.

8.3 Ethics and fashion in today's marketplace

A report by the New Economics Foundation in conjunction with the Co-operative Bank in the UK illustrates that the ethical consumer market is currently growing significantly, revealing that product categories which specifically cater for the ethical market currently enjoy inflated market share value (Doane, 2001). This report developed the UK's first ethical purchasing index (EPI) as a means to investigate the value and growth of the ethical consumer market. This index, however, neglects the context of fashion and clothing. More specifically, it is noted that the hypothetical 'basket of goods', which formed the basis of the EPI, did not include any fashion articles or indeed clothing of any description, therefore, neglecting to place a value on these product categories. Instead, the basket of goods represented the following seven consumer product groups: food, fuel and light, housing, household goods, personal items, transport and subscriptions, that is donations to charities and charity shop sales (Doane, 2001). Although it could be argued that the inclusion of 'charity shop sales' may comprise clothing purchases, it must be acknowledged that charity shops do not solely sell clothing garments but also stock a variety of household products such as crockery and books. Consequently it is suggested here that in failing to address the value of ethical clothing purchases, the EPI in turn neglects to address the role that clothing and fashion plays within the ethical consumer market.

As ethical consumerism continues to become a significant force in the marketplace, businesses are increasingly alerted to the ethical issues and concerns that are of particular relevance to the fashion industry. These issues relate more generally to sweatshop production in developing countries where workers are often forced to work excessively long hours, for below living wages, enduring inhumane working conditions (e.g. Anon, 1997; Weadick, 2002). In response to the continual fears over garment workers' rights, as evidenced by the well-documented boycott cases against Gap and Nike, many consumers are now demanding fairer trade practices and improved codes of conduct. In terms of textile production, concerns exist surrounding the environmental impact of production and the impact on workers' health. Recognising the potential for more 'ethical' fabrics a number of fashion retailers, including Marks and Spencer (Marks and Spencer, 2002) and the Italian fashion company Missoni (Watson, 2001) have introduced organic cotton fashion ranges. Watson (2001) argues that in the same way as organic food products have become popular it is inevitable that consumers will extend the scope of their organic purchases to organic textiles. The use of fur and leather in fashion production has been viewed as an ethical concern for some time, more recently, additional concerns surrounding the treatment of rabbits farmed for angora wool and the culling of endangered reptiles for their skins have also emerged (Watt, 2000; PETA, 2002).

The lack of attention devoted to ethical clothing and fashion purchases within the EPI, as discussed above, is also mirrored within the marketplace where clothing which addresses the above issues is significantly under-represented (Anon, 1997; Law, 2000; Weadick, 2002). Most concerning, however, is the fact that a number of fashion chains, including Next and Espirit in the UK, which previously sold more ethically conscious clothing ranges, produced using ecologically friendlier materials and organic textiles, have now withdrawn stock of these styles (Anon, 1997). In doing so, these companies have further restricted ethical choice in the marketplace; therefore, forcing concerned individuals to seek alternative mainstream retailers or gain information on 'substitute' ethical traders (Anon, 1997). This difficulty in ethical clothing choice was illustrated in the quote provided at the beginning of this chapter, and is a key issue in this context.

In investigating the ethical consumer market, it is apparent that this particular sector is currently undergoing a significant period of growth. However, despite the fact that an increased number of consumers have become alerted to the ethical and environmental issues associated with consumer society, very limited research has been carried out to establish ethical consumers' views and attitudes with regards to the fashion industry. Moreover, although a number of ethical consumer organisations in the UK, including the Ethical Consumer Research Association in their publication *Ethical Consumer*, regularly document the various ethical issues associated with the fashion industry in general, it remains unclear how these issues influence ethical consumers' decision-making with regard to the purchase of fashion garments.

8.4 Ethical consumers and clothing in the UK

Due to the very specific nature of ethical decision-making in fashion and clothing choice, a purposive sample of ethical consumers was obtained from subscribers to ethical consumer organisations, *Labour Behind The Label* and *Ethical Consumer* magazine and from retail outlets located in Edinburgh and Glasgow, Scotland, which consider ethical issues in relation to clothing. This sample was used throughout all stages of the research. In order to gain an understanding of ethical consumerism in relation to fashion, it was deemed necessary to initially employ an exploratory research method. Two focus group interviews were conducted in Edinburgh and Glasgow. In accordance with the advice presented by Krueger (1988), the focus groups comprised of seven and nine participants. By conducting focus groups of this size, it was not only possible to encourage each member to feel sufficiently confident to air their views but also ensured a diversity of opinions was sought (Greenbaum, 1998). Following the completion of the focus group interviews a short questionnaire was administered to verify at an individual level the various issues discussed.

Seven individual in-depth interviews were conducted to explore more deeply the series of complex issues raised in the group discussions. All data were recorded and fully transcribed. Following the completion of the qualitative research stage a postal question-naire was employed to elicit the salient beliefs underlying intention to purchase ethically produced clothing items. One hundred and thirty questionnaires were distributed and resulted in 31 useable responses. This elicitation stage was designed to gain an insight into beliefs in this area, thus such a sample size is in keeping with previous litera-ture (e.g. Sparks and Shepherd, 1992). This approach is outlined in full in Ajzen and Fishbein (1980).

8.5 Research findings

8.5.1 Focus groups and in-depth interviews

In accordance with the grounded theory approach (Easterby-Smith *et al.*, 2002), the quali-tative data was analysed in relation to the concepts and issues raised. The identified themes were:

- the *ethical issues* associated with the purchase of clothing garments;
- the participants' *attitudes towards fashion*;
- their resultant *behaviour*;
- the *difficulties* the participants' encounter in attempting to adhere to their ethical beliefs;
- the significance of *normative influences* in their decision-making process;
- the *feelings* they experience when attempting to purchase 'ethical' clothing garments.

These issues will be discussed in turn.

8.5.2 Ethical issues

The focus group discussions revealed that ethical consumers' concerns regarding clothing and fashion did not exist in isolation. This supports previous research that highlights the importance of self-identity in ethical consumer behaviour (e.g. Sparks and Shepherd, 1992; Shaw *et al.*, 2000). Participant's stated that they were anxious about a number of issues including the use of chemicals in the production of textiles, the general ethos of various fashion retailers, the use of animal skin and fur, and the general conduct of the fashion industry:

> GW: ... there's a lot of issues concerning the chemicals which they [textile producers] use in production and where they dispose of chemical wastage. I also have some issues with the use of angora and snakeskin.

> AT: Well some clothing stores have been found to give money to whichever government is in power. I don't think that that is particularly ethical. It indicates that that company may get preferential treatment and may be let away with behaving in manner which other companies can't get away with.

> SS: I think there is a lot of concern over the use of animal skins like leather. I definitely wouldn't buy anything made of fur. The same can also be said for the use of wool. In many occasions sheep are treated very badly in order that we can use their wool, I don't think there's a need for that.

The in-depth interviews revealed a number of participants regard exploitative produc-tion practices as an appendage of 'corporate responsibility'. Many demonstrated a sense of ethical obligation to others, namely textile workers, supporting findings elsewhere in the context of food purchasing (Shaw and Clarke, 1999; Shaw *et al.*, 2000; Shaw and Shiu, 2003):

> *CF*: ... the most significant issue is related to the reputation of the company ... what does the company represent. Have they been found using child labour? What conditions are their factories in?

> *ET*: If you were to ask me which was the most prevalent issue for me I would have to say corporate responsibility and the whole ethos of the company itself. I don't like clothing retailers which opt for cheap production facilities ... some of the big conglomerates use sweatshops and dreadfully inhumane practices during the manufacturing stages. I don't agree with that.

8.5.3 Attitudes towards fashion

The majority of the focus group participants held very negative views towards the fashion industry. A number of individuals' stated that their dislike for the fashion industry was related to the fact that they perceive the sector as being dictatorial and superficial:

> *CE*: If people wanted to look good for themselves then they would have a clear idea in their mind what they wanted to wear ... but that isn't what happens because people follow a fashion because they are persuaded to wear that. They're like sheep, it's totally pathetic, can they not think for themselves? They think that by following fashion they will gain acceptance and approval from society [crossing arms and turning head away from group]. Honestly, I think it's totally pathetic.

> *SS*: I think the thing I don't like about the fashion industry is this nagging pressure. You know it's all about being told what to wear and when that I don't like ... Then it gets to the point where it's hard to pinpoint whether that's actually how you want to look or whether you think you want to look a certain way because the fashion industry is telling you to look that way.

Although the above participants both present negative views towards the fashion industry, the latter participant is aware that she is influenced by fashion. In contrast, the former participant completely abhors the entire concept of fashion and would never allow himself to be persuaded to follow fashion trends. Despite being initially rather adamant in expressing their dislike for the fashion industry when presented with the ethical clothing catalogue, Green Fibres, a number of participants stated that they did not perceive the styles illustrated as being particularly 'fashionable':

> *RP*: Ethical styles are so limited. There's no colour or style. I mean I wouldn't say that those styles [pointing to brochure] are particularly fashionable.

While it is highly probable that the focus group participants genuinely believe that they are not interested in fashion, the above statements indicate an acknowledgement that clothing offers symbolic, as well as functional qualities; features synonymous with the concept of fashion. These findings appear to contradict previous research by Dickson (1999) which concluded that, when presented with the opportunity to purchase an ethically produced garment, the majority of ethical consumers claim that they are not influenced by the style of the garment. In presenting issues relating to the 'power' of fashion industry, it is implied that the participants' dislike of the sector is actually related to an aversion to multinational corporations as opposed to the concept of fashion itself.

8.5.4 Behaviour

Consistent with previous research (e.g. Shaw and Clarke, 1999), a number of the focus group participants stated that, due to the difficulties identified above they are often unable to make an 'ideal' choice, but instead settle for products which they *believe* may adhere to their ethical values. In particular, one participant claimed that her dislike for the clothing styles produced by ethical retailers had forced her to adopt a 'shopping criteria', although as highlighted below this criteria can vary in complexity among participants:

> *VB*: A lot of the time it's just about maintaining a balance … you can't adhere to all your beliefs but you've just got to decide what's more important. For example, I buy some clothes from Marks and Spencer. I don't like the company itself, but I think that most of their products are made in the UK, and that's an important issue for me; it means I'm not supporting sweatshops.

> *MB*: I generally look at five different criteria; who makes it, who supplies it, quality, durability and the cost … by the way, if something doesn't correspond with my ethics then I won't buy it, it's as simple as that.

Although the focus group participants agreed that they followed similar style checklists, many recognised that they could not always adhere to their beliefs and were occasionally forced to purchase an 'unethical' product. Others where forced to adopt more drastic measures. In particular, two focus group participants had become so 'mentally exhausted' trying to buy suitable ethical clothing garments that they postponed buying new clothes for as long as possible:

> *MB*: I hate shopping and I guess that's because I can't find a retailer which I'm confident fits with my beliefs. I find myself looking for clothes which will last me for ages so that I don't have to endure the agony which is shopping. The T-shirt I'm wearing I bought it in 1981. I go with practicality, not what looks good or what's in fashion. I found a shop that sold leather look shoes that looked quite hard wearing, I bought 10 pairs.

> *CF*: I tend to wear clothes until they actually fall apart and then I'll buy more. To be quite honest, I buy clothes as a means of covering me up and keeping me warm and that's it. I don't have any other agenda, whether that be fashion or otherwise.

Although a number of focus group participants agreed that they also viewed the exercise of shopping for clothes as rather daunting, one in-depth interviewee was keen to point out that she was not motivated to purchase clothes purely for their functional value but instead desired clothes which portrayed her desired self-image:

> *VB*: I live in a consumer society and I like to buy new things like everyone else. I wouldn't be happy wearing the same clothes for years and years. I like pretty things and I like to look pretty. I don't like being dictated to by the fashion industry, but I want my clothes to look attractive, not old and tatty.

8.5.5 Difficulties

Both the focus group and the in-depth interview participants regularly made reference to the fact that, in attempting to purchase ethical clothing products, they are often faced with difficult and challenging decisions. These difficulties are related to the issue of *choice* within the ethical clothing market, the availability of *information*, *trust*, the existence of legitimate corporate *ethical codes of conduct* and the higher *prices* charged for ethical clothing alternatives. These difficulties will be discussed in turn.

In identifying the issue of choice as being a significant obstacle, focus group participants referred to the difficulties they encounter in attempting to purchase ethically produced clothing products, suitable for formal, business and social occasions:

> *RP*: The thing is, I work in an office and I need to look quite smart. I mean
> there are a few ethical clothing retailers about now but they only sell really
> casual, kind of hippy clothes.

As the focus group discussions progressed, the participants claimed that the difficulties they encounter with regard to the purchase of clothing garments, is more closely related to the availability of information than choice. Further, in-depth interviewees considered the ability to trust the information presented:

> *ET*: The thing is that it's difficult to know which companies actually use those
> [unethical] types of facilities. It's all kept very hush hush. Then sometimes when
> you find a good company, you're later told that they've actually been bought
> over by a disreputable company and that's pretty disheartening.
>
> *PF*: I mean I would really like to buy more organic stuff, you know like tops and
> stuff, but you don't even know whether it's really organic.

Referring to organisations' codes of conduct, one in-depth interviewee commented that, while many fashion retailers' use ethical codes of conduct to present themselves as being more 'ethical', the lacking of a formal regulatory system casts doubt over the accuracy of such policies:

> *VB*: … published ethical policies are a bit dodgy because they usually get found
> out that they're not all that great. I guess the only way round it would be to
> introduce a regulatory committee. You know a body that really monitors these
> companies.

Offering a solution for such 'inadequate' ethical policies, a number of in-depth interviewees stated that they would like to see more ethical organisations, such as *Labour Behind The Label* and the *Ethical Consumer* magazine, working with fashion retailers to endorse specific clothing retailers. Greenpeace (2002), for example, alert consumers to food manufacturers that are known to use genetically modified crops. Although the availability of such information will inevitably assist ethical consumers in seeking out 'ethical' food products, the lack of similar guidelines with regard to fashion retailers results in consumers feeling misinformed and confused. Expanding upon the difficulties they encountered in attempting to make ethical clothing purchases, a number of focus group participants also made reference to the fact that ethical clothing choices are generally more expensive than mainstream clothing garments. Likening the ethical clothing market to the ethical food market, one focus group participant stated:

> *RC*: … the thing about ethical clothes is that they're so expensive as well. That
> can really put you off … I've got used to spending more on organic food … but
> I can't bear spending more on ethical clothes.

It could be argued that the participants' concerns regarding the cost of ethically produced clothing garments, reflects and supports those presented by a number of fashion companies. More specifically, because organic materials are generally more expensive to produce and harvest, many fashion retailers are slow to introduce such ranges fearing that consumers will not be prepared to spend more for ethically produced garments.

8.5.6 *Normative influences*

In discussing the role that normative others play in influencing and promoting their ethical views, the focus group participants indicated that they each received varying levels of support for their ethical beliefs from others:

> *GM*: She [my partner] started me off on this ethical crusade … We both kind
> of support each other to be ethical. If I miss something, she'll say I don't think
> we agree with x company … I heard they do this or that.
>
> *VB*: My friends tend not to give a monkeys about my views, apart from winding
> me up about it a lot, but I don't care what they think anyway.

Although ethical retailers, such as The One World Shop and Bishopton Trading, were all regarded as being positive influences, a large number of focus group participants referred to multinational companies in a very negative and hostile manner. This is consistent with the research of Shaw and Clarke (1999) exploring ethical consumption in a grocery context.

8.5.7 *Feelings*

All participants often felt 'frustrated' that they could not purchase garments that fitted their ethical criteria; however, all experienced contentment in knowing that they had at least 'attempted' to buy ethically:

> *SS*: I think the important thing to get across is that when you do make an
> unethical clothing purchase, as ethical consumers we are aware of it. OK I
> usually feel quite frustrated but I don't feel guilty. We can't always avoid these
> unethical situations but the fact is that we're at least thinking about the
> consequences of the purchase.

The participant below uses second-hands as a means of justifying the acquisition of clothing and of reassuring herself that, although she is compromising her ethical beliefs, the purchase is not entirely 'unethical'. Presenting a similar line of argument, another in-depth interviewee described how she had purchased fur from a second-hand store, where animal welfare concerns could be compromised, however, under no circumstances could she purchase a Gap or Levi product. While there may be no apparent logic to explain her actions, the individual appears to have 'made sense of the situation' in her own mind, by developing her own set of guidelines:

> *VB*: Second-hand shops are great. If I see an outfit in a high-street store that I
> really like, I know that if I wait long enough I can get it in a second-hand
> store. Because the clothes are second-hand it's like they're recycled and that
> means it's like ethical now, you don't feel so bad that it's really from a
> mainstream shop.

8.5.8 *Salient beliefs*

The findings discussed above present a valuable insight into the issues ethical consumers consider in decisions to purchase clothing items. Although many ethical issues were raised as being of concern, when asked to prioritise their concerns, the questionnaire administered after the qualitative discussions revealed that 14 out of the 16 participants identified the issues relating to workers' rights and the condition of production facilities, in short sweatshop production, as being of 'most important' to them. The remaining two participants viewed this issue as being 'important'. Using this concern as a behavioural focus, the elicitation questionnaire, revealed the salient beliefs underlying this concern.

In terms of the salient beliefs underlying behavioural intention to avoid the purchase of garments produced in a sweatshop the next time they went shopping for clothing, partici-pants referred to the belief that they would have a clear conscience, minimise human abuse, withdraw support from non-ethical manufacturers and support local economies. Normative beliefs revealed that ethical organisations, friends, family and church groups would be supportive of this choice. Multinationals were named as a group who would not be supportive off this behavioural intention. Although these findings reveal that participants are highly motivated to avoid the purchase of clothing garments produced in a sweatshop, the control beliefs identified a number of difficulties associated with this behaviour, namely lack of information (especially concerning country of origin), lack of choice, limited availability, high price, location of 'ethical' retail outlets and lack of fashionability of ethical ranges. Although control factors impact on the achievement of a behavioural goal (Ajzen, 1991), Shaw *et al.* (2000) reveal that although the consumer may be faced with difficulties in decision-making, the extent to which these issues affect the individuals behaviour depends on whether the issue is central to their self-identity and on the strength of their ethical obligation. For example, where ethical obligation is perceived as being stronger than the identified control factor(s), it is highly likely that this obligation will overrule the opposing control issues and result in the individual carrying out the given behaviour. The results of this questionnaire reveal a high level of ethical obligation for all but one of the participants. Beliefs are considered important as underlying final behaviour, and further, the results reported at this stage support and substantiate the qualitative findings discussed above.

8.6 Conclusions and implications

Consistent with the theory of self-identity (e.g. Sparks and Shepherd, 1992; Shaw *et al.*, 2000), this research has revealed that ethical consumers associate many ethical issues with the purchase of fashion and clothing garments which influence their decision-making. Problematic, however, is a combination of limited ethical clothing ranges, high prices, an absence of independent company monitoring and insufficient product information, which means individuals are rarely able to make an 'ideal' choice, resulting in feelings of 'frustration' and 'confusion'. In situations where individuals are unable to purchase ethical clothing garments, these consumers maintain that they rarely experience feelings of guilt, rather demonstrating a sense of ethical obligation (e.g. Shaw *et al.*, 2000) continue to be motivated in their ethical consumption. When asked to comment on the clothing garments available from the limited number of ethical retailers, a number of participants argued that the fashionability of ethical clothing styles often fell short of their expectations. Thus, while ethical consumers commonly present the argument that they are not influenced by fashion or the fashion industry, their references to the 'fashionability' of clothing garments implies some affiliation. It could be argued that as part of a consumer society, despite their intentions to escape the allure of fashion, the consumers' responses imply that they have subconsciously become enticed into the very industry that they claim to dislike.

Despite the fact that a number of industries, including the food sector, have recognised ethical consumerism as a source of competitive advantage, few fashion companies appear to have acknowledged, or embraced, the ethical consumer movement. Furthermore, as ethical consumers remain dissatisfied with the style of ethically produced clothing garments, it appears imperative that fashion companies recognise the emergence of this rather 'untapped' niche market. Although the research findings indicate negative views of multinational organisations, it is argued here that this should not deter the fashion industry from focusing attention on developing ethical product ranges. On the contrary, in the same way as organic and fair trade grocery products have become a regular feature in most multinational supermarkets, it remains apparent that there is scope for multinational clothing companies to do the same. While it is argued that fashion companies must actively seek to present a more 'socially and ethically aware' attitude, one cannot ignore the fact that, by its very nature, fashion is rather wasteful of resources and, therefore, can be considered 'unethical'. In the same way, as an ethically conscious consumer can justify the purchase of a second-hand fur coat on the basis that it is 'recycled', it is highly probable that a similar justification process could be employed when the consumer is faced with the opportunity to purchase an 'ethically produced fashion garment'.

Regardless of how these companies embrace the notion of 'ethics', these organisations cannot underestimate the expectations of society's increasingly discerning customers. In particular these companies must recognise that ethical consumers are not only demanding that clothing garments are produced in a humane working environment, but are also challenging manufacturers, retailers and the government to provide them with validated ethical policies which meet their demands. Arguably, it is only in achieving these rigorous specifications that the fashion industry can ever hope to win over the increasing numbers of ethical consumers.

Although the findings of this research present an important insight into the various issues ethical consumers associate with the purchase of clothing garments, it is acknowledged that they do not provide an exhaustive insight into the issue of fashion, clothing and ethical consumption. It is recommended that future research build on current findings through the development of a large-scale quantitative study. This could be achieved using the Model of Ethical Consumer Decision-Making which has been successfully applied in the context of fair trade grocery choice (Shaw and Shiu, 2003). In particular, the elicited beliefs revealed through the present research provide the groundwork for the development of such an instrument. This model in the context of ethical clothing choice would serve to develop and substantiate current findings using a more broad-based respondent sample. As stated at the beginning of this chapter:

> It is just really difficult trying to be an ethical consumer. I mean I guess the food sector has kind of got it cracked but the fashion industry seems a bit more off-the-beaten track. There is just so much to consider when you buy clothes, where it is produced, how it is produced, what it is made off. It is difficult, it is just difficult!

References

Ajzen, I. (1991) The theory of planned behaviour. *Organisational Behaviour and the Human Decision Process*, **50**, 179–211.

Ajzen, I. and Fishbein, M. (1980) *Understanding Attitudes and Predicting Social Behaviour*. UK, Prentice-Hall.

Anon (1997) Clothes shops: corporate responsibility. *Ethical Consumer Magazine*, December, 6–12.

Anon (2002) Why buy ethically? An introduction to the philosophy behind ethical purchasing. www.ethicalconsumer.org, 29 April.

Bohdanowicz, J. and Clamp, L. (1994) *Fashion Marketing*. UK, Routledge.

Daft, R. (1995) *Understanding Management*. UK, The Dryden Press.

Dickson, M.A. (1999) US consumers' knowledge and concern with apparel sweatshops. *Journal of Fashion Marketing and Management*, **3**(1), 44–45.

Dickson, M.A. (2001) Utility of no sweat labels for apparel consumers: profiling label-users and predicting their purchases. *Journal of Consumer Affairs*, **35**(1), 96–119.

Doane, D. (2001) Taking flight: the rapid growth of ethical consumerism. *New Economics Foundation*. London.

Easey, M. (2002) *Fashion Marketing*. UK, Blackwell Science Ltd.

Easterby-Smith, M., Thorpe, R. and Lowe, A. (2002) *Management Research: An Introduction*. UK, Sage Publications.

Foxall, G.R. and Goldsmith, R.E. (1994) *Consumer Psychology for Marketing*. UK, Routledge.

Gabriel, Y. and Lang, T. (1997) *The Unmanageable Consumer*. UK, Sage Publications.

Greenbaum, T.L. (1998) *The Handbook of Focus Group Research*, UK, Sage Publications.

Greenpeace (2002) www.greenpeace.org

Kalafatis, S.T., Pollard, M., East, R. and Tsogas, M.H. (1999) Green marketing and Ajzen's theory of planned behavior: a cross-market examination. *Journal of Consumer Marketing*, **16**(5), 441–460.

Krueger, R.A. (1998) *Focus Groups: A Practical Guide for Applied Research*. UK, Sage Publications.

Law, C. (2000) The poisoned legacy of the cotton T-shirt. *The Times* (London), 26 April, p. 27.

Marks and Spencer (2002) Marks and Spencer Home Page. Corporate and Social Responsibility www2.marksandspencer.com/thecompany/ourcommitmenttosociety/environment. 24 April.

Maslow, A. (1970) *Motivation and Personality*. Harper and Row.

Mason, T. (2000) The importance of being ethical. *Marketing*, 26 October, p. 27.

Mintel (1994) The green consumer. *Mintel Special Report*.

Mullins, L. (1996) *Management and Organisational Behaviour*. UK, Pitman Publishing.

PETA (2002) Activists storm Paris fashion show. www.petaonline.org/search/news/row.asp

Shaw, D.S. and Clarke, I. (1999) Belief formation in ethical consumer groups: an exploratory study. *Marketing Intelligence and Planning*, **17**(2), 109–120.

Shaw, D.S. and Duff, R. (2001) Ethics and social responsibility in fashion and clothing choice. *European Marketing Academy Conference*, Portugal.

Shaw, D.S. and Shiu, E. (2003) Ethics in consumer choice: a multivariate modelling approach. *European Journal of Marketing*, **37**.

Shaw, D.S., Shiu, E. and Clarke, I. (2000) The contribution of ethical obligation and self-identity to the theory of planned behavior: an exploration of ethical consumers. *Journal of Marketing Management*, **16**, 879–894.

Smith, N.C. (1990) *Morality and the Market: Consumer Pressure for Corporate Responsibility*. UK, Routledge.

Sparks, P. and Shepherd, R. (1992) Self-identity and the theory of planned behavior: assessing the role of identification with green consumerism. *Social Psychology Quarterly*, **54**(4), 388–399.

Watson, L. (2001) Wear and care. *The Scotsman (Edinburgh)*, 17 October, p. 8.

Watt, J. (2000) Style: to die for. *The Guardian*, 24 March, p. 2.

Weadick, L. (2002) Sweating it out. *Ethical Consumer Magazine*, **76**(April/May), 12–15.

Webb, J. (1992) *Understanding and Designing Marketing Research*. UK, Academic Press.

Study questions and guideline answers

1. **Consider how in the context of fashion/clothing involvement in decision-making could increase significantly for an ethical consumer?**

Traditionally consumers have been seen as going through a number of 'cognitive stages'. For ethical consumers additional layers of decision-making would be exhibited within these stages.

Need recognition/problem awareness
Developing awareness of a product want/need. Some ethical consumers would even question their own wants. These are sometimes referred to as ethical or voluntary simplifiers, who seek to reduce their consumption levels for ethical reasons.

Information search
In order to identify alternative ways of problem solution a search may be internal or external. An internal search involves a review of relevant information from memory, including, for example personal experience and marketing communications. If a satisfactory solution is not found, then an external search is necessary. Given that ethical concerns are often ongoing and subject to change, information is critical to the ethically concerned consumer. Information could be obtained from newspapers, news programmes, documentaries,

specialist magazines like *Ethical Consumer*, environmental/ethical pressure groups, charities, some labelling, ethical clothing retailers, etc. External searching for information is critical in a fashion context where the label does not give full details of place(s) of production and codes of conduct are deemed often as a public relations exercise.

Consumer ethical concerns often do not exist in isolation but rather are interlinked, for example fair trade benefiting poorer producers vs. loss of local textile production.

The need for information to make an informed choice raises issues of information overload where there is too much information that is likely to be complex and exhibit conflicting imperatives. Also important is trust and credibility of information sources.

Evaluation of alternatives

Traditional criteria – price, quality, style and convenience (e.g. inexpensive fashionable clothes vs. child labour).

Consumers might or might not know about the wide range of issues typically included among the concerns of their affluent culture. An individual might consciously decide to assiduously avoid animal-based products but do nothing about trade inequities. Although aware of fair trade clothing products and being disposed to the underpinning arguments they chose to give their effort to animal rights by choosing to avoid fur, leather and wool. The opposite would be equally possible. Thus, due to the range of often-complex issues individuals often need to prioritise competing ethical concerns one above the other.

Purchase

Where to purchase? Mainstream or alternative retailer? Is the item(s) readily available? Is there a choice of 'ethical' retailer? Question 3 explores this issue in more detail.

Post-purchase evaluation of decision

- *Feeling* – guilt if the consumer does not make an ethical purchase, disheartened if there is difficulty in obtaining ethical products, perhaps due to availability issues, and isolation if important others do not share ethical concerns. Alternatively, good feeling can be derived from doing something about ethical beliefs, making a difference and contributing to change.
- *Product performance* – has the product performed/functioned as required both materially and semiotically. Ethical products can be bought to demonstrate to others the consumer's ethical concerns.
- *Company performance* – for example has the company moved on their ethical stance?

2. **Identify all of the important criteria in ethical consumer decision-making in fashion/clothing choice. Considering these criteria what do you judge to be the most favourable 'place' of purchase?**

Important criteria in decision-making which consist of both traditional and ethical issues to be considered:

- *Traditional criteria* – price, quality, style, convenience, etc.
- *Ethical criteria* – child labour, animal welfare, environment, working conditions, wages, corporate social responsibility, etc.

Ethical retailers

In terms of ethical criteria alternative ethical retailers exist including those that provide fair trade, organic or animal-free clothing ranges. Individuals may opt to buy from alternative retailers so they take a more active role in ethical concerns and through a desire to support alternative outlets. Further, these outlets expose consumers to ethical issues and may not survive if consumers do not support them, thus reducing ethical choices in the marketplace. Problems with some of these retailers, however, include a price that is often higher, they are not always readily accessible (often Internet or mail order based), may not be convenient if you cannot try garments on and they are limited in styles. Second-hand outlets may also be selected as they provide recycled clothing; however, you cannot ensure where the product first originated. The consumer needs to consider what is more important to them the benefits of reusing clothing or the benefits of original ethical production.

Mainstream retailers

Ethical consumers may opt to purchase from mainstream or high-street retailers to exhibit demand for ethical products and expose others to that demand. They may keep pressurising mainstream retailers to provide ethical alternatives. This would expose those consumers who would not go to alternative outlets to ethical alternatives. Further the high street is where most people shop so for ethical alternatives to enjoy wider success they need to get into the mainstream market (this is what happened for fair trade and organic foods).

3. **Exploring the ethical concerns surrounding child labour and consumer's ability to 'vote' in the marketplace what could be regarded as a socially responsible consumer response to this issue?**

Ethical principles reflect the cultural values and norms of society. The increase in globalisation has resulted in exposure to other cultural values and norms, one of which is child labour. Where cases of child labour have been uncovered for products produced for our consumption, consumers must decide whether to boycott the company(s) concerned or continue purchasing.

Boycott

To continue purchasing would send a vote to the marketplace that you were happy with that company and its practices. Children should not have to work they should go to school. Further, children should not be working to produce cheap products for Western consumption or to provide profits for Western companies.

Purchase

In some cultures children need to work to help support their families, thus working is necessary to survival. A child working is a normal part of the culture in some societies thus you are judging an aspect of that culture as wrong. The decision to stop purchasing could result in a child(ren) losing their job(s), in such a situation they may end up in more dangerous employment such as prostitution. Consumers should not boycott without first asking employees. There may be issues they are unaware off, such as the factory may be negotiating better conditions for workers. A boycott may result in a company relocating from an area resulting in loss of jobs. Although to continue purchasing is registering a positive vote you could couple that vote with action to let the company know that you wish them to change their practices. Action could include letter writing, protesting, joining a campaign group, etc. and ensuring the company knows you are a consumer of their products. Thus, instead of boycotting you could pressure the company to provide educational opportunities for young employees.

Chapter 9

A contemporary analysis of global luxury brands

Tim Jackson

Aims

The aims of this chapter are:

- to present an overview of contemporary issues facing the global luxury goods industry;
- to analyse the links between fashion and luxury;
- to provoke discussion over the credibility of mass-marketing luxury brands.

9.1 Introduction

This chapter aims to present an overview of contemporary issues facing the luxury goods industry. It reviews the links between fashion and luxury goods, and the concept of luxury in an apparently overloaded luxury market. There is a breakdown of four leading luxury brand groups although it should be noted that the large groups such as LVMH are always reviewing their company and brands portfolios. It is possible that in the currently weak global economic climate, LVMH and others may divest some brands from their portfolios thus changing the current structure of the group.

9.2 Luxury or fashion?

Today there is a strong association between the notions of luxury and fashion, as the two sectors have grown increasingly close over the last decade. However, the two concepts are not necessarily complementary as fashion is ubiquitous and ephemeral whereas luxury is rare, special and often timeless. The linkages arise, for many people these days, through their increased awareness of brands that have been revived or repositioned in the luxury brands sector. For example, brands such as Louis Vuitton, Gucci and Burberry have become highly desirable since their turnarounds in the 1990s. All possess a significant heritage based on quality and yet have successfully used fashion positioning to revitalise their brand offers.

The relationship between fashion and luxury exists in people's minds for many reasons including the fashion dynasty at the heart of many luxury brands. Names such as Chanel, Balenciaga, Givenchy and Yves Saint Laurent are fashion icons in their own right although they are also highly prestigious luxury brands with diversified portfolios of products. Contemporary designers such as Tom Ford, John Galliano, Alexander McQueen and Marc Jacobs reinforce the fashion association as they provide creative direction for the luxury

Table 9.1 International designers and luxury brand groups

Designer	Luxury brand group	Design label(s)
John Galliano	LVMH	Christian Dior and own
Tom Ford	Gucci Group NV	Gucci/YSL Rive Gauche
Alexander McQueen	Gucci Group NV	Alexander McQueen
Marc Jacobs	LVMH	Louis Vuitton and own
Julien Macdonald	LVMH	Givenchy and own
Miuccia Prada	Prada	Prada and Miu Miu
Christian Lacroix	LVMH	Emilio Pucci and own

Source: www.style.com

brands which employ them. Table 9.1 indicates the relationship between leading international designers, the luxury brand groups with which they are associated and the different labels that they work on.

Many of these designers work on collections for an established house and produce ready-to-wear (RTW) collections under their own names. John Galliano designs his own collection and is also responsible for the RTW and couture collections for Christian Dior. Following his appointment by Bernard Arnault in 1996 his role in Christian Dior is artistic director. This means that he has full responsibility for the creative direction of the Christian Dior brand including, advertising and store design and presentation. This broadening of the design role beyond solely the product is a common feature in LVMH, where Christian Lacriox and Marc Jacobs have similar roles within Emilio Pucci and Louis Vuitton. It is also the same for Tom Ford within the Gucci Group who, as the Creative Director of both Gucci and Yves Saint Laurent, is responsible for the design of all products, advertising, store design, visual display and fashion public relational (PR) activities for both the houses. These wider activities are clearly designed to create coherent brand statements within the luxury market. Tom Ford is a great exponent of such a holistic approach to branding:

> I realised a long time ago that one can either design a dress or design a brand. The exercise of designing is still the same: the same creativity, the same eye, and the same intuition are still needed, but the parameters are different. For me, there was never an option: a dress does not exist in a void, it exists in a world, and its context can radically alter its effect or its success, or its appropriateness, for that matter you must have the right product, but you must also have it beautifully produced in beautiful stores at the right time, priced in a manner that the customer perceives its value and it must be delivered with the most perfect service.
>
> Tom Ford, *International Herald Tribune Fashion Conference* (2001)

The fashion dimension of many luxury brands is further underpinned by regular global media coverage of the work and actions of their celebrity designers. For example, bi-annual fashion weeks in New York, London, Paris and Milan, together with the couture shows in Paris provide perfect media positioning opportunities for the brands to display the latest collections of their celebrity designers. These will normally feature eye-catching, provocative and directional pieces to move the brand forward and court publicity. In these instances, the statement 'all publicity is good publicity' is true as brands inject 'edginess' into their images via controversy. Further, the personalities of the designers themselves add to the positioning and image of the host brands. Many top designers appear to be exotic individuals and their designs equally mysterious. Media interest is also aroused when leading designers become associated with major fashion houses, creating great news stories, which are inevitably supported by arresting photographs of extravagant personal style, attendance of parties and runway collections. For example, the brand Christian Dior is as likely to be featured in fashion media as much for interest in its Artistic Director and Chief Designer, John Galliano, as it is for its dresses. Similarly, designers such as Tom Ford (Gucci Group NV), Stella McCartney (Gucci Group NV) and Julien Macdonald (LVMH/Givenchy) are regularly in the news due to interest in celebrity. This may be due to interest both in them and those who wear their designs at high-profile events such as film and music awards ceremonies. The designers' glamorous lifestyles and the lifestyles of those who wear their clothes reinforce consumers' aspiration and desire for the products which have exclusive and luxurious associations.

Further, fashion apparel and accessories are uniquely associated with luxury in a way that most other products are not, primarily because of the heritage of haute couture. It is common these days for there to be a 6-month waiting list for the latest 'must have', limited edition handbag form a particular luxury brand. Haute couture itself is inextricably linked to luxury after the early couturiers in Paris produced exclusive clothing for the very wealthy in society. Indeed many would argue that modern fashion began with the early couturiers such as Henry Worth and Paul Poiret who provided the wealthy elite of French and English society with exclusive designs, in the late 19th century. The subsequent evolution of couture and RTW designer collections has contributed to the strong association between fashion and luxury. However, throughout the 20th century the luxury industry has grown, consolidated and diversified to embrace designer labels from Asia, such as Comme des Garcons and the US, including Marc Jacobs.

In essence luxury brands have employed high-profile fashion designers to boost the allure of their products at a time in history when more consumers have been able to afford to buy luxury products.

9.3 What is luxury?

Luxury can mean many things according to one's point of view. In common usage it refers to an indulgence where something is experienced infrequently because it is expensive or rarely accessible. Such constraints have traditionally meant that luxury is associated with exclusivity and that conspicuous ownership or usage of a luxury brand's product is an indication of status. This fits with the theory of conspicuous consumption, conceived by Thornstein Veblen in the 19th century, which states that the reason for buying and owning goods was for prestige as opposed to consumption (in line with their function). Luxury goods have historically been made with the finest raw materials involving natural fabrics such as wool, cashmere, silk and the finest cottons for apparel products. However, new smart fabrics are providing luxury product designers with new opportunities to innovate.

However, the concept of exactly what constitutes luxury has changed over time as people in Western and selected Asian societies have become wealthier. In many Western countries it is now common for a household to possess two cars, satellite television, a digital video device (DVD) player, home computers and assorted designer fashion products ranging from clothing to perfumes. Although some of these products may appear to be essential to their owners, the selection of brand often has less to do with function and more to do with status.

However, in an increasingly crowded luxury goods market some believe that new ways of defining luxury are needed. Bulgari have diversified into hotels with an emphasis on well-being in the luxury residential experience they plan to offer. Sir Paul Smith, a strong critic of 'luxury overload' created by the big global luxury brands' marketing activity, sees luxury as something rare and personal. Certainly there is a danger that many of the big luxury brands' groups sacrifice real exclusivity for a formulaic approach to generating increased sales revenues. After all, if luxury is everywhere then true luxury is nowhere.

9.3.1 What is a luxury brand?

In theory a luxury brand should be easy to define. One would expect it to refer to a business that is distinctively associated with the world of luxury through its heritage, products and image. However, although luxury brands produce and sell a range of products ranging from apparel to Champagne the sector encompasses six product categories (Saviolo and Testa, 2000):

1. Fashion and leather goods
2. Watches and jewellery
3. Perfumes and cosmetics
4. Wines and spirits
5. Selective or other retailing
6. Other businesses (often associated with the arts).

These six categories closely reflect those listed on the LVMH web site (www.lvmh.com) to describe the make up of the LVMH Group. Examples of the range of companies included under these categories can be found later in the chapter where some of the major luxury groups are discussed.

Luxury goods are generally those which are in the top sector across a range of products including clothing, jewellery, watches, leather goods, cosmetics, fragrances and other personal goods (Lloyd-Jones, 1998). Further, luxury goods are characterised by exclusivity, premium prices, image and status, which combine to make them desirable for reasons other than function. A further perspective is provided through Morgan Stanley Dean Witter's view of the key ingredients that comprise a luxury brand. Their view is that the key ingredients are:

- Global recognition
- Critical mass
- Core competence and other products
- High product quality and innovation
- Powerful advertising
- Immaculate store presentation
- Superb customer service.

Source: Kent *et al.* (Morgan Stanley Dean Witter 2000)

Although not generally included in luxury goods categories, certain brands of motorcar are certainly luxury products. Porsche, Mercedes and Cadillac are all names that one immediately associates with image status and wealth in today's lifestyle-driven society. They meet all the conventional criteria required to be luxury goods in that they possess image and status, are priced at a premium and can be exclusive (depending on the particular model). However, the brands do not diversify significantly beyond the car market. A number of luxury brands of cars have been bought up by the larger mass-market producers in the motor industry for reasons that are similar to those of the predatory luxury fashion groups such as LVMH, Richemont and Gucci Group. Namely that the luxury brands benefit from the financial muscle of their parent group owners and the parent groups benefit from the status and quality of the brands. Volkswagen owns Bentley, Lamborghini and

Bugatti, Fiat owns Ferrari, and BMW owns Rolls Royce (*The Economist*, 2002). Interestingly neither Volkswagen nor Fiat is perceived to be a luxury brand and BMW is really a mass-market brand now, albeit a quality one.

9.4 Brand personality

Marketing theory states that a brand is a distinctive and recognisable name or symbol, which has some meaning and value for its customers. Businesses spend millions of dollars each year trying to project an appropriate image of a brand to their customers in order to differentiate one brand from another. Increasingly this differentiation leads to the individual brands developing 'personalities', which appeal to market segments or groups of customers. In addition to benefiting from powerful advertising imagery and designer personality, many luxury brands also capitalise on the perceived characteristics of their indigenous national identity.

9.5 National image

Nation branding is not a new concept but one which was conceived by Jean Baptiste Colbert, the Finance Minister in the reign of King Louise XIV of France. He first devised the 'Made in France' cachet as part of a series of measures to protect French exports and boost the pay and conditions of the French artisans (Lewis, 2002).

Luxury brands can benefit from an association with national identity. Each of the principal fashion cities Paris, Milan, New York and London is a focal point for the expression of unique national identities and attitudes. These conduits of cultural and fashion expression deliver a unique image to indigenous brands. 'French chic', 'Italian style' and 'British creativity' are all equivalents of brand values that help contribute to people's perception of the value of a product. Such national perceptions are based on the country's heritage, industrial focus and popular conceptions supported by the media and individual's travelling experiences (Table 9.2).

Rather like a business, a country's branding can change over time. Forty years ago 'Made in Britain' was considered to be a statement of quality, a claim that has sadly been undermined over time following the decimation of the UK's manufacturing base. With manufacturing a low priority for all UK governments in the latter half of the 20th century, a lack of investment into training, technology and infrastructure has resulted in overseas sourcing and many British companies being sold to foreign owners in order to survive. Britain is known for its fashion retailers and their ability to produce affordable, cutting-edge, high-street fashion. Equally, British consumers are more adventurous than their European and US counterparts, adopting new looks with little concern for the constraints of tradition and some may argue, aesthetics and good taste. However, Britain is derided

Table 9.2 Perceived national image

Country	Associated image
Italy	Art/culture
France	Art/culture
USA	Bigger/better/cheaper
Switzerland	Reliability/quality/chic
Germany	Efficiency/engineering
Japan	Aesthetic/tradition/modernity

Source: Morgan Stanley Dean Witter (2000)

for its inability to produce competitively priced designer wear in the same way the Italy can. This explains why so many British designers move their runway shows and production abroad to countries such as Italy, a country which maintains its strong manufacturing roots (Rickey, 2002). The majority of British fashion consumers prefer to buy the diffusion lines of designers, such as those available in Debenhams and the Autograph collection in M&S, or low-priced imitations of designer styles produced and sold through retailers like Topshop and Zara. There may be many reasons for this including a general lack of interest in heritage or traditional style, through to the higher prices charged by many brands in the UK for all sorts of products including fashion.

Morgan Stanley Dean Witter refers to the UK's image as being associated with traditional country living. This is an image that some foreign consumers buy into and has been the core concept to brands such as Hackett, Purdy (Richemont Group) and Burberry. However, in the case of Burberry the brand went through significant repositioning and re-branding in 1997 and is now a thriving contemporary business. A more contemporary image for the UK is one that is based on invention and creativity. *London Fashion Week* is regarded as being the exciting and radical, if 'poor relation', in the round of *International Fashion Weeks*, where new design talent can be found. It is unsurprising then that UK design talent is recognised for its creativity and employed by the better funded and commercially focused European luxury brands.

France is still considered to be the home of luxury goods industry, despite the strength of Italy and America. This is in part due to its heritage, being the home of artisan fashion skills and the centre of haute couture. France has sustained its apparel industry despite facing the same global competitive threats of cheaper production countries. Even throughout the occupation of the Second World War, La Chambre Syndicale De La Couture was still active. The Chambre Syndicale runs a Paris couture school to train designers and technicians of the couture trade. The school provides fashion education and training, supports the French fashion industry and is a great source of skilled labour and fresh talent for the couture houses. Today the luxury goods industry employs 200,000 people in France and is responsible for providing the second largest surplus in their balance of payments (www.comité-colbert.com). The Comité Colbert is the French luxury goods association that oversees the international promotion of its 67 members, with the objective of making them better known throughout the world. Its members produce over 10.67 billion Euros and include such companies as Celine, Chanel, Christian Dior, Guerlain, Givenchy, Leonard and Hermes (*ibid.*).

9.6 Quality and heritage

Product quality and heritage are two of the key characteristics that have traditionally defined a luxury brand. Many luxury brands with a long history have retained the artisan skills and customised manufacturing processes that have long been replaced with mass production by mass-market brands. In this respect heritage and authenticity have evolved from the early roots of the companies when craftsmanship was central to their success. Hermes was founded in 1837 by Thierry Hermes as a small business manufacturing harnesses and Louis Vuitton began manufacturing leather goods in 1854. Today Hermes is an elegant, classic luxury brand best known for its leather goods, and silks although it has diversified into a wide range of luxury products across all markets. Heritage is also linked to the soul or DNA of a brand. Suzy Menkes has referred to the powerful Chanel DNA created by 'Coco' Chanel and used by Karl Lagerfeld to develop 'endless variations on her image'. (Jackson, 2002)

Aldo Gucci, the son of the Founder of Gucci company Guccio Gucci, once said that quality is remembered long after price is forgotten (Forden, 2000).

Table 9.3 Global luxury goods sales by region

Europe	35%
USA	25%
Japan	20%
Rest of the world	20%

Source: Morgan Stanley Dean Witter (2000)

Historically countries have developed specialisations in the manufacturing of luxury goods. France and Italy are known for their artisan skills in leather goods and apparel production. France has a stronger heritage in perfume and cosmetics going back to some of the earliest couturiers at the end of the 19th century. Switzerland has the greatest design and production competence in watches and is strong in jewellery along with France and Italy.

9.7 Main markets

Today's wealthy Western economies offer much higher standards of living than in the immediate post Second World War period. In fact in the 1950s the luxury goods market was narrower in scope and more clearly focused on a smaller number of customers. The world of luxury was for the few who had lifestyles and access to wealth that was out of the reach and experience of the masses (Lloyd-Jones, 1998). Today there are approximately seven million High Net Worth Individuals (HNWIs) throughout the world that represent a primary market for luxury brands. These are individuals who have liquid financial assets in excess of US $1 million.

These consumers of luxury goods are more numerous and more widely dispersed geographically with the main markets being Europe, USA and Japan. Table 9.3 provides an approximate percentage breakdown of luxury goods sales by region.

9.8 Structure of the luxury goods industry

9.8.1 The major groups

The 1980s and 1990s were a period of significant change for the luxury goods industry as many of the exclusive deign houses and brands consolidated under one or other of the major luxury groups. The four dominant luxury brand groups are Moët Hennessy Louis Vuitton LVMH, Richemont, Gucci Group and Prada. In each case a luxury group has emerged from a series of strategic takeovers. This multi-brand approach to growing a business involves buying brands where there is a strategic logic, instead of investing in and growing a single brand. Key players in the formation of two groups, LVMH and Gucci Groups, are Bernard Arnault (LVMH), Francois Pinault (Pinault-Printemps-Redoute) and Domenico De Sole. Francois Pinault and Domenico De Sole became unlikely partners in 1999, as PPR struck an alliance with Gucci to buy its shares and so halt a takeover by Arnault's LVMH Group.

9.8.2 Moët Hennessy Louis Vuitton or LVMH

Moët Hennessy Louis Vuitton, or LVMH as it is more commonly known, is the largest of the European luxury brand groups. It is a group that is made up of many iconic brands representing a variety of commercial sectors after a series of mergers and acquisitions. Its mission is to represent the most refined qualities of Western 'Art de Vivre' around the world and be synonymous with both elegance and creativity.

The group operates in five principal sectors, namely:

1. Wines and spirits
2. Fashion and leather goods
3. Perfumes and cosmetics
4. Watches and jewellery
5. Selective distribution.

The product categories of LVMH and the other activities are given in Table 9.4.

Many of the brands now owned or operated by LVMH have a significant brand heritage in their own right. For example, the wine brand Château d'Yquem can be traced back to 1593 and Ruinart is the oldest Champagne brand, founded in 1729. Givenchy is a good example of a major fashion label, which has been taken over by LVMH as part of its multi-brand strategy. Givenchy is known equally well for its couture collections as it is for its perfumes. It is typical of a brand with a strong heritage that has been made contemporary by modern and innovative designers. The house began in 1952 as Hubert de Givenchy presented his first collection in Paris (De Agostini, 2000). He was successful very quickly

Table 9.4 LVMH Companies and brands (March 2003): product categories and brands

Wines & spirits	Fashion & leather goods	Perfumes & cosmetics	Watches & jewellery	Selective retailing	Other activities
Moët & Chandon	Louis Vuitton	Parfums Christian Dior	Tag Heuer	DFS	Tajan
Dom Pérignon	Loewe	Guerlain	Ebel	Miami Cruiseline Services	DI Group
Mercier	Celine	Parfums Givenchy	Zenith	Sephora	Connaissance des Arts
Ruinart	Berluti	Kenzo Parfums	Christian Dior	Le Bon Marché	Art & auction
Veuve Clicquot	Kenzo	Laflachère	Fred	La Samaritaine	sephora.com
Canard-Duchêne	Givenchy	Bliss	Chaumet		eLuxury
Krug	Christian Dior	Benefit Cosmetics	Omas		
Château d'Yquem	Christian Lacroix	Fresh	LVMH/De Beers (*joint venture*)		
Hine	Stefano Bi	Make Up For Ever			
Newton	Emilio Pucci	Michael Kors Fragrances			
Cape Mentelle	Thomas Pink	Marc Jacobs Fragrances			
Chandon Estates	Marc Jacobs	Kenneth Cole Fragrances			
Cloudy Bay Hennessy Mount Adam	Donna Karan Fendi	Acquadi Parma			

Source: www.lvmh.com

and struck up a close association with Audrey Hepburn who inspired him, wore his clothes and facilitated great publicity as an international film star. In 1957, the first perfumes were launched; Le de Givenchy and L'Interdit (*ibid.*). The perfume collection has developed to include the more modern Amarige and Organza products. Over time the house has been lead by some very high-profile British designers including John Galliano, Alexander McQueen and more recently Julien Macdonald who took over as *Chief Designer* in 2001.

9.8.3 Gucci Group NV

In 1996, the Gucci Group NV was formed following its divestment from Intercorp and has been developed into a major luxury brand group under the management of Domenico De Sole and Tom Ford. In common with the LVMH multi-brand strategy, Domenico De Sole favoured growing Gucci's business through buying and investing in strong and complementary brands. This was to avoid over extending and potentially diluting the Gucci brand, a problem which Gucci had faced in the 1970s. Today Tom Ford oversees Gucci and more recently the YSL brand following the retirement of Yves Saint Laurent from the fashion world. The Gucci Group comprises many brands while the Gucci Division refers to Gucci's own label products, approximately 45 per cent of which are leather goods. Within the group there is a combination of iconic names such as YSL and Balenciaga and contemporary designers including Alexander McQueen.

The product categories and brands of the Gucci Group are given in Table 9.5.

Another luxury group is Richemont, which is a Switzerland-based company formed in 1988 when Rembrandt Group of South Africa spun off its international operations. Few consumers may have heard of Richemont, but most would be familiar with the brands in its group, which include Dunhill, Chloe and Cartier. It inherited a number of its brands from the Vendome Luxury Group, which is now a subsidiary of Richemont. The group is much more focused on high-end jewellery and watches than any of the other multi-brand groups. It is also represented in those markets by many established and specialist brands unlike other groups which possess fashion brands that have extended into the product categories of watches and jewellery (Table 9.6).

There are many reasons for the consolidation of brands into luxury groups most of which are concerned with business and are examined later in this chapter. While this book is concerned with fashion, luxury products extend beyond the boundaries of apparel accessories and cosmetics.

Another dimension of the globalisation of brands is the evolution of family-owned artisan-based businesses into a 'corporate family' of brands within a luxury group, such as LVMH,

Table 9.5 The Gucci Group NV (March 2003): product categories and brands

Fashion & leather goods	Perfumes & cosmetics	Watches	Jewellery
Gucci	YSL Beaute	Boucheron	Boucheron
Yves Saint Laurent	Roget & Gallet	Gucci	
Sergio Rossi	Oscar de la Renta	YSL	
Bottega Veneta	Van Cleef & Arpels	Bedat & Co	
Alexander McQueen	Fendi		
Stella McCartney	Boucheron		
Balenciaga	Alexander McQueen		
	Ermengildo Zegna		

Source: www.guccigroup.com

Table 9.6 The Richemont Group of brands (March 2003): product categories and brands

Jewellery	Accessories	Watches	Clothing
Cartier	Cartier	Cartier	Chloé
Van Cleef & Arpels	Montblanc	Piaget	Hackett
Piaget	Dunhill	A. Lange & Sohne	Dunhill
	Lancel	Vacheron Constantin	Old England
	Chloe	Jaeger-LeCoultre	Purdey
	Hackett	Panerai	Shanghai Tan
	Old England	Baume & Mercier	
	Purdey	IWC	
	Shanghai Tan	Dunhill	
	Montegrappa	Montblanc	
		Van Cleef and Arpels	

Source: www.richemont.com

Table 9.7 Composition of the Prada Group's brand portfolio

Brand	2001 net revenues (%)
Prada/Miu Miu	83
Jil Sander/Church's/Helmut Lang	16
Alaia/Car Shoe/Genny	1

Source: Bertelli, *International Herald Tribune Conference* (2002)

Table 9.8 Prada brands' product contribution to group revenue

Product category	2001 net revenues (%)
Bags and accessories	39
RTW	35
Shoes	25
Other	1

Source: Bertelli *International Herald Tribune Conference* (2002)

Gucci and Richemont. Each group has a shared creative direction and a clear profit goal. Whereas once the focus of an individual brand was principally on 'the product' it has shifted to ensuring 'shareholder value' for the group.

9.8.4 Prada

Prada was formed in 1913 when it started producing leather goods and opened its first Prada boutique in Milan. Since then it has become a multi-brand group with 10 brands across a range of product categories, although it has maintained its privately owned status. In common with companies in many sectors it has held back from flotation due to the volatility of global stock markets (Table 9.7).

The business operates principally in the product categories of fashion clothing (RTW), shoes and accessories (Table 9.8).

Brand	Product categories						
	Bags	Accessories	Shoes	RTW	Eye-wear	Skincare	Fragrance
Prada	☺	☺	☺	☺	☺	☺	
Miu Miu	☺	☺	☺	☺	☺		
Jil Sander	☺	☺	☺	☺	☺	☺	☺
Helmut Lang	☺	☺	☺	☺	☺		☺
Genny		☺	☺	☺	☺		☺

Figure 9.1 The expanding Prada Group product portfolio
Source: Bertelli *International Herald Tribune Conference* (2002)

9.8.5 Multi-brand expansion

The expansion of luxury brands throughout the 1970s and 1980s was largely achieved through the use of licensing in order to increase sales. In the 1990s control over the manufacturing and retailing of luxury products was important to the success of individual luxury brands. Today the focus is on brand management as luxury groups aim to grow sales with a range of prestige brands, each with different investment needs and cost structures. In the luxury sector the multi-brand strategy is an effective means of increasing sales without the risk of over-extending individual brands.

The sheer diversity of product categories and global distribution across the various brands within a group means that at least some part of the business is guaranteed to be doing well. There are however significant problems with managing a diverse group of brands with broad product portfolios and varying investment needs and profit potential. Generally, predatory companies believe they can improve the performance of the target company through synergies, investment in growing the business, cutting out costs and improving efficiency.

Another trend in the luxury goods industry has been brands or luxury brand groups seeking a stock market listing. The rationale for this is to access significantly greater financial resources in order to generate growth. Sales growth costs money as it depends on investment in product design, production facilities, distribution and image communication. The latter is particularly important for luxury brands which have a higher advertising to sales spend than mass-market fashion retailers. Typically luxury brands' advertising budgets are between six and 12 per cent of sales. As investment levels increase so, businesses need to reach a critical mass in size of turnover and scale of operations to manage the costs and generate the required return on investment.

Once a brand or group of brands becomes a public company then it has to grow its business to satisfy shareholder expectations and return on investment requirements. The dilemma then becomes how to grow the business without over-exposing and thus diluting the brand(s). There is going to be a limit to the growth of a luxury brand and so companies build a portfolio of brands to generate the revenues and profits. However, some in the industry would argue that is risky to diversify into new product markets until a business has become a market leader in its core business.

Another benefit of the multi-brand strategy is the opportunity to access new markets through taking over new businesses. Prada is an example of a multi-brand group that has been able to enter a new market through its newly acquired brands. Figure 9.1 shows the group's entry into the fragrance market following takeovers of the Jil Sanders, Helmut Lang and Genny brands.

9.8.6 Management and creative partnerships

A key factor in the success of a luxury business is achieving the right balance between creativity and business management. Ralph Toledano, Chairman and Chief Executive Officer of Chloe believes

> There is almost no example of a successful story in our industry which is not based on a foundation of two people. In France, Christian Dior becomes very quickly the duo Christian Dior and Jacques Rouet; Yves Saint Laurent is the pair of Yves Saint Laurent and Pierre Bergé; in the past 20 years Chanel is certainly personified by Karl Lagerfeld, but Alain Wertheimer is discretely running the business.
>
> Toledano, *International Herald Tribune Conference* (2001)

This also holds true in the case of the Gucci Group where Domenico De Sole runs the business and Tom Ford is responsible for all things creative. It is the same for Prada where Patrizio Bertelli and Miuccia Prada have similar roles to those in Gucci.

9.8.7 Distribution

Traditionally, luxury brands have used a combination of selective licensing, wholesaling and retailing to sell products to their global customers. Wholesaling has tended to target-specific department stores and boutiques with an appropriate market profile. Such strategies have enabled brands to achieve global coverage relatively quickly, which is important since global recognition is a key success factor for a luxury brand. It is more difficult for a luxury brand to succeed if it is only located in one place as its customers tend to be global travellers. However, towards the end of the 1990s many luxury brands realised the importance of managing the customer experience at the point of sale. The best opportunity for them to do this is through their own retail outlets. These are known as directly operated stores in the luxury goods industry.

Directly operated stores enable brands to reinforce their image communication through establishing a physical presence in a prestige shopping location and to influence its customers' shopping experience at the point of sale. The latter is important when customers feel the need for greater product knowledge as a consequence of higher-price points. Product merchandising, innovative store design and visual merchandising of the selling space all help create the magic and theatrical ambience needed to present an impression of luxury.

However there is a distinction between *hard products* (which include watches and jewellery) and *soft products* (which include apparel and cosmetics). In general, soft products are sold through retail outlets either directly operated of franchised whereas hard products tend to be sold through wholesaling to specialists. Table 9.9 shows the different emphasis in choice of distribution between two of the largest luxury brands. Historically, Louis Vuitton has preferred to sell through its own stores.

Table 9.9 Distribution channels for Gucci and Louis Vuitton in 2000

Brand	Wholesale soft brands	DOS/franchise
Gucci Division	262	186
Louis Vuitton	37	310

Source: Merrill Lynch (2002)

However, it is interesting to note that Gucci Timepieces used a network of 6500 selected distributors to wholesale its watches through (Merrill Lynch, 2002). This reinforces the point that consumers tend to purchase watches and jewellery from independent specialist boutiques or department stores.

9.9 Luxury unlimited?

Throughout 2002 there has been continued debate within the luxury goods industry and associated media, over the 'democratisation of luxury' and the implications for many modern luxury brands. The concerns centre on the broadening of the customer base for many brands to include aspirational customers who are not typical buyers of luxury brands' products. Such customers tend to buy small items such as accessories in order to be seen owning a prestige label. However such customers only identify with the brand on a superficial level creating the potential for them to desert the brand according to fashion trends. Umberto Angeloni, the Chief Executive Officer for the Bironi Group, has recognised this and expressed concern at brands building their businesses on sales derived from such a broader customer base. In his view,

> the downside of the more aggressive version of such a global brand strategy has been: (a) growing dilution, both of a brand's customer base (no longer only affluent) and of its essence (no longer related to the core product or to its cultural identity), (b) diminishing loyalty on the part of the consumer (brand substitution). The rather extensive sales declines experienced by some global brands during the past 12 months may be explained by these factors. In other words, it would seem that a good proportion of what was sold in the last 10 years was 'aspirational demand' of 'quasi-luxury products' by mainstream consumers. This demand is intrinsically more volatile in times of recession (Angeloni, 2001). As if to support this the innovative American designer Roy Halston remarked, at the height of his fame in the 1970s, that You're only as good as the people you dress (Arnold, 2000).

Sir Paul Smith, arguably England's most commercially successful international fashion designer has been very critical of the expansion of many luxury brands through what he describes as 'corporate roll-outs'. At the *Annual International Herald Tribune Luxury Conference* in Paris last year he said,

> Everybody is doing it: There is luxury overload. Luxury used to be rare and special, but there is too much of it with the corporate roll-outs. Whether you are in Harrods or Tiffany there is not one chic customer.
>
> Menkes (2002)

His view undoubtedly supports the argument that for real luxury to exist its accessibility must be restricted. This view is slightly at odds with that of Ralph Lauren whose label is founded on the concept of an aspirational lifestyle. To him the very word 'luxury' is outdated:

> The word luxury is almost old fashioned. I have a very different philosophy on luxury – to me it is the right pair of jeans that fit well and could be any brand. I call it design led quality.
>
> Menkes (2002)

Another American fashion executive, Rose Marie Bravo of Burberry, is also a believer in the concept of 'accessible luxury' as expressed through the ubiquitous Burberry check, which she has helped to make desirable again.

A final thought is a pragmatic statement about luxury from Tom Ford. In an interview with the fashion writer Colin McDowell in 2002 he said,

> The sad thing about exclusivity is that it's a luxury that a successful firm can't afford. Fashion businesses are based on product. No sales means no business.
>
> McDowell (2002)

This is of course the ultimate dilemma facing any luxury brand.

References

Arnold, R. (2000) Luxury and restraint: minimalism in 1990s fashion. In White, N. and Griffiths (eds), *The Fashion Business, Theory, Practice, Image, Berg.* Oxford International Publishers Ltd.

Angeloni, U. (2001) *International Herald Tribune Conference (Fashion 2001 – The Business and The Brand)*, Hotel George V, Paris.

Bertelli, P. (2002) *International Herald Tribune Conference (Fashion 2002 – Luxury Unlimited)*, Hotel George V, Paris.

De Agostini (2000) *Fragrance and Fashion.* Silverdale Books. *The Economist* (2002) Every cloud has a silver lining. 23 March, pp. 83–85.

Ford, T. (2001) *International Herald Tribune Conference (Fashion 2001 – The Business and The Brand)*, Hotel George V, Paris.

Forden, G. S. (2000) *The House of Gucci.* UK, Morrow Publications.

Jackson, T. (2002) Gucci Group – the new family of luxury brands. *International Journal of New Product Development and Innovation Management*, June/July, 161–172.

Kent, C., Macdonald, S. and Deex, M. (2000) Luxury status, achieving and exploiting it. *November Industry Report*, Morgan Stanley Dean Witter.

Lewis, E. (2002) Nation branding – national pride and prejudice. *Brand Strategy*, June, 20–21.

Lloyd-Jones, T. (1998) *Luxury Goods Retailing – Strategies for Global Growth.* London, FT Retail and Commerce.

McDowell, C. (2002) Tom Ford, he's got it. *Sunday Times Style Magazine*, 8 September, pp. 29–32.

Menkes, S. (2002) Is luxury's triangle eternal? *International Herald Tribune*, 5 December.

Merrill Lynch (2002) *Lap of Luxury – Do Giant Stores Mean Giant Killers?* 20 February.

Rickey, M. (2002) Is this the godfather of British fashion? How to spend it? *Weekend Financial Times*, October, p.10.

Saviolo, S. and Testa, S. (2000) *Le Impresse del Sistema Moda.* Italy, Etas, pp. 70–80.

Toledano, R. (2001) *International Herald Tribune Conference (Fashion 2001 – The Business and The Brand)*, Hotel George V, Paris.

Web sites
www.comitecolbert.com
www.guccigroup.com
www.lvmh.com
www.richemont.com
www.style.com

Study questions and guideline answers

1. What does luxury mean?

For luxury to have any real meaning it must refer to something rare or special, which is experienced infrequently. As society has become more open and egalitarian, so fewer products and brands are 'out of reach' for the ordinary person. This greater brand awareness and achievable aspiration has created problems for many 'luxury brands' that are positioned as exclusive labels. A number of leading figures in the fashion and luxury industry are arguing that the word luxury is no longer relevant. Patrizio Bertelli, of Prada, has suggested that the industry moves away from using the term and focus on changes in people's lifestyles to generate new product and service opportunities. However, it is a natural human condition that some people will want to be different from others and may chose to define this through the ownership of rare and beautiful things.

2. How is a luxury brand different from a fashion brand?

Although most luxury apparel and accessories are also referred to as high-end fashion, it is not the case that all luxury brands' products are fashion oriented. For example the LVMH luxury brands group includes brands that sell wines and spirits and Richemont includes luxury brands that sell pens and even shotguns. The relationship between haute couture and luxury brands has provided a strong fashion designer dimension to luxury. The relationship between luxury, designers and fashion has become more complex and involved over recent years as fast-changing mass-market fashion is frequently inspired by the 'high-end' designer collections of the luxury brands' fashion houses. It is not uncommon to see Topshop's own-label cleverly reproducing Marc Jacobs. Chanel and Bulgari are some of the brands whose products are not really accessible to the average person, with the exception of their fragrance products.

3. What are the pros and cons of pursuing a multi-brand strategy?

A luxury brand may grow its business through buying other luxury brands to allow it to increase its sales revenues without risking individual brand dilution through overexposure. A luxury brand may be able to access important design talent and production facilities through the acquisition of a new brand. Similarly, a luxury group may be able to enter a new market more effectively through the existing business activities of a newly acquired brand. However, there are risks associated with this as new businesses may have different corporate cultures and methods of working. For example, when Prada Group acquired the Jil Sander brand, the designer Jil Sander left the label. Some in the industry believe that if the multi-brand acquisition is a diversification then it should only be attempted if the predatory brand is a market leader in its core-business area. This is to avoid any weakening of the core-business activity that might arise from investing in the takeover target.

Chapter 10

International bank retailing: identifying cross-cultural differences in consumers' service-quality expectations

Anne Smith

10.1 Introduction

Over two decades ago, Carman and Langeard (1980) argued that out-of-country market expansion is a more risky strategy for a service firm than, for example, concentric diversification or new service development in existing markets. Similarly, they show how out-of-country expansion is more risky for a service business than it is for a manufacturer of physical items. A major element of risk relates to the mode of market entry. Since a feature generally attributed to service industries is 'inseparability' or 'simultaneous production and consumption'[1] there is less potential for lower-risk entry modes such as exporting. Consequently, the potential for incremental expansion is less than for physical goods, and a higher level of commitment of financial and other resources is required. Risk also increases with lack of familiarity with the features of diverse environments, for example, political and legal imperatives; nature of the infrastructure and business customs and practice. As risk increases so too does the need for valid and reliable information for decision-making and control. Yet many authors have commented on the lack of research concerning international services (Eriksson *et al.*, 1999; Knight, 1999). McGoldrick and Ho (1992) for example, state that 'reliable, comparative information on market conditions remains a major problem; retailers must often base location decisions abroad on far less sophisticated information than their location decisions at home' (p. 61). Further, they add, 'why should retailers assume that the same pattern of needs and solutions will apply worldwide?' (p. 72).

Conversely, service quality has been described as the most researched area of services marketing (Bitner, 1993). A major reason for such interest is the underlying assumption that

---

[1] The product is consumed as it is produced and therefore requires the physical presence of both service provider and consumer.

consumers' service-quality perceptions, satisfaction and behaviours, such as word-of-mouth recommendation and repeat patronage, are related. Yet, despite a considerable amount of mono-cultural research, very little is known as to how consumers from different cultures evaluate service quality and how this relates to their intended and actual behaviour.

A fundamental decision area for international service management is whether, and to what extent, adaptation of products and processes is necessary for the various markets in which they operate. Consumer research is a vital component in determining service design and evaluation, but there are considerable problems involved in collecting and analysing cross-cultural data as will be highlighted later.

10.2 Aims

The aims of this chapter are:

■ to examine how consumers from different cultures evaluate services and some of the issues involved in collecting such information;
■ to examine how consumers' service-quality expectations might differ across cultures;
■ to explore how relationships between consumer perceived service quality and behaviour might vary cross-culturally;
■ to highlight the problems of cross-cultural data collection and in particular, to study
  – the need for equivalence,
  – the potential impact of response styles when establishing data comparability.

In particular, the focus will be on banking services, an industry which Donthu and Yoo (1998) argue is one of the most dramatic examples of service internationalisation, and specifically on retail or consumer banking. Many examples and illustrations, however, are drawn from other service industries and are also relevant to discussion of retailing of physical goods – fashion, grocery, etc. Griffin *et al.* (2000) have argued that a consistent finding of research into consumers' shopping and their interaction with retail environments is that 'value derives not only by the acquisition of goods, but also through the degree of gratification derived from the process itself' (p. 34). Yet little research in retailing focuses on the service process (Homburg *et al.*, 2002). This chapter emphasises the importance of the service encounter, defined by Solomon *et al.* (1985, p. 100) as 'face-to-face interactions between a buyer and a seller in a service setting'. They emphasise the dyadic nature of service interactions and the central element of role performances. Further, they argue, 'the root cause of many provider/client interface problems is the failure of participants to read from a common script' (Solomon *et al.*, 1985, p. 102). As discussed later, since definitions of culture emphasise differences in values, beliefs and behaviours there is significant potential for common scripts to differ cross-culturally. First through the context of banking, and other forms of retailing, within the international services sector will be examined.

10.3 International retailing within a services context/the impact of technology

The growing emphasis on service-sector internationalisation has focused attention on groupings reflecting differences relevant to international management (see e.g. Patterson and Cicic, 1995; Lovelock and Yip, 1996; Cicic *et al.*, 1999). Lovelock and Yip (1996) for example, suggest three types of services:

■ *People processing* – which involves tangible actions to customers.
■ *Possession processing* – which involves tangible actions to physical objects.
■ *Information-based services* – which involves collecting, manipulating, interpreting and transmitting data to create value.

The authors suggest that the degree of international adaptation is the highest when 'people processing' is involved. The classification of Patterson and Cicic (1995), along with the two dimensions of 'degree of tangibility' and 'degree of face-to-face contact' emphasises that the costs and risks of internationalisation are perceived as higher by organisations supplying highly intangible (or pure) services. These require a local presence, together with a high degree of customisation through personal contact, in markets which potentially exhibit cultural distance from the country of origin. A potential location within the matrix for both retail banking and clothing/grocery retail is illustrated in Figure 10.1.

Clearly, although one type of service delivery may dominate in a particular sector, such categorisations need not necessarily be industry specific (as e.g. the UK Standard Industrial Classification (SIC) codes). Developments in information technology may reduce the need for personal interaction and consequently for the proximate location of branches/outlets. As the nature of retail banking, grocery and clothing retail potentially changes (as illustrated in Figure 10.1) with alternative modes of delivery, so too do the criteria which consumers evaluate and the nature of the standardisation/adaptation decision.

Where tangible goods are a key feature of the service transaction, these will form an important element of consumer evaluation. The requirement to adapt tangible goods for the different needs of national markets is well documented (see e.g. Keegan, 1996) and is not the focus of this chapter. Rather it is the nature of the intangible service element which augments the physical product and is comparable with other service operations such as retail banking. Indeed the diversification strategies of many retailers into financial services, illustrates the existence of some common service features. Additionally, as will be discussed later, researchers (Parasuraman *et al.*, 1988, 1991, 1994a) have sought to establish generic criteria and traits which consumers evaluate across all service industries. It is the way in which these differ across cultures which is of interest here. An additional feature illustrated by Figure 10.1 is the potential for retailing organisations to adopt technology-based distribution methods in order to reduce costs and/or increase market share. Again adaptation of this strategy may be necessary for national markets, in view of differences in cultural acceptance of technology-based services.

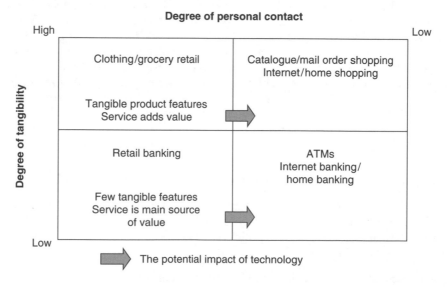

Figure 10.1 Categorising retail banking and other forms of retail distribution within an international services context

Source: Adapted from the two-dimensional matrix of Patterson and Cicic (1995)

A number of researchers have examined attitudes towards technologically delivered banking services in a variety of countries. Polatoglu and Ekin (2001) for example, consider the importance of Internet banking to the banking sector of an emerging economy such as Turkey. It might be assumed that cultural differences will erode over time as national income increases, globalisation advances and requirements for convenience and speed replace traditional modes of behaviour as banking customers around the world 'homogenise'. de Mooij and Hofstede (2002) however, argue that although differences in national wealth can explain differences in ownership and usage of products up to a point; culture becomes a more useful explanatory variable after that point is reached. They highlight how cultural factors impact on the ways in which the Internet is used, and that acceptance of the Internet, and in particular e-commerce, varies in ways which can be explained by differences in the cultural factors described in the next section.

10.4 Examining cross-cultural differences: problems of defining and classifying culture

Ingold (1999), states that 'no concept is more contentious in cultural anthropology than the concept of culture itself' (p. 191). He describes the compilation, over 30 years ago, of 161 different definitions since which time the number has continued to increase. Similarly, Usunier (1996) describes how 'many definitions have been formulated for culture: because it is a vague abstract notion, there are many candidates for the ultimate definition' (p. 4). Among those which he highlights are, Linton's (1945) 'learned behaviours' which are 'shared and transmitted by members of a particular society' and Goodenough's (1971) emphasis on 'beliefs or standards'.

This lack of consensus underlies the complexity involved in distinguishing between, and comparing across cultures. In the comparative service-quality studies discussed in this chapter, nation is often used as a proxy measure for culture, although the two are not synonymous. Religious norms and beliefs, for example, transgress national boundaries while behaviours and standards of groups (e.g. by ethnicity) within one nation may be distinguished. Naroll (1970) argues that it is often difficult to define the boundaries of a particular culture or to identify exactly which of several competing cultures an individual belongs to. Gerrard and Cunningham (1997) for example, found differences between Muslim and non-Muslim customers of Singapore banks, particularly relating to attitudes towards payment of interest. Individuals may therefore be from one culture (as defined by nation) but exhibit characteristics that more closely resemble the norms of others. Conversely, the intra-cultural heterogeneity of needs and preferences, attributed to differences in age, gender, income level, etc., is well recognised and forms the basis of the segmentation and targeting strategies of the retail banks.

While acknowledging the inherent complexity of examining 'cross-cultural' consumer attitudes and behaviour, service-quality researchers generally adopt Hofstede's (1980, 1991) original typology of individualism/collectivism, masculinity/femininity, power distance and uncertainty avoidance (for an explanation of these cultural characteristics see Figure 10.2). Hofstede's study of IBM's worldwide subsidiary employees conducted in the late 1960s/early 1970s classified 55 countries according to four variables (see Figure 10.3) highlighting the need to adapt management theories and practices to differences in these cultural dimensions.

Typically, service-quality studies will attempt to distinguish between countries exhibiting high scores on individualism and low scores on power distance such as Great Britain, the US and Australia, and those where the converse is true; for example, Hong Kong, India and Singapore (see later sections for details of these studies). Individual comparisons also focus on differences in other dimensions including long-term/short-term orientation (The Chinese Culture Connection, 1987). Later added to Hofstede's original four dimensional, long-term-oriented cultures (often a feature of East Asian countries) have a pragmatic

Power distance – The extent to which the less-powerful members of organisations and institutions (like the family) accept and expect that power is distributed unequally (i.e. inequality defined from below).

Individualism versus collectivism – Individualism on the one side versus its opposite; collectivism is the degree to which individuals are integrated into groups. In individual societies, ties between individuals are loose and individuals look after themselves and immediate families. Collectivist societies involve strong loyal cohesive groups (often extended families).

Masculinity versus femininity – Refers to the distribution of roles between the sexes .... The women in feminine countries have the same modest, caring values as the men; in the masculine countries they are somewhat assertive and competitive, but not as much as the men, so that these countries show a gap between men's values and women's values.

Uncertainty avoidance – Deals with a society's tolerance for uncertainty and ambiguity ... indicates to what extent a culture programmes its members to feel either uncomfortable or comfortable in unstructured situations (i.e. situations which are 'novel, unknown, surprising and difficult').

Figure 10.2 Hofstede's four original cultural dimensions
Source: Hofstede (1994) also see Hofstede (1980, 1991)

	PD	**UA**	**I**	**M**
UK	35	35	89	66
USA	40	46	91	62
Australia	36	51	90	61
Hong Kong	68	29	25	57
India	77	40	48	56
Singapore	74	8	20	48

Measured on index scales from 0 to 100.
Notes: PD, power distance; UA, uncertainty avoidance; I, individualism versus collectivism; M, masculinity versus feminity.

Figure 10.3 Extract of values of Hofstede's four original cultural dimensions for countries examined in service-quality studies
Source: Hofstede (1980)

future – oriented perspective valuing thrift and perseverance. Short-term orientation implies a respect for tradition and a conventional historic or short-term perspective. de Mooij and Hofstede (2002) state that usage of several financial products is related to this cultural dimension. Long-term-oriented cultures, for example, prefer cash or debit cards, whereas consumers with a short-term orientation (e.g. from the UK and US) prefer credit card transactions.

Further distinctions are made between high and low context cultures (Hall and Hall, 1990). The former, which describes Eastern/Asian cultures, adopts less verbal communication modes, whereas the latter (Western cultures) endorse more explicit communication which is direct and unambiguous. As service encounters typically involve personal interaction, it follows that expectations of communication patterns, together with other service features, will vary among cultures.

10.5 Determinants of consumers' service-quality evaluation

Over the last two decades, mono-cultural studies have focused on a wide range of service industries, including retail banking, to examine some key questions with respect to consumers' service-related attitudes and behaviours. These same questions are now being addressed by cross-cultural researchers who aim to identify similarities across, and differences between, various cultural groups. Consumer-perceived service quality is generally defined and conceptualised as a comparison by consumers of their expectations of a service with their perceptions and which results in a service gap. (In order to measure this gap, a multi-item measurement scale – SERVQUAL – was developed. As this has been adopted by the majority of cross-cultural studies discussed later, for those not familiar with the scale, the key features are outlined in the Appendix.) Culture has been described as a key variable in determining service expectations as these relate to the norms of a particular consumer group. They represent what consumers feel is appropriate to a particular situation, that is, what 'should be done' or 'what is important to them'.

When exploring the nature of the service features (or traits) which consumers evaluate, a general distinction is made between process (how the service is delivered) and outcome (what is delivered). Mattila (1999) in her study of hotel services found an overall difference in the relative weighting of process and outcome between Asian consumers, who were more concerned with the quality-of-service interactions, that is the process dimension, and Westerners who were more interested in rapid completion of service process and more focused on outcomes. Other researchers (e.g. Kettinger *et al.*, 1995; Imrie *et al.*, 2000) have also suggested an 'Asian factor' focusing on courtesy/politeness. Winsted (1997a) describes how 'courtesy', as a feature of service delivery, can be expected to be of greater importance to Japanese consumers due to their focus on harmony and status. She describes eight potential service encounter dimensions (i.e. authenticity, caring, control, courtesy, formality, friendliness, personalisation and promptness) which will impact on service encounter satisfaction according to the cultural values of the respondent. With respect to authenticity, for example, she argues that this is of much more importance to the satisfaction of US customers than for those from Japan due to the US focus on individualism and the Japanese focus on harmony, privacy and roles.

A substantial amount of research in the UK and elsewhere has examined the nature of bank customers' service satisfaction and quality expectations. Johnson (1997) for example (based on Herzberg *et al.*'s (1959) approach of distinguishing between 'satisfiers' and 'dissatisfiers') describes how for U.K. consumers, increasing the speed of processing information and customers will have a positive impact on satisfaction. Many mono-cultural researchers have examined the broad dimensions/determinants underlying consumers' evaluation of retail-banking services (see e.g. Leblanc and Nguyen, 1988; McDougall and Levesque, 1994; Bahia and Nantel, 2000), and like those researchers focusing on other service sectors (e.g. Finn and Lamb (1991) examine the dimensionality of service quality within a retail setting) often adopt the SERVQUAL methodology (Parasuraman *et al.*, 1988, 1991). Based on the tenet that five generic interrelated dimensions underlie consumer' service-quality evaluation, this model focuses largely on the service-delivery process. Only the reliability dimension includes traits more easily associated with outcome, that is the service is performed when promised and dependably (for an explanation of the five service-quality dimensions see Figure 10.4).

Although criticised by many researchers who suggest that there are more (Carman, 1990) or fewer (Mels *et al.*, 1997) dimensions, this model remains central to both mono-cultural and, more recently, cross-cultural studies of consumers' service-quality evaluations. Indeed, administration of the SERVQUAL questionnaire to respondents from different cultures has been commonplace. Yet rarely are perceived differences attributed to cultural factors.

> *Tangibles* – Physical facilities, equipment and appearance of personnel.
> *Reliability* – Ability to perform the promised service dependably and accurately.
> *Responsiveness* – Willingness to help customers and provide prompt service.
> *Assurance* – Knowledge and courtesy of employees and their ability to inspire trust and confidence.
> *Empathy* – Caring, individualised attention the firm provides its customers.

Figure 10.4 The SERVQUAL dimensions
Source: Parasuraman (1988)

   Two studies (Donthu and Yoo, 1998; Furrer *et al.*, 2000) however, have specifically examined the service expectations of retail-banking consumers from a variety of cultures.[2] Both assessed respondents' cultural characteristics by reference to Hofstede's classification criteria and adopted the SERVQUAL model. Although there are a number of disparities between the two studies, their findings indicate that the relative importance of service-quality dimensions varies according to cultural background. Donthu and Yoo, for example, describe how individualistic consumers will typically require higher levels of service quality and value responsiveness, speed and efficiency. They argue that these customers are more independent and self-centred and, due to their drive and self-responsibility ethic, demand that others be efficient.

   Furrer *et al.* (2000) emphasise the importance of distinguishing between male and female customer-contact staff with respect to the masculinity/femininity dimension of Hofstede, since expectations of gender roles differ. Secondly, the need to stipulate whether frequent or infrequent service encounters are the norm for that particular service organisation/customer relationship. They argue, as does Donthu and Yoo, that consumers will generally perceive less risk and uncertainty when engaged in frequent encounters, therefore expectations (particularly those related to cultural levels of uncertainty avoidance) may differ across service sectors. Finally, when addressing the relationship between power distance and service-quality expectations, the nature of the perceived power relationship between service provider and consumer should be assessed. (For example, for retail banking, service employees may be perceived to have expert power as opposed to grocery retail.) It is argued that weak customers from cultures which exhibit high power distance (i.e. those who accept and expect that others will be more powerful) are more likely to tolerate service failure and to value assurance as a service feature.

   A recent emphasis in the mono-cultural literature has been on the retail environment or 'servicescape' (see McGoldrick and Pieros, 1998; Baker *et al.*, 2002; Turley and Chebat, 2002). The usual focus is on the shopping environment but there is evidence that retail banks are adopting branch design ideas from the fashion retail sector (Fischbacher and Smith, 2001) Mattila's (1999) study of hotel customers, suggests that those from Western cultural backgrounds are more likely to rely on tangible cues from the physical environment than Asian customers when evaluating service quality. Cross-cultural retail-banking studies suggest differences in the role of tangibles – physical facilities, appearance of staff in consumer evaluation. It is suggested that, in cultures with a large power distance, tangibles which help to maintain distance are important to 'weak' customers and to those from individualistic cultures who also prefer to maintain a distance between themselves and the service provider (Furrer *et al.*, 2000). The ways in which perceptions of space and

---

[2]Donthu and Yoo (1998) include respondents from the US, Canada, Great Britain and India. Furrer *et al.* (2000) include masters level students from the US and Switzerland, together with a range of international students, including a number based in Singapore.

Segment	Cultural profile	Major expectations of service quality
Followers	Power distance (M) Collectivism (H) Masculinity (H) Uncertainty avoidance (N)	Assurance Most important
Balance seekers	Power distance (L) Collectivism (H) Masculinity (N) Uncertainty avoidance (N)	Moderate importance to all dimensions except tangibles which are low
Self-confidents	Power distance (L) Individualism (H) Femininity (M) Uncertainty avoidance (L)	Reliability and responsiveness are important; low importance to assurance
Sensory seekers	Power distance (H) Individualism (M) Masculinity (H) Uncertainty avoidance (L)	Extremely high importance to tangibles only
Functional analysers	Power distance (L) Individualism (M) Femininity (H) Uncertainty avoidance (H)	Extremely high importance to reliability and responsiveness; moderate importance to empathy

Notes: For power distance/individualism/collectivism/masculinity/femininity/uncertainty avoidance H, high; L, low; N, neutral; M, medium.

Figure 10.5 Cross-cultural differences in service-quality expectations: potential for international market segmentation of retail-banking services
Source: Extract from Furrer *et al.* (2000)

proximity vary cross-culturally have been described by Hall (1966) and have implications for retail design. Cultural differences with respect to colour schemes, queuing systems, etc. should also be recognised (see Usunier, 1996).

Furrer *et al.* (2000) suggest cultural groupings of retail-banking consumers that could be used as the basis for international market segmentation. Although based on a relatively small sample, these findings suggest the potential for developing service-quality strategies which are appropriate to consumer requirements of differing national cultures (see Figure 10.5).

A final consideration relates to the exact nature of staff behaviours which consumers evaluate within the broad dimensions described earlier. Behaviours are important elements of 'culture' and, it has been suggested, may be more problematic for service organisations who are involved in inter-cultural service delivery – where consumers from one culture encounter service providers from another, for example, airlines, restaurants, retailers and banks. Findings from one study (Stauss and Mang, 1999) however, suggest that inter-cultural encounters can be perceived as less problematic than intra-cultural encounters. They explain this finding in terms of attribution theory – in inter-cultural encounters consumers may explain differences or service 'failures' in terms of their own lack of knowledge and understanding. For intra-cultural encounters however, consumers expect behaviours which concur with their own cultural values and beliefs. Consumers from high context cultures, for example, will emphasise elements of non-verbal communication such as posture, hand gestures and facial expression. Winsted (1997a) describes how behaviour in Japan is formalised and ritualised politeness is extremely important, but friendliness may be considered impolite. Additionally, customers accustomed to great power distance, and who see themselves in a superior position will judge a service employee's behaviour as an affront if they perceived an attitude of superiority (Stauss and Mang, 1999). Despite the considerable number of mono-cultural studies, which have examined service quality determinants/dimensions, only recently have researchers begun to address the nature of consumers' expectations of service behaviours and to examine whether these differ across service industries and cultures. Examination of consumers' own service-related behaviours (such as repeat patronage) however, has been of major interest.

10.6 Relationships between consumers' service-quality evaluation and their behaviour: evidence of cross-cultural differences

Of substantial interest to both researchers and management are the relationships between consumers' service experiences and evaluations, and consequent service-related behaviours and attitudes. A substantial number of mono-cultural studies have examined the relationships depicted in the simplified representation below (see Figure 10.6). The relationship between the constructs 'service quality' and 'satisfaction', for example, has been hotly debated over the years in term of pattern of antecedence, causality, temporal distinctions, etc. (for further discussion see e.g. Oliver, 1993; Bitner and Hubbert, 1994; Gotlieb *et al.*, 1994; Parasuraman *et al.*, 1988, 1994b; Spreng and Mackoy, 1996; Zeithaml *et al.*, 1996).

Service quality is often conceptualised as a cognitive evaluation and satisfaction, as a more emotional or affective response, resulting from the consumers' reaction to that evaluation. One determinant of expectations is price (Gronroos, 1984; Voss *et al.*, 1998) and the role of perceived value in consumer decision-making has also been widely discussed (Zeithaml, 1988; Cronin Jr *et al.*, 2000). Cronin *et al.* (2000), for example, include in their model (i.e. sacrifice) a measure of the monetary and non-monetary price associated with the acquisition and use of a service. They argue that the three concepts – service quality, service value and satisfaction – must all be considered in order to understand consumers' behavioural intentions. The nature of these concepts can be expected to differ across cultures. A comparison of Chinese and US shoppers, for example, found that the former are more willing to expend more time and energy in comparing prices and products (food products in this case) to obtain better quality and value (Ackerman and Tellis, 2001).

Behaviours of interest to researchers, and management, include reduced price sensitivity, word-of-mouth recommendation and particularly customer retention which is an important and reliable source of economic performance (for further discussion of the relationship between customer satisfaction, loyalty and firm profitability see e.g. Reichheld and Sasser, 1990; Reicheld, 1996; Fornell, 1992; Zahorik and Rust, 1992). Assessment of behavioural intention as an indicator of actual behaviour is a problematic area in

Figure 10.6 A simplified model of the suggested relationships between consumers' service evaluations and related behaviours

mono-cultural research (and potentially more problematic in cross-cultural research as will be discussed later). The link between intention and action is often tenuous. Many studies focus on the theory of reasoned action of Fishbein and Ajzen (1975) where the salience of other persons', group or society norms and the desire to conform to their norms are emphasised. Tests and adaptations of this model suggest that there are other variables that have effects on behaviour that are not mediated by behavioural intentions. (In particular, previous behaviour has been found to influence future behaviour, and in one study (Ajzen and Madden, 1986) was found to be the best single direct predictor of future behaviour.) Further variables have been suggested, including a total of 14 by Bagozzi and Warshaw (1986) that would argue Chaiken and Stangor (1987) result in a virtually different model.

Despite this often lack of association, researchers typically collect behavioural intentions data as an indicator of the relevance of perceived service quality, as a behavioural determinant and also as a test of scale validity. Parasuraman *et al.* (1988) when developing SERVQUAL, for example assessed respondents' intention to recommend the service firm to a friend. Additionally, they enquired about the past behaviour in terms of whether the respondent had ever reported a problem with the service. (The purpose here was to associate higher perceived quality with the fact that the consumer had not reported a problem.)

Perceived service-quality relationships (of the nature illustrated in Figure 10.6) are often examined across a range of industries to assess their generalisability as discussed earlier, yet few have been generalised across cultures. Most service-quality studies have been developed in the US and can be expected to reflect the dominant culture of the sampled respondents.[3] Substantial differences are likely to exist however, in the ways in which consumers from different cultural backgrounds conform to the relationships described and the underlying assumptions inferred by the model (Figure 10.6). Researchers have described cultural differences for example, with respect to complaint behaviour (Richins and Verhage, 1985). Winsted (1997a) highlights that Japanese customers are reluctant to insist, or negotiate, because this is embarrassing and does not promote 'wa' (harmony). They will smile and conceal negative emotion. Consequently, they will be less willing to complain about services than the US customers for whom, being in control is important and confrontation is acceptable. Usunier (1996) highlights how the codes and rituals which distinguish cultures allow for a compromise between two extreme positions:

■ *Affective cultures* – expressing emotions is legitimate and useful for action.
■ *Neutral cultures* – needs to be separated from action.

Word-of-mouth communication is particularly important in service industries where, compared to tangible goods, experience qualities dominate.[4] The propensity for collectivist cultures to be reliant on word-of-mouth information and in particular, the dominant role of the family and social networks in choice behaviour has been examined. Money and Gilly (1998) for example, highlight how in Japan's highly collectivist, high uncertainty avoidance and high context culture, the role of word-of-mouth referral in the small/medium firm's bank-selection process is far greater than for similar US-based firms. Gregory (2000) describes how Japanese mothers generally maintain greater control over their childrens' consumption than do American mothers who encourage independent consumption. The greater role and influence of the Chinese family in the young consumers' choice of banking institution, when compared to the UK, is also documented

---

[3] The problems of describing cultures as equivalent to nations were discussed earlier.
[4] It is often noted that, unlike physical goods, consumers can often do little to evaluate services prior to consumption (i.e. services are low in search properties) and therefore can only evaluate them post-consumption.

(Smith and Chan, 1996). Consequently, relating these factors back to the statements of complaining behaviour and word of mouth in the SERVQUAL questionnaire:

1. respondents from more *individualist cultures* can be expected to have reported a problem if they have received poor service *but*
2. be less likely than those from *collectivist cultures* to engage in positive word of mouth if they have received good service.

These suppositions are confirmed by one of the few service-quality studies to examine cross-cultural differences in behavioural intention. Liu *et al.* (2001), with respect to retail banking found that bank customers from higher power distance and more individualistic cultures had a lower intention to praise when service is good. When service is poor however, those from individualistic cultures have a higher intention to switch service provider or give negative word of mouth. Conversely, customers from higher uncertainty avoidance and long-term orientation cultures have a higher intention to praise good service. Whereas those customers from masculine and high uncertainty avoidance cultures, who receive poor service, have a lower intention to switch, and the latter to give negative word of mouth, or to complain.

As discussed earlier, there is a complex link between behavioural intention and behaviour. One factor which will be considered later is the impact of cultural differences on the research method adopted for collecting behavioural intentions, and other data. However, the importance of equivalence in cross-cultural research will be addressed first.

10.7 Collecting cross-cultural perceived service-quality research data

Much of the evidence with respect to cross-cultural differences in consumers' service-quality expectations, evaluative criteria, etc. is derived from studies based on the SERVQUAL methodology (e.g. Kettinger *et al.*, 1995; Wetzels *et al.*, 1995; Caruana *et al.*, 1998; Donthu and Yoo, 1998; Furrer *et al.*, 2000). Other researchers have adopted alternative methodologies, for example, observation (Mattila, 1999), critical incident technique (Stauss and Mang, 1999) and other qualitative approaches such as focus groups and in-depth interviews (Winsted, 1997a, b).

A key concern for researchers is to establish comparability of data sets, ensuring that differences (or similarities) are a representation of respondents' beliefs, attitudes, etc., rather than artefacts of the research design. In particular the need for equivalence in all aspects of the research design and the potential for cross-cultural differences to emerge as a result of the chosen research method should be recognised.

10.7.1 Cross-cultural research: the need for equivalence

A fundamental consideration of cross-cultural research is that of establishing equivalence and thus comparability. The many types of cross-cultural equivalence (e.g. construct, sample, translation…) impact on all elements of the research programme. (For discussion of the nature of various elements of equivalence relevant to cross-cultural studies, see Craig and Douglas (2000); Usunier (1996, Chapter 5); specifically related to service-quality studies refer to Smith and Reynolds (2002).) Construct equivalence for example, requires that the behaviour, product or idea to be investigated must exist in all the cultures under consideration and must be meaningful in those cultures (Segall *et al.*, 1990; Malhotra, 1993). One element of construct equivalence – conceptual equivalence – refers to the comparability of meaning. Service-quality studies may lack conceptual equivalence due to cultural differences in the interpretation of behaviour. In the 1980s/1990s, for example, UK retailers, in their customer care training programmes, emphasised the importance of staff–customer eye-contact during the service encounter. This was an expression of individualised attention and concern for the customer. Lack of eye-contact is, however, an indication of politeness in many Eastern cultures. Failing to identify this difference would result in incorrect interpretation of customer perceptions data. Similarly, the Western emphasis on speed of service and responsiveness has been shown to be less important to other cultures who value politeness. Mono-cultural researchers (Cronin and Taylor, 1992) have advocated that perceptions data alone is sufficient for establishing consumers' service-quality evaluations. It is clear therefore, that exploratory research is required for each cultural group of interest. Transporting a measurement scale cross-nationally without substantial investigation of underlying concepts is likely to result in lack of both construct equivalence and the related scale (or item equivalence, i.e. the scale) may fail to measure the same phenomenon uniformly across cultures since items may mean different things to different groups. Closely allied to these problems is that of establishing translation equivalence. The nuances of language create considerable problems for international research generally. It can only be hoped that the example of Cateora (1993) below, from a Japanese hotel has lost meaning in the translation:

> You are invited to take advantage of the chambermaid
>
> Cateora (1993, p.118)

Further problems in assessing comparability relate to the potential for differences in response styles across cultures.

10.7.2 Assessing the potential impact of response styles on cross-cultural service-quality data

According to Cronbach response style is a

> habit (or momentary attitude) causing the examinee (i.e. respondent) to earn a score different from the one he would earn if the same question were presented in a different form
>
> Cronbach (1950, p. 175).

Response styles may take many forms, for example, extreme response style (ERS); that is, tendency to respond at extreme scale points; acquiescence (yea-saying), that is the tendency to agree to statements regardless of content, and the converse, opposition (nay-saying) … Clearly if a particular response style is a feature of one of the cultural groups under consideration this will affect measurement equivalence and result in incorrect inferences being made from the data. Two features should be recognised when service-industry management collect cross-cultural data:

1. Likert-type scales (i.e. of the nature of the SERVQUAL scale) tend to be the most problematic in terms of response styles.
2. Cross-cultural differences in response style have been detected.

Respondents from collectivist cultures for example have been found to avoid extremes (Chen *et al.*, 1995) and those from Asian countries (China, Japan and Hong Kong) to be more likely to use the middle response categories than Western respondents (USA, Germany and UK) (Si and Cullen, 1998; Shiomi and Loo, 1999).

Consequently, differences in response styles can affect many aspects of research findings and result in poor decision-making. They could, for example, impact on the number and nature of apparent service-quality dimensions/determinants produced by statistical analysis; account for observed differences (or similarities) between cultural groups; be responsible for apparent relationships within the data, for example, between service-quality perceptions and behavioural intentions. A number of statistical techniques exist which enable the cross-cultural researcher to address these problems (for further discussion see Reynolds, 1999; Smith and Reynolds, 2002), one solution however is to adopt alternative (and preferably) multiple data collection methods.

Evaluation of service quality/satisfaction can focus on an overall evaluation of experiences of a service provider over time, or on a specific encounter. Critical incidents 'technique' has been used to assess service quality/satisfaction both mono-culturally (see e.g. Bitner *et al.*, 1990; Keaveney, 1995) and more recently, cross-culturally. Stauss and Mang (1999) argue for the superiority of CIT for measuring quality perceptions of customers from different cultures, as it is more likely to achieve conceptual equivalence. This approach allows the respondent to focus on a specific encounter, and to identify a specific incident(s), defined by Bitner *et al.* (1990) as 'an observable human activity that is complete enough in itself to permit inferences and predictions to be made about the person performing the act' (p. 73).

By questioning consumers about particular satisfying or dissatisfying encounters it is argued that the benefits of a deeper understanding of positive and negative service behaviour may be gained. CIT avoids the often, reductionist approach of survey questionnaires which may constrain a respondent to express themselves within a framework developed in another culture and the problems of response styles described earlier. All research methods, though, have their own problems and deficiencies. CIT can suffer from subjectivity of interpretation and the problems of low-role involvement – the respondent, particularly in frequent service encounters, may be unable to relate any critical incidents. Cross-culturally, too, respondents' willingness to criticise; to be polite to the interviewer, etc., can be expected to influence findings. Other methods, such as observation, offer significant benefits to the cross-cultural researcher (Craig and Douglas, 2000). Mattila (1999) suggests, however, from her study of consumers, evaluation of hotel services, that culture-based rules governing display of emotions provide 'plausible explanations' for differences in observed behaviours. Consequently, using expressed emotions such as smiling and eye-contact, as an indicator of service satisfaction might be restricted to Western customers.

10.8 Conclusion

Cultural differences between countries have been problematic for European banks in their internationalisation strategies (Nellis *et al.*, 2000) whereas market similarities have been an important determinant of the internationalisation strategies of the US credit card companies (Worthington and Edwards, 2000). The need to understand national cultures, in an industry in which the importance of the customer–client relationship is crucial, is well recognised. This chapter has largely focused on the service process and it is clear, from the few studies which have emerged, that consumers' expectations of that process will vary across cultures. As will preferences for financial products, attitudes towards technology-based service delivery, etc. Culture is however, a complex phenomenon and an understanding of how consumers of diverse value systems form their service-quality/satisfaction evaluation, and thus determine related attitudes and behaviours are embryonic.

Universality of consumer behavioural theories, models and measurement instruments, often developed in the US, has been questioned (Van Raaij, 1978; Lee and Green, 1991). This chapter has highlighted how typical assumptions, such as the relationships between service satisfaction and word-of-mouth communication and complaining behaviour, do not necessarily transcend cultures. Reliable and valid research data is essential for understanding consumers' requirements and for building and maintaining relationships which, Nellis *et al.* (2000) argue, relates to comparative advantage in international retail banking. Such information is required for key decision-making areas such as market segmentation and positioning strategies; service and retail design; product and distribution planning; training policies and resource allocation generally. There are also important implications for the location of decision-making, autonomy for local managers and staff, etc. Customer satisfaction/service-quality evaluation data is often an important source of control information triggering the need for re-design of service. Yet collecting such data is potentially problematic. An awareness of these problems and issues – the need for equivalence and an appreciation of the potential for response styles and other biases to distort data and affect comparability – should enable retail-bank management to more meaningfully identify cross-cultural differences in consumers' service-quality expectations.

Appendix

The SERVQUAL scale

Described as a 'generic' scale for measuring consumer-perceived service-quality (Parasuraman *et al.*, 1988) SERVQUAL (a self-administered questionnaire) has been applied and tested across a wide range of service industries and nations.

The scale has in fact been revised a number of times due to the development activity of its authors and the criticisms advanced by researchers who have attempted to apply it. The original version (Parasuraman *et al.*, 1988) included 22 items, designed to measure five dimensions (see Figure 10.4): reliability, responsiveness, empathy, assurance and tangibles; assessed by a seven-point Likert scale, anchored by end points labelled 'strongly agree' and 'strongly disagree', and presented in two formats – one for expectations and then repeated for consumer perceptions. Expectations were defined as experience-based norms (Woodruff *et al.*, 1983) for example:

> they should provide their services at the time they promise to do so.

Half of the statements were presented in a negative format, an approach often suggested by scale designers in order to encourage the respondent to read the items carefully and prevent, for example, 'yea-saying' biases. Once the respondent has completed both sections of the questionnaire, a gap score can be calculated which represents the evaluation of service quality on an individual item, dimension, and on aggregate, for example,

	Strongly disagree					Strongly agree	
Banks should have modern looking equipment	1	2	3	4	5	⑥	7
This bank does have modern looking equipment	1	2	3	④	5	6	7

Quality gap $= 4 - 6 = -2$

Consequently, questions relating to overall perceptions of service quality can then be correlated with these scores highlighting causes of poor-quality evaluations. Similarly, questions relating to behavioural intentions for example, 'intention to re-attend' would provide both an understanding of service-quality-related behaviour and assessments of concurrent validity.

Later developments (Parasuraman *et al.*, 1991, 1994a) included some changes to scale content; removal of negative phrasing and rewording of expectations statements. Many problems and issues have been raised by the administration of SERVQUAL within mono-cultural environments (for further discussion see Asubontang, 1996; Smith, 1995, 1999); however, it is the application of scales cross-culturally which is of interest here.

References

Ackerman, D. and Tellis, G. (2001) Can culture affect prices? A cross-cultural study of shopping and retail prices. *Journal of Retailing*, **77**(1), 12–14.

Ajzen, I. and Madden, T.J. (1986) In Chaiken, S. and Stangor, C. (1987) Attitudes and attitude change. *Annual Review of Psychology*, 575–630.

Asubontang, P., McCleary, K.J. and Swan, J.E. (1996) SERVQUAL revisited: a critical review of service quality. *Journal of Services Marketing*, **10**(6), 62–81.

Bagozzi, R.P. and Warshaw, P.R. (1986) In Chaiken, S. and Stangor, C. (1987) Attitudes and attitude change. *Annual Review of Psychology*, 575–630.

Bahia, K. and Nantel, J. (2000) A reliable and valid measurement scale for the perceived service quality of banks. *International Journal of Bank Marketing*, **18**(2), 84–91.

Baker, J., Parasuraman, A., Grewal, D. and Voss, G.B. (2002) The influence of multiple store environment cues on perceived merchandise value and patronage intentions. *Journal of Marketing*, **66**(2), 120–141.

Bitner, M.J. (1993) Tracking the evolution of the service marketing literature. *Journal of Retailing*, **69**, 61–103.

Bitner, M.J. and Hubbert, A.R. (1994) Encounter satisfaction versus overall satisfaction versus quality. In Rust, R.T. and Oliver, R.L. (eds), *Service Quality: New Directions in Theory and Practice*. New York, Sage Publications, pp. 72–84.

Bitner, M.J., Booms, B.H. and Tetreault, M.S. (1990) The service encounter: diagnosing favourable and unfavourable incidents. *Journal of Marketing*, **54**(January), 71–84.

Carman, J.M. (1990) Consumer perceptions of service quality: an assessment of the SERVQUAL dimensions. *Journal of Retailing*, **66**(1), 33–55.

Carman, J.M. and Langeard, E. (1980) Growth strategies of service firms. *Strategic Management Journal*, **1**(January–March), 7–22.

Caruana, A., Ramaseshan, B., Ewing, M.T. and Rouhani, F. (1998) Expectations about management consultancy services: testing the assumption of equivalence across Australian and Singaporean firms. *Journal of Professional Services Marketing*, **18**(1), 1–10.

Cateora, P.R. (1993) *International Marketing*, 8th edition. Boston, Irwin.

Chaiken, S. and Stangor, C. (1987) Attitudes and attitude change. *Annual Review of Psychology*, 575–630.

Chen, C., Lee, S. and Stevenson, H.W. (1995) Response style and cross-cultural comparison of rating scales among East Asian and North American students. *Psychological Science* **6**(3), 170–175.

Cicic, M., Patterson, P.G. and Shoham, A. (1999) A conceptual model of the internationalization of services firms. *Journal of Global Marketing*, **12**(3), 81–106.

Craig, C.S. and Douglas, S.P. (2000) *International Marketing Research*, 2nd edition. John Wiley and Sons, Ltd: Chichester.

Cronbach, L.J. (1950) Further evidence on response sets and text design. *Educational and Psychological Measurement*, **10**, 3–31.

Cronin Jr, J.J., Brady, M.K., Hult, G. and Tomas, M. (2000) Assessing the effects of quality, value and customer satisfaction on consumer behavioural intentions in service environments. *Journal of Retailing*, **76**(2), 193–216.

Donthu, N. and Yoo, B. (1998) Cultural influences on service quality expectations. *Journal of Service Research*, **1**(2), 178–186.

Eriksson, K., Majkgård, A. and Sharma, D.D. (1999) Service quality by relationships in the international market. *Journal of Services Marketing*, **13**(4/5), 361–375.

Finn, D.W. and Lamb, C.W. (1991) An evaluation of the SERVQUAL scales in a retailing setting. *Advances in Consumer Research*, **18**, 483–490.

Fischbacher, M. and Smith, A.M. (2001) Creating a design strategy: the complexity of the new service development process. *International Journal of New Product Development and Innovation Management*, March/April, 59–77.

Fishbein, M. and Ajzen, I. (1975) *Belief, Attitude, Intention and Behaviour: An Introduction to Theory and Research*. Addison-Wesley Publishing.

Fornell, C. (1992) A national customer satisfaction barometer: the Swedish experience. *Journal of Marketing*, **56**(January), 6–21.

Furrer, O., Liu, B.S.-C. and Sudharshan, D. (2000) The relationships between culture and service quality perceptions: basis for cross-cultural market segmentation and resource allocation. *Journal of Service Research*, **2**(4), 355–371.

Gerrard, P. and Cunningham, J.B. (1997) Islamic banking: a study in Singapore. *International Journal of Bank Marketing*, **15**(6), 204–216.

Goodenough, W.H. (1971) In Usunier, J.C. (1996) *Marketing Across Cultures*, 2nd edition. Europe, Prentice-Hall.

Gotlieb, J.B., Grewal, D. and Brown, S.W. (1994) Consumer satisfaction and perceived quality: complementary or divergent constructs? *Journal of Applied Psychology*, **79**(6), 875–885.

Gregory, R.M. (1999) Consumer socialisation, parental style and development. Timetables in the United States and Japan. *Journal of Marketing*, **63**(3), 105–119.

Griffin, M., Babin, B.J. and Modianos, D. (2000) Shopping values of Russian consumers: the impact of habituation in a developing economy. *Journal of Retailing*, **76**(1), 33–52.

Gronroos, C. (1984) A service quality model and its marketing implications. *European Journal of Marketing*, **18**(4), 36–44.

Hall, E.T. (1966) *The Hidden Dimension*. New York, Doubleday.

Hall, E.T. and Hall, M. (1990) *Understanding Cultural Differences*. Yarmouth, MA, Intercultural Press.

Herzberg *et al*. (1959) In Johnston (1997) *op cit*.

Hofstede, G. (1980) *Culture's Consequences: International Differences in Work-Related Values*. Beverly Hills, CA, Sage Publications.

Hofstede, G. (1991) *Cultures and Organisations: Software of the Mind*. London, McGraw-Hill.

Hofstede, G. (1994) The business of international business is culture. *International Business Review*, **3**(1), 1–14.

Homburg, C., Hoyer, W.D. and Fassnacht, M. (2002) Service orientation of a retailer's business strategy: dimensions, antecedents, and performance outcomes. *Journal of Marketing*, **66**(4), 86–111.

Imrie, B.C., Durden, G. and Cadogan, J.W. (2000) Towards a conceptualisation of service quality in the global market arena. *Advances in International Marketing*, **10**(Suppl. 1), 143–162.

Ingold, T. (1999) Social relations, human ecology, and the evolution of culture: an exploration of concepts and definitions. In Lock, A. and Peters, C.R. (eds), *Handbook of Symbolic Evolution*. Oxford, Blackwell Publishers, Chapter 7, pp. 178–203.

Johnston, R. (1997) Identifying the critical determinants of service quality in retail banking: importance and effect. *International Journal of Bank Marketing*, **15**(4), 111–116.

Keaveney, S.M. (1995) Customer switching behaviour in service industries: an exploratory study. *Journal of Marketing*, **59**, 71–82.

Keegan, W.J. (1989) In *Global Marketing Management*, 4th edition. Englewood Cliffs, Prentice-Hall International, Chapter 12.

Kettinger, W.J., Lee, C.C. and Lee, S. (1995) Global measures of information service quality: a cross national study. *Decision Sciences*, **26**(5), 569–588.

Knight, G. (1999) International services marketing: review of research, 1980–1988. *Journal of Services Marketing*, **13**(4/5), 347–360.

Leblanc, G. and Nguyen, N. (1988) Customers' perceptions of service quality in financial institutions. *International Journal of Bank Marketing*, **6**(4), 7–18.

Lee, C. and Green, R. (1991) Cross cultural examination of the Fishbein behavioural intentions model. *Journal of International Business Studies*, **22**(2), 289–305.

Linton, R. (1945) In Usunier, J.C. (1996) *Marketing Across Cultures*, 2nd edition. Europe, Prentice-Hall.

Liu, B.S-C., Furrer, O. and Sudharshan (2001) The relationship between culture and behavioural intentions toward services. *Journal of Service Research*, **4**(2), 118–129.

Lovelock, C.H. and Yip, G.S. (1996) Developing global strategies for service businesses. *California Management Review*, **38**(2), 64–86.

Malhotra, N.K. (1993) *Marketing Research: An Applied Orientation*. Englewood Cliffs, NJ, Prentice-Hall.

Mattila, A.S. (1999) The role of culture and purchase motivation in service encounter evaluations. *Journal of Services Marketing*, **13**(4/5), 376–389.

McDougall, G.H. and Levesque, T.J. (1994) Benefit segmentation using service quality dimensions: an investigation in retail banking. *International Journal of Bank Marketing*, **12**(2), 15–23.

McGoldrick, P.J. and Ho, S.S.L. (1992) International positioning: Japanese department stores in Hong Kong. *European Journal of Marketing*, **26**(8/9), 61–73.

McGoldrick, P.J. and Pieros, C.P. (1998) Atmospherics, pleasure and arousal: the influence of response moderators. *Journal of Marketing Management*, **14**, 173–197.

Mels, G., Boshoff, C. and Nel, D. (1997), The dimensions of service quality: the original European perspective revisited. *The Service Industries Journal*, **17**(1), 173–189.

Money, R.B. and Gilly, M.C. (1998) Explorations of national culture and word-of-mouth referral behaviour in the purchase of industrial services in the United States and Japan. *Journal of Marketing*, **62**(4), 76–87.

de Mooij, M. and Hofstede, G. (2002) Convergence and divergence in consumer behaviour: implications for international retailing. *Journal of Retailing*, **78**, 61–69.

Naroll, R. (1970) *Main Currents in Cultural Anthropology*. New York, Appleton-Century-Crofts.

Nellis, J.G., McCaffery, K.M. and Hutchinson, R.W. (2000) Strategic challenges for the European banking industry in the new millennium. *International Journal of Bank Marketing*, **18**(2), 53–63.

Oliver, R.L. (1993) A conceptual model of service quality and service satisfaction: compatible goals, different concepts. *Advances in Services Marketing and Management*, **2**, 65–85.

Parasuraman, A., Zeithaml, V.A. and Berry, L.L. (1988) SERVQUAL: a multiple-item scale for measuring consumer perceptions of service quality. *Journal of Retailing*, **64**(1), 12–40.

Parasuraman, A., Berry, L.L. and Zeithaml, V.A. (1991) Refinement and reassessment of the SERVQUAL scale. *Journal of Retailing*, **67**(4), 420–450.

Parasuraman, A., Zeithaml, V.A. and Berry, L.L. (1994a) Alternative scales for measuring service quality: a comparative assessment based on psychometric and diagnostic criteria. *Journal of Retailing*, **70**(3), 201–230.

Parasuraman, A., Zeithaml, V.A. and Berry, L.L. (1994b) Reassessment of expectations as a comparison standard in measuring service quality: implications for future research. *Journal of Marketing*, **58**(February), 6–17.

Patterson, P.G. and Cicic, M. (1995) A typology of service firms in international markets: an empirical investigation. *Journal of International Marketing*, **3**(4), 57–83.

Polatoglu, V.N. and Ekin, S. (2001) An empirical investigation of the Turkish consumers' acceptance of Internet banking services. *International Journal of Bank Marketing*, **19**(4/5), 156–165.

Reichheld, F.F. (1996) *The Loyalty Effect: The Hidden Force Behind Growth, Profits and Lasting Value*. Boston, MA, Harvard Business School Press.

Reichheld, F.F. and Sasser Jr, W.E. (1990) Zero defections come to services. *Harvard Business Review*, September/October, 105–111.

Reynolds, N.L. (1999) *An investigation of response styles in the cross-national environment: the impact of changing scale format on measurement equivalence*. Ph.D. Thesis, University of Wales, Swansea.

Richins, M. and Verhage, B. (1985) Cross cultural differences in consumer attitudes and their implications for complaint management. *International Journal of Research in Marketing*, **2**, 197–205.

Segall, M.H., Dansen, P.R., Berry, J.W. and Poortinga, Y.H. (1990) *Human Behavior in Global Perspective: An Introduction to Cross-Cultural Psychology*. UK, Pergamon Press.

Shiomi, K. and Loo, R. (1999) Cross cultural response styles on the kirton adaptation. *Innovation Inventory, Social Behaviour and Personality*, **27**(4), 413–420.

Si, S.X. and Cullen, J.B. (1998) Response categories and potential cultural bias: effects of an explicit middle point in cross-cultural surveys. *The International Journal of Organisational Analysis*, **6**(3), 218–230.

Smith, A.M. (1995) Measuring service quality: is SERVQUAL now redundant? *Journal of Marketing Management*, **11**(3), 257–276.

Smith, A.M. (1999) Some problems when adopting Churchill's paradigm for the development of service quality measurement scales. *Journal of Business Research*, **46**, 109–120.

Smith, A.M. and Chan, C.K. (1996) *A cross-cultural study of students' expectations of banking services*. Working Paper, University of Sheffield, October.

Smith, A.M. and Reynolds, N.L. (2002) Measuring cross-cultural service quality: a framework for assessment. *International Marketing Review*, **19**(5), 450–481.

Solomon, M.R., Surprenant, C., Czepiel, J.A. and Gutman, E.G. (1985) A role theory perspective on dyadic interactions: the service encounter. *Journal of Marketing*, **49**(Winter), 99–111.

Spreng, R.A. and Mackoy, R.D. (1996) An empirical examination of a model of perceived service quality and satisfaction. *Journal of Retailing*, **72**(2), 201–214.

Stauss, B. and Mang, P. (1999) Culture shocks' in inter-cultural service encounters? *Journal of Services Marketing*, **13**(4/5), 329–346.

The Chinese Culture Connection (1987) Chinese values and the search for culture-free dimensions of culture. *Journal of Cross-Cultural Psychology*, **18**, 143–164.

Turley, L.W. and Chebat, J.C. (2002) Linking retail strategy, atmospheric design and shopping behaviour. *Journal of Marketing Management*, **18**, 125–144.

Usunier, J.C. (1996) *Marketing Across Cultures*, 2nd edition. Europe, Prentice-Hall.

Van Raaij, W.F. (1978) Cross-cultural methodology as a case of construct validity. In Hunt, M.K. (ed.), *Advances in Consumer Research*, Vol. 5. Anne Arbor, pp. 693–701.

Voss, G.B., Parasuraman, A. and Grewal, O. (1998) The roles of price, performance and expectations in determining satisfaction in service exchanges. *Journal of Marketing*, **63**(October), 46–61.

Wetzels, M., de Ruyter, K., Lemmink, J. and Koelemeijer, K. (1995) Measuring customer service quality in international marketing channels: a multimethod approach. *Journal of Business and Industrial Marketing*, **10**(5), 50–59.

Winsted, K.F. (1997a) The service experience in two cultures: a behavioural perspective. *Journal of Retailing*, **73**(3), 337–366.

Winsted, K.F. (1997b) Service encounter expectations: a cross-cultural analysis. *Journal of Transnational Management Development*, **2**(4), 5–32.

Woodruff, R.B., Cadotte, E.R. and Jenkins, R.L. (1983) Modelling consumer satisfaction processes using experience based norms. *Journal of Marketing Research*, **XX**(August), 296–304.

Worthington, S. and Edwards, V. (2000) Changes in payments markets. Past, present and future: a comparison between Australia and the UK. *International Journal of Bank Marketing*, **18**(4/5).

Zahorik, A.J. and Rust, R.T. (1992) Modelling the impact of service quality on profitability: a review. In Swartz, T.A., Bowen, D.E. and Brown, S.W. (eds), *Advances in Services Marketing and Management*, Vol.1. Greenwich, CT, J.A.I. Press, pp. 247–276.

Zeithaml, V.A. (1988) Consumer perceptions of price, quality and value: a means-end model and synthesis of evidence. *Journal of Marketing*, **52**(July), 2–22.

Zeithaml, V.A., Berry, L. and Parasuraman, A. (1996). The behavioural consequences of service quality. *Journal of Marketing*, **60**(April), 31–46.

Study questions and guideline answers

1. **Suggest reasons why the senior management of an international retail bank might prefer national managers to determine the nature of service delivery in the branch/outlet. Or why they may prefer to standardise service internationally.**

Reasons for national managers to determine service delivery include the following:

- Local managers will be aware of local cultural characteristics which require adaptation of service delivery, for example consumers may prefer speed of response as opposed to more informal staff interaction.
- Decision-making at the local level will encourage flexibility and customer responsiveness.
- The service encounter involves staff–customer interaction. An understanding of staff values and assumptions is therefore essential.
- Will encourage autonomy, potentially improving motivation, morale and therefore customer service. Reasons for a standardised approach include:
  (a) lower costs (e.g. training programmes);
  (b) a unified corporate image (i.e. consistency for the international customer).
  (c) a unified corporate culture. ...

2. **Suggest how a knowledge of Hofstede's cultural dimensions would assist senior management in determining the nature and degree of national adaptation of service delivery.**

Hofstede suggests that countries can be grouped according to cultural dimensions and that these groups will exhibit similarities:

- Service-quality researchers have suggested that expectations of service quality differ according to these cultural dimensions in terms of, for example, relative emphasis on service process and outcome; comparative importance of dimensions of service quality (e.g. reliability, responsiveness, tangibles, etc.).
- Such information can assist management in determining the need for adaptation of, for example, the design of the retail outlet, staff interpersonal skills, use of technology, etc.

3. **An international retail bank has conducted a customer satisfaction survey in a number of countries. The questionnaire included the 'SERVQUAL' scale to measure service-quality expectations and perceptions and measures of behavioural intentions.**

   The results from country A suggest that service-quality levels are higher in country B but intentions to recommend the bank to friends is lower *and* customers from country C perceive poorer service-quality levels than country D but were not more likely to say that they would complain.

   Suggest reasons for these findings.

Possible reasons would include the following:

- Other constructs which might impact on the service-quality/behavioural intention relationship have been omitted (e.g. satisfaction, value).
- There could be problems in the research design, for example, scales which are likely to encourage response styles may have been used.
- The results may be indicative of cultural differences in consumer behavioural intentions.

For example, Country A may have a more individualist culture than country B. Country C may exhibit higher uncertainty avoidance than Country B.

There may be fewer alternative retail-banking facilities in Country C.

4. **A number of researchers have suggested that a methodology involving critical incidents technique would be more appropriate for comparative cross-cultural research than a questionnaire survey. To what extent would you agree with this view?**

CIT typically evaluates a service encounter whereas questionnaires (e.g. SERVQUAL) typically assess the respondent's view of multiple encounters over time (although this need not necessarily be the case):

- Benefits of CIT include – in-depth qualitative analysis, avoidance of researcher-determined criteria.
- Problems of CIT include – cost, subjectivity of interpretation; sample size; relevance to low-involvement services, etc.
- Benefits of questionnaire surveys include – lower cost; increased sample size; ease of comparing findings from different groups, etc.
- Problems include – spurious findings due to response biases, misinterpretation of scale items, etc.
- For any methodology, the need to establish the various type of equivalence should be emphasised.

Chapter 11

Retail positioning and store image

Grete Birtwistle

Aims

The aims of this chapter are:

- to define retail positioning and store image;
- to determine store image attributes;
- to explore methods for measuring store image;
- to explore store image congruency.

11.1 Introduction

The economic rationale for creating strong market positioning is based on the theory that congruence between the objectives of market-positioning strategies and consumer perception of store image results in customer loyalty towards a store (Samli and Lincoln, 1989). The argument is based on the assumption that retailers strive to attract consumers to their stores with an image created by emphasising particular factors, such as merchandise quality or store design, and that this is effective if the chosen factors are those deemed important by the targeted customers. Individuals are influenced by their surroundings and retailers can manipulate the marketing mix to persuade consumers that gratification will be achieved through purchase of promoted goods.

11.2 Retail positioning

> A company selects its market position as its response to its understanding of the needs, desires and behavioural characteristics of its targeted customers. This requires a coordinated 'statement' to be made to the customer through merchandise selection, trading format, customer services and customer communication.
>
> Harris and Walter (1992, p. 3)

Positioning is defined 'as the design and implementation of a retail mix to create an image of the retailer in the customer's mind relative to its competitors' (Levy and Weitz, 1998). Store or brand image acts by communicating social signals of symbolic nature which provide the market positioning of a retailer with psychological importance, as brand ownership transfers the image of the brand to the owner (Schiffman and Kanuk, 1994). Strategic positioning concerns the identification of image dimensions that add unique value in the eyes of the targeted consumer (Wortzel, 1987). Consequently, understanding the way target consumers react to marketing communications and monitoring their effectiveness have become a focus of research activity.

Jobber (2001) suggests that successful positioning is based on four concepts:

- *Clarity* – The position must be clear to the target market by the way it is communicated to the customer and in the way it offers a differential advantage.
- *Consistency* – Consumers must receive marketing communication, which is consistent and does not change from year to year.
- *Credibility* – The positioning of a brand must be credible to the target market, especially when retailers are trying to change market positioning.
- *Competitiveness* – Two factors are important to retailers: the need to have a stylish image to distinguish the brand from the competition, and the need to have a reputation for product quality which is acknowledged by consumers.

Market positioning, based on price, product differentiation and service provision, is central to the competitive strategy of multiple retailers (Walters and Laffy, 1996). The main technique for determining consumer perception of retailer market positioning is to utilise perceptual mapping. This depicts different retailers over two or three dimensions, such as price, design and quality. The significance is that when the market positioning has been identified and compared with immediate competitors, the retailer can decide how best to re-affirm positioning (Easey, 2002). Focused differentiation is the way retailers can target a market by understanding the lifestyle of its customers (Porter, 1985).

11.3 Store image

Store image has been identified as one of the most important marketing mix variables (Greenley and Shipley, 1988). Understanding store image is a complicated process, yet vitally important for retail managers.

The seminal paper of Martineau (1958) on store image suggests that consumers perceive retail stores to have personalities, and that these are created from a combination of store layout and architecture; symbols and colours; advertising and sales personnel. Martineau (1958, p. 47) describes store image as 'the way in which the store is defined in the shopper's mind, partly by its functional qualities and partly by an aura of psychological attributes'. The study proposes that consumers choose a store with the image that most reflects their own self-image and, consequently, the importance for retailers to understand why shoppers perceive stores differently and how marketers can manipulate store image factors to influence store choice.

Kunkel and Berry (1968, p. 22) define store image as 'the total conceptualised or expected reinforcement that a person associates with shopping at a particular store' and conclude that image is gained through experience and thereby learned. This behavioural approach illustrates the view that consumers will react in a deliberate way to a given set of stimuli.

A behavioural approach is proposed by James *et al.* (1976, p. 25) and caused them to define store image as 'a set of attitudes based upon the evaluation of those store attributes deemed important by consumers'. Concordant with Kunkel and Berry (1968) they conclude that the perception of store image is based on individual experiences in a store, by talking with friends, or by seeing advertisements and window displays. Hence, store image is here identified to be the conceptualised perception that a person associates with shopping at a particular store, grounded on a combination of functional and psychological attributes deemed important to the individual.

11.3.1 Factors contributing to store image

Store image research can be divided into conceptual and behavioural research. The first endeavours to discover factors contributing towards the concept of store image; the second considers differences in store positioning and retailer image as well as the association between store image and consumer behaviour. Hansen and Deutscher (1977) observe store image terminology to be confusing and recommend a three-level classification of image measurement to be used: *dimension*, *component* and *attribute*. By 'dimension' they mean the largest element, for example merchandise; by 'component' they refer to the selection of merchandise; and 'attributes' would signify the brands stocked by the retailer. They suggest that there would be less confusion, and studies could be compared if researchers were more specific in classification of image elements. The study of three department stores of Kunkel and Berry (1968) led them to identify store image to consist of 12 dimensions consisting of a number of components (Table 11.1). Furthermore, they propose that different combinations of dimensions and components describe the image profile of a retailer.

As a result of a review of 19 store image studies, Lindquist (1974) created a list of nine store image dimensions and calculated the frequencies of categories mentioned by researchers (Table 11.2). The review concludes the most important image factors to be merchandise dimensions, consisting of selection, quality, pricing, and fashion and style.

Table 11.1 Kunkel and Berry's store image dimensions

1. Price of merchandise	7. Other convenience factors
2. Quality of merchandise	8. Services
3. Assortment of merchandise	9. Sales promotions
4. Fashion of merchandise	10. Advertising
5. Sales personnel	11. Store atmosphere
6. Location convenience	12. Reputation on adjustments

Table 11.2 Store image attributes

The most frequently cited attribute dimension including the contributing components	Frequency in %	Other attribute dimensions	Frequency in %
1. Merchandise		2. Service	27
– Selection	42	3. Clientele	–
– Quality	38	4. Physical facilities	–
– Price	38	5. Convenience	35
– Fashion and style	27	6. Promotion	–
		7. Store atmosphere	–
		8. Institutional	–
		9. Post-transaction	–

Source: Adapted from Lindquist (1974).

Two other components, general service and sales-clerk service, are identified as the next most important factors.

Hansen and Deutscher (1977) base their work primarily on the store image dimensions identified by Lindquist (1974) and examine the importance of different attributes in two different retail sectors, grocery and department stores. While similar attributes are identified for both sectors, the order of priority is found to be different. In both cases, the most important attribute is the dependability of the product. However, for supermarket shoppers, features that stress utility and time-pressures like store cleanliness, easy accessibility of products and speed of checkout are significant factors. This finding is in contrast to department store shopping, where value for money and product quality are perceived as highly important. Hence, store image attributes should be prioritised for each retail sector and practitioners should note the most important and least important dimensions to optimise capital investment.

Arnold *et al.* (1997, p. 112) conducted extensive store choice surveys over two decades across a number of different retail sectors. They propose that differences exist across sectors and that some variances occur within sectors. The *primary attributes* identified in all sectors were location, price and assortment and the *secondary factors* were quality, service, value and sales promotions. The order in which these attributes are prioritised depends on the sector. The authors hypothesise that variances within retail sectors relate 'to the degree of competitive market structure differentiation, that is, the extent to which competitors in a particular market differ from each other on a specific store choice attribute'. In addition, an important factor is the consumer lifestyle and self-image which may dictate to retailers the combination of attributes required by different customer segments.

Mazursky and Jacoby (1986) suggest that consumers form a set of beliefs about a store and decide whether a shopping environment is reflective of the type of store from which they want to be seen to purchase. Hence, if a retailer can identify those store attributes that appeal to a segment of consumers, it is possible to manipulate the physical and/or the psychological image components to attract those consumers without loosing the existing customer base. If a retailer uses a marketing strategy with store positioning criteria different to the selection criteria of the targeted consumer, sales may be lost and the marketing budget wasted. Retailer intention of store positioning is not necessarily the same as consumer perception, since it is the opinion of the targeted consumer that is important and thus, should be identified by the retailer.

11.4 Measurement of store image

Store image has been measured by applying techniques such as open-ended questions, attitude scaling, multi-attribute models, multi-dimensional scaling (MDS) and conjoint analysis. By appraising a store for retail image it is possible to compare it with the main competitors or to utilise the results for a longitudinal study.

Zimmer and Golden (1988) point out that though some consumer perceptions of store image are attribute-specific, others have a holistic perception of image and yet others have an apprehension of a behavioural or product/brand-related nature. They note that most mentions are affective descriptions and propose that as images are of a complex nature it is difficult for consumers and retailers to describe factors contributing to store image and this in turn makes it harder to measure perception of image. Thus, it is important for researchers to consider the design and the measurement techniques of a survey and these must be taken into consideration when drawing conclusions based on the results.

11.4.1 Open-ended techniques

In most studies, researchers have utilised a limited number of attribute dimensions to compare results with those of close competitors. Hence, the image dimensions to be measured have first to be identified. Zimmer and Golden (1988) recommend employing an unstructured measurement technique using open-ended image data to identify elements of image attributes important to consumers for a specific retail sector. When salient dimensions have been identified researchers can commence to measure the image of a store. The assumption is that consumers are aware of these and are prepared to state them. However, research indicates that some respondents may falsify their answers to improve their own image (Townsend, 1991). Furthermore, open-ended questions demand a good verbal ability from the respondent and this may reduce the reliability of a study. The use of unstructured measurement techniques requires difficult coding processes that may introduce subjectivity in the grouping stages. Nevertheless, the advantage of using qualitative methods for exploring store image is that it does not limit image dimensions and ensures that variables relevant to respondents are utilised.

11.4.2 Attitude scaling techniques

The semantic differential scale was developed by Thurstone (1929) and improved by Osgood *et al.* (1957). It has been used extensively to measure consumer perception of store image and is administered by applying either a five- or seven-point bipolar scale. Extremes are defined by opposites like 'good value' and 'poor value'. The problem with the process is that respondents are uncomfortable in using the negative end of the scale even if this demonstrates an accurate attitude towards the store in question (McDougall and Fry, 1974).

Staple scales, have been applied to studies, where respondents evaluate the importance of an attribute in describing it by a single adjective, and then allocating it a value from zero to ten or one to seven, and where the higher numbers signify 'extreme importance'. By applying staple scales, measurements indicate how well a store fulfils consumer expectation. Studies, administering scales with pre-selected attribute criteria, force consumers to respond to characteristics they might not have thought of themselves. This lack of objectivity can skew the results as they are influenced by the selection of salient attributes (Zimmer and Golden, 1988).

11.4.3 Multi-attribute models

Bass and Talarzyk (1972, pp. 93–94) adapted the Fishbein model, of 'Attitude-toward-Object', to be suitable for measuring attitudes towards a brand and concluded that it proved to be more reliable in predicting consumer preferences than demographic, personality or general attitude models. It is their belief that the model deals with attitude as a unidimensional concept, which provides a holistic measurement of the individual attitude to a brand. They describe the equation as 'a function of the relative importance of each of the product attributes and the beliefs about the brand on each attribute'.

The adapted model can also be utilised to measure store image as well as brand image, by substituting stores for brands (James *et al.*, 1976). Thus, the model measures store image as a function of the importance of a number of store attributes and the evaluation of these for a particular store. The model is represented by the equation:

$$A_s = \sum_{i=1}^{n} W_i B_i$$

where A_s is the attitude towards a particular store; W_i, the weight of importance of attribute i; B_i, the evaluative aspect or belief towards attribute i for a particular store and n, the number of attributes important in the selection of a given store.
Source: James *et al.* (1976)

The model measures store image by analysing the 'evaluation of all salient aspects of the store as individually perceived and weighted' (Doyle and Fenwick, 1974, p. 40).

The researcher has to establish relevant attributes to be measured either through exploratory research or by selecting attributes established from previous findings. However, not all consumers find the same attribute dimensions equally important and market segmentation can be included in store image studies to enable a re-formulation of the marketing strategy.

11.4.4 Multi-dimensional scaling

The MDS techniques have been used to make visual presentations of results to advise retailers of their own image and that of the competition. Similarity data are collected for two stores using a scalar instrument and then analysed by an MDS programme. The presentation of the results is by a spatial representation to inform interested parties of the differences in consumer perceptions between competitors in terms of image dimensions (Van Auken and Lonial, 1991). Doyle and Fenwick (1974) applied the technique to establish a two-dimensional perceptual map of store positioning for different grocery outlets. Jain and Etgar (1976) later applied MDS techniques to surveys administered in department stores and presented the results on a three-dimensional map.

A major study utilising MDS compared positioning strategies in a number of retail sectors (Davies and Brooks, 1989; Davies, 1992a). These findings were displayed on two-dimensional maps and based on a number of attributes identified to be relevant for each sector. The survey identified the positioning of a perceptual 'ideal store' and compared this with a number of retail companies within the sector. Although MDS techniques can be employed as a diagnostic tool (Van Auken and Lonial, 1991) the spatial representations are difficult to understand. Furthermore, they are based on consumer current store choice criteria, which may well change over time.

11.4.5 Conjoint analysis

Since Green and Srinivasan (1978) applied conjoint analysis to marketing problems, it has become a standard method for understanding and predicting consumer choices and comprehending trade-offs made by customers in their purchase decisions (Louviere, 1994). The most important reason for using conjoint analysis in formulating marketing strategy is its predictive capability in evaluating interacting salient factors. In addition, conjoint analysis allows for segmentation of responses and identification of homogeneous groups within the overall targeted group of customers, potentially enabling more efficient marketing communications based on consumer preferences (Amirani and Gates, 1993).

Conjoint analysis enables a concept to be decomposed into a number of variables important to consumers in decision-making. It is presumed that the consumer evaluates store image as a holistic concept and that important factors are appraised as a 'bundle of attributes' (Hair and Anderson, 1985). This type of attribute-anchored conjoint model has the advantage of conceptualising the 'Gestalt nature' of measurement of overall store preference (Green and Desarbo, 1978).

To administer a conjoint survey, a set of profile cards are designed containing all the chosen features (i.e. attribute dimensions). Green (1977) notes attributes chosen for the analysis should be 'benefits' sought from the product or service. Each feature has a minimum of two different levels. Respondents evaluate each profile by ranking these in order of preference or by rating them on a scale. The analysis estimates the contribution of each feature to the decision process and evaluates the trade-offs between a number of specified features at different levels.

For example, a conjoint analysis could identify the trade-off respondents make in store choice decision. The approach involves asking each respondent to express a level of preference for a hypothetical store description, which is summarised in terms of a number of features (e.g. store location) and stating a specific level for that feature (high-street or within an out-of-town shopping centre).

There are five stages in a basic conjoint analysis study (Lehmann *et al.*, 1997):

1. establish attributes;
2. assign attribute levels;
3. design profile cards;
4. design questionnaire and administer;
5. evaluate customer's preferences, segment size and utilities.

In the analysis it is possible to determine which features are the most important to customers and also which level of each feature is preferred. By using the results from a conjoint analysis, the retail mix and store positioning can be manipulated by the retailer to suit ever-changing consumer expectations. By employing this technique to generate market research data it is possible to understand the principal dimensions involved in store choice and to evaluate how customers make their purchasing decisions. The technique, utilised with a small sample of customers, enables identification of individual sub-segments within a large group of customers, which in many cases are believed to be homogenous, that is all with fairly similar demographic profiles and views of the retail chain.

Applied market research studies have used conjoint analytical techniques to evaluate retail positioning for supermarket chains, banks, sports and leisure services, service stations, fast food outlets, convenience stores and the entertainment sector (Johnson, 1997).

11.5 Store image studies in fashion retailing

In the following sections, fashion retailer strategies are discussed in terms of the main factors identified by Lindquist (1974). These are 'price of merchandise'; 'quality of merchandise'; branding, which includes 'selection' and 'fashion and style'; service provisions; store environment, which includes 'physical facilities' and 'store atmosphere'; and customer communications, which includes 'promotions', 'institutional' and 'post-transactions'.

11.5.1 Price of merchandise

The price points of merchandise are important because they can attract or deter the target market. If prices are too low the retailer may send confusing messages and potential customers may view products as being of poor or low quality. In contrast, promoting high-price points can encourage consumers to shop around to find products offering better value for money. Some consumers may feel high prices indicate better quality and more exclusiveness.

'Value for money' is the key criteria consumers use to compare stores where value is defined as the balance between price and product quality and includes the additional effects of other store characteristics such as selection of stock, service, accessibility and store atmosphere (Verdict, 1994). There are two principle ways of changing the 'value' of merchandise to the customer: by reducing price points while keeping product quality consistent or by holding price points stable and improving product quality (Gale and Klavans, 1985).

11.5.2 Quality of merchandise

Perceived product quality is an idiosyncratic value judgement with respect to the fitness for consumption which is based upon the conscious and/or

> unconscious processing of quality cues in relation to relevant quality attributes
> within the context of significant personal and situational variables.
>
> Steenkamp (1990, p. 317)

Consumer perception of merchandise quality is increasingly important as an element of the marketing strategy for fashion retailers since customers are willing to pay a premium for consistently high product quality (Evans, 1995).

In fashion retailing, image positioning is important because the product expresses something about the wearer. The old adage 'we are what we wear' still holds true for fashion clothing. Many consumers buy brands that project their self-image or the image to which they aspire (Hite and Bellizzi, 1985); they do not buy clothes just for functional qualities. Individual selection of clothing has been described as 'a personal signature that symbolically communicates the social identity that a person seeks to project and is a reflection of the personality of the wearer' (Thompson and Chen, 1998, p. 162). Thus the quality of the purchased fashion clothing is important as it communicates something about the wearer.

11.5.3 Branding

The concepts of branding national and private labels have been extensively researched (Doyle, 1991; or De Chernatony and McDonald, 1998). Such studies have focused primarily on the grocery sector with less investigation of the issues for fashion retailers (Moore, 1995). De Chernatony and McDonald (1992, p. 237) define a brand as 'an identifiable product, service, person or place, augmented in such a way that the buyer or user perceives relevant, unique added values which match their needs most closely'. The interacting attributes, which contribute to this image of a brand, are formulated from factors important or aspirational to the consumer.

The attributes or points of difference define the product in the mind of consumers and give an image or an aspirational lifestyle to which the customer can relate (Evans, 1989). When a brand is communicated through advertising, packaging and merchandising, it aims to create confidence (Doyle, 1991) and minimise the purchasing risk to the consumer. Such attributes, it is held, are particularly important when buying fashion products (De Chernatony and McDonald, 1998). Successful brands in fashion retailing create an image or are perceived by the consumer as having a 'personality' and can command a premium, allowing the retailer greater opportunity to maximise profitability with less need to discount prices (Doyle, 1991). Moreover, lifestyle branding sends out social signals, which can incorporate symbolic connotations of status and affluence, and are utilised to attract customers by attempting to satisfy these aspirations (Lewis and Hawskley, 1990; Fernie *et al.*, 1997).

For fashion retailers, maintaining a sustainable competitive advantage will be dependent on translating company core values into a coherent brand strategy. De Chernatony and McDonald (1998) maintain that a retailer may adopt either an *added value* or *cost-driven* strategy. Value-added brands are positioned to exceed the functional value of the product. Applied to fashion retailing, this may be achieved through innovations in style and design, by improvements in product quality or through store ambience. Staffing levels and the provision of skilled and knowledgeable staff may also be considered important.

In contrast, a cost-driven strategy attaches little symbolic value to the product. Low price remains the primary focus and is achieved via bulk orders, less work on individual garments, cheaper materials and by limiting ranges. Costs-driven strategies are reinforced at store level by reduced staffing, provision of minimal staff training and tight management control. Davies (1992b) maintains that to be deemed a brand, as opposed to merely a product label, a product or retailer must satisfy four criteria:

- *Differentiation* Does the consumer differentiate the brand positively in comparison with the main competitors?

- *Premium price* – Has the brand an image for quality that enables the retailer to command a premium price?
- *Separate existence* – Can the brand be valued, used, sold or licensed separately from the business owning the brand name?
- *Psychic value* – Does the brand offer augmented symbolic value to the customer?

A successful brand should meet all these criteria otherwise the name can only be perceived as a label for different ranges. Brands themselves can be divided into two broad categories: national/manufacturer brands and retailer brands.

11.5.3.1 National/manufacturer brands

National/manufacturer brands are designed, manufactured, and in the majority of instances, marketed by the supplier. The objective is to establish an image and create a demand for the product by communicating directly with the consumer (Levy and Weitz, 1998). Suppliers of national brands have to build in cost to cover advertising and promotion. However, these ranges stocked by a number of retailers in the same area can lead to increased competition and reduced margins. Hence, many UK retailers have decided to invest in their own retail brand.

11.5.3.2 Retailer brands

Historically, private-label or own-label merchandise has had a poor image, perceived by the consumer to be of a lower quality than national brands. However, in recent years retailer brands have improved greatly (Davies, 1992b). In the fashion sector this has been due primarily to retailers becoming more involved in product creation and investing in their own design, buying and marketing teams (Levy and Weitz, 1998).

Fashion retailers have the choice of selling either national- or private-label brands or a combination of both. The retailing of own-labels can increase the control the retailer has over the supply chain allowing greater direction to be exercised over the choice of fabrics, construction, quality control and distribution. It also provides the retailer with an intangible symbolic differentiator that is difficult to replicate (Moore, 1995).

Although the retail outlet may be a brand, some retailers prefer to develop a number of lifestyle brands that target different customer groups. Some retailers use the store name as the product name and only promote the one brand to their targeted customers, thus, the retail outlet becomes the brand. A typical example of this is Next Retail Ltd. with their label 'Next'. In contrast, the Dorothy Perkins, TopShop/Man and Burton Menswear stores prefer to promote a combination of national- and own-label brands and the retailer names in this situation would not fulfil Davis (1992b) criteria to be brands.

Retail branding is concerned not only with the branding of products and services offered by the firm, but with the retail company as a whole, and it is crucial since many customers purchase brands not products. It involves the development and maintenance of product and company values and beliefs that are coherent, appropriate, distinctive and attractive to customers in their attainment of differentiation and customer loyalty (Murphy, 1992). These values and beliefs in the brand are communicated to the customer via product quality, packaging, product presentation and store environment.

11.5.4 Service provisions

Service quality is a contributor to consumer perception in all interactions between customers and staff, and these evaluations contribute towards the perceived image based on a number of store visits. Many consumers do not have the time to compare product quality, but may rely on friends or sales staff to influence them. Advice to the consumer may help to sell the merchandise, particularly if the purchase is perceived as being of a high-risk nature. Thus, it is not surprising that many multiple retailers are turning to staff service provision to differentiate themselves in the high street (Turnbull and Wilson, 1989). It has also been acknowledged that customers have different needs and that retail employees need to adapt their approach to customers to satisfy individual requirements (Beatty *et al.*, 1996). In addition, the cost–benefit ratio of enhanced service provisions needs to be estimated and controlled since additional services may in effect reposition the company or not be required by the target customer.

Service is accepted as being a key differentiator between retailers (Zeithaml *et al.*, 1990). Increasing loyalty and retaining customers is understood to be more efficient than developing new customer business (Gould, 1995). In trying to manage service it becomes important to decide whether to prioritise the hard or the soft factors. Some companies stress the hard factors of customer segmentation and communication; measuring service standards; benchmarking; information management and procedural systems. Others emphasise the soft factors and point out the significance of customer relationships; listening to customers; culture of organisations; empowerment; support systems and appreciating staff contributions (Cook and Macaulay, 1997).

In retailing the soft factors of customer service are difficult to manage and are the real differentiators between retailers. Creating an acceptable working environment in a company where the lowest-paid staff has the highest contact with customers is vital (Richer, 1996). The customer-service level provided by any organisation cannot be imposed on staff, it is a result of the culture, the company structure and the human resource policy (Broadbridge, 1996). Staff have to enjoy work and be motivated to provide excellent customer service. Empowerment can aid employees to be motivated, but suitable reward, staff development and communication systems also have to be in place.

Customers' complaints are important in any organisation. By monitoring the type of complaints and reacting to them quickly retailers can minimise future complaints and customer's dissatisfaction. Refund or complaint policies are marketing tools that lead to increased loyalty if dealt with to the customer's satisfaction (Ward *et al.*, 1998). Refund and exchange policies are very similar in all the major fashion retailers; the main difference is the way these policies are implemented at store level. In reality, if customers feel they have been treated badly or made to jump through unnecessary hoops when returning goods, they are unlikely to shop with that retailer again. Companies that recognise the importance of the lifetime value of a customer realise that retaining customers is a good investment.

Although both quality and price and, therefore, value are still very important, service is becoming the most significant differentiator, particularly in fashion retailing where staff can have high customer contact. The real key to increasing customer's satisfaction is to 'balance customers' expectations and perceptions and close the gaps between the two' (Zeithaml *et al.*, 1990, p. 33).

11.5.5 Store environment strategy

Store design is a competitive tool used to attract customers and enables retailers to communicate a clear identity which lead to customer loyalty and increased profitability. Customers evaluate the total product offer, which incorporates both the product factors, merchandising and the store environment. Hence, the setting in which it is sold will influence the perception of a brand (Kelley and Hoffman, 1997).

Fashion retailers find window displays the most effective way of attracting potential customers into their store as it is the initial communicator of brand image. Retailers now design their windows to allow passers-by to see the store interior behind the displays. Store layouts are important in projecting and reinforcing the image and thus, influencing the purchase decision. The retail environment attempts to create an atmosphere or a 'mood' that coerces the customer into purchasing. Some studies have suggested that consumers enjoy surprise, innovation and intrigue and this has led to fashion retailers having frequent store refits to create clear, distinctive and memorable brand identities (Bruce and Cooper, 1997; Moore and Lochhead, 1998).

Occasionally a brand needs to be repositioned due to poor sales performance or changes in customer requirement. Retailers can change their market position by identifying new target markets or by gaining differential advantage. Intangible repositioning can be made by changing branding, level of customer service, store environment or customer communications. Davies and Liu (1995) argue that well-trained staff and store design are two efficient techniques for successful repositioning in contrast to media advertising, which appears to be less effective. Design has become part of the business strategy to optimise profit potential by attracting new and retaining existing customers. Design has brought added value to the shopping experience.

11.5.6 *Customer communication*

Customer communication to identify expectations and needs is an important part of any marketing strategy. It is not enough to monitor and analyse complaints and complements, forward looking companies set up systems to encourage customers to voice their views on the company, its products and service, and to seek suggestions on how customers' satisfaction might be increased (Cook, 1997). Another method has been to improve in-store communication via better merchandise labelling to explain features and benefits of new products, fabrics or finishes as well as providing care instructions. Thus, customers can obtain information without having to approach staff.

11.6 Store image congruency

Osman (1993) examined consumer attitude to store choice and noted that it is affected by the store rating on each of the contributing store image attributes. The argument is that if retailers meet or exceed expectations, customers will have a positive experience, make repeat purchases and increase their loyalty towards the store. Conversely, a low degree of congruence between the image perceived by the customer and the intended market positioning could, potentially, be an indicator of future problems.

Employee perception of the company image influences not only the way they serve customers, but also the way they discuss the company with their family and friends. Thus, congruence of image is an important area for further research, as staff have often been shown to perceive their company image differently from that of their customers (Samli and Lincoln, 1989).

Pathak *et al.* (1974) compared consumer and retailer perception of the image of four department stores. Results indicated that managers had a good understanding of consumer opinion with regard to tangible aspects of the merchandise, but were less certain of customers' perception of symbolic factors, such as store atmosphere. Furthermore, Samli and Lincoln (1989) found divergence when they compared retail manager and consumer perceptions. Overall, they found managers to have a more positive image of the store, although on some factors they had a lower opinion than customers. They conclude that total congruence is not likely but that it highlights the importance of evaluating differences in perception. In contrast, May (1974) identified consumers to have a more favourable perception than managers on many attributes. This is credited to the fact that retailer staff are in the store regularly and, maybe, have a more realistic view or tend to be more critical than consumers.

Congruence of store choice evaluations is considered to be important in optimising retail resource hence, it is important to identify differences in employee and customer image perception. Retailers should take notice when the image perception of employees is lower than that of the customers on specific attributes. It is advantageous for retailers to employ staff with a positive perception of the store, its products and the environment in which they work. In addition, there is a relationship between the propensity of staff to purchase goods from the store in which they work, and customer reaction to the product. Thus, staff purchases can be an early indicator of consumer preference on new ranges and be used as a management control system.

The standard marketing response to heterogeneous markets is segmentation; one of the major contributions of marketing thought to modern business practice (Lockshin *et al.*, 1997). Segmentation research helps retailers to identify behavioural differences within their customer target groups. Consumer levels of involvement with the buying decision vary. This can range from being highly involved in the act of purchasing by seeking specific low-risk brands with the right image, to being less involved in the selection of products and more conscious of price and value. Customer clusters have been found on the continuum between this dichotomy and it is important for retailers to understand the different levels of involvement within their targeted customer groups. Hence, it is recommended that retail companies assess how well they are anticipating the perceived importance of store image attributes and the extent to which they satisfy their customers by regularly measuring store image congruity.

11.7 Conclusion

Empirical studies have identified store image dimensions, components and attributes, and indicate the precise mix to be different for retailers, not only between retail sectors but also within a sector. Arguably there is a relationship between image perceptions and market share, profit margin and sales turnover. Thus, it is essential for retailers to identify the specific combination of image attributes demanded by their customers to ensure a strong image and effective market positioning.

It is difficult to compare store image studies due to the variety of method and research designs utilised. Multiple fashion retailers conduct market research, on a regular basis to evaluate customer's attitudes towards the product and service provision. However, there is some evidence to show that measuring the importance of different attributes is not always satisfactory since respondents are inclined to assess everything as relatively important and, hence, results provide minimal variance (Johnson, 1997). This is why more sophisticated survey techniques such as conjoint analysis prove valuable. Furthermore, the added benefit of including segmentation research can help inform retailers on the requirements, behaviour and attitudes of their targeted customers.

Consumers purchase from those stores that come closest to the individual specification of determining choice factors. These concepts must influence retailers in deciding the strategy for the retail mix of product quality, service provision and store environment to best satisfy their target market.

Customer segmentation and market positioning are closely linked. Store positioning is the development and implementation of the retail mix to create an image of the retailer in the mind of the targeted consumer that is more positive than that of its competitors. The apparent success some retailers have achieved is attributed to the image and 'street cred' of the brand typified by the number of people becoming advocates for these retailers.

Research into store image has undoubtedly served to inform retailers on positioning strategies for their outlets, enabling them to differentiate their stores in terms of their products, their prices, or the services they offer. While empirical research has demonstrated a link between product quality and market share (Buzzell and Gale, 1987) there is less evidence of a clear relationship between store image, store choice and customer loyalty. However, a strong retail position and perceived store image do tend to lead to greater customer through-flow and hence profitability.

References

Amirani, S. and Gates, R. (1993) An attribute-anchored conjoint approach to measuring store image. *International Journal of Retail and Distribution Management*, **21**(5), 30–39.

Arnold, S.J., Tigert, D.J. and Handelman, J.M. (1997) *Competitive Market Structure Differentiation and Store Choice Attribute Determinacy*. Paper presented at the *Retailing: End of a Century and a Look to the Future*, St. Louis, Missouri.

Bass, F.M. and Talarzyk, W.W. (1972) An attitude model for the study of brand preference. *Journal of Marketing Research*, **9**(February), 93–96.

Beatty, S.E., Mayer, M., Coleman, J.E., Reynolds, K.E. and Lee, J. (1996) Customer–sales associate retail relationships. *Journal of Retailing*, **72**(3), 223–247.

Broadbridge, A. (1996) Female and male managers – equal progression? *The International Review of Retail, Distribution and Consumer Research*, **6**(3), 259–279.

Bruce, M. and Cooper, R. (eds) (1997) *Marketing and Design Management*. London, International Thomson Business Press.

Buzzell, R.D. and Gale, B.T. (1987) *The PIMS Principle*. New York, Free Press.

Cook, S. (1997) *Customer Care*, 2nd edition. London, Kogan Page.

Cook, S. and Macaulay, S. (1997) Customer service: what's a smile got to do with it? *Managing Service Quality*, **7**(5), 248–252.

Davies, G. (1992a) Positioning, image and the marketing of multiple retailers. *The International Review of Retail, Distribution and Consumer Research*, **2**(1), 13–34.

Davies, G. (1992b) The two ways in which retailers can be brands. *International Journal of Retail and Distribution Management*, **20**(2), 24–34.

Davies, G.J. and Brooks, J.M. (1989) *Positioning Strategy in Retailing*. London, Paul Chapman.

Davies, G., and Liu, H. (1995) The retailer's marketing mix and commercial performance. *International Review of Retail, Distribution and Consumer Research*, **5**(2), 147–165.

De Chernatony, L. and McDonald, M.H.B. (1992) *Creating Powerful Brands*. Oxford, Butterworth-Heinemann.

De Chernatony, L. and McDonald, M.H.B. (1998) *Creating Powerful Brands: In Consumer, Service and Industrial Markets*. Oxford, Butterworth-Heinemann.

Doyle, P. (1991) Branding. In Baker, M.J. (ed.), *The Marketing Book*, 2nd edition. Oxford, Butterworth-Heinemann.

Doyle, P. and Fenwick, I. (1974) How store image affects shopping habits in grocery chains. *Journal of Retailing*, **50**(4), 39–52.

Easey, M. (ed.) (2002) *Fashion Marketing*, 2nd edition. Oxford, Blackwell Science.

Evans, M. (1989) Consumer behaviour towards fashion. *European Journal of Marketing*, **23**(1), 63–69.

Evans, R.J. (1995) Quality versus cost – lessons for the late 1990s. *Managing Service Quality*, **5**(1), 6–10.

Fernie, J., Moore, C., Lawrie, A. and Hallsworth, A. (1997) The internationalization of the high fashion brand: the case of Central London. *Journal of Product and Brand Management*, **6**(6), 151–162.

Gale, B.T. and Klavans, R. (1985) Formulating a quality improvement strategy. *Journal of Business Strategy*, **5**(Winter), 21–32.

Gould, G. (1995) Why it is customer loyalty that counts (and how to measure it). *Managing Service Quality*, **5**(1), 15–19.

Green, P.E. (1977) A new approach to market segmentation. *Business Horizons*, **20**(1), 66–73.

Green, P.E. and Desarbo, W.S. (1978) Additive decomposition of perceptions data via conjoint analysis. *Journal of Consumer Research*, **5**(June), 58–65.

Green, P.E. and Srinivasan, V. (1978) Conjoint analysis in consumer research: issues and outlook. *Journal of Consumer Research*, **5**(September), 103–123.

Greenley, G.E. and Shipley, D. (1988) An empirical overview of marketing by JK retailing organisations. *Service Industries Journal*, **8**(1), 50–66.

Hair, J.F.J. and Anderson, R.E. (1985) *Multivariate Data Analysis with Readings*, 2nd edition. Macmillan.

Hansen, R.A. and Deutscher, T. (1977) An empirical investigation of attribute importance in retail store selection. *Journal of Retailing*, **53**(4, Winter), 59–72, 95.

Harris, D. and Walters, D. (1992) *Retail Operations Management – A Strategic Approach*. Hemel Hempstead, Prentice-Hall.

Hite, R.E. and Bellizzi, J.A. (1985) The psychological relationship between self-image, product image, and store image with regard to retailing. *Mid-South Business Journal*, **5**, 7–11.

Jain, A.K. and Etgar, M. (1976) Measuring store image through multidimensional scaling of free response data. *Journal of Retailing*, **52**(4, Winter), 61–70.

James, D.L., Durand, R.M. and Dreves, R. (1976) The use of a multi-attribute attitude model in a store image study. *Journal of Retailing*, **52**(2, Summer), 23–34.

Jobber, D. (2001) *Principles and Practice of Marketing*, 3rd edition. Maidenhead, McGraw-Hill.

Johnson, M. (1997) *Retail Positioning Techniques*. Research International.

Kelley, S.W. and Hoffman, K.D. (1997) An investigation of positive affect, prosocial behaviors and service quality. *Journal of Retailing*, **73**(3), 407–427.

Kunkel, J. and Berry, L. (1968) A behavioral conception of retail image. *Journal of Marketing*, **32**(October), 21–27.

Lehmann, D.R., Gupta, S. and Steckel, J.H. (1997) *Marketing Research*. Reading, MA, Addison-Wesley.

Levy, M. and Weitz, B.A. (1998) *Retailing Management*, 3rd edition. Boston, Irwin McGraw-Hill.

Lewis, B. and Hawskley, A. (1990) Gaining a competitive advantage in fashion. *International Journal of Retail and Distribution Management*, **18**(4), 21–32.

Lindquist, J.D. (1974) Meaning of image. *Journal of Retailing*, **50**(4), 29–38; 116.

Lockshin, L.S., Spawton, A.L. and Macintosh, G. (1997) Using product, brand and purchasing involvement for retail segmentation. *Journal of Retailing and Consumer Services*, **4**(3), 171–183.

Louviere, J.J. (1994). Conjoint analysis. In Bagozzi, R.P. (ed.), *Advanced Methods of Marketing Research*. Cambridge; MA, Blackwell.

Martineau, P. (1958) The personality of the retail store. *Harvard Business Review*, **36**(1), 47–55.

May, E.G. (1974) Practical applications of recent retail image research. *Journal of Retailing*, **50**(4), 15–20, 116.

Mazursky, D. and Jacoby, J. (1986) Exploring the development of store images. *Journal of Retailing*, **62**(2), 145–165.

McDougall, G.H.G. and Fry, J.N. (1974) Combining two methods of image measurement. *Journal of Retailing*, **50**(4, Winter), 53–61.

Moore, C.M. (1995) From rags to riches – creating and benefiting from the fashion own brand. *International Journal of Retail and Distribution Management*, **23**(9), 19–28.

Moore, C. M., and Lochhead, M. (1998). The management of retail design: demystifying the activity. *Journal of Consumer Studies and Home Economics*, **22**(3), 121–130.

Murphy, J.M. (1992) What is branding? In Murphy, J.M. (ed.), *Branding: A Key Marketing Tool*, 2nd edition. Basingstoke, Macmillan, pp. 1–12.

Osgood, C.E., Suci, G.J. and Tannenbaum, P.H. (1957) *The Measurement of Meaning*. Urbana, IL, University of Illinois Press.

Osman, M.Z. (1993) A conceptual model of retail image influences on loyalty patronage behaviour. *International Review of Retail, Distribution and Consumer Research*, **3**(2), 133–148.

Pathak, D.S., Crissy, W.J.E. and Sweitzer, R.W. (1974) Customer image versus the retailer's anticipated Image: a study of four department stores. *Journal of Retailing*, **50**(4), 21–28, 116.

Porter, M.E. (1985) *Competitive Advantage; Creating and Sustaining Superior Performance*. New York, Free Press.

Richer, J. (1996) *The Richer Way*, 2nd edition. London, Emap Business Communications.

Samli, A.C. and Lincoln, D. (1989) Management versus customer perception of image. In Samli, A.C. (ed.), *Retail Marketing Strategy: Planning, Implementation, and Control*. New York, Quorum, pp. 193–205.

Schiffman, L.G. and Kanuk, L.L. (1994) *Consumer Behavior*, 5th edition. Englewood Cliffs, NJ, Prentice-Hall.

Steenkamp, J.-B.E.M. (1990) Conceptual model of the quality perception process. *Journal of Business Research*, **21**, 309–333.

Thompson, K.E. and Chen, Y.L. (1998) Retail store image: a means-end approach. *Journal of Marketing Practice: Applied Marketing Science*, **4**(6), 161–173.

Thurstone, L.L. (1929) Theory of attitude measurement. *Psychological Review*, **36**, 222–241.

Townsend, B. (1991) Consumers don't always do what they say. *American Demographics*, **13**(April), 12–13.

Turnbull, P.W. and Wilson, D.T. (1989) Developing and protecting profitable customer relationships. *Industrial Marketing Management*, **18**(August), 233–238.

Van Auken, S. and Lonial, S.C. (1991) Multidimensional scaling and retail positioning: an appraisal. *International Journal of Retail and Distribution Management*, **19**(3), 11–18.

Verdict (1994) *Retail Fashion Images* (Special Report). London, Verdict Research Limited.

Walters, D. and Laffy, D. (1996) *Managing Retail Productivity and Profitability*. Basingstoke, Macmillan Press.

Ward, P., Sturrock, F., Schmidt, R.A. and Lea-Greenwood, G. (1998) *To Shop or Deshop: Motivational Aspects of Product Returns*. Paper presented at the Academy of Marketing, Sheffield Hallam University.

Wortzel, L.H. (1987) Retailing strategies for today's mature marketplace. *Journal of Business Strategy*, **7**(4), 45–56.

Zeithaml, V.A., Parasuraman, A. and Berry, L.L. (1990) *Delivering Quality Service: Balancing Customer Perceptions and Expectations*. New York, The Free Press.

Zimmer, M.R. and Golden, L.L. (1988) Impressions of retail stores: a content analysis of consumer images. *Journal of Retailing*, **64**(3), 265–293.

Study questions and guideline answers

1. **Make a critical analysis of store image attributes important to customers for a number of sectors/retailers. Justify your selection. Design a method of measuring store image for a retailer of your choice.**

Students are expected to be able to identify store image attributes important to different sectors. In addition, they should be able to identify these for a number of retailers with different retail positioning within a sector. They should be able to justify the selection of attributes, which the retailer can manipulate for the required market positioning which will suit the target market. Students should use one of the methods described to enable them to measure store image for a retailer of their choice.

2. **Discuss the positioning of Marks and Spencer's clothing offer. How is this communicated to the customer?**

Students should evaluate the market positioning of the different Marks and Spencer product lines, such as Per Una and Autograph (see Menswear lines). The positioning of these can be discussed and how the retailer tries to provide marketing communication through labelling, fixtures and fittings, and carrier bags.

3. **Identify a number of retailers that have strong store positioning and justify why these retailers could be a brand.**

Using the four criteria of Davies (1992a), students should select a number of retailers such as Next, TopShop/TopMan, H&M and Zara or Mango and evaluate which of these retailers can be called a brand. The justification should be based on examples for each retailer for each of the criteria.

4. **Discuss why store image congruency is important. Illustrate your answer with examples.**

The text demonstrates that there is not one view on store image congruency. However, store image attitude measurement comparisons between retail management, staff and customers is important to enable the retailer to measure the strength of market positioning and to enable quick identification of problem areas. Students should be able to evaluate the importance of store image congruency by using examples from existing retailers.

Chapter 12

Fashion retail trends in Hong Kong

Alice W.C. Chu and Kit-lun Yick

Aims

The aims of this chapter are:

- to show the current retail environment in Hong Kong;
- to discuss common fashion retailing format in Hong Kong;
- to examine the contemporary trend in fashion retailing strategies;
- to identify the practice of fashion retailers in response to the market change.

12.1 Introduction

Before the Chief Secretary has announced to strategically position Hong Kong as a fashion design centre, Hong Kong was already recognised as a shopping haven for overseas tourists. In the past decades, the fashion industry has been developing at a fast pace. Except the import of renowned international fashion brands, many local manufacturers have established their own brands successful in this market and most of them have already internationalised their business overseas and to Chinese mainland. The growth in this retail business is due to the constant demand of fashion merchandise from Hong Kong shoppers. Many international fashion brands also set up their stores in Hong Kong not only to satisfy these fashion-conscious shoppers but also to use this as a window for China market. However, with the over-development of fashion retailers, the fashion retailing business is more than saturated and the competition is becoming very fierce. It is observed that any fashion retailers without strong brand identity and good product mix find it difficult to survive in this market where the consumers are very price and fashion-conscious.

12.2 Background

The wholesale and retail industry is one of the biggest service industries in terms of number of establishment and employment in Hong Kong. In 2000, there were about 73,000 business undertakings in the main wholesale and retail services, employing some 288,000 people. The wholesale and retail industry generated about HK$44.7 billion value added in 1999, or 3.9 per cent of Hong Kong's gross domestic product (GDP).

As stated in the *First Quarter Government Economic Report 2002*, the local consumer spending remained subdued due to the rising unemployment and wage restraint. On a

Table 12.1 Value indices of retail sales in Hong Kong

	1996	1997	1998	1999	2000	2001	2002 (Jan–May)
Value index	120.2	126.1	105.0	96.6	100.2	99.0	95.3
Volume index	112.2	113.4	94.5	93.1	100.8	102.0	99.8

October 1999 to September 2000 = 100

year-on-year comparison, private consumption expenditure (PCE) slackened to a 0.6 per cent in real terms in the first quarter of 2002 over a year earlier. In fact, with the reference from Table 12.1, retail sales started to decline after the Asian financial crisis. The value index dropped almost 10 points in 1998 and it is still in a downward trend. A few reputable department stores, mostly Japanese, have gone into liquidation. Automotive, clothing and footwear sales dropped more than 30 per cent (Icon Group International, 2000). Although Hong Kong's retailers are trying harder than ever to improve service and courtesy standards to attract customers, the situation is not optimistic. Local consumers are still worried about job security, income uncertainty and weakness in the asset markets, these factors depress their sentiment to spend. Furthermore, consumer prices are even expected to drift lower in the near term since its downturn in late 1998. When competition in a slackened retail market is keen, together with a reduced labour income and a sluggish property market, retailers will face a very difficult time for the coming years.

Such economic environment has given the retail business a hard time. Many fashion stores closed down after 1997 as the consumption power has dropped tremendously. With the increase of the unemployment rate – up to 7 per cent by the end of 2002, the high percentage of salary cuts, and devaluation of property market, most of the consumers in Hong Kong have changed to be very conscious in spending. Due to the fear of losing job, among all levels of workforce, the future of fashion retail business is not optimistic and fashion retailers have to be very competitive in order to survive in this marketplace.

12.3 Development of fashion retail format in Hong Kong

The change of fashion retail format evidenced the change of the economy, and the consumer behaviour of local people. Regarding retail institutions, retailers can be classified on the basis of their ownership, merchandise, size, affiliation, location and operational characteristics, etc. The diversity and complexity of business formats found in the retailing industry preclude developing a mutually exclusive classification that clearly differentiates each type of retailer (Lewison, 1997). In the case of fashion retailing in Hong Kong, some of the common formats include:

- department store,
- historical development of Hong Kong department stores,
- speciality chain,
- discount store,
- boutiques.

12.3.1 Department store

Department store is a large retail unit with an extensive assortment of goods and services that is organised into separate departments for purpose of buying, promotion, customer service and control. As defined by Levy and Weitz (1996), department stores are retailers that carry a wide variety and deep assortment, offer considerable customer services and are organised into separate departments for displaying merchandise. Lewison (1994), however, defined department store as a large retailing institution that carries broad variety of merchandise lines with a reasonably good selection within each line. The US Bureau of Census gives a much clearer definition of a department store, in which it is a retail establishment that employs at least 50 people and has sales of apparel and soft goods amounting to at least 20 per cent of total sales. Moreover, the merchandise assortment must include some items in each of these lines: furniture, home furnishings, appliances; a general line of apparel for the family; household lines and dry goods.

In Hong Kong, as defined by the Census and Statistics Department, department stores are regarded as all establishments which engage in the retail of a variety of consumer goods of which foodstuffs or clothing are not predominant. Sales persons should be available to assist or promote sales of goods in some or all sections of the department stores. In Hong Kong, there are department stores that serve the high-end segment such as Lane Crawford and Seibu, and also department stores that target the mass market such as Jusco, Wing On. Most of them offer a wide range of products, from food, clothing and accessories to electrical appliances.

12.3.2 Historical development of Hong Kong department stores

The *department stores industry* is an important segment of the retail sector of Hong Kong because it evidenced the change of fashion retail business here. The first local-financed department store, Sincere Department Store, was opened in 1900. It was the first time that Hong Kong people had ever experienced such a large variety of merchandise with modernised facilities in one store. Seven years later, Wing On Department Store entered the retail market. They were both family-based department stores which brought an early taste of Western-style, wide-assortment retailing to an area accustomed to numerous small shops, each selling only a few product categories (McGoldrick, 1990). In 1938, the first Chinese-financed department store, China Products Co. Ltd., entered the market. Later, in 1960s, there was an emergence of the Chinese-style department stores including Yue Hwa, Chung Kiu and the Chinese Product Emporium Ltd. During the mid-1960s, the dominant situation was no longer maintained as Japanese-style department stores entered the Hong Kong market. Daimaru was the first Japanese department store to open in Hong Kong at Causeway Bay, which targeted middle-class customers with its spacious shopping space and expensive brand names. Thereafter, Japanese-style department stores set up their branches in Hong Kong continuously and rapidly. Shortly, it captured 50 per cent of market share in the industry and had great impact on both Chinese- and Hong Kong-styled ones.

Starting from late 1960s, Hong Kong's economy had grown rapidly and people became more quality and image-conscious. Many department stores thus imported reputable and branded merchandise from European countries and expanded the scale in order to spread out the operating cost. Large Japanese mega-stores from Yaohan, UNY and Jusco became the operating format in Hong Kong. The competition of the Hong Kong department stores industry became more severe. Meanwhile, British-style department stores began to enter Hong Kong market and the first comer was Dodwell Co. Ltd. In late 1980s to early 1990s, many department stores like Wing On and Yaohan and Jusco continued to open their branches. However, Japanese-style department stores still captured 80 per cent of the market share in the industry and became the market leader due to their wide product varieties, higher product quality, better customer services, and more preferred image of fashionable and modern style. By the end of 1993, Sogo introduced Jumbo Sogo. With a total retail space of 360,000 square feet, which combined the original Sogo and became the largest department store in Hong Kong. Three years later, the New Face by Sogo opened which aimed at

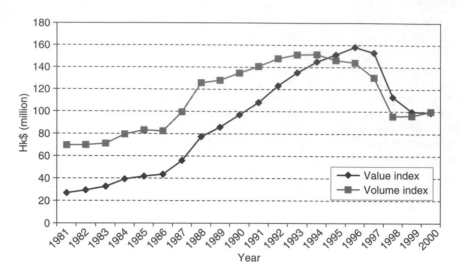

Figure 12.1 Value and volume indices of department store (1999/2000 based)
Source: Census and Statistic Department

young and fashionable people with high disposable incomes (Chan, 1993, 1996). It is also noteworthy trend, that leased departments have become a way of increasing the proportion of sales areas (Diamond and Pintel, 1996).

However, the successful development of Japanese department stores was not lasting. Many Japanese department stores in Hong Kong have either closed or scaled back their operations since 1995 (Fulford, 1998). In 1995, Mitsukoshi closed its Tsim Sha Tsui store because of the severe financial problems in its home market. Isetan also closed in 1996. In November 1997, Yaohan department store went into liquidation due to its Japanese parent company collapsing under huge debts in September (Diola *et al.*, 1997). In 1998, Matsuzakaya and Daimaru closed in August and December, respectively, due to global restructuring and serious debts caused by severe competition and recession (Lam, 1998).

In spite of the specific closure reason for specific companies, there are some common reasons of closure. Firstly, the high rent may have been the major cause of closure (Kwong, 1998). Secondly, due to the Asian economic crisis, consumers' confidence has been hit hard by growing fears of unemployment and the declining in stock. Consumers therefore were not willing to spend (Tsang, 1998). The decline in tourist spending in Hong Kong due to a sharp fall in visitor arrivals from Japan and other Asian countries was another reason (Ng, 1998). Although some of the local department stores tried to establish spin-off stores for capturing the younger market, most of them failed. They include Express from Lane Crawford and Signature from Sincere.

Figure 12.1 and Table 12.2 show the value and volume indices of department store between 1981 and 2000. Comparing with one of the famous local department store, (Wing On's past performance, in Figure 12.2, it shows that the popularity of such a kind of format is decreasing after the change of the retail environment and the consumer taste.

12.3.3 Speciality chain

A traditional speciality store concentrates on a limited number of complementary merchandise categories and provides a high level of service (Levy and Weitz, 1996). By carrying a narrow variety but deep assortment, they offer customers a better selection and sales expertise in that category than department or discount stores can provide. According to

Table 12.2 Value and volume indices of department store (1999/2000 based)

	1981	1982	1983	1984	1985	1986	1987	1988	1989	1990
Value index	26.8	29.2	32.6	39.1	41.6	43.4	55.8	77.3	85.9	97.1
Volume index	69.6	69.9	71.1	79.4	83.2	82.4	99.5	125.8	128.2	134.7
	1991	1992	1993	1994	1995	1996	1997	1998	1999	2000
Value index	108.2	123.4	135.3	145.2	151.5	158.3	153.2	113.0	100.0	99.0
Volume index	140.9	147.8	151.4	151.8	146.4	144.2	130.8	95.7	96.2	100.2

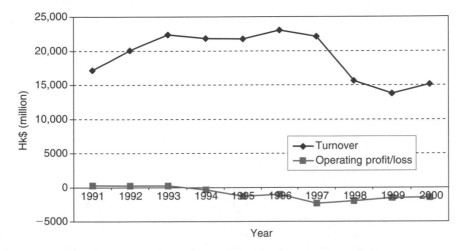

Figure 12.2 Turnover and operating profit/loss of Wing On department store
Source: Annual Report of Wing On Company International Limited (1991–2000)

Segal (1994), every successful speciality retailing format starts with a unique idea that strikes consumers as new, fresh and different. Retail ideas become ego expressions of the people involved in creating, nurturing and developing them. A retail idea reflects a particular approach to product selection, display, merchandising store design and customer service. The speciality store retailers attempt to serve all consumers in one or a limited number of market segments.

In Hong Kong, some of the largest local fashion speciality chains are Giordano, Esprit, Bossini, G2000, Moiselle, Wanko, etc. For example, Esprit is a leading international fashion lifestyle brand with a distribution network of over 6500 stores and outlets in 40 countries worldwide. Esprit targets young, fashion-conscious, trendy and energetic customers. As stated by their marketing assistant, Miss Sarina Hung, their customers are those who pursue personal clothing taste, and prefer the fashion dressing code of 'mix and match'. The age range of the target segment is between 18 and 40 years old, and of both sexes. Other than large-scale fashion chain stores, there is a large number of small-scale fashion speciality stores in Hong Kong. Ice House is a typical example of small-scale speciality store targets at oversized customers. Their product sizes (waist sizes) range from 28 to 50 inches, including ready-to-wear, casual wear and executive wear. Small stores are ranked as the second popular store type for consumers after chain stores. Most small stores (named as boutique) are selling unique merchandise and provide personalised services, one can always find innovative products among these shops. They are very popular among young consumers who look for trend and style.

Except local fashion brands, international brands and designer brands have also established their specialities chain in Hong Kong. Prada, Miu Miu, Louis Vuitton, Celine, Dior and Giorgio Armani are some of the examples. Recently, Georgio Armani opened his second largest flagship store in Hong Kong. A lot of international fashion brands treat Hong Kong as the 'window' for China, as it is viewed as the most important destination for them to develop in this 21st century.

By looking at the success of this institution, speciality chain stores will be one of the popular formats in the future. Basically, customers in Hong Kong are concerned about the convenience of a retail site. Chain operations can enhance this advantage. Development of shopping malls also speeds up the chain expansion. Working females who face a lack of time like the speciality store's focus on merchandise mix, as it saves them time in making purchase decisions.

12.3.4 Discount store

A discount store is a general merchandise retailer that offers a broad variety of merchandise, shallow assortments, limited service and low prices. Discount stores tend to concentrate on lower- to middle-income consumers. They offer brands that are typically less fashion-orientated than brands in department stores. Targeted to meet the needs of the economy-minded consumer, the discount stores use mass-merchandising techniques that enable it to offer discount prices as its major consumer appeal (Rinne and Swinyard, 1995). Most of these small stores sell branded merchandise at a lower price. They carry the overruns and end-of-season product from famous brands and distribute them in an office site located in the central business district. Off-price and factory outlets are common formats selling such discounted items. In order to upkeep their image, some fashion brands only launch discount sales in their office rather than traditional retail sites. The purpose of this is to clear season-end products, and price reductions can be up to 90 per cent off. Currently, even the big fashion retailers such as Joyce and Dickson Co. Ltd. have also opened discount stores in both business districts and neighbourhood shopping malls. Joyce warehouse and Dickson discount mall are examples in this format. For attracting pedestrian traffic, mall developers such as Wharf (Holdings) Ltd. also joins this discounting game. In the Harbour City (one of the largest shopping malls in Kowloon), the developer regularly chooses the third floor of an office building connected to Harbour city as a discount sales outlet for their tenants. Following the change in the shopping behaviour of local people and keen competition, fashion retailers have become very conscious in their pricing strategy, as it must reflect the value of the product and services provided.

12.3.5 Boutiques

A boutique is a type of speciality store that sells fashion apparel and accessories selected for a group of specific customer. In French, 'Boutique' means 'little shop usually carrying few-of-a-kind merchandise' (Jernigan, 1990). The rise in the number of boutiques is an example of the changing attitudes of today's customers. They expect and want more from their purchases, including not only practicality but also individuality. Boutiques are much like speciality stores, but they are smaller and appeal to more limited target markets. Such stores are small operations with distinct personalities, and they provide a unique product assortment that usually consists of special types of goods (Hasty and Reardon, 1997).

In Hong Kong, there are many small and independent boutiques. A lot of them are run by the proprietor. Boutiques can normally be found in shopping mall like Mong Kok Shopping Centre and on the street. Most of the boutiques target the budget-minded customers. The merchandise found in these boutiques is mainly manufactured locally or imported from China. Some boutiques may also sell imported goods from Italy or Japan. Other boutiques selling lower-price fashion products are also popular among the shoppers in Hong Kong. These boutiques change the fashion merchandise very fast so as to generate sales through the inventory turn. Most of these boutiques do not pay much attention on the quality, as the life cycle for the product is short. However, trend and styles are their main concern. These boutiques usually target to young consumers in their teens or twenties. Currently, due to high rental charges of traditional retail sites, some of these small boutiques have located in the upper floor of office buildings. These are named as 'upstairs' stores and they have become more and more popular among those new fashion designers with limited budget. The boutique format seems to be prevalent in the coming future as this kind of small store can personalise their service to individual customer.

12.4 Contemporary trends in fashion retailing strategies in Hong Kong

Since the 1980s, there has been dramatic change in the retail environment. Hong Kong's economy has undergone a remarkable transformation and the services sector has now taken over from manufacturing as Hong Kong's main enterprise. Among, the wholesale and retail industry has become one of the biggest service industries in Hong Kong. Anticipated with considerable changes in socio-economic trends and technological revolution, the retail environment has also undergone radical change. Retail companies have grown at an unprecedented scale and are increasingly becoming international corporations. Consumers have become more affluent and demanding. In Hong Kong, shopping is widely accepted as an increasingly leisure-based activity. New retail formats have emerged, reflecting a response to these demands and to the changing requirements of retailers in the evolving business, fiscal and planning environment. Nevertheless, the economic crisis in 1997 and 2001 has brought a tremendous impact on the consumption power of the general public. Today, consumers make apparel expenditures much more cautiously than in the past. Fashion retailers therefore have to alter their retail operations and/or implement different strategies in order to cope with the changing needs of their consumers. As stated by Lewison:

> To survive in the contemporary world of retailing, retail formats must adapt rapidly and creatively to the dynamics of the marketplace. Past and current winners in the field of retailing have been those that have best identified emerging unsatisfied needs for consumers and developed innovative merchandising and operating strategies and practices to satisfy them. Today, successful retailers are those who make a habit of adaptation, based on an ever-deepening knowledge of their marketplace and their consumers, to whom they will listen, learn from, and respond.
>
> Lewison (1997)

In respect to the dramatic change of retail environment in Hong Kong, some fashion retailers have expanded their existing markets and developed new market segments to increase their market share. Some retailers have developed large single stores selling a wide range of goods to satisfy the fashion needs of the consumers. Anyhow, some of the more visible retail trends are discussed below.

12.4.1 Rapid and continuous flow of product development

In the late 1980s, the fashion industry implemented quick response (QR) strategy to achieve quick and precise replenishment of fast-selling merchandise by means of computerised partnerships between fabric suppliers, apparel producers and retailers. Now, because of advanced communication systems which facilitate the rapid transfer of fashion news, fashion-forward consumers see new fashion trends and want them immediately. This rapid transfer of demand places pressure on the whole manufacturing–distribution chain to be able to respond more quickly than ever before. In order to serve the customer more effectively by focusing on the customer's needs, retailers want to reduce the time required to get merchandise produced and to the retail sales floor. Nevertheless, speed is not the only advantage in today's market environment. Fashion merchandising has increasingly moved away from the traditional cycles and, instead, has evolved more and more towards a continuous flow of new products (Jarnow and Dickerson, 1997). Also, by taking the guesswork out of reordering, many companies place small orders for consumer style testing and replenish only the styles which sell. Kurt Salmon Associates (KSA), a leading consulting firm for the fashion industries, has also predicted that in the year of 2000 and beyond, products will be more customised rather than mass produced where one or a few sizes are expected to fit all. Many consumers are tired of the 'sameness' and exerting a new independence. They are more likely to define their own styles and more likely to resist being dictated to by industry.

Not only with increased customisation of products and service, Frings (1999) also stated that the 1990s were referred to as the value decade. Consumers are value driven, demanding more for less. As Mackey McDonald, President and CEO of VF Corporation, noted, 'The consumer is now in control' (Maycumber, 1995). Consumers make apparel expenditures much more cautiously than in the past and are not easily manipulated by promotional efforts geared to encourage them to buy things they do not need or want.

In Hong Kong, the phenomenon of rapid and continuous product development has been widely adopted by the local fashion retailers. A typical example is Veeko – a ladies apparel company – who design, manufacture and retail under their own-brand names Veeko and Wanko. The company was established in 1984 as a small manufacturer/wholesaler of ladies apparel with 10 staff in Hong Kong and now, it has become one of Asia-Pacific region's largest chains of ladies' fashion, with over 120 outlets in Hong Kong, Macau, Taiwan, Singapore and mainland China. From 1996 to 2001, sales increased six times from HK$59 million to HK$345 million. The company aims to meet the clothing needs of today's modern woman, who wants good value for money. Mr. C.M. Chung, the Chairman and Managing Director of Veeko stated that shortening the turnaround time from sourcing to production is one of their major marketing strategies (Chan, 2000, 2001). To satisfy the constant glamour for new outfits, the company implements a QR programme which enables the company taking only 2½ months on average – far shorter than the average 6 months of some retailers – to source the textiles, design and produce the ensemble and display them in its outlets. This quick turnaround time has made the company a leader of the latest fashion while allowing it to reduce the risk of excess inventory. In view of its product development strategy, the company has an in-house design team which produces three sets of new designs under its brands every 2 weeks. Mr Chung also emphasised that the company would like to maintain their competitive price policy but add value to the products by selecting high-quality imported fabrics. To be profitable, the company has its own manufacturing facilities accompanied with a marketing strategy which aims at responding demand of the market swiftly in order to control costs.

12.4.2 Store size (mega-store approach of one-stop shopping)

One-stop shopping is the marketing strategy of broadening the retail offering to meet consumer's expanding needs. By expanding the number of product options, retailers try to increase the size of their total market by appealing to several sub-markets and thereby attempting to satisfy more of the specific shopping needs of several individual market segments. In this expansion process, the one-stop merchandiser attempts to develop a more general-purpose retailing format that will satisfy the needs of most consumers (Lewison, 1997). Regarding the one-stop shopping approach, line extension (extending the selection of product items within the retailer's existing product lines), line addition (adding more desirable product items to the retailer's traditional merchandise mix) and/or format combinations (combining two or more compatible retailing formats) can be accomplished. To cope with the increase in the offerings, the store size has been increased from below one thousand square feet to several thousands.

The recent development of Esprit is a typical example of broadening its merchandise mix to meet customer's expanding needs. At its headquarters in Hong Kong, Esprit is engaged in the design, sourcing, retail and wholesale distribution of quality and lifestyle product under the global brand name of *Esprit*. Its name is promoted as a 'lifestyle' image, and products bearing the Esprit brand are designed to reflect the latest trends in colour, silhouette, fabric and item co-ordination. In Hong Kong, they have 149 retail outlets. Other than offering an extensive range of women's, men's and children's apparel, customers may also find footwear, accessories, skin- and body-care products, cosmetic and beauty products under the Red Earth brand name, timewear, eyewear, socks and tights, bed and bath products, jewellery, and hair saloons, etc. in some of their mega-stores. Another example is Benetton. In 1999, the Benetton and Sisley Mega-Store were opened at Tsim Sha Tsui (one of the famous shopping district in the Kowloon Pennisula), offering clothing, handbags, shoes, sunglasses and other accessories. Mexx also has its mega-store (around 7000 square feet) in Festival Walk – a 1-million square feet shopping mall located in Kowloon Tong. Giorgio Armani also opened the second largest flagship store in Hong Kong by the end of 2002. Except increasing the room for merchandise display, this kind of mega-store has also helped create new concepts for the fashion brands. Typical example is azona a02 which is the one of the local fashion brands bringing in household accessories and furniture to be sold on the floor. The basic philosophy is to build up a unique brand image and attract the shoppers to browse the store. Such a kind of concept store needs bigger space for displaying a wide collection of merchandise. As a result, with the increase in product assortment, the trend of setting up bigger stores will persist. To this end, the location of such stores is very critical because pedestrian traffic flow and rent are the main concerns for setting up such a size of a store.

12.4.3 Portfolio retailing

Sheth (1983) has stated that no single retailing approach is likely to be sufficient in the future simply because markets are diverging more and more with respect to wants, needs and buying power. A portfolio retailer therefore operates multiple types of retail formats, each with individual-tailored merchandising programme designed to serve the specific needs of a different target group (Kopp *et al.*, 1989). In other words, the portfolio retailer operates a collection of separate and specialised retail businesses specifically suited for and focused on selective consumer segments (Lewison, 1997). Recently, portfolio retailing is also regarded as a growth strategy that enables a retailer to gain an important competitive advantage of flexibility. An example of Hong Kong portfolio retailer is the Veeko Group. Other than the QR programme (discussed above), the company has set up shops and outlets under three different brands. Its portfolio includes Wanko (products for ladies executive wear), Veeko (designed for trendy young ladies) and i-Miix (a recent product diversification of casual and fashionable wear for young ladies). Another local retailer with similar approach is Texwood. The company diversified its products and opened an outlet namely Texwood Menswear which targets aged 28–40 customers with middle/high-price products.

Moiselle is also a successful example of ladies' fashion wear retailing in Hong Kong. In 1997, the company firstly introduced a local designer's label 'Moiselle' for ladies' fashion wear targeted to capture the retail market of young ladies and professionals above the age of 20 in Hong Kong. The company has all along emphasised on top-quality material, updated European design, variety of choices, adequate sizes, top-class customer services and reasonable attractive prices. In 2001, the company started to diversify the products to meet the needs of different age groups. Its portfolios are: 'moi', 'imaroon' and 'M.kids'. While the 'Moiselle' products appeal to more mature women who look for a versatile and feminine style in day-wear which fits into their lifestyle and evening-wear for occasional events, the 'moi' caters for the nine-to-five needs of young female professionals, who are fashion-conscious, with clothing offered at competitive prices. The 'imaroon' targets at young working women with simple fashion and basic wear with less extravagant decoration in timeless styles. The 'M.kids' as suggested by the name, is children's wear.

Other local fashion brands with longer history such as Giordano and G2000 have practised such portfolio retailing for some time. Under the G2000 group, brands include U2 and U2 Women while Giordano Group carries Giordan Ladies, Blue Star Exchange and Giordano. By managing a collection of retail businesses, these portfolio retailers gain an important competitive advantage, that of flexibility (Lewison, 1997).

12.4.4 Target marketing

Targeting marketing is the strategy of focusing the retailer's efforts on a select group of customers and employing a penetration strategy to serve 'all' of the individual needs of a given market segment (Lewison, 1997). Fashion retailers are increasingly embracing target marketing as it helps identify marketing opportunities better. They can develop the right product, adjust their prices, distribution channels and advertising to each target market efficiently. According to Kolter (1985), target marketing starts with market segmentation which is the act of dividing a market into distinct groups of buyers who might require separate products or marketing mix. The second step is market targeting which is the act to select and evaluate which segment to enter. The third step is product positioning which is the act to formulate a competitive positioning for the product and a detailed marketing mix.

In the past, Wing On Department Store marketed itself as a family store, catering to family needs. Recently, the company started repositioning itself to attract younger customers and regain the market share by opening a new mega-store of 'Wing On Plus'. The store adopts a totally different and fresh approach to provide a new shopping experience and excitement for its shoppers so as to meet the retail challenge in the new millennium. U2 Women (UWN) from U2 is also another example of target marketing. While U2 Women targets the busy, self-assured and confident city woman in Hong Kong, it offers more fashionable and feminine apparels for the urban woman. U2 mainly focuses on providing stylish casual wear for trend-led women and men who are outgoing, young-at-heart. The segmentation using age and lifestyle is an effective way to segment the fashion market by individual fashion brands.

12.4.5 Polar retailing

Polar retailing is the tendency for retail organisations to evolve around either the speciality store format or formats that employ mass-merchandising techniques within a large store facility (Lewison, 1997). In fashion retailing, some retailers offer excitement, service and education. Although some fashion retailers offer moderate price points and safe but uninspiring fashion assortments, many others are defining a viable and well-differentiated polar niche that should enable them to prosper despite the turbulence in the retail industry. For example, Moiselle aims at female consumers who look for feminine styles of clothings, while G2000 have repositioned their image from smart casual wear to modern city wear. Their collections offer highly versatile co-ordinating pieces and refined separates that fulfil the consumers' need across their career wardrobe and relaxed occasions. Both companies are more focused on their consumers and entertain their individual needs. Niche marketing becomes the very technique for enhancing the competitiveness of these fashion retailers.

12.4.6 Store environment

Many fashion retailers realise that the design of store environment is an important element of marketing strategy, retailers strive to develop consumer-orientated store environments which have been identified as a potential competitive advantage. They strive for a differential advantage on variables that are most likely to be store-choice factors as determined by the expectations of consumers in the target market. As a result, many fashion retailers spend millions of dollars periodically designing and refurbishing their stores because the central challenge lies in understanding the needs of consumers, and hence providing the store environment that appeals to consumers' need. Since Hong Kong customers rank shopping as their favourable pastime, a retailer should provide a retail environment which can lure these customers to enter. Thus the unique environment offered may be influential to the consumer's store-choice decision (Darden *et al.*, 1983). Furthermore, store environmental design is particularly important for retailers when the number of competitive outlets increases; or when product entries are aimed at distinct social classes or lifestyle buyer groups. In a study of department store image of Hong Kong and Shanghai, it was revealed that store atmospheric design is one of the elements to develop a 'sense of prestigious and high quality' (Chan and Leung, 1996). It indicated that store environment affects the store choice of the customers in upscale market segment.

Store environment has undergone a tremendous change in the past decade. With the change in consumer demand, many Hong Kong-fashion brands have tried to create a unique environment to attract their target audience to stay longer. They started to pay attention to the international trends on the interior design and window display. In the 1980s, most fashion brands used wood for interior decoration. In the 1990s, store design of fashion retailers changed from using brown wood backgrounds to white ones. Benetton is one of the examples. During that time, most designer brands inclined to minimalism and this trend has also affected the local fashion retailers such as Bossini and Girodano. Having the concept that keeping shoppers longer in the store can promote sales, many fashion stores have increased the aisle width and the store size so as to provide a comfortable and spacious environment for shopper to browse and purchase.

On the other hand, some new fashion retailers made use of the store design to create a store atmosphere that corresponds to their brand personality. One of the most innovative fashion retailers – Izzue of IT Group has given up the conventional way of using bright lighting to illuminate the store space. Instead, they decorate the store like a warehouse with dim light (Ho, 2000). Such approach created a mood of mystery and relaxation which has gained acceptance by their young consumers. Today, other fashion retailers aiming at young consumer groups have followed this approach. Apart from the change in the intensity of lighting, another brand of this group, i.t., has chosen the bright orange fixture to match with black wall and white floor in the store design. Such attempt of using strong colour contrast to attract consumer attention has made the store image very outstanding among its competitors.

The age of the cookie-cutter store is over. Fashion retailers that clearly communicate well-established and understandable identities have the best chance of meeting the expectations of consumers (Lewison, 1997b, p. 656). This applies to the fashion retailers in

Hong Kong as the market is saturated and the competition is keen. Intratype and intertype competition push most retailers to build up a unique image for differentiation. Creating a pleasing store atmosphere with the latest custom-designed fixture becomes one of the effective tools to enhance the brand's image. Many fashion retailers have put particular emphasis on store apparel, visual merchandising and invests continuously to maintain their store's image. All these efforts are made to ensure every store is delivering a pleasurable shopping experience to their target audience.

12.4.7 Globalisation

Over the past two decades, due to the saturation of the local markets, a lot of fashion brands from the US and Europe have been motivated to set up store globally. Fashion retailers are the most international of retailers, as was noted by Doherty (2000), who recognised that the international expansion of fashion retailers outweighs the foreign market activities of retailers operating with other product sectors. In Hong Kong, one can find many of these international fashion retailers operating stores beyond their borders. Examples include Prada, Miu Miu, Louis Vuitton, Celine, Christian Dior, Giorgio Armani, Moschino, Escada, Tommy Hilfiger, Guess? and DKNY, etc. These international brands aim to use Hong Kong as a platform to China. Facing the same situation, many local fashion brands also went global in the past decade. Most of them opened stores in the Southeast Asian countries such as Singapore, Malaysia, Taiwan, Thailand, Indonesia, Korea, Philippines, etc. Some may go further to countries in the Middle-east and Central America. Following the opening up of retail markets in China, these fashion brands have begun to develop their stores there. One of the most successful brands is Baleno. Baleno is owned by a listed company in Hong Kong called Texwinca. Texwinca is principally engaged in the production and sales of dyed yarns and knitted fabrics. It expanded its business into casual wear retailing by acquiring the trademark of Baleno in June 1996. After repackaging the image, Baleno introduced a new collection of casual wear with clean and fashionable designs for both sexes. Over the past few years, Baleno has expanded rapidly in China. In 2003, the company operates 535 stores in this market and has become one of the famous brands there. The success of this brand is due to its low-price strategy, low cost of operations, mass appeal, design and good quality.

Today, many fashion brands have successfully built up their image in mainland China through franchising. Esprit, G2000, Veeko and Wanko, etc. are some examples. Any retailer who is intending to expand internationally, or who is already operating in different countries, is likely to have a keen interest in franchising as this mode of entry can reduce the risk of failure and cost of operations (Manaresi and Uncles, 1995). For local or foreign fashion brands, this mode of entry is regarded as effective for geographical expansion because it capitalises the established brand by duplicating its successful operation format to new markets. However, it would be a mistake to assume that globalisation is as easy as opening the box and re-creating concepts already tested in the domestic market. The unique economic, cultural and political environment of the individual market should be considered and certain a degree of adaptation to the market concerned is unavoidable. The 1.2 billion of population in China is very tempting for both local and international fashion retailers, it lures many of them to start their operation in China even without making profit. Operational problems still existed but most of the fashion retailers are optimistic of the future as this market provides ample room for future growth of the business.

12.4.8 Electronic tailing

Shopping in the bricks-and-mortar store has been one of the favourable leisure activities for women. These stores offer them a wide variety of merchandise to choose and an enticing shopping environment. Such kind of retail channel therefore becomes a dominant venue for consumers to purchase whatever merchandise they need over the past two decades. With the emergence of other formats of retailing, consumers' shopping behaviour has changed and in today's market, both offline and online shopping models co-exist due to the need of individual market segments.

Although the burst of dot.com bubble has broken, the dreams of many firms who want to generate more sales through this channel (i.e. the trend of using such format to build up the brand awareness) is still very common among fashion retailers in Hong Kong. Brands such as Baleno, Giordano and G2000, etc. have already had their own web site. Baleno's web site is for advertising purpose while Giordano's and G2000's also perform retail function. Both brands have been established in Hong Kong for more than a decade. Their brands are familiar among local shoppers. By using Yahoo, Giordano sells merchandise online. G2000 has set up its own online stores for both brands – U2.com.hk and g2000.com.hk. Both of them offer sales of merchandise to foreign countries in US dollars. It seems that the company wants to draw non-local shoppers through this channel of distribution. Whatever these objectives are, one thing is sure, they no longer only take the web site as a promotional medium, but also as a sales channel.

Due to the limitation of the geographical size of Hong Kong, the development of online stores will not be as fast as that in Europe and the US. Shoppers in Hong Kong want fast delivery and convenient location especially for fashion items. The chain store therefore is the most favourable shopping channel for local shoppers. Online purchasers are most likely limited to be fashion leaders, as they like to find unique apparel with special design through browsing online stores worldwide. Though the trend will not be prevailing in the near future, the tendency for consumers to look for fashion information is becoming common, presently due to the high computer literacy among the younger generation. It cannot be denied that e-mail has become the essential communication tool nowadays, however electronic tailing (e-tailing) may need to take some time to be developed as a favourable channel for fashion shoppers.

12.5 Conclusion

To be a leading fashion retailer in the Hong Kong market is not easy as there are many new players entering into the market constantly. Foreign fashion retailers are also expanding their presence in Hong Kong in preparation to their entry to the Chinese market. Faced with unfavourable economic conditions and a group of cautious consumers in the domestic markets, both local and foreign fashion retailers should be more innovative in managing their business. A customer-centred approach to marketing strategy is one of the keys to retail success. Analysing the customer preferences will customise the offerings to individual needs and this helps promote the sales. Building up a strong brand image will create enormous opportunity for business investors to wholesale and franchise the firm's products. The success of fashion retailers lies in the development of core competence which is not easy to be copied. However, change seems to be the ever-lasting element for running this business and the long-term success is built on how quick and effective the retailers adapt to these changes.

References

Amna K., Sanjay, S. and Sheri, B. (1999) The ownership effect in consumer responses to brand line stretches. *Journal of Marketing*, **8**(8).

Chan, K. (1993) Jumbo sogo ready to take off next week. *Hong Kong Standard*, 19 November.

Chan, K. (1996) Ambitious and bullish its new face. *Hong Kong Standard*, 30 November.

Chan, Y.L. (2000) *Hong Kong Economics Daily*, 10 August.

Chan, Y.L. (2001) *Hong Kong Economics Daily*, 8 November.

Chan, K.K. and Leung, Y.L. (1996) *A study of department store image in Hong Kong and Shanghai*. Hong Kong Baptist University, Business Research Centre, Papers on China Series CP96015.

Darden, W.R., Erdem, O. and Darden, D.K. (1983) A comparison and test of three causal models of patronage intentions. In Darden, W.R. and Lusch, R.F. (eds), *Patronage Behaviour and Retail Management.* , New York, North Holland, pp. 29–43.

Diamond, J. and Pintel, G. (1996) *Retailing*, 6th edition. Prentice-Hall,

Doherty, A.M. (2000) Factors influencing international retailers market entry mode strategy. *Journal of Marketing Management*, **16**, 223–45

Duikam, R., So, A. and Bruning, H. (1997) Yaohan goes into liquidation. *Hong Kong Standard*, 21 November.

Frings, G.S. (1999) *Fashion : From Concepts to Consumer*, 6th edition. Prentice-Hall, Chapter 13, pp. 287–308.

Fulford, B. (1998) Japan retailers opt out of Hong Kong. *South China Morning Post*, 5 March.

Goldstein, C. (1990) High stakes. *Far Eastern Economic Review*, 8 June.

Hasty, R. and Reardon, J. (1997) *Retail Management*, International Edition. McGraw-Hill, Chapter 1, p. 31.

Ho, W.H. (2000) Izzue – the 3rd stop. *The Economics Daily*, 24 January.

Icon Group International (2000) Retailing in Hong Kong: a strategic entry report, 2000. *Icon Group International, Inc. Report.*

Jarnow, J. and Dickerson, K.G. (1997) *Inside the Fashion Business*. Prentice-Hall, Chapters 1 and 2, pp. 1– 68.

Jernigan, M.H. (1990) *Fashion Merchandising and Marketing*. Macmillan.

Joseph, A.R. (1995) Branding: a trend for today and tomorrow. *Journal of Product and Brand Management*, **4**(4), 48–55.

Kolter, P. (1985) *Marketing Management: Analysis, Planning, and Control*, 5th edition. Prentice-Hall.

Kopp, R.J., Eng, R.J. and Tigert, D.J. (1989) A competitive structure and segmentation analysis of the Chicago fashion market. *Journal of Retailing*, **65**(Winter), 496–515.

Kwong, J. (1998) Little Japan set for major face-lift. *South China Morning Post*, 15 March.

Lam, W. (1998) Daimaru stores to close with loss of 400 jobs. *South China Morning Post*, 26 June.

Levy, M. and Weitz, B.A. (1996) *Essentials of Retailing*. McGraw-Hill, Chapter 1, pp. 2–83.

Lewison, D.M. (1997a) *Retailing*, 6th edition. Prentice-Hall, Chapter 2, p. 45.

Lewison, D.M. (1997b) *Retailing*, 6th edition. Prentice-Hall, Chapters 15 and 16.

MacPherson, K.L. (1998) *Asian Department Stores*. Curzon Press, Chapter 2, pp. 47–65.

Manaresi, A. and Uncles, M. (1995) Retail franchising in Britain and Italy. In Mcgoldrick, P.J. and Davies, G. (eds), *International Retailing: Trends and Strategies*. Pitman Publishing, p. 152.

Maycumber, G. (1995) Add value or die, says VF president McDonald, 16 February , p. 9.

McGoldrick, P.J. (1990) *Retail Marketing*. McGraw-Hill, Chapter 4, pp. 109–119; Chapter 5, pp.123–128.

Ng, D. (1998) Retail sales slump 15pc. *Hong Kong Standard*, 25 July.

Perkin, I.K. (1989) Japanese fuel local retail boom. *South China Morning Post*, 27 December.

Rinne, H. and Swinyard, W.R. (1995) Segmenting the discount store market: the domination of the difficult discount core. *The International Review of Retail, Distribution, and Consumer Research*, April, pp.123, 146.

Segal, G. (1994) Crate and barrel: success develops from a unique idea. *Retailers on Retailing, Lessons from the School of Experience*, p. 85.

Seibert, R. (1991) Arthur Andersen retailing issues. *Letter*, March.

Sheridan, M. (1990) There's much more in store. *Asian Magazine*, 21 September.

Sheth, J.N. (1983) Emerging trends for the retailing industry. *Journal of Retailing*, **59**(Fall), 14.

Tan, L.H. (1989) How the Japanese are winning the retailing war. *Asian Finance*, 15 January.

Tsang, D. (1998) Association sees years of woe for shops. *South China Morning Post*, 29 June.

Wing On Annual Reports (1991) Wing On Company International Limited.
Wing On Annual Reports (1992) Wing On Company International Limited.
Wing On Annual Reports (1993) Wing On Company International Limited.
Wing On Annual Reports (1994) Wing On Company International Limited.
Wing On Annual Reports (1995) Wing On Company International Limited.
Wing On Annual Reports (1996) Wing On Company International Limited.
Wing On Annual Reports (1997) Wing On Company International Limited.
Wing On Annual Reports (1998) Wing On Company International Limited.
Wing On Annual Reports (1999) Wing On Company International Limited.
Wing On Annual Reports (2000) Wing On Company International Limited.

Study questions and guidelines answers

1. **What kind of retailing strategies seem most likely to prevail within Hong Kong for the next few years?**

- Globalisation will continue due to the sluggish local market.
- Target marketing seems unavoidable due to the keen competition and very demanding local consumer.
- Chain store operations enhance convenience for shopping.
- QR allows fast delivery of popular merchandise.
- Polar retailing helps identify the niche of the market.
- Portfolio retailing reduces the risk during turbulence time.
- Big size operation allows a one-stop-shop environment for local customers.
- Attention paid to store design will be more.

2. **Why is franchising considered to be an effective mode of entry to the fashion market in China?**

- Reduce risk.
- Reduce cost of entry.
- Capitalise on the established brand.
- Local franchisees understand the market.
- Expand faster.

3. **How do the local fashion retailers achieve rapid and continuous flow of new products?**

- Shortened turnaround time from sourcing to production.
- Maintain competitive price.
- Build up a strong design team to develop new designs continuously.
- Offer value-added products (e.g. using high-quality imported fabrics).
- Develop their own manufacturing facilities (enabling better control of cost and time).

Chapter 13

Retail in the USA: the environment and consumer purchase behaviour

Trevor J. Little and Traci May-Plumlee

Aims

The aims of this chapter are:

- scope of the US retail complex;
- consumer behaviour in a department store;
- purchase and evaluative criteria;
- interpreting and synthesising purchase data.

13.1 Introduction

The US retail complex provides apparel and other products to 280 million people and is often recognised as the largest single market in the world. Nevertheless, the US consumer with relatively high personal consumption expenditures (PCEs) demands good value at retail. The high demands of the consumer provide an impetus for providing the consumer with desirable product at affordable prices. While the US retail sector has always been at the forefront of technology and customer service, the past two decades have shown a major effort to bring products to the consumer at even more competitive pricing and variety.

The US retail complex is a well-developed enterprise and of the top 200 global retailers, 45.5 per cent are in the US (Table 13.1). Furthermore, taking into consideration the sales of the top 200 global retailers, 52.7 per cent of the sales are in the US (Table 13.2). These tables illustrate the global retailing positions for a number of countries with organised retail industries. Four years ago, more than half (53 per cent) of the top 200 retailers operated in only one country while today, only 44 per cent remain single-country merchants. This globalisation trend can only intensify in the years ahead. The benefits of increased sales and greater economies of scale are too large to be ignored.

Table 13.1 Top 200 retailers by country of origin

Country	% of top 200 retailers by origin
USA	45.5
Japan	12.0
UK	9.0
Germany	6.5
France	5.5
Canada	3.3
Italy	3.0
Other Europe	11.5
Other	5.5

Source: Stores Online (January 2003)

Table 13.2 Sales by country for the top 200 retailers

Country	% sales of top 200 retailers
USA	52.7
Germany	10.3
France	8.9
UK	7.8
Japan	6.6
Canada	1.5
Italy	0.7
Other Europe	8.5
Other	3.0

Source: Stores Online (January 2003)

Table 13.3 Retail sales of apparel

	Department	Discount	Chain	Speciality	Total
1990	51.2	84.3	35.1	95.9	266.5
1991	50.6	92.1	34.5	97.4	274.6
1992	51.3	103.4	36.1	104.2	295.0
1993	51.7	114.8	38.3	107.4	312.2
1994	53.7	128.1	40.3	110.4	332.5
1995	54.4	140.7	41.6	111.4	348.1
1996	55.6	151.5	41.7	115.3	364.1
1997	55.4	168.9	41.7	119.6	385.6
1998	56.5	185.9	41.1	126.9	410.4
1999	55.2	205.5	42.7	135.1	438.5
2000	56.9	221.7	42.7	142.7	464.0

Source: AAFA (2003)

The US retail sales of apparel have continued to increase from 1990 through 2000 as shown in Table 13.3. Table 13.3 shows the breakdown of sales for the major channels of distribution for soft goods and the values are given in US$ billions (AAFA, 2003). The discount stores, often referred to as the mass merchants, and the speciality stores account for the increasing sales while the sales from traditional department stores remain flat. Sales through chain stores have increased about 20 per cent over the 11-year period.

This chapter explores the US retail trends from three perspectives:

- the supply network,
- the retail technology,
- the consumer.

13.2 The supply network

The soft goods supply chain has undergone a significant transformation in the past two decades. The US retail firms have been the major drivers of the transformation to a more efficient and more effective way to bring the right product to the consumer. The supply network is often characterised by being too long and lacking timely response to the changing consumer demand. A significant amount of research has been devoted towards understanding the soft goods supply network and changing it from a push system of supply to a pull system of demand. The retail demand chain operates on the premise that as consumers purchase apparel at retail, the merchandise is replenished quickly from a demand-activated supply network. In this way, the retailer is responsive to the consumer demand while maintaining the appropriate levels of inventory in the supply network.

There is a continuing trend for the large US retailers to reduce the number of preferred suppliers. Reducing the number of suppliers involves several strategies including the rationalisation of the supply network, eliminating suppliers with less than satisfactory product and performance, and strengthening the remaining suppliers with volume commitments adequate to yield price competitiveness.

13.3 Retail technology

Technology has become a major enabler in forging a responsive demand chain. Foremost among the technologies is point-of-sale (POS) data capture through the use of bar-coded product identification on all apparel merchandise. The scanned bar-coded label data is often provided to the vendor at the end of each business day or, alternatively, accumulated and analysed by the retail firm to decide the reorder activity required. The barcode may be superseded by radio frequency identification (RFID) technology in the foreseeable future as the cost and physical size of RFID tagging are now in line with retail requirements. Retail investments in RFID technology are at an early stage but this technology has great potential for merchandise tracking, carton inventory checking as well as product security and as a counterfeit technology.

Electronic-commerce (e-commerce) solutions have lowered the transaction costs in placing purchase orders, providing advance shipping notices and payment of invoices. This trend is continuing with the increasing use of the Internet as a vehicle to conduct e-commerce. While e-commerce has lowered the transaction cost, that is, the cost of personnel engaged in performing purchase order, invoice reconciliation, payment activities, etc. there has been a corresponding increase in information technology (IT) investment. The retail technology systems are focused on the stock levels in the store and in the supply network. Of particular interest is the ability to minimise stock-outs through the use of POS data and real-time tracking of merchandise on order.

Customer-relationship management (CRM) has been advocated as an enhanced customer retention and loyalty strategy. In CRM, the retailer connects their POS data with customer profiles enabling personalised up-sell and cross-sell presentation as well as uniform delivery of their loyalty programmes. Recent surveys have shown that CRM initiatives are among the most important to the US retailers today. CRM analytical systems produce reports on customer trends, buying patterns and loyalty issues. In difficult economic times, companies are looking for ways to either retain or do more business with their current customers. Other areas of demand chain innovation include dynamic pricing, markdown optimisation and providing diversification in product, format or service.

Real-time price management and optimisation technology can monitor specific stock keeping units (SKUs) to adjust local markdown scheduling, evaluate consumer response to promotions and optimise sales and margin capture without resorting to deep discounting. As retailers invest in IT solutions, the competitive capability has increased significantly. Retailers have a range of analytical and management tools that leverage real-time transaction data to improve operating efficiency, fleeting margin opportunities and aggressively manage risks. Out-of-stock and supply chain network solutions track inventory flux through the POS and alert store personnel to stock-outs, even with lower safety stock reserves. Real-time price management and optimisation solutions also monitor specific SKUs to evaluate promotion response and adjust local markdown scheduling, optimising sales and margin capture while reducing deep discounting. Throughout the 1990s, US retailers aggressively reduced their inventories by a total in excess of $500 billion through the use of improved supply chain techniques and ITs (Stores Online, 2003).

The concept of selling to consumers over the Internet has also changed dramatically in just these last few years. Retailers realise that the Internet can be used as a communication channel with their customers. Additionally, retailers value the Internet as an advertising medium by which shoppers research the product prior to the purchase decision. The Internet is turning into a customer service tool that helps attract consumers to the store environment as well as a vehicle for direct purchase.

Retailers in the US continue to improve their systems and business practices in an industry-wide effort under the auspices of Voluntary Inter-industry Commerce Standard (VICS). VICS was established in the mid-1980s to begin developing voluntary standards for new business practices (VICS, 2003). VICS continues to promulgate a number of recommended guidelines and voluntary standards for business practices ranging from e-commerce transaction sets to product-related business practices. In general, the guidelines and voluntary standards developed under the auspices of VICS seek to place responsibility for a business practice at the place in the supply network where least cost will occur in its implementation. Examples of business practices that have been developed by VICS include product marking, floor-ready merchandise, collaborative planning with forecast replenishment, supply network logistics and Internet commerce. Each of these new practices seeks to improve the overall efficiency of the supply network and implement systems that permit the retailer and supply network to effectively respond to the needs and wants of the consumer.

13.4 The customer

When a customer enters a retail store, that individual may or may not purchase a product. A number of factors come into play in determining whether or not a purchase will occur. Among those factors, three are chosen for discussion here; purchase intent, price promotion, and the criteria used by the customer in evaluating a product for purchase.

Engle *et al.* (1995) describe the relationship between purchases and purchase intent by characterising the specificity of the intent. They describe purchases as fully planned, partially planned or unplanned:

- A fully planned purchase occurs when the product and the brand were selected prior to physically seeking the product.

- A partially planned purchase occurs when consumers have selected the product, but not the brand prior to entering the purchase environment.
- An unplanned purchase occurs when product and brand are selected in the purchase environment.

Simply because a customer has intent to purchase a product that does not necessarily mean that the purchase will be made. It is not unusual for differences to exist between consumer demand (desire for and intent to purchase a product) and purchases recorded at the POS. This difference can be attributed to inability to locate the desired product, unavailability of the product, an unacceptable price, stock-out situations or other intervening circumstances. Figure 13.1 depicts the various possible purchase intent/purchase scenarios.

Frequently, in practice and in academic research, product sales are taken to be an accurate reflection of consumer demand. In reality, consumers may not be able to find a desired product and purchase a substitute, or purchase nothing at all. Schary and Christopher (1979) developed a model of behaviour of consumers confronted with a stock-out. Consumers' responses included buying a different size, a different brand, a different product, postponing the purchase, deciding not to buy at all and searching elsewhere for the product. In a similar study completed 12 years later, Emmelhainz *et al.* (1991) identified nearly identical types of consumer responses to stock-outs, emphasising that 40.5 per cent of the consumers studied either delayed their purchases or went to another store.

Promotional pricing has been shown to influence consumer purchasing behaviour including willingness to substitute brands. Price promotions are known to temporarily increase sales of promoted brands, and to reduce sales of substitute brands in some product categories (Dodson *et al.*, 1978; Moriarity, 1985; Kumar and Leone, 1988; Preston and Mercer, 1990; Walters, 1991). Brands with a large market share seem especially likely to gain share at the expense of competitors' brands when prices are reduced (Walters, 1991). However, brand loyal consumers may be less likely to switch brands due to price promotions, but the behaviour is not always consistent across brands or products (Grover and Srinivasan, 1992). It has also been established that consumers learn to buy only during price promotions when those promotions occur frequently (Krishna *et al.*, 1991).

13.5 Case study

A case study provides an opportunity to examine how consumers behave in a retail environment. This case study examined purchase behaviour of consumers regarding the purchase

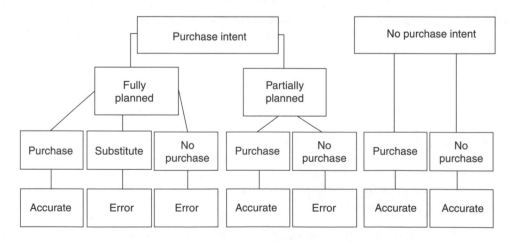

Figure 13.1 Purchase intent and purchase scenarios (after Engle *et al.*, 1995)

of bras over a 2-week period. The brand owned by top four manufacturers are given in Table 13.4.

The bra category is very intensive in terms of SKUs with one style requiring multiple SKUs. A typical style may have, for example, six band sizes, four cup sizes and three colours producing 72 separate SKUs for one style. Data was collected in a large department store in the South-eastern US over a 2-week period in the fall.

A total of 338 female consumers were approached to participate in the study. Of those, only 33 declined to participate. Therefore, although the sample was self-selecting, the participation rate was over 90 per cent. Interviews with 10 participants were incomplete, containing only pre-shopping data, so were eliminated from the sample. In addition, two participants who were shopping exclusively for mastectomy products, available in only one brand, were dropped, resulting in a final sample of 293. The sample was 79.9 per cent Caucasian ($n = 234$), with an additional 15 per cent African-American ($n = 44$) and 0.3 per cent other ($n = 1$), with 4.8 per cent ($n = 14$) unidentified. Of the 288 subjects for which age estimates were available nearly half, 47.9 per cent ($n = 138$), were estimated to between 30 and 55 years old, with the remainder approximately evenly distributed between the under 30 and over 55 categories, 27.4 per cent ($n = 79$) and 24.7 per cent ($n = 71$), respectively. Over half, 66.6 per cent ($n = 195$), of the sample shopped in the intimate apparel department between noon and 6:00 p.m. Evening hours between 6:00 and 9:00 p.m. attracted the next largest number of shoppers, 18.8 per cent ($n = 55$) while the remaining 14.7 per cent ($n = 43$) shopped between 10:00 a.m. and noon.

For those consumers who planned to purchase, the evaluative criteria provided in the pre-shopping interview were the first indication of attributes considered in the purchase decision. In addition, those consumers indicated evaluative criteria which were important in making their selections at time of purchase. Participants who indicated no purchase intent during the pre-shopping interview, yet purchased, provided evaluative criteria for their selections as well. If consumers who pre-planned did not purchase, they indicated reasons for not completing the anticipated purchase.

13.5.1 Bra purchase evaluative criteria

Table 13.5 summarises the frequency of evaluative criteria provided by all participants who purchased regardless of intent expressed in the pre-shopping interview. Table 13.5 includes all attributes specified upon entering the department as well as those reported during or immediately following purchase. As is clear from Table 13.5, certain evaluative criteria were cited by bra consumers as considerations in the purchase decision.

13.5.2 Purchase intent and evaluative criteria

Table 13.6 reports the evaluative criteria cited by participants separated by purchase intent and specificity of that intent. Pre-selected product and fully planned intent groups represent participants who had specified a brand in the pre-shopping interview. Partially

Table 13.4 Brands owned by top four manufacturers

Warnaco	Maidenform	VF	Sara Lee
Warners	Maidenform	Vanity Fair	Playtex
Olga	Lillyette	Vasarette	Hanes Her Way
Calvin Klein	Trueform	Bestform	Wonderbra
Marilyn Monroe	Oscar de la Renta		Bali
	Flexees		Champion

Table 13.5 Evaluative criteria for bra purchases*

	%	n		%	n
Extrinsic-BI			*Intrinsic-AD*		
Brand	41.2	70	Colour	31.8	54
Price/sale	17.6	30	Style	30.0	51
Extrinsic-S			Appearance/attractiveness	15.3	26
Used before	8.8	15	Fabrication	8.8	15
Acceptable substitute	2.9	5	*Intrinsic-TD*		
Situational factors	2.9	5	Fit/sizing	69.4	118
			Comfort	30.0	51
			Construction	20.6	35
			Durability/wearability	2.4	4
			Care	0.6	1

*Numbers and percentages for each criteria are expressed independently in relation to total purchasers (*n* = 170), each of whom indicated multiple criteria

Table 13.6 Purchase intent groups and evaluative criteria

Pre-selected/ fully planned	%	n	Partially planned	%	n	Unplanned	%	n
Extrinsic-BI								
Brand	24.8	66	Brand	1.6	3	Brand	3.6	1
Price/sale	3.0	8	Price/sale	8.6	16	Price/sale	21.4	6
BI total	27.8	74		10.2	19		25.0	7
Extrinsic-S								
Used before	4.1	11	Used before	2.2	4	Used before	0.0	0
Other	1.5	4	Other	2.7	5	Other	3.6	1
S total	5.6	15		4.0	9		3.6	1
Intrinsic-AD								
Colour	12.8	34	Colour	9.7	18	Colour	7.1	2
Style	12.0	32	Style	10.2	19	Style	0.0	0
Attractiveness/ appearance	2.3	6	Attractiveness/ appearance	8.6	16	Attractiveness/ appearance	14.3	4
Fabrication	0.4	1	Fabrication	6.5	12	Fabrication	7.1	2
AD total	27.4	73		34.9	65		28.6	8
Intrinsic-TD								
Fit/sizing	25.6	68	Fit/sizing	25.8	48	Fit/sizing	7.1	2
Comfort	9.0	24	Comfort	12.4	23	Comfort	14.3	4
Construction	3.3	9	Construction	10.8	20	Construction	21.4	6
Durability/care	1.1	3	Durability/care	1.1	2	Durability/care	0.0	0
TD total	39.1	104		50	93		42.9	12
Grand totals		266			186			28

planned intent includes participants who indicated they were shopping for a bra, but did not specify brand. As can be seen in Figure 13.2, intrinsic-technical design (Intrinsic-TD) was the most important evaluative criteria category for all intent groups. Intrinsic-aesthetic design (Intrinsic-AD) was the second most important category for the partially planned and unplanned intent groups. For those who had fully planned purchases, extrinsic-brand image (Extrinsic-BI) and Intrinsic-AD were equally important. Extrinsic-BI

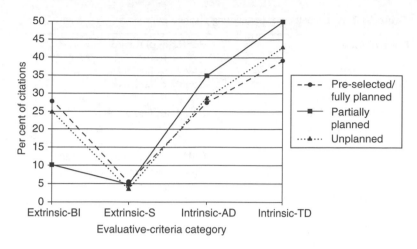

Figure 13.2 Purchase-decision profile for consumers in a department store

criteria were much less frequently cited by the partially planned group, where Intrinsic-TD criteria were especially important. Extrinsic-situational (Extrinsic-S) evaluative criteria were much less frequently cited than the other categories for all intent groups.

13.5.3 Unfulfilled purchase intent and criteria substitution

Table 13.7 summarises reasons provided by those who had indicated intent to purchase but did not do so, or wanted additional products which were out of stock. This provides another indication of the evaluative criteria and their impact on the purchase decision. Again, the importance of intrinsic criteria to the purchase decision is in evidence with 83 per cent of the reasons given for not purchasing being references to intrinsic-evaluative criteria. Inability to find the correct size was by far the most commonly cited reason for failure to complete a planned purchase, emphasising the importance of sizing/fit. This is consistent with data reported in the trade literature. Consumers cited inability to find the correct size (67 per cent) and poor fit (75 per cent of females) as reasons for not purchasing products (Kurt Salmon Associates, 1998). Failure to locate the desired style was also a commonly cited reason for not completing planned purchases; 84 per cent of survey respondents in the Kurt Salmon Associates (1998) study indicated that inability to find satisfactory styles was a reason for not purchasing apparel products.

One survey question was directed at assessing the substitutability of different evaluative criteria. Purchasers were asked if the product or products purchased were exactly what they wanted, or how they differed from the ideal. A relatively small percentage, 19.4 per cent (*n* = 52) of purchased products were described as differing from the ideal. This suggests that many of the evaluative criteria are not very substitutable for bra consumers. Although intrinsic criteria are most often cited as criteria used in the purchase decision, they also seem to be more substitutable than extrinsic criteria.

Differences expressed by those who purchased a less than ideal product are summarised in Table 13.8. As can be seen, when bra consumers purchased an alternative, it most likely differed in style or colour. Although the meaning of a difference in colour is quite clear, the term style meant many different things to the consumers surveyed. When participants described the styles they intended to purchase in the pre-shopping interview, responses ranged from specific style numbers, to general style categories (such as minimiser), to construction details (such as no under wire). Thus, a difference in style could have very diverse meanings.

Table 13.7 Reasons for not completing planned purchases

Fully planned		Partially planned	
Could not find size	22	Could not find size	17
Could not find style	9	Could not find style	5
Could not find brand/style	4		
Could not find colour	3	Could not find colour	3
Could not find brand	2		
Did not have more	2		
		Did not find exactly what wanted	4
		Situational factors	5
		Not comfortable	1

Table 13.8 Differences between purchased product and ideal

Expressed differences	expressed differences (%)	total purchases (%)	*n*
Style	34.6	6.7	18
Colour	19.2	3.7	10
Size/fit	11.5	2.2	6
Construction	7.7	1.5	4
Fabrication	5.8	1.1	3
Brand, colour and size	3.8	0.7	2
Brand	3.8	0.7	2
Not for self, for another	3.8	0.7	2
Brand and style	1.9	0.4	1
Style and size	1.9	0.4	1
Other	5.8	1.1	3
Total			52

The design checklist completed for purchased products recorded much of the styling and construction information which could be discerned from POS data. Table 13.9 reports the styling information for purchased products, separated by manufacturer. The data reinforces the complexity of understanding intrinsic design-evaluative criteria.

As is clear from Table 13.9, products with certain intrinsic-design features are purchased more frequently than others. However, the proportions are not identical across manufacturers. For example, Manufacturer 1's consumers primarily purchase products with comfort straps and straps with stretch insets, while consumers of other manufacturers' products select bras with plain elastic straps. Demi and push-up bra styles are more frequently purchased by consumers of Manufacturer 3's bras than those of other manufacturers. Manufacturer 3's consumers also purchase a larger proportion of bras with moulded and padded cups than consumers of other brands. Consumers of bras produced by Manufacturers 1 and 2 purchased a larger proportion with full-figure fit than consumers of other brands.

Bra consumers surveyed used a limited range of salient evaluative criteria in evaluating bras for purchase, some more frequently than others. Fit/sizing and brand, the two most frequently cited evaluative criteria, are of particular interest. Although sizing/fit was the most often cited consideration in a purchase as well as the most frequently cited reason for not purchasing, bra consumers' unwillingness to substitute brands makes it apparent that many were only searching within the pre-selected brand. Therefore, size and brand are both extremely important criteria. During the bra purchase decision, intrinsic-evaluative criteria

Table 13.9 Aesthetic and technical design features of purchased products

Feature	Mfr1 (n)	%	Mfr2 (n)	%	Mfr3 (n)	%	Mfr4 (n)	%	Other (n)	%	Total (%)
Strap type (totals)	115		45		42		51		9		
Elastic inset	35	30.4	8	17.8	14	13.3	6	11.8	1	11.1	24.4
Comfort strap	33	28.7	7	15.6	7	16.7	3	5.9	0	0	19.1
Elastic	19	16.5	24	53.3	15	35.7	25	49.0	5	55.6	33.6
Cami	16	13.9	0	0	1	2.4	7	13.7	1	11.1	9.5
Non-stretch	9	7.8	6	13.3	5	11.9	7	13.7	0	0	10.3
Other	3	2.6	0	0	0	0	3	5.9	2	22.2	3.0
Strap placement (totals)	113		45		42		50		7		
Standard	105	92.9	42	93.3	40	95.2	46	92	7	100.0	93.4
Other	8	7.1	3	6.7	2	4.8	4	8	0	0	96.6
Strap adjustment (totals)	113		45		42		49		7		
Back	62	54.9	35	77.8	30	71.4	35	71.4	6	85.7	65.6
Front	47	41.6	10	22.2	12	28.6	9	18.4	1	14.3	30.5
None	4	3.5	0	0	0	0	5	10.2	0	0	3.9
General structure (totals)	115		45		42		54		9		
Standard	94	81.7	43	95.6	14	33.3	42	77.8	6	66.7	75.1
Minimiser	7	6.1	0	0	2	4.8	1	1.9	0	0	3.8
Sports	4	3.5	1	2.2	0	0	0	0	1	11.1	2.3
Demi	4	3.5	1	2.2	15	35.7	3	5.6	0	0	8.7
Push-up	3	2.6	0	0	10	23.8	3	5.6	0	0	6.0
Other	3	2.6	0	0	1	2.4	5	9.3	2	22.2	4.2
Cup type (totals)	115		45		42		54		9		
Seamed	64	55.7	39	86.7	34	81.0	13	24.1	6	66.7	58.9
Moulded	48	41.7	6	13.3	8	19.0	40	74.1	2	22.2	39.2
Other	3	2.6	0	0	0	0	1	1.9	1	11.1	1.9
Cup padding (totals)	115		45		42		54		9		
Non-padded	97	83.4	37	82.2	11	26.2	36	66.7	9	100.0	71.7
Padded cup	15	13.0	8	17.8	21	50.0	18	33.3	0	0	23.4
Push-up pads	3	2.6	0	0	10	23.8	0	0	0	0	4.9
Under wire (totals)	115		45		42		54		9		
Under wire	66	57.4	45	100	33	78.6	36	66.7	7	77.8	70.6
No under wire	49	42.6	0	0	9	21.4	18	33.3	2	22.2	29.4
Fabric (totals)	115		45		42		54		9		
Satin	51	44.3	10	22.2	14	33.4	11	20.5	0	0	32.6
Satin and lace	35	30.4	17	37.8	23	54.8	6	11.1	3	33.3	31.7
Sheer and lace	11	9.6	0	0	1	2.4	8	14.8	0	0	7.5
Lace	7	6.1	0	0	0	0	4	7.4	2	22.2	4.9
Cotton	6	5.2	0	0	2	4.8	6	11.2	1	11.1	5.7
Sheer	2	1.7	0	0	0	0	9	16.7	0	0	4.1
Knit and lace	1	.9	9	20.0	2	4.8	9	16.7	3	33.3	7.5

(continued)

Table 13.9 *Continued*

Feature	Mfr1 (n)	%	Mfr2 (n)	%	Mfr3 (n)	%	Mfr4 (n)	%	Other (n)	%	Total (%)
Embedded satin	1	.9	9	20.0	0	0	0	0	0	0	3.8
Sheer and knit	0	0	0	0	0	0	0	0	0	0	1.5
Other	1	.9	0	0	0	0	0	0	0	0	0.8
Closure (totals)	*115*		*45*		*42*		*54*		*9*		
Back	111	96.5	45	100.0	33	78.6	41	75.9	8	88.9	89.8
Front	0	0	0	0	8	19.0	12	22.2	1	11.1	7.5
None	4	3.5	0	0	1	2.4	1	1.9	0	0	2.6
Full-figure (totals)	*115*		*45*		*42*		*54*		*9*		
Full-figure fit	46	40.0	16	35.6	6	14.3	3	5.6	0	0	26.8
Regular fit	69	60.0	29	64.4	34	85.7	51	94.4	9	100.0	73.2
Support insert (totals)	*115*		*45*		*42*		*54*		*9*		
Has insert	10	8.7	3	6.7	0	0	0	0	0	0	4.9
No insert	105	91.3	42	93.3	42	100.0	54	100.0	9	100.0	95.1
Love knot (totals)	*115*		*45*		*42*		*54*		*9*		
Knot	0	0	11	24.4	0	0	0	0	0	0	4.1
No knot	115	100.0	34	75.6	42	100.0	54	100.0	9	100.0	95.9

Mfr-Manufacturer

comprise the bulk of attributes considered. These evaluative criteria represent attributes which are determined directly by decisions made during the product-development process and so emphasise the importance of all consumer inputs.

Evaluative criteria used by the bra consumers surveyed mapped directly to the universal evaluative criteria discerned through content analysis of published research. This reinforces the contention that some criteria are indeed universal for apparel products, being used by consumers to weigh alternatives prior to purchase. Bra consumers cited post-purchase evaluation (repeat purchase) as criteria in their weighing of alternative products for purchase. This fact supports the assertion that other evaluative criteria are unique to the product.

The evaluative criteria of size, brand, colour, style and price are discernable through a POS record of purchases. Though price was less frequently cited as a purchase consideration by bra consumers, the impact of the sale on purchases makes it clear that price is a consideration. Purchase records contain SKU level data identifying the particular style purchased. For the manufacturer, a style has meaning in terms of the products' structure, so would provide insight into product features which were most widely purchased. For those involved in vendor-managed inventory (VMI) programmes on the scale of an entire department, similar information may be discernable for competitor's products as well.

13.5.4 Shopping and purchasing patterns

More than half of the intimate apparel shoppers, 58 per cent ($n = 170$), purchased bras during their visit to the department. Of those, 55.3 per cent ($n = 94$) purchased one bra, 35.3 per cent ($n = 60$) purchased two and 9.4 per cent ($n = 16$) purchased three or more. Only 22 of those purchasing multiple bras purchased two identical bras and one purchased three which were identical. Another 23 purchased two bras which were identical styles in

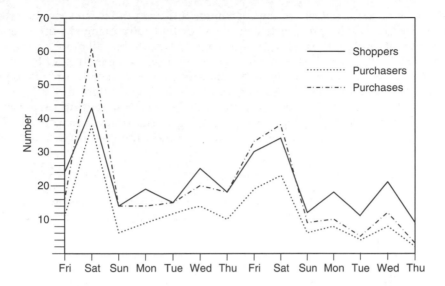

Figure 13.3 Purchase patterns over a 2-week period

Table 13.10 Participants' reported purchase intent

	n	%
Intent	234	79.9
Pre-selected product	(28)	(9.6)
Fully planned	(77)	(26.3)
Partially planned	(129)	(44.0)
No intent	59	20.1

different colours, and four purchased three in identical styles but different colours. The total number of shoppers and the subset of those who purchased each day are shown in Figure 13.3. The percentage of shoppers who purchased each day ranged from a high of 88.4 per cent on a Saturday to a low of 25 per cent on a Thursday.

13.5.5 Shoppers intent and purchase behaviour

Table 13.10 summarises the purchase intent as reported by each participant during the pre-shopping interview. The no-intent category includes participants who responded anything but 'yes' when asked if they were shopping for a bra. As can be clearly seen, upon entering the department the majority of participants indicated some level of intent to purchase.

Kurt Salmon Associates (1998) reported a similar percentage (70 per cent) of consumers indicated that they entered a store knowing what they wanted.

A fully planned purchase is one in which the brand as well as the product was planned prior to purchase, while the product but not the brand is pre-selected in a partially planned purchase. For bra consumers, the pre-selected product purchase-intent category was added. This category included consumers who reported seeking a specific style number within a brand. Note that numbers in parentheses on the table indicate a breakdown of the intent. As the planning is completed prior to shopping and regardless of whether the purchase is culminated, these descriptions of the extent of purchase planning can be considered as characterisations of the specificity of the consumers' intent to purchase a product. Brands sought by participants who pre-selected products or had fully planned purchase intent, manufacturers that produce those brands, and brands purchased by all purchasers are identified in Table 13.11. Again, numbers in parentheses represent a breakdown of the numbers in the preceding rows. As can be clearly seen in the table, 97 per cent of the brands sought by shoppers and 95.9 per cent of purchases were produced by four manufacturers.

As is clarified by Figure 13.4, the proportion of shoppers purchasing each manufacturer's product varies from the proportion expressing intent to purchase product. This is due in part to the large number of those in the fully planned intent group who did not find

Table 13.11 Brands sought and purchased by shoppers

Manufacturer and brand	expressing intent (%)	Number expressing intent	of shoppers purchasing* (%)	Number of shoppers purchasing
Manufacturer 1	*61.9*	*65*	*47.0*	*80*
Brand 1	(26.7)	(28)	(24.7)	(42)
Brand 2	(1)	(1)	(2.3)	(4)
Brand 3	(30.5)	(32)	(14.7)	(25)
Brand 4	(3.8)	(4)	(5.3)	(9)
Manufacturer 2	*15.2*	*16*	*20*	*34*
Brand 5	(15.2)	(16)	(20)	(34)
Manufacturer 3	*11.4*	*12*	*17.7*	*30*
Brand 6	(4.8)	(5)	(11.2)	(19)
Brand 7	(5.7)	(6)	(5.9)	(10)
Brand 8	(1.0)	(1)	(0.6)	(1)
Manufacturer 4	*10.5*	*11*	*27.1*	*46*
Brand 9	(4.8)	(5)	(17.1)	(29)
Brand 10	(5.7)	(6)	(10)	(17)
Other	*1.0*	*1*	*4.7*	*8*

*Percentages do not sum to 100% as purchasers may have purchased multiple brands

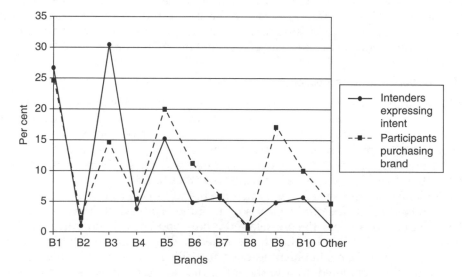

Figure 13.4 Comparisons of intent and purchase by brand

what they wanted to buy. In addition, shoppers who partially planned their purchases ended up selecting brands in the store.

13.5.6 *Translating intent to behaviour*

Those who had pre-selected products or fully planned purchases primarily purchased the chosen brand, or did not purchase. Thus, consumer intent expressed on entering the purchase environment does not necessarily match the purchase behaviour for bras. Table 13.12 and Figure 13.5 document the specificity of purchase intent and the ultimate purchase behaviour for participants who indicated intent to purchase a specific brand. Only five who intended to purchase a specific brand substituted another brand when making a purchase. Those consumers switched manufacturers as well as brands, although probably unknowingly.

Expressed purchase intent seems to translate into purchases of about 60–70 per cent. Expressed lack of intent is seen to translate into purchases of about 20 per cent. Figure 13.6 illustrates that a greater proportion of those with purchase intent purchased multiple products than those who had indicated no purchase intent.

Intenders who did not purchase ($n = 76$) represent over 25 per cent of the sample. Twenty-six of those were seeking a specific brand of product, and 13 were seeking a specific brand and style. Purchases are an accurate reflection of intent for three-fourths of the sample only. However, it may be the case that this shadow demand would be captured by POS data at some point in time. Just over 76.3 per cent ($n = 58$) of intenders who did

Table 13.12 Brand purchase intent and purchase behaviour

	Pre-selected product		Fully planned	
	n	%	*n*	%
Purchased brand	15	53.7	46	60.76
Substituted brand	0	0	5	6.33
Did not purchase	13	46.43	26	32.91
Total	28		77	

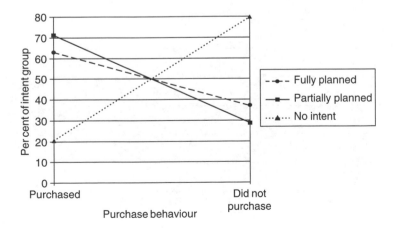

Figure 13.5 Purchase behaviour compared with intent to purchase

not purchase indicated a strategy for proceeding. Of those, the majority indicated they would continue to attempt purchase by either shopping elsewhere (67.2 per cent), returning later (19.0 per cent) or ordering the product (1.7 per cent). Failing to complete a purchase during one visit to a store is not necessarily an indicator of change in intent, though it does represent shadow demand not captured with POS data.

Another way to examine purchase behaviour in relation to intent is presented in Figure 13.7 and Table 13.13. The strategy focuses exclusively on those participants with fully planned intent, reporting how that intent translates to actual purchases by presenting a translation percentage. The translation percentage is expressed in terms of both purchasers and total number of bras purchased by fully planned intenders. Over half of the purchases of multiple identical bras, or ones differing only in colour, were made by this group which comprises only about 36 per cent of the sample. Though purchase quantities are quite small for some brands, greatly impacting the calculation of translation percentage with a purchase or two, it is clear that translation percentages are improved when total purchases are considered. Disregarding the 'other' manufacturer category, which was

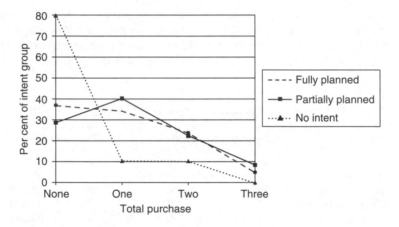

Figure 13.6 Purchase Intent compared to purchase of multiple products

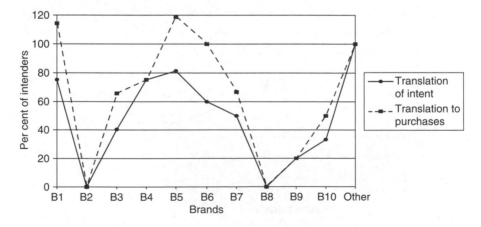

Figure 13.7 Translation of fully planned intent into purchases

based on one purchase, Manufacturer 2 had the best record for translating intent to purchase, though some potential sales were still missed.

Translation of intent to purchase can also be examined by looking at relationship between purchase intent and purchase for all purchasers. As is shown in Figure 13.8, 54 per cent of the purchasers had partially planned intent and selected the product in the store. Another 27 per cent purchased the desired brand, selecting the style in the store. The small percentage that purchased the exact brand and style specified was due in part to the inability of those with intent to find their size in the desired brand and style.

Table 13.13 Translation of intent to purchase

Manufacturer and brand	Number of intenders	Number that purchased	translation of intent (%)	Number purchased by intenders	translation to purchases (%)
Manufacturer 1	65	36	55.4	56	83.6
Brand 1	(28)	(21)	(75.0)	(32)	(114.2)
Brand 2	(1)	(0)	(0.0)	(0)	(0.0)
Brand 3	(32)	(13)	(40.6)	(21)	(65.6)
Brand 4	(4)	(3)	(75)	(3)	(75)
Manufacturer 2	16	13	81.2	19	118.7
Brand 5	(16)	(13)	(81.2)	(19)	(118.7)
Manufacturer 3	12	6	50.0	9	75.0
Brand 6	(5)	(3)	(60.0)	(5)	(100.0)
Brand 7	(6)	(3)	(50.0)	(4)	(66.7)
Brand 8	(1)	(0)	(0.0)	(0)	(0.0)
Manufacturer 4	11	4	36.4	5	45.4
Brand 9	(5)	(2)	(20.0)	(2)	(20.0)
Brand 10	(6)	(2)	(33.3)	(3)	(50.0)
Other	1	1	100.0	1	100.0

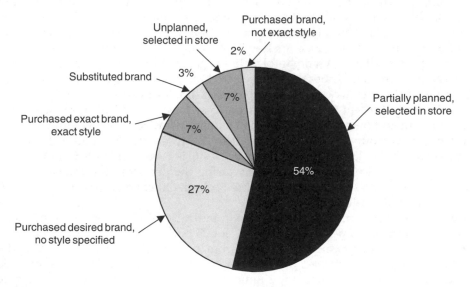

Figure 13.8 Overall purchase behaviour for bra purchases

Table 13.14 Brands purchased by shoppers

Manufacturer/brand	n	purchases (%)
Manufacturer 1	116	43.4
Brand 1	(65)	(24.3)
Brand 2	(4)	(1.5)
Brand 3	(38)	(14.2)
Brand 4	(9)	(3.4)
Manufacturer 2	45	16.8
Brand 5	(45)	(16.8)
Manufacturer 3	42	15.7
Brand 6	(29)	(10.8)
Brand 7	(12)	(4.5)
Brand 8	(1)	(0.4)
Manufacturer 4	55	20.5
Brand 9	(36)	(13.4)
Brand 10	(19)	(7.1)
Other	10	3.7

13.5.7 Total purchases

In previous sections, purchase behaviour has been examined in relation to the purchaser. Since many shoppers purchased multiple products, total product purchases provide an alternative means of examining purchase behaviour in relation to the evaluative criteria discernable through POS data. The next few paragraphs describe total purchases in terms of brand, style, size, price and colour. Table 13.14 presents total purchases segmented by manufacturer. As shown in the table, 96.4 per cent of the bras purchased came from four manufacturers; 79.5 per cent of the purchases were comprised of only the five most frequently purchased brands. This dominance by a few brands is consistent with preferences expressed by shoppers who had fully planned purchase intent.

Examining purchases by style number proved uninformative. Within the total of 268 purchases, 130 different style numbers were purchased. Nearly half of the style numbers, 49.2 per cent ($n = 64$), were purchased just once. Only a dozen style numbers were purchased more than five times. Examination of structural features related to style and construction (intrinsic criteria) is more informative regarding bra consumers' choice of style.

The large percentage of shoppers who selected their purchases in the store emphasises the importance of understanding the purchase decision for those in product development. Figures 13.9–13.12 present the purchases separately for each manufacturer segmented by purchaser intent and outcome. The variation among manufacturers is of interest.

White was the colour of choice for purchasers, representing over half of the purchases as can be seen in Table 13.15. The dominance of white is consistent with 56.1 per cent of the participants who indicated a colour choice during the pre-shopping interview, as is the position of beige as the second most purchased colour. Other colours purchased tended to be staple rather than fashion colours.

Consumers' intent to purchase was a strong indicator of ultimate purchase behaviour barring intervening circumstances. However, for 25 per cent of the sample, circumstances intervened to prevent planned purchases from occurring. Inability to locate desired product due to stock-outs in size, colour, brand or style was the primary reason reported by bra consumers for not completing anticipated purchases. Stock-outs have a strong impact on the accuracy of purchases for capturing consumer demand, contributing greatly

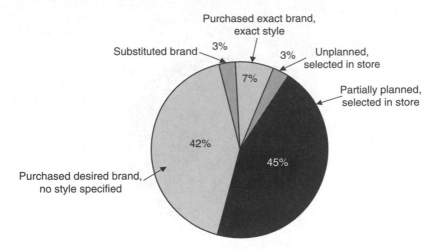

Figure 13.9

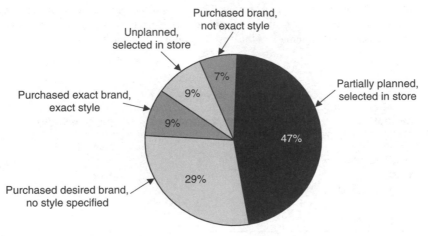

Figure 13.10

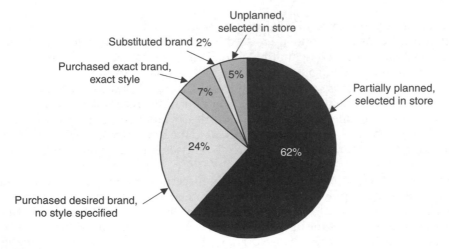

Figure 13.11

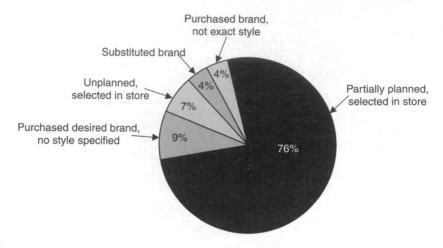

Figure 13.12

Figures 13.9–13.12 Purchase behaviour broken down by manufacturer aggregate data, such as that provided by market research services, may be less valuable to manufacturers than their own record of purchases for understanding how consumers of their products-use evaluative criteria

Table 13.15 Colour of purchased bras

Colour	Number purchased	purchases (%)
White	143	53.4
Beige, taupe, fawn	48	17.9
Black	29	10.8
Ivory, cream, champagne	28	10.5
Other	17	6.3
Beige or white	3	1.1

to the amount of 'shadow demand' not captured with a purchase. Translation percentages indicate that these consumers who are missed with POS data are not only loyal but also significant consumers, inclined to multiple purchases of the favoured product.

POS data represents a rich source of data readily available to industry. Strategies for using the data to manage inventory beyond replenishment and product development have been undertaken with incomplete understanding of the meaning of a consumer purchase. Information contained in POS data includes evaluative criteria of brand, style, sizing/fit, colour and price shown to be important to the bra consumer. The three intrinsic criteria of sizing/fit, colour and style are directly impacted by the merchandise selection process.

Bra consumers' style preferences are less easily discerned from a purchase. Although a complete record of styles purchased is contained in POS data, the quantity of styles purchased creates challenges in interpreting the data. The usefulness of POS data for studying consumers' style preferences for bras may be improved by grouping styles according to features. Similar attributes across styles, brands, stores and/or regions, may be tallied to provide a more concrete measure of the styles purchased by consumer.

Table 13.16 Colour of products

White	Brown
Black	Taupe/fawn
Nude	Grey
Print	Champagne
Ivory/cream	Fashion

The importance of brand and price as evaluative criteria emphasise the necessity that product and brand development occur in conjunction. Brand was a critical criterion in many consumers' purchase of bras, and many searched for appropriate size and fit only within the preferred brand as evidenced by their unwillingness to substitute brands. Consumers' indication of previous product use as evaluative criteria, as well as their specification of a specific brand and style in expressing purchase intent suggests that brand loyalty may be enhanced by positive evaluation of previously purchased products.

Content analysis of published research resulted in identification of universal attributes, or evaluative criteria, considered by consumers in reaching a purchase decision. Considerations reported by survey participants confirmed the validity of the identified universal criteria. Similarities and differences between consumer demand, expressed through intent, and consumer purchases were characterised. The pie diagram of Figure 13.8 clearly demonstrates that over half of the product selections were made in the store, in a large part based on intrinsic criteria.

13.5.8 Garment-sector profile

The five most frequently purchased brands accounted for 79.5 per cent of the 272 bra purchases. In addition, 96.4 per cent of the bras came from four manufacturers. Examining purchases by style number, as is commonly done in industry, proved uninformative as 130 different style numbers were purchased.

Nearly half of the style numbers, 49.2 per cent ($n = 64$), were purchased just once and only a dozen were purchased more than five times. Consequently, a product-attribute analysis was undertaken. Tracking attributes over time, each attribute recorded was plotted over time to explore purchase patterns for the 2-week period studied. Results of the analysis of colour ($n = 272$) and fabrication ($n = 268$) of the bras purchased are shown in Figures 13.13 and 13.14. Table 13.16 lists the colours of the purchased products. Figure 13.13a shows the number of bras of each of the top four colours purchased each day. This strategy for looking at the attribute of colour makes it easy to see that white was the predominant colour purchased. In Figure 13.13b, colours were grouped into colour families, and all of the colours presented in Table 13.16 were included. In this figure, the importance of fashion as well as basic colours becomes apparent. In Figure 13.13c, colour groups are charted as a percentage of total sales each day. This way, purchase patterns can be examined without the variation that results from differing numbers of daily purchases and from the generally declining trend in total purchases per day that occurred over the period of the study. Examined this way, beige seems to be a more important colour group. However, an analysis based on percentages must be undertaken with caution because misleading patterns can result when the number of purchases is very small. For example, a dramatic change in colour preference on the 29th is suggested by Figure 13.13c until one realises that only three purchases, two to one consumer, are reflected in the chart. Table 13.17 presents the fabrications of all of the products purchased.

Figure 13.14a–c examines fabrication as a product attribute. Figure 13.14a illustrates that lace with satin and patterned satin dominate when individual fabrications are plotted

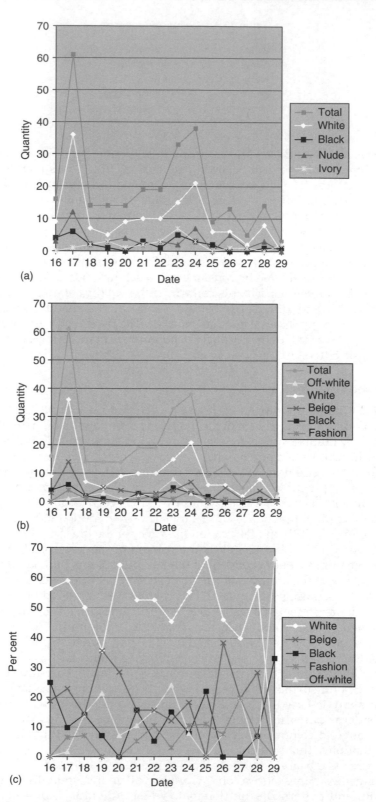

Figure 13.13 Colours of products: (a) major colours; (b) grouped colours and (c) white (sold best)

Table 13.17 Fabrications of products

Lace	Part lace
Patterned satin	Satin
Sheer	Velvet
Cotton	Embroidered satin
Satin/sheer	Lace/sheer
Lace/satin	Embroidered sheer
Lace/cotton	Knit
Satin/knit	Lace/patterned satin
Lace/knit	Sheer/knit
Other	

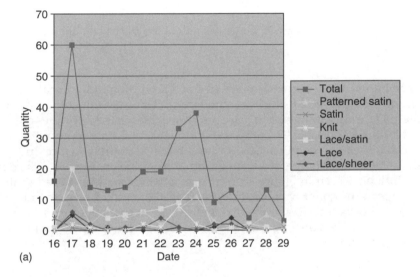

(a)

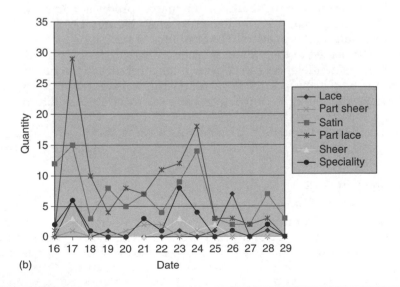

(b)

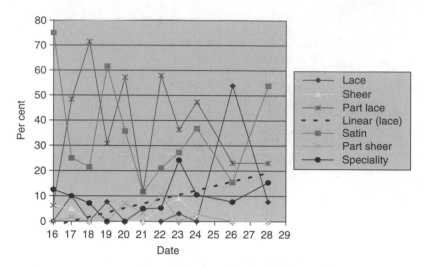

Figure 13.14 Fabrication of products: (a) fabrication; (b) grouped and (c) satin and lace

over time. In Figure 13.14b, purchases are grouped according to similarities in fabrication, and preference for products featuring some lace is clear. As with colour, grouping products by shared fabrications helped to tease out similarities in the attributes of purchases. In Figure 13.14c, the importance of both satin and lace are clear, and an interesting change over time can be seen in the purchases of bras fabricated entirely in lace. In Figure 13.14c, days with fewer than 10 purchases were dropped from the analysis to reduce the disproportionate influence seen in Figure 13.13c. Also, a trend line was added to illustrate the general change in the quantity of lace bras purchased over the 2 weeks studied. Although 2 weeks is too short a time to assume that an increase in preference for lace bras is occurring, the chart does demonstrate the potential of the technique for identifying trends in preferences for attributes.

13.5.8.1 Variation among manufacturers

To examine the differences in attributes of purchased products among manufacturers, the 2 weeks of purchase data were examined overall. Figures 13.15 and 13.16 provide examples of the results of this analysis. The attributes of strap type ($n = 263$) and general structure ($n = 269$) related to the universal criteria of style/design provide examples of this analysis. Note that differences can be seen in the attributes of the purchased products when broken down by manufacturer. For manufacturers, exploring purchase data for an entire category, as well as for their own lines, can provide additional information regarding opportunities for new products.

However, considering foundation garments as a category-for-category management would yield aggregate POS data that would disguise these manufacturer differences.

13.5.9 Forecasting attributes

Currently, most firms rely on style numbers to track product sales, sell through and to plan the product offerings for future seasons. This work investigates forecasting consumer purchases based on attributes of products purchased. This type of data analysis is not presently undertaken by either commercial market research firms or by manufacturers.

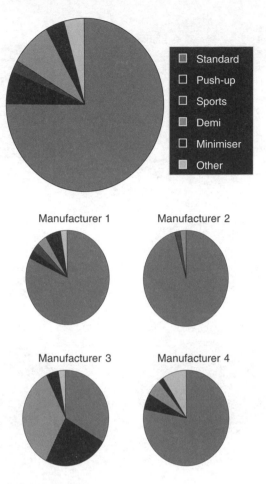

Figure 13.15 Attribute analysis by manufacturers

Consequently, much information regarding consumer preferences is ignored by the current practice of tracking style numbers.

Figures 13.17–13.20 examine the potential for forecasting attributes for new product development. The assumption is made that purchase patterns were established by the end of the 2-week period in which the data was collected. Attributes examined were typical of apparel products and included colour, fabrication and a number of design attributes. Each of the figures shows the percentage of each attribute purchased at 2 weeks (*total*) and at intervals during the data collection period. It can be seen in Figure 13.17 that the percentage of each colour purchased can be accurately predicted after the 8th day of purchase. Fabrication of purchased bras was accurately predicted after only 2 days, as seen in Figure 13.18. Prediction of purchases related to specific style features required up to 9 days, as seen in Figures 13.19 and 13.20. As can be clearly seen in each of the figures, a very strong indication of the attribute distribution is achieved after only 3 days. The data required to predict purchases by attribute appears to be somewhat indirectly related to the dominance of one option within that attribute; that is, when one option is represented in half or more of the purchases, more data is needed to characterise overall attribute distribution.

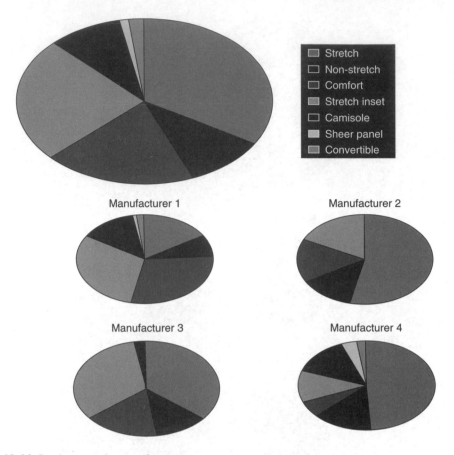

Figure 13.16 Product type by manufacturers

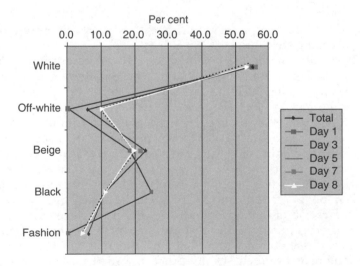

Figure 13.17 Cumulative colour distribution

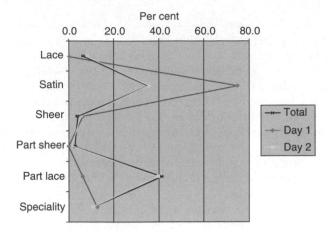

Figure 13.18 Cumulative fabrication distribution

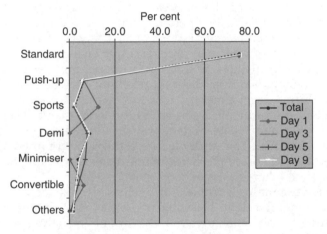

Figure 13.19 Cumulative structure distribution

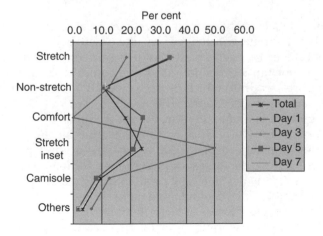

Figure 13.20 Cumulative strap-type distribution

13.6 Discussion

Results of the current research suggest that gaining insight into consumer preferences for particular products via analysis of style numbers has limited potential. Consumers' style/design preferences are not easily discerned by simply tracking the style numbers of products purchased. Although POS data provides a complete record of style numbers sold in nearly all cases, the huge array of different style numbers purchased creates challenges in interpretation. A vast amount of data would be required to identify style preferences and, even then, an understanding of characteristics shared by the purchased products would not be achieved. New technologies such as CRM will permit retailers to better manage the merchandise mix to yield increased consumer satisfaction. Developing a database of style attributes for purchase preference analysis and for collaboratively developing new products would be beneficial.

Results also suggest that the usefulness of purchase data for studying consumers' style/design preferences may be improved by tracking and analysing the attributes of purchased styles. For manufacturers, analysis of attributes would provide insight into product features that were most widely purchased. Data from multiple retail outlets would show differences in attributes of preferred styles across geographical and demographic consumer groups. Over a long period of time, changes in preference for attributes could be identified, as suggested by Figure 13.13c. Analysis of product attributes could provide an ongoing sense of consumer preferences, of changes in those preferences over time, and could assist in making product and product-mix decisions during product development. Combining data from different retail outlets would facilitate analysis and targeting product during development.

Purchases can be forecast by attributes with little more than a week of data, in some cases less. Additionally, only 3 days of data provide a very strong indicator of the attributes of upcoming purchases. This attribute forecasting would provide adequate time for retailers, manufacturers and suppliers to optimise sales by changing the product and colour mix based on the shared sales data.

Each strategy for examining attributes of purchased products holds the potential to yield new and meaningful insight. The value of examining attributes in a variety of ways is illustrated by the examples in Figures 13.13–13.20. For an analysis similar to that shown in Figures 13.13 and 13.14, many additional attribute groupings could be examined before conclusions were reached regarding specific trends. In this case, for example, all products containing satin could be grouped. Or products with lace components could be compared to those without.

If product-attribute data is analysed in aggregate for a category, even more insight into consumer purchase behaviour is achieved, as illustrated by Figures 13.15 and 13.16. Currently, this is not done. Through investment in resources that provide category-wide data development, opportunities in colour and size could be identified. An example of such a resource is SportsTrendInfo which provides weekly SKU specific POS data for the active and athletic wear segments (Conrad, 1999).

An increasing number of manufacturers are working with retailers in VMI programmes (Mautner, 2001). Companies with VMI programmes should be able to analyse purchases and provide style and attribute data to the merchandising and product-development functions. Retailers could use the information to order additional merchandise featuring specific attributes, or to jointly develop new product with their suppliers.

The potential applicability of POS purchase data for bringing input from the consumer into the product-development process as described above moves consumers from multiple markets much closer to the manufacturer. In an increasingly global marketplace, POS data may provide a means of acquiring input from consumers in distant markets, particularly since there is evidence to suggest that the apparel purchase-decision process is similar across cultures (Wagner and Ettenson, 1989). Use of POS data may help manufacturers to more easily adapt product lines for diverse markets.

References

AAFA (2003) American Apparel and Footwear Association, Arlington, VA. www.americanapparel.org

Conrad, A. (1999) Designing for demand: SCM dream or reality. *Apparel Industry Magazine*, May, SCM-6–SCM-11.

Dodson, J., Tybout, A. and Sternthal, B. (1978) Impact of deals and deal retraction on brand switching. *Journal of Marketing Research*, **15**(February), 72–81.

Emmelhainz, M., Stock, J. and Emmelhainz, L. (1991) Consumer responses to retail stock-outs. *Journal of Retailing*, **67**(2, Summer), 138–147.

Engle, J., Blackwell, R. and Miniard, P. (1995) *Consumer Behaviour*, 8th edition. Fort Worth, TX, The Dryden Press.

Grover, R. and Srinivasan, V. (1992) Evaluating the multiple effects of retail promotions on brand loyal and brand switching segments. *Journal of Marketing Research*, **29**(February), 76–89.

Kumar, V. and Leone, R. (1988) Measuring the effect of retail store promotions on brand and store substitution. *Journal of Marketing Research*, **25**(May), 178–185.

Krishna, A., Currim, I. and Shoemaker, R. (1991) Consumer perceptions of promotional activity. *Journal of Marketing*, **55**(April), 4–16.

Kurt Salmon Associates (1998) *KSA's Consumer Pulse*. Atlanta, GA, Kurt Salmon Associates.

Mautner, N. (2001) Retailers rely on suppliers for inventory management. *Inside Fashion*, **11**(5), 4.

May-Plumlee, T. (1999) *Modeling apparel product development using consumer purchase criteria*. Ph.D. Thesis, North Carolina State University, Raleigh.

May-Plumlee, T. and Little, T.J. (1998) No-interval coherently phased product development model for apparel. *International Journal of Clothing Science and Technology*, **10**(5), 342–364.

May-Plumlee, T. and Little, T.J. (2001) Consumer purchase data as a strategic product development tool. *Journal of Textile and Apparel, Technology and Management*, **1**(3), http://www.tx.ncsu.edu/jtatm

Moriarty, M. (1985) Retail promotional effects in intra- and interbrand sales performance. *Journal of Retailing*, **61**(3), 27–46.

Preston, J. and Mercer, A. (1990) The evaluation and analysis of retail salespromotions. *European Journal of Operational Research*, **47**, 330–338.

Schary, P. and Christopher, M. (1979) The anatomy of a stock-out. *Journal of Retailing*, **55**(2), 59–70.

Stores Online (2003) National Retail Federation. www.stores.org

VICS (2003) Voluntary Inter-industry Commerce Standards, Lawrenceville NJ, www.vics.org

Wagner, J. and Ettenson, R. (1989) Apparel purchase decisions: a cross-cultural comparison of Chinese and American consumers. *Association of College Professors in Textiles and Clothing Proceedings*, Vol. 46, p. 121.

Walters, R. (1991) Assessing the impact of retail price promotions on product substitution, complementary purchase, and interstore sales displacement. *Journal of Marketing*, **55**(April), 17–28.

Index

Page numbers in **bold** refers to figures and tables.